War Memorial

War Memorial

The Story of One Village's Sacrifice

from 1914 to 2003

CLIVE ASLET

VIKING

an imprint of

PENGUIN BOOKS

VIKING

Published by the Penguin Group
Penguin Books Ltd, 80 Strand, London WC2R ORL, England
Penguin Group (USA) Inc., 375 Hudson Street, New York, New York 10014, USA
Penguin Group (Canada), 90 Eglinton Avenue East, Suite 700, Toronto, Ontario, Canada M4P 2Y3
(a division of Pearson Penguin Canada Inc.)
Penguin Ireland, 25 St Stephen's Green, Dublin 2, Ireland (a division of Penguin Books Ltd)
Penguin Group (Australia), 707 Collins Street, Melbourne, Victoria 3008, Australia
(a division of Pearson Australia Group Pty Ltd)
Penguin Books India Pvt Ltd, 11 Community Centre, Panchsheel Park, New Delhi – 110 017, India
Penguin Group (NZ), 67 Apollo Drive, Rosedale, Auckland 0632, New Zealand
(a division of Pearson New Zealand Ltd)
Penguin Books (South Africa) (Pty) Ltd, Block D, Rosebank Office Park,
181 Jan Smuts Avenue, Parktown North, Gauteng 2193, South Africa

Penguin Books Ltd, Registered Offices: 80 Strand, London WC2R ORL, England

www.penguin.com

First published 2012
001

Set in 12/14.75 pt Bembo Book MT Std
Typeset by Jouve (UK), Milton Keynes
Printed in Great Britain by Clays Ltd, St Ives plc

A CIP catalogue record for this book is available from the British Library

ISBN: 978-0-670-92153-9

www.greenpenguin.co.uk

MIX
Paper from
responsible sources
FSC
www.fsc.org   FSC™ C018179

Penguin Books is committed to a sustainable
future for our business, our readers and our planet.
This book is made from Forest Stewardship
Council™ certified paper.

ALWAYS LEARNING   **PEARSON**

To Howard Barkell and Barbara Weeks,
keepers of the Lydford flame

'What a shame, they are mostly boys.'

Remark by a nurse overheard when Private
E. Smith disembarked from his troopship
at Le Havre, on his twenty-first birthday,
during the First World War

Contents

List of Illustrations

1. Lydford's church choir and bell ringers on an outing, 1908 (*Barbara Weeks*)

2. Villagers outside the Post Office, *c*.1914 (*Barbara Weeks*)

3. Tourists in front of the White Lady falls in Lydford Gorge (*Plymouth and West Devon Record Office*)

4. The Lydford village band (*Graham Huggins*)

5. Archie Huggins, in the tropical kit with which the Royal North Devon Hussars were issued before going to Gallipoli in September 1915 (*Graham Huggins*)

6. Archie Huggins's grandfather, Roger (*Graham Huggins*)

7. The Huggins family, stonemasons and builders (*Graham Huggins*)

8. Charlie Berry's widow, Polly, on a picnic outside Lydford in the 1920s (*Fred Hammett*)

9. Charles Sargeant Jagger's bas-relief of the Battle of Gheluvelt, 31 October 1914 (*Imperial War Museum ART 2287*)

10. Horse ambulance at Courcelette, on the Somme, summer 1916 (*Library and Archives Canada*)

11. Sam Voysey in the uniform of a territorial cadet (*Marilyn Griesemer*)

12. Sam Voysey with his two daughters, shortly after his family arrived in Canada (*Marilyn Griesemer*)

13. The family Sam Voysey left behind, 1916 (*Marilyn Griesemer*)

14. The ruins of the sugar factory, Courcelette, September 1916 (*Canadian War Museum*)

15. Lieutenant Richard Radford Turner (*George Radford*)

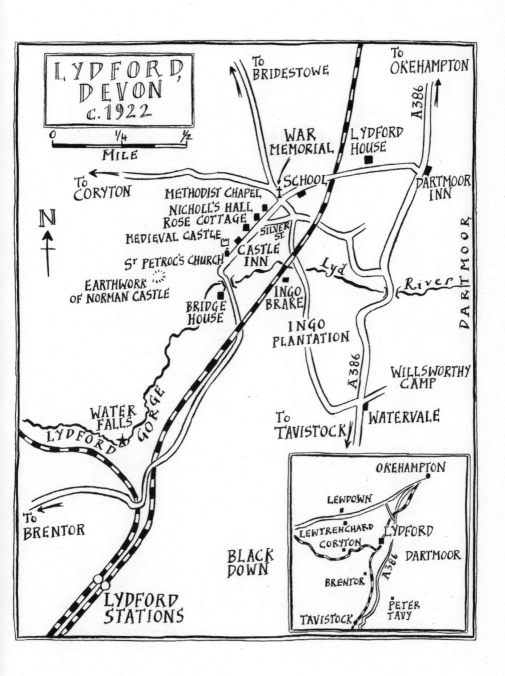

LYDFORD, DEVON c.1922

0   ¼   ½
MILE

N

To BRIDESTOWE
To OKEHAMPTON
A386

WAR MEMORIAL
LYDFORD HOUSE
To CORYTON
SCHOOL
DARTMOOR INN
METHODIST CHAPEL
NICHOLL'S HALL
ROSE COTTAGE
SILVER ST.
MEDIEVAL CASTLE
ST PETROC'S CHURCH
CASTLE INN
Lyd
River
DARTMOOR
EARTHWORK OF NORMAN CASTLE
BRIDGE HOUSE
INGO BRAKE
INGO PLANTATION
A386
WILLSWORTHY CAMP
WATER FALLS
LYDFORD GORGE
To TAVISTOCK
WATERVALE
To BRENTOR
BLACK DOWN
LYDFORD STATIONS

OKEHAMPTON
LEWDOWN
LEWTRENCHARD
CORYTON
LYDFORD
DARTMOOR
A386
BRENTOR
TAVISTOCK
PETER TAVY

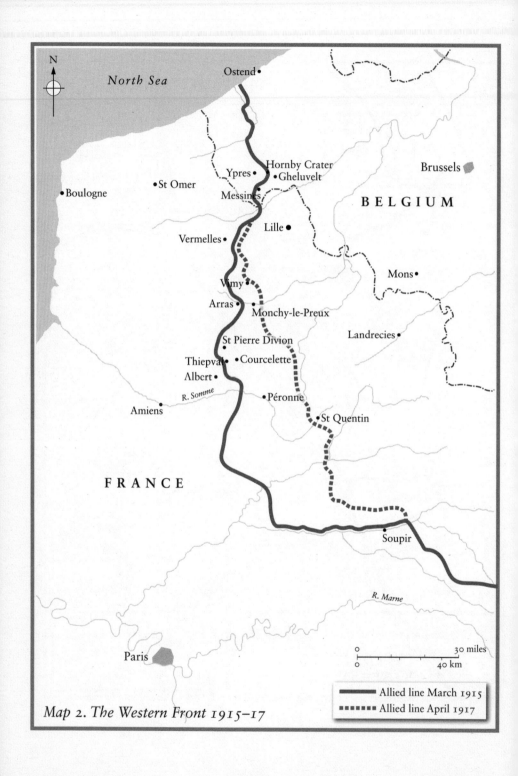

N

North Sea

Ostend •

Hornby Crater
Ypres •   • Gheluvelt
• St Omer
Messines •

Boulogne •

Lille •

Vermelles •

Brussels

BELGIUM

Mons •

Vimy •
Arras •   • Monchy-le-Preux

Landrecies •

St Pierre Divion •
Thiepval •   • Courcelette
Albert •

R. Somme

Amiens •

• Péronne

FRANCE

• St Quentin

Soupir

R. Marne

Paris

0   30 miles
0   40 km

Map 2. The Western Front 1915–17

━━━━ Allied line March 1915
▪▪▪▪▪ Allied line April 1917

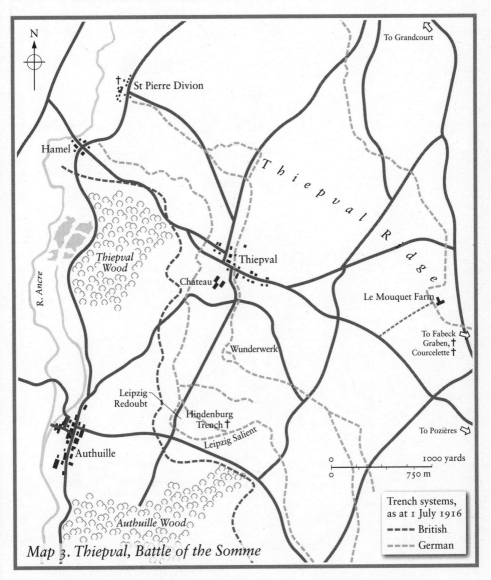

Map 3. Thiepval, Battle of the Somme

Charlie Berry died in the Hindenburg Trench; Dickie Petherick died at St Pierre Divion; Sam Voysey died near Le Mouquet Farm; Mancel Clark died at Courcelette.

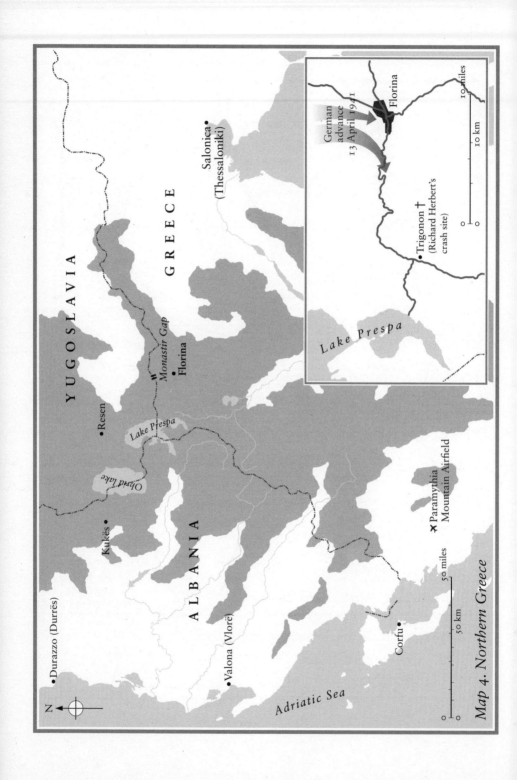

Inset map labels:

Florina

German advance
13 April 1941

Trigonon †
(Richard Herbert's
crash site)

Lake Prespa

10 miles

10 km

0

Main map labels:

YUGOSLAVIA

GREECE

Salonica
(Thessaloniki)

Monastir Gap

Florina

Resen

Lake Prespa

Ohrid Lake

Kukës

ALBANIA

Valona (Vlorë)

Durazzo (Durrës)

✈ Paramythia
Mountain Airfield

Corfu

Adriatic Sea

N

50 miles

50 km

0

Map 4. Northern Greece

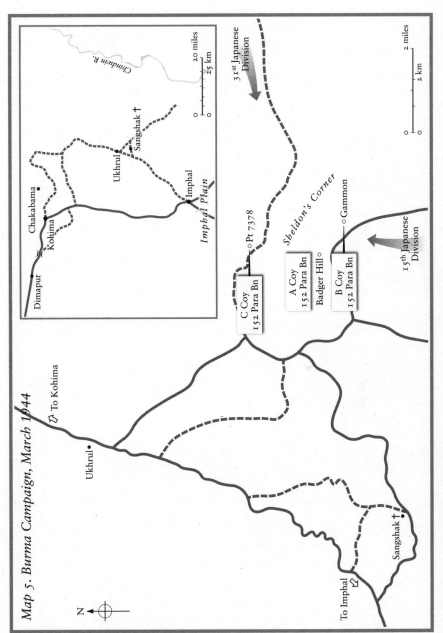

Map 5. Burma Campaign, March 1944

Richard Gillett died at Sangshak.

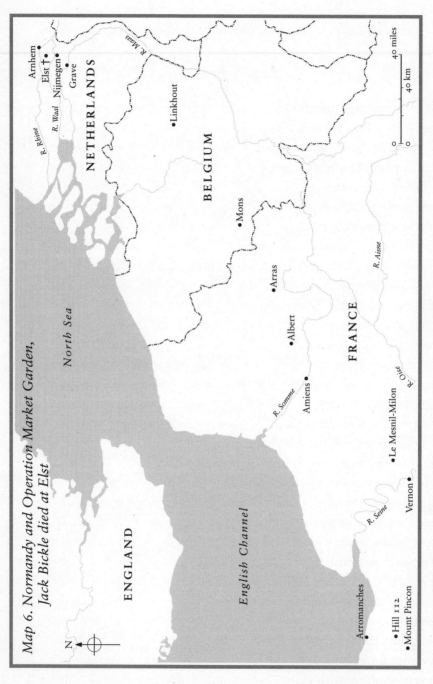

Map 6. Normandy and Operation Market Garden, Jack Bickle died at Elst.

The 4th Battalion Somerset Light Infantry landed at Arromanches on 23 June 1944. Jack Bickle, aged eighteen, joined them at Le Mesnil-Milon in early September and was killed at Elst.

Preface

One of my earliest memories is of the war memorial at the church where I grew up. As I read the names out loud, wondering who they could have been, my mother told me, in hushed but urgent tones, to desist: it might upset any friends or family members of the dead who overheard. War memorials are a familiar sight in Britain, particularly its villages. I still look at the rolls of honour, trying to picture the world that the fallen came from, what they did on active service and how the village coped with its grief. I am not alone in doing so. Although none of the soldiers who fought for the British army in the First World War are now alive, and the ranks of those who took part in the Second World War are thinning, the number of people who participate in Remembrance Day ceremonies is rising. More visitors explore the battlefields each year. In our secular and libertarian age, desecration of a war memorial – whether by a protester swinging on a flag or by a scrap metal merchant melting down a bronze plaque – evokes outrage of the kind that Ancient Greece visited on Alcibiades.

War memorials are not defunct. New conflicts add new names.

I wrote this book to answer the questions that occurred to me as a child, sitting next to my mother in the parish church. Who were the individuals behind the names? What were their stories? I took a village war memorial almost at random: the one at Lydford in Devon. I knew nothing about the twenty-three names attached, in bronze letters, to the granite cross. The names themselves consisted simply of surname and initials, without so much as rank or regiment. I did know that Lydford, having been a Saxon burgh, was an exceptionally interesting place historically, with a precipitous gorge owned by the National Trust. It is on the edge of Dartmoor, and I had no objection to spending time there. I imagined that it had made its living principally from agriculture until the fairly recent past, and would therefore be a settled place, with many of the families represented on the cross still resident in the village. In one respect the war memorial was unusual: it had names from the Falklands and Iraq.

This book is the result of my researches into family history and military and naval archives. I close it with reluctance because each of the individuals with whom I have been living in the course of writing this book has become close to me. I continue to wonder about them. I took Lydford as, so to speak, a random sample of one – a representative example of what must be more than 10,000 village war memorials in the country. Other villages might be different, but the character of this one in the first half of the twentieth century turned out to be not at all what I had expected. I had assumed the population at the time of the First World War to have been deeply rooted in its birthplace. It wasn't. Some village names are on the memorial, familiar from parish records and the logbook of the school. But the two stations at the railway junction – dismantled so completely that a casual visitor would not know the junction had ever been there – brought new families. Other young men, unable to find employment following the closure of the mines, in a countryside blighted by agricultural depression from the 1870s, left the village. Two of them had already emigrated to Canada by 1914, and they died fighting with Canadian regiments. They were remembered by their families in Lydford.

By contrast, some of the Second World War names, although recorded on the war memorial, have been forgotten by the modern village. They were not traditional village people, but occupied some of the big houses on the outskirts for a time; they went to boarding schools. I could find nobody who knew about the three Herbert brothers, beyond their presence on the war memorial.

The book became a record of memory and social change.

Virtually no memorials to ordinary soldiers existed before the First World War. They were created, as I explain in Chapter 8, as the result of what might now be described as a 'Princess Diana moment', an unfamiliar display of feeling for a nation that, at the beginning of the twentieth century, was even more emotionally tongue-tied than it was at the end of it. Memorials arose almost as a folk movement, as communities across Britain sought to express the trauma of their grief. They continue to be bearers of meaning.

I feel privileged to have come close to the lives of twenty-two men and one woman. The loss of some of them is still raw. It has made me realize that, as my mother knew, the symbolism of a war memorial is highly charged. My generation has lived through half a century of prosperity, not having to think much about the wars fought by the professional armed services in our name. This has given a new and no less profound resonance to war memorials. While continuing to embody simple patriotism, they also keep facts about which we might not always be comfortable in the public eye. With time, memory fades. Families at home may never have known what their loved ones experienced at the front. My task is to reconstruct those experiences, those lives. Neither the people nor their tales are always what you would expect.

They remind us, in the words of the nurse quoted at the beginning of this book, that – oh so sadly – 'they are mostly boys'.

On With the Show

∽ WILFIE FRY ∽

Wilfie Fry had been looking forward to the Pony Show on 3 August 1914. Fourteen years old, he had just left the village school at Lydford, on the north-west side of Dartmoor. 'Withdrawn – gone to work' was generally the laconic comment in the school logbook when a boy's departure was noted. Wilfie, like the majority of children, did not merit an entry. Yet he had been a promising pupil – only from too poor a family to allow him to stay in education. It was a good school, as such schools went, and had been run since it was built in 1878 by the moustachioed, musically inclined William Kenner, whose inspiration it had been to start a village band, with uniforms and drum. Kenner always won praise from the governors for the discipline and tone of the school, as well as the 'beautiful singing of hymns'. Classes, according to the logbook, were held in English, Arith[metic], Geog[raphy], History, Singing, Drawing, Needlework – taught by Mrs Kenner to the girls – Drill and Object Lessons, the last being adapted to the surroundings of the school and the pupils' prospects: Seed, Roots, Leaves, Insects, Frog, Animals on a farm, Birds on a farm, Railroad, Ships, Post Office, Needles, Brushes, Thermometer, and so on.

It was a programme that promoted neatness and proficiency above ambition.

Mr Kenner could not be accused of sentimentality towards his young charges. 'Thos Bickle deceased' is the minimal note that explains the permanent absence of a seven-year-old boy who had tumbled into the river Lyd. But that may reflect the exasperation of a man for whom keeping up attendance was always something of

a struggle. It was apt to fall during the season for picking whortleberries; or when Lydford Fair came around; or if a menagerie passed
along the turnpike; or when the temperance Band of Hope paraded
in Tavistock, seven miles away. This being Dartmoor, windows
would often be blown in by the wind, and it could be cold. Wet
clothes would be piled on the stove, with the pasties that the children
had brought for lunch warming above them. If the recalcitrant
caretaker, Mrs Stanbury, had failed to light the fire, lessons would
continue in bitter temperatures and the pasties were eaten cold. There
may have been a degree of relief when 'Mrs Stanbury deceased' was
noted in the logbook – she had left, some might have thought, to
tend other fires – but the stove probably still got blocked, filling the
schoolroom with smoke or not lighting at all.

When the snow was up to the top of the hedgerows, children from
the outlying farms, who would otherwise stride out for two miles
each way across the wild moor, could not come. In fact the village
was cut off from the outside world altogether, sometimes for weeks.
Even this was no excuse for Wilfie. The Frys lived in one of the grey-
walled cottages that make up the centre of Lydford, sparsely furnished
with deal tables, dresser and chairs. A zinc bath was filled from kettles
for the family ablutions once a week. His parents were house-proud:
their dwelling had won a prize from Squire Radford and two other
prominent citizens for being the 'best decorated cottage' at the time
of George V's coronation in 1911.

One of Wilfie's first ventures in the world of work had been to
plant some yew trees in the churchyard of St Petroc's, the square-
towered, granite-built parish church; a hundred years later they are
still there. But he was probably destined to follow the trade that had
well served his father, Frank, and grandfather, Edmund, before him:
thatching. Frank Senior, as he should be called – Wilfie had been
christened Frank Wilfred – also made the occasional sixpence by
attending to a different kind of thatch: he cut hair when needed,
under the glass verandah at the back of the cottage. He is not remembered for his suaveness of manner. 'Keep your head still,' he would
advise children (as the handshears and clippers – sharpened on the
whetstone by the door and probably also used for sheep – tugged at

the roots), 'or I'll cut your bloody ear off!' Perhaps his skill with the scissors was inherited. Wilfie's grandfather used to win prizes for sheep-shearing – until the day in January 1903 when Edmund lost his footing on a cottage roof in Lydford and crashed to the ground. The fall killed him, depriving the church choir of one of its best voices.

Lydford had been Edmund's adopted village; he had originally come from Lezant in Cornwall in search of work, bringing with him the traditional songs which he had grown up with, not all of them polite to the ears of Victorian gentlefolk. Sometimes the squire-vicar of the neighbouring parish of Lewtrenchard, the tireless Sabine Baring-Gould, formed an audience. Baring-Gould built his own country house-cum-vicarage, fathered fourteen children with the beautiful young factory girl whom he had made his bride (and educated for her place in the gentry), wrote 'Onward Christian Soldiers' and other hymns, and produced over a hundred books. One of these was *Songs and Ballads of the West* which, long before Cecil Sharp, gathered together the folk songs Baring-Gould heard in Devon.

In 1914, with unemployment rife and a war looming, work was not everything for Wilfie. It had been a glorious summer for a boy on Dartmoor, whose spare time was spent looking for birds' nests, bathing in streams, fishing and sliding down the steep sides of Lydford Gorge. If he was like the children of a slightly later generation (now old men), he would have commandeered the long trough that the Hugginses used for feeding their sheep and put it against the wall of the late-Norman castle. It formed a convenient ladder. Once on top of the battlements, a supply of corks from the hundreds of beer bottles left behind the Castle Inn would have made convenient ammunition, as he repelled the attacks of other village boys – until his mother bore down, threatening a different kind of warfare supplied by the flat of his father's hand.

From the battlements, the boys could look down on the village street, observing that some of the roofs had holes in them. In 1900, Sabine Baring-Gould had described Lydford's 'ruinous condition', referring particularly to the walls that had been made of stones from the moor, piled one on top of the other, without mortar to hold them together or stop the draughts. The place, he wrote disparagingly, looked like 'an Irish village' – and if you were an order-loving clergyman of the Church of England, supported by a large private income, nothing worse could be said than this. After thirty years of agricultural slump, farm rents were too low for the estates which owned the farmhouses and cottages in Lydford to make adequate repairs. Holes in roofs should have made work for thatchers – only Lydford increasingly chose to forego the expense. Slates from the quarry at Coryton were cheaper. They were not perfect slates – flaking in the least suggestion of a wind, and finally disappearing altogether – but they were good enough at the price.

Throwing corks from the top of the castle was an unstructured activity: the Pony Show, which the village shared with the neighbouring Brentor, was an event. It was not just an event for Wilfie. Lydford was a farming village. Flocks of sheep blocked the road and held up traffic – such traffic as there was. Little went through the village except horse-drawn carts, and there were few enough of those (which was just as well, because the steep, narrow road down to the bridge over the gorge was difficult to negotiate). There were five farmyards: what are now dwellings were then often barns. People who did not farm for a living kept 'fowls', or some pigs and a couple of cows. You could see the pigsties on the one village street, as well as smell them. Animals were slaughtered in a shed near the brook. Afterwards their meat was salted in trundles for future use, as in medieval times. Nothing was wasted. It was not unknown for an animal to escape into the field, in which case the butcher had to fetch his gun and cut the beast up where it fell. The village also knew about horses. There were around 60,000 of them in Devon, two-thirds of them used on farms. To a country boy, a pony was as familiar as a bicycle was to his town counterpart between the wars.

After ten or twelve hours on the land, the men came home and, as soon as they did so, went outside again to dig their vegetable gardens; it was how they fed their families. The women went out early to milk the cows, selling the milk from zinc churns into which the householder inserted a pint dip to extract the desired quantity of the creamy liquid. Housewives scalded milk to make their own cream and butter. In portrait photographs, young men sometimes posed as blades about town, in starched collars, swinging a cane, but they look happier with their sleeves rolled up, a cigarette in the corner of the mouth, handling the sheep. If there was one thing that could be expected to quicken Lydford's pulse it was the opportunity to admire some 238 horses, 68 sheep and 11 sheepdogs at the Pony Show.

For adults as much as children, Lydford's entertainments were homespun. Every so often there were socials and dances, organized by the Cricket Club, with the admirable Mr Kenner at the piano. Socials raised money for the Methodist Chapel, while Temperance meetings sought to terrify the wayward – not that the wayward would have gone (it was left to the irreproachably virtuous members of the Band of Hope to chill the blood or stimulate the tear ducts with their recitations and hymns). After the annual New Year's Day pigeon shoot at the Dartmoor Inn, the year went on in a round of chapel anniversary teas, Sunday school treats, amateur theatricals and harvest festival suppers, with lists of presents for any wedding that might take place being published in the local newspaper. No wonder so many people went to the Pony Show. In a calendar so limited in its excitements, this was one of the highlights. It was one of the best shows in the South-West.

Tied to their cottages by their animals, and with little money to spare, Lydford rarely took a holiday. So the bank holiday that came every August would have been a day to savour, even if it had not, for the last quarter of a century, brought the Pony Show. Expectation had been mounting ever since one of the builders in the village had begun to construct the grandstand and show ring on Farmer Medland's fields. The site lay near the railway station – or rather, the two railway stations, for this was a junction at which both the Great Western Railway (GWR) and the London and South Western Railway (LSWR) had a station with their own stationmasters and porters, signalmen and platelayers; the rival companies even had their own bridges. The railway-owned cottages formed a hamlet unto itself. It was so wet down there that the railway track had to be laid on faggots to stop it from sinking into the marsh. But it provided a stretch of level ground. Some of the judges made the journey from the local metropolis of Tavistock. This year, the committee promised more events, and so more prizes, than ever before – a silver hot-water jug for the best hunter colt in the district, a pound for the best Dartmoor pony, two guineas for the best carthorse. The ladies were not forgotten. Whatever violence was being practised elsewhere in the country by suffragettes in pursuit of the vote, the dames of Lydford – its damsels too – were kept busy with musical chairs:

> . . . a source of great amusement and no little excitement, as lady after lady proved the odd one out, and at last the struggle for supremacy lay between those expert and well-matched horsewomen, Miss Calmady-Hamlyn and Miss Imogen Collier. The Band intensified interest in the result by prolonging its strains, and when the music suddenly ceased the two ladies made a dash for the vacant 'chair', and Miss Calmady-Hamlyn secured the first prize, amid much cheering.

It had been worth competing for: the winner folded three large cream and brown one-pound banknotes into her purse. Musical chairs did not, however, offer much of a diversion for boys. Wilfie Fry would surely have preferred watching male teams test their strength in the tug of war. In other years, such as 1911, the tug of war had been on horseback, with the young Lydford stonemason and hussar, Archie Huggins, cutting a dash.

Despite every effort of the committee, this year's Pony Show was not all that it might have been. It was not just that it rained: it does, in Devon. The spectators, three deep around the show ring, merely pulled their hats lower over their heads and their waterproof capes more tightly around their shoulders during deluges. Whatever their individual trade or calling, they were all outdoor people, powerfully shod in hobnailed boots, and it would take more than a spot of rain to distract them from the best pen of ewes or agricultural foal. When Lydford walked up over the springy turf to watch sheepdogs marshalling a flock on Black Down, it had no terror of damp feet. Besides, the crops needed the rain. No, the problem lay with the crowd.

The Frys, the Bickles, the Stanburys, the Pethericks, the Hugginses, the Mays, the Stephenses were there in force. These were village families, their names recurring whenever a tea was need for church or chapel, or a Sunday school treat laid on. They were joined by the usual number of visitors who spent their summer in the area, often measuring their stay in months rather than weeks. Visitors were becoming important to the village economy. They came to admire the white gush of the waterfall plunging down Lydford Gorge, and to peer into the Devil's Cauldron in which the river Lyd seems to boil. You could venture out over the Cauldron on a plank, hung on chains – a delight to boys who liked to swing on it. Occasionally, one of the bank holiday crowd fell in, usually being fished out uninjured – although in 1881 an 'elderly lady' of forty-nine who came with the Charles Church Lay Help Association became a martyr to 'natural beauties', pitching head first into the stream where, watched help-lessly by a housemaid, she met her death. Lodgings, declared Ward and Lock's *Dartmoor Guide* of 1913, could be had at many of the houses and cottages of the neighbourhood. Each year, the Lydford Manor Hotel published a list of the highly respectable guests who were residing there. The Hunters from Cheltenham, a family of eight, stayed for seventeen weeks at Armstor House, finding it all most satisfactory, according to Mrs Hunter's entry in the guest book. Improvements in the postal service (including an afternoon delivery) had been welcomed as benefitting such folk, although the village could still fall down. Until the Pony Show, the summer of 1914 had been so unaccountably dry that the Manor Hotel ran out of water to make tea: its genteel guests had to drink beer.

Visitors could turn into residents. William Widgery, the Victorian artist and connoisseur of Devon scenery, had made Lydford his home. Having started his working life as a stonemason, Widgery began painting in his leisure hours. Although untrained, he made such a success of his cattle pictures and Dartmoor scenes that he built him-self an Italianate villa outside the village (the end of its garden would periodically become enveloped in clouds of smoke as a steam train rattled unseen, but not unheard, through the deep cutting and under the bridge). His son Frederick, also a painter, lived on there after William's death in 1893. Other substantial houses followed. Sharptor, designed by E. G. Warren of Exeter in 1901, was one of the best of them. Mr Finch of Exeter had employed the Bickle family to build it; Mr Bickle Senior had caused 'great amusement' by a spirited rendition of 'Little Brown Jug' at the dinner to celebrate the completion of the house given at the Dartmoor Inn. The Bickles, though, may have overextended themselves; William Bickle of Bickle and Sons was declared bankrupt the next year.

Some new people had come into the area to work. There was a whole community of them around the railway junction, meeting in their own Bible Christian chapel. The nature of their employment meant that they came and went: in March, the GWR's stationmaster had been promoted to a similar post at Wrangaton, in the south of the county. Word of jobs, when any were to be had, could travel a long way. Edward Whitford was a Gloucestershire man who had been living in Ealing, West London; he had recently come to act as foreman at the sawmills that Squire Newman had established to serve his plantations at Coryton, a straggling settlement next to Lydford. Dating from the 1840s, the plantations were then reaching maturity. Whitford's brother Frederick Whitford was one of the stationmasters at Lydford Junction.

As usual at the Pony Show, there was a good showing of khaki. Officers strolled down in their polished field boots from the camp at Willsworthy, on the moor above the show fields, established as part of Britain's effort to up its game after the Boer War (it had a rifle range to practise the marksmanship in which it was felt the imperial force had been outclassed). What with the officers, the villagers, the summer visitors and folk who had walked, ridden or, conceivably, motored from Okehampton or Tavistock, the grandstand was nearly full. But the committee must have felt a sad absence of bustle. In other years, ranks had been swelled by excursion trippers, arriving on special trains. They did not come this year. It was nothing to do with the rain; the trains had been cancelled. Habitués of the village Reading Room may have guessed the cause from the weekly *Tavistock Gazette*. Among the fashion plates for bathing costumes (with a proper allowance of form-concealing woollen skirt), a consideration of the 'question of the moment' – Should women go to boxing matches? –

and an announcement about the Pony Show, the issue of 3 July had run the headline in heavy type:

ASSASSINATED. ARCHDUKE FRANCIS AND HIS WIFE SHOT. REVOLVER AFTER BOMB FAILURE.

Sarajevo must, at that distant time, only a month earlier, have seemed almost unimaginably remote from Devon. But as world events unfolded, the connection – to some, at least – became plain. West Country folk expected to hear Drake's Drum (emblazoned with the Elizabethan seafarer's coat of arms, it was said to beat of itself when the country was in danger). The government began to plan for mobilization.

Lydford was no stranger to war. Indeed, it owed its existence to it. Originally Lydford had been rather more than a village: it was one of the fortified burghs founded by Alfred the Great as part of his defensive strategy against the Danes. If a member of the Royal Flying Corps had taken you up in one of its string-and-sealing-wax planes, you would have seen that the Saxon layout had not changed. The village street is Saxon, the lanes that run off it are Saxon, and the town bank that the Saxons heaped up as an encircling defence still survives. That crack in the landscape which is Lydford Gorge opens with such suddenness, and goes so deep, that it forms its own microclimate. No attacker would have been able to swarm up this sheer-sided ravine and arrive in fighting condition at the top. Even Wilfie's friends, attacking the Norman castle under a hail of beer-bottle corks, would have been out of breath. The Saxons improved the position by building a wooden fortress whose earthworks, joining up with the town bank, survive beside St Petroc's Church. A spring that still flows gave water.

Saxon Lydford was even sufficiently important to mint its own silver pennies, the largest collection of which is now in Scandinavia, presumably there as part of the protection money that bought off the Danes. They show King Ethelred, hair sticking up in a Mohican crest, styled as a Roman emperor; a facsimile can be seen in the dining room of the Castle Inn. King Alfred's successors may not have been of the same mettle as him, but Lydford held its own. When the Vikings gave battle here, the people of Lydford town won.

Now war was once more in the rain-heavy air. Squire Calmady-Hamlyn of Bridestowe, a relation of the winner of musical chairs, captured the spirit when toasting the judges at the Pony Show luncheon. Referring to the European crisis, he made a sporting analogy: while he would not like to place the winners too exactly he would give England, France and Russia in the order named, with Germany unplaced. He was loudly cheered.

So what was the character of this village over whose leaky roofs storm clouds were both literally and metaphorically louring? The Castle Inn is aptly named. Just as Lydford had two railway stations, it also had more than one castle. The second, gaunt and square, is generally identified with the 'strong house' built by Edward I to detain royal prisoners in the mid-1190s; partly rebuilt in the thirteenth century, it came to serve as the gaol for the notorious Stannary Court. This court regulated the tinners of Dartmoor, on the principle that the King would not interfere with their activities as long as the Exchequer received a regular payment. The gaol had a deservedly evil reputation. Lydford Law became a byword for arbitrary justice: malefactors would be hanged and tried later, to save the expense of keeping them until the Assize could hear the case; prisoners were not given the benefit of doubt because, as Mr Toad's judge might have said, there clearly wasn't any. In 1520, Richard Strode, a tinner who was also an MP, was confined there for daring to propose in parliament that the tinners might restrict their activities in order to prevent the mouths of rivers from silting up. He had an unpleasant time of it, and the principle of parliamentary privilege was established as a result.

For centuries, Lydford thrived on tin. But by 1660, the proud, autocratic burgh, overtaken militarily by Launceston and commercially by Okehampton and Tavistock, is recorded as having 'dwindled now into a mean and miserable village'. The position had not improved by the end of the nineteenth century when a Devonshire historian wrote: 'Some scattered houses, a few green mounds, a crumbling ruin – these are modern Lydford.' In the 1870s, what might be taken at first glance as the third castle was built, to designs by the architect of the Law Courts, G. E. Street. This turreted building was the rectory, occupied for half a century by Revd George S. Thorpe, who may have had private means but still took his threadbare shirts to a village seamstress to have the collars turned.

In his invariable rusty black suit and black hat, Revd Thorpe, who asked young Wilfie to plant the yews, presided over one of the largest parishes in England. It extended as far as Princetown, fifteen miles away, enthusiastically developed by a Duchy of Cornwall surveyor as a holding station for Napoleonic prisoners of war, which closed after 1815, only to reopen as a civilian prison in 1851. (During the First World War it was converted to house conscientious objectors.) Every so often, the Lydford constable was instructed to watch the railway line during prison escapes, sometimes handcuffing recaptured prisoners to the kitchen table of his police house to await recovery. It was the prison's grimly proud boast that no prisoner ever got away.

So big was Lydford parish that inhabitants of outlying villages had to tramp for a dozen miles over the moor to reach St Petroc's Church: hence the sombre track known as the Lychway, or Way of the Dead, over which coffins were carried. In bad winters, when the Lychway was impassable, bodies had to be salted like the bacon and stored until conditions improved. Before the Victorian Age of Faith, snow would blow in through the gaps in the church wall, covering the altar. It should not be brushed off, proclaimed the curate one Christmas Day, because, 'God has spread His table.' There had been no resident rector before Revd Thorpe – and even he preferred not to be resident during the winter months, letting the rectory, hiring a locum and travelling to warmer climes. He got into trouble for being away too much, supposedly 'on urgent medical advice' as a result of 'the overstrain due to the great exertions he had made on behalf of the Parish for nearly 12 years', and said he would see the Bishop about getting a more suitable living. But there is an inertia about Devon villages, and he never moved.

Whatever feelings the rector may have had about the level of amenities at Lydford in 1914, the village was less primitive than it had been. A water supply had been provided by Daniel Radford, a successful Victorian coal merchant who had bought Lydford Gorge. The new water supply took the form of what looked like a couple of large tombstones set with taps. Householders still had to carry their buckets home, but they no longer hauled them up from a well or dipped them among the wildlife of the Saxon spring beside the town bank.

But Lydford was poor. Sometimes it barely scratched a living. The tin from which it used to prosper had given way to copper and other minerals. For a time, it was worth mining the silver that could be found in small quantities – perhaps the silver from which the Saxons had made Lydford pennies had been mined locally. When the copper boom of the 1860s passed, interest grew in a material that had previously been discarded as part of the waste: arsenic. It could be used to make an insecticide against the boll weevil that ruined the cotton crop in the southern United States, and it was exported in barrels. The first centre of arsenic production in the world was in Cornwall, but West Devon surpassed it. Arsenic gave some of the mines around Lydford a new lease of life – if such an expression can be used of a deadly material – and a few were still going in the early twentieth century. Brought to the surface, the ore was crushed into a powder which was then burnt. As the vapour snaked its way through long flues, a residue was deposited on the sides. Once it had built up to a sufficient depth, a worker, handkerchief across mouth, was sent in to scrape it off. Eventually even that source of employment came to an end. Devon miners then often followed their trade, travelling to work in mines elsewhere in Britain or overseas. Some sought their fortunes in the American and Australian gold rushes.

Farming had been doing badly for decades. The slump started in the 1870s. British agriculture could not compete with an increasingly global trade in commodities. Wheat came from Canada, beef arrived – first on the hoof and then in refrigerated ships – from South America, sheep from New Zealand. Britain exported the products of her heavy industries and fed herself from the Empire. Four-fifths of wheat flour came from overseas; it has been calculated that Britain's own farmers could only feed the nation for 125 days a year. The life of an agricultural labourer had not changed much since Stephen Duck wrote *The Thresher's Labour* in the eighteenth century. Steam traction engines pulled ploughs and operated chaff-cutting machinery on the big, highly capitalized enterprises of the High Farming movement. But the farms around Dartmoor were small, their land too hilly to be tilled by machine, their tenants too poor to innovate. (As late as the 1950s Devon fields were still being sown broadcast, as they were in the Bible.) For farmers, an independent breed who believed in standing on their own two feet, the economic conditions demanded exceptional measures: the National Union of Farmers was founded in 1908.

The economic tides which brought railway workers and foresters to Lydford carried others away. Richard Hobbs used to grow vegetables for a living. The market garden had been started by his father, William Hobbs, and was continued after William's death by Richard, his mother Mary, and a male servant named Bert Walter. It cannot have been easy – not least because the household included Hobbs's sister Maud who, born with a deformed spine, was 'unable to work'. Mary had been born at Lydford, but Richard never lived there; the family had moved down the fringe of the moor to Budge Hill at Whitchurch by 1891 when Richard, born at Tavistock, was two. In the summer of 1915, during a period of leave from the Devonshire Regiment, he married Louise Powlesland, daughter of a platelayer on the railway at Lydford Station; he was then still a gardener but living at Compton, on the edge of Plymouth. Perhaps Plymouth offered a bigger market for the vegetables.

With such poor prospects at home, some Lydford families moved further than Compton. R. J. Weaver of Okehampton, advertising as a 'Hairdresser, Tobacconist and SHIPPING AGENT', offered free passage and guaranteed employment for farmhands and domestic servants in Canada and Australia. It must have seemed a beguiling prospect. Others followed the traditional route, going beyond Compton to Plymouth itself and thence to sea. George Metters had been a stoker on Royal Navy ships since he joined in 1889. Shovelling coal all day, stokers often died before old age, and George was no exception. His last voyage was on HMS *Jupiter*, sent as an icebreaker to Archangel in 1915; thereafter he was confined to shore, not with a lung condition but a nervous complaint, until his death in 1916, aged forty-six. His name joins those of the dozen others who never came home after the First World War.

The tradition of seafaring continued. Poor Alfred Stanbury – known, in the confusing Lydford manner, as Jimmy – was the son of a platelayer at Lydford Station, sent to the Prince of Wales Sea Training Hostel for Boys for the Merchant Navy at Limehouse at the age of fourteen. He was only seventeen when his ship, the SS *Ahamo*, hit a mine off the Norfolk coast in 1941.

The men and women who emigrated, or otherwise left Lydford, carried a memory of it in their hearts, and Lydford kept a memory of them. Glasses were raised to absent friends.

Friends present, so far as the Pony Show on 3 August 1914 was concerned, would never forget it. This was the day on which Germany invaded Belgium and declared war on France. In the course of the afternoon, word was rushed down from Willsworthy that the army had mobilized. As Lieutenant Colonel G. S. Meadows of Belgrove, Lamerton, remembered when addressing a Pony Show audience in 1924, 'The various officers present from the neighbouring camps had to clear out,' and the show was, 'very nearly broken up.' War was declared on Germany at 11 p.m. the next day.

Later that week, when the *Tavistock Gazette* carried the news of the declaration of war, it was kept well away from the front page which, as was usual for the date, consisted of advertisements – for the Diabolo cream separator (capacity 27 gallons an hour, price £4 15s), boots and leggings, and R. Stranger and Sons' Holeproof Clothing. The report appeared between a dressmaking pattern for the pyjama suit – the 'latest thing in underwear for ladies . . . now recognised as the most ideal and hygienic night garment' – and 'Gardening Notes'. This gave an air of unreality to these tumultuous events. Many people expected the war to be over by Christmas.

Unlike the European powers, Britain had only a small standing army; Wilfie Fry had no reason to suppose he would be affected. Although some eager youths lied about their age to sign up – 'Come back tomorrow when you're nineteen,' the recruiting sergeants would tell under-age hopefuls, with a wink – fourteen was too young even to fudge. But when conscription was introduced in 1916, the age was lowered to eighteen (Wilfie would be eighteen in 1918).

Wilfie did not have much of a war. Sometime before March 1917, aged seventeen, he went to Plymouth and signed up with the Duke of Cornwall's Light Infantry. He was sent first to a training battalion in Wiltshire, then to another, formed by the Royal Warwickshire Regiment, at Larkhill. While he was there he caught pneumonia, perhaps weakened by the epidemic of Spanish influenza which swept Europe, killing more people than died under arms. Wilfie died at the age of eighteen, without having left the country.

When Lieutenant Colonel Meadows, perhaps not a master of public speaking, gave his address at the 1924 Pony Show, he remarked: 'Lots of us have forgotten the men who went out from this Show and never came to this Show again. I ask you to bear that in mind.' But Lydford had not forgotten Wilfie, who made the ultimate sacrifice. He was buried in the churchyard near the yews that he had planted; his name is on the granite cross of the war memorial.

2

The Dashing Hussar

⟝ ARCHIE HUGGINS ⟞

At the beginning of the twentieth century, Lydford Cricket Club was a typically village affair, playing in a bumpy meadow and keeping its scores in a book from Gamage's department store. The squire generally opened the batting, but never seemed to make more than a few runs, setting an unambitious standard for those who came after him. The Lydford team was no match for the bowlers from neighbouring Mary Tavy. But occasionally a young man would stride to the crease who made the scorer's heart leap. This was Archie Huggins, a stonemason who is remembered even now for his big hands, just one of which could stretch around, and pick up, an old-fashioned leather football. Photographs show that these hands were attached to equally formidable forearms and biceps. Archie, unlike Squire Radford, was a big hitter who would knock the ball to the boundary, or sometimes out of the cricket ground. One day in August 1901, as a lad in his early teens, he soared to a total of forty-eight runs. For Lydford, that was something to celebrate.

Yet Archie's cricket was as nothing to his football. While not above playing for the Lydford Park Rangers – he was probably on the legendary team that won all but one of its twenty-four matches – his impregnability in defence earned him a larger stage. Archie was the sterling right back of the Tavistock Football Club, otherwise known as the Lambs, who often 'saved the day' and 'won . . . unstinted praise from both friend and foe'. There is still a tribal memory that 'running into Archie was like hitting a brick wall'.

Soon after he was eighteen, Archie joined the Royal North Devon Hussars, one of the yeomanry regiments that had been raised in response to Prime Minister William Pitt's call for volunteers for home defence after France declared war in 1793. At that time, half the regular army was overseas, much of it in tropical stations that were wracked by sickness. What was needed was a 'species of Cavalry' consisting of 'gentlemen and yeomanry who would not be called upon to act out of their counties except under pressure of invasion or urgent necessity'. Under the inspiration of Lord John Rolle, a dozen troops were formed around Devon, later reorganized as squadrons in Barnstaple (the regimental headquarters), Torrington, South Molton and Bideford. When no invasion came, the yeomanry nevertheless proved their worth to the government by suppressing the unrest at home (parish constables were hardly equal to a rioting mob). Since the officers of the yeomanry were magistrates or the relations of magistrates, with the other ranks being farmers, they could be expected to deal robustly with cases of rick-burning and other threats to property. Across the country, the record was not always a noble one; it was a yeomanry regiment, the worse for drink, that rode down an unarmed crowd in the Peterloo Massacre of 1819.

The Devon yeomanry were more likely to be found on escort duty, whether taking a condemned man to the gallows or Lord Nelson to his hotel. Very fine they must have looked, in their flamboyant uniforms of dark blue with scarlet facing and white lace (or silver for officers). Their tall scarlet headgear (the distinctive busby bags) were set off with a white plume. But by the end of the nineteenth century they were regarded as something of a comic opera turn.

Then came the British disasters in the Boer War. The yeomanry regiments were hastily re-formed, as 'the farmers of Britain were called to go overseas to meet the farmers of the veldt'. From now on, the yeomanry were expected to behave like soldiers, with exercises under canvas rather than at fashionable watering-holes, proper musketry training, a new title – the Imperial Yeomanry – for those willing to serve overseas, and khaki uniforms of loose-fitting tunic and riding breeches (the latter with blue velvet stripes down the seams, supposedly to prevent farmers from wearing them around their yards). It was a serious force that Archie had joined, though nobody would have said it was as smart as one of the fashionable cavalry regiments, for which a private income was necessary. Leonard Gamlen joined on 20 August 1914 and wrote an account of his experiences, now in the Barnstaple Museum. Waved off by three maiden aunts fluttering handkerchiefs, and patriotically endorsed by the domestic staff, he was attired in clothes that had been carefully chosen to suggest a 'sporting agriculturalist'.

One of the attractions of the yeomanry was that the government helped with the costs of a horse. Archie had probably been riding Dartmoor ponies since he was a boy, beginning, if the example of other Devon lads is anything to count on, by jumping aboard without either bridle or saddle, hoping that he would be able to stop in due course – and if not, tumbling off. Early experiences of that kind would have qualified him for his role later in life as a member of one of the daring, bare-back equestrian tug-of-war teams who competed at county shows.

Every so often, the polished field boots and peaked caps of the hussars were exchanged for striped football jerseys. Naturally, Archie was a member of a regimental team, and it is in this persona that we see him in a photograph taken outside a bell tent at an army camp, perhaps on Salisbury Plain, in 1907. He stands in the back row, his beefy arms folded; the players have been joined by a handful of NCOs, one of whom carries a swagger stick. Archie was a corporal, rising to become a sergeant before 1915; perhaps it was an NCOs' team.

Everyone in Lydford knew the Hugginses. Archie was one of thirteen children, the fourth youngest, born in 1887, two years after the twins, Baron and Laura. They all crammed into a cottage just over the parish boundary, in Bridestowe (although when Archie was born the eldest, Lily, might have followed the usual route for village girls and gone into service, relieving a little of the pressure on the accommodation). There were two bedrooms, the children squeezing into beds where they could find them, whether in a bedroom, on the landing outside, or in the kitchen or parlour downstairs. There had been Hugginses in this part of Devon since the mid-eighteenth century. They had come to work in the mines, extracting tin and other minerals from the rocks under the surface of Dartmoor. But before long they had changed jobs, preferring to avoid the sudden fluctuations that bedevilled mining and choosing to work instead with another aspect of the geology of Dartmoor, visible to anyone who crosses it. Granite.

Despite the turf, the gorse and the rain, Dartmoor is not all green. In places the granite rears up into tors – strangely shaped stacks or columns that suggest a menagerie of archaic beasts that some Snow Queen has turned to stone. They are the stumps of larger outcrops that, over millennia, have been stripped of all but their innermost, peculiar core. Elsewhere granite just lies around. Humps of it push through the covering of peat and grass, somewhat as though a great herd of grey-backed elephants is sleeping, restlessly, below the turf. So stone was there for the taking – if, that is, you were a commoner and you could get it.

It was a slow and laborious process to separate a useful slab of granite from its bed. The stonemason took a chisel and, turning it at each blow, drilled a hole in the rock; then he made another a few inches away. This was followed by a third, and so on, until there was a whole line of holes. Into each of them he would then hammer a feather and tares. This instrument consisted of two wings of soft metal – the feathers – with a point of hard steel between them. The hammer made the metal 'sing'. After the feathers and tares had all reached the same note, there would come the thud that indicated the stone had split – in theory, along the line of the holes that had been drilled. But the split did not always go according to plan, and Dartmoor is littered with broken stones that were never dragged off the moor. Hauling a slab on to a cart, using chains pulled by a horse, was itself a significant undertaking (I have spoken to the granddaughter of a stonemason whose fingers caught in the chains and left him with a crippled hand while doing so). Archie would have been well used to splitting and hauling granite. No wonder he had such big hands.

As stonemasons, the Hugginses perhaps shared an affinity with far earlier inhabitants of the area, one of whose tools – a rare hammer-axe made in the third millennium BC – was found by Archie's great-nephew, Graham Huggins, near the Dartmoor Inn in 1977. The hammer-axe is made of stone. Stone remained part of the fabric of Dartmoor life long after Devon's reluctant entry into the machine age. It was the material that built Lydford's cottages, farmhouses, barns and outhouses, before the advent of concrete block in the twentieth century. Traditional Lydford's restricted palette – grey touched with silver, pink and charcoal – is that of the colours of the stone on the moor. Aesthetically it was harmonious, but the housing stock left much to be desired.

Archie worked with his father, Roger, and his brothers Baron, Gilbert and 'Bird'. In his mid-seventies, Roger Huggins wore a bowler hat and corduroys, and sported long whiskers. He was often seen with his Jack Russell in his wooden wheelbarrow. The sort of work that he and his sons had on hand can be seen from a surviving account book: replastering at Bridge House for Mr Radford; clearing out the chimney at Forda Mill. Missing roofing slates had to be put back after storms. The slates came from Coryton and tended to flake, each storm reducing their thickness until one or two would disappear completely every time a strong wind blew up. 'Baron and Arch rep roofs' is a typical entry. As masons, they could fashion a garden sun-dial if required, but usually supplied 'granite heads' or lintels over door or window openings for five shillings each. A granite roller or gatepost fetched just half a crown. It was not much, considering the trouble that had to be taken in wresting the blocks from the moor.

But, as we have seen, Archie also had his hours of relaxation. And so it is that one evening in January 1914 we find him in the village Reading Room, playing billiards for a church team against one captained by his brother Harry. He is twenty-seven years old. The church team loses, but, true to form, Archie saves their honour by demolishing his opponent. February followed January, the year rolled on, and Lydford went about its usual pursuits: planting vegetables; regretting that the mine at Peter Tavy, where the Huggins forebears once worked, should have gone into receivership; congratulating Mr Browning, stationmaster at Lydford's Great Western Railway for several years, on his appointment as stationmaster at Wrangaton, South Devon; attending (if Tory) the Primrose League's whist drive, an evening of cards and Conservatism. Archie, though, has other things on his mind.

In late spring, he marries Lily Wonnacott in St Petroc's Church. Not only does he quit his parents' overcrowded cottage, but he leaves Lydford altogether. He and Lily make their new home at South Tawton, further around the shoulder of Dartmoor and five miles closer to the town of Okehampton where a stonemason could find more work than in Lydford. But barely had the couple settled into their cottage when Germany invaded Belgium. The Tavistock Football Club announced that it would defer 'all football until December, or until the war is over'. Like most people, it expected the fighting to be over by Christmas.

Five hours before the British ultimatum to Germany had expired, the Royal North Devon Hussars had been ordered to mobilize. Some officers, such as the machine-gun officer, Captain the Hon. Hugh Money-Coutts, a former MP, later Lord Latymer, succeeded in reaching regimental headquarters at Barnstaple that night. Money-Coutts, however, had a motorcar. Corporal Huggins probably joined A Squadron at Torrington the next day. Men were desperate to join them – Barnstaple was:

> . . . brimming over with warlike enthusiasm. You could hardly show
> yourself abroad without someone plucking at your sleeve, and asking
> if there was not room for just one more recruit. But we were only
> a little below our establishment numbers, and vacancies were few.

All ranks numbered 459 men, short only of 3 captains and 14 other ranks. Hastily, the officers did their best to ensure that the regiment had the necessary equipment. For Money-Coutts, this meant finding adequate transport for his machine guns: to his fury, the purchase officer had only succeeded in providing a couple of lumbering farm carts which would not have been able to keep up with the cavalry. With the help of a local doctor, he stood at the top of a hill, assessing the personality of the locals driving past. Those who were most likely to be patriotically disposed were simply asked for the loan of their vehicles. They willingly gave them, neither side realizing that they would not be returned for a year.

Officers checked the items that the men were supposed to supply for themselves. A toothbrush without bristles might be produced, or a boot full of holes, or thin evening socks. Often, they put off buying replacements for as long as possible. 'It was a very harassing arrangement for the squadron leaders.'

On the Glorious Twelfth of August, first day of the grouse-shooting season, the North Devons were in a stuffy troop train, heading away from the moor (where sportsmen did attempt to shoot grouse in the early twentieth century) to Winchester, which – despite the improbability of any Germans appearing there – was suffering an invasion scare. Next day they were ordered to proceed directly to Essex, where it was thought the Germans were about to land. Money-Coutts with his machine guns, on their inelegant but serviceable wagons, arrived ahead of the rest and, having eaten, immediately turned in. But alas, as he remembered:

> . . . not for long. At midnight, August 13th–14th, came a banging at my door, and a peremptory summons: 'Turn out, the Germans are coming!'
>
> This was quite exciting, and really made the pulse beat quicker, half asleep though one was. As I was dressing, the Adjutant came up to my room and showed me the War Office telegram, 'Admiralty expect a landing tonight.' He gave me the Colonel's orders about my guns, which I got out of the carts and placed in position on the main road; two Cossack posts were sent out – one under the charge of the Regimental, consisting of two servants, a cook and an Army Service Corps driver; the other, under the Headquarters' Quartermaster-Sergeant, of a sanitary man, the doctor's orderly, two Headquarters' clerks, and the Colonel's groom. Some of them were given a little hasty instruction about loading a rifle, and we felt we were safe against surprise – from the Germans, anyhow. All kinds of surprises from our own side were possible.

Eventually Money-Coutts dozed off in a ditch beside his guns. The invasion never came, but the episode shows how real the possibility seemed to the War Office, which remained subject to scares for the rest of the year. Archie and his comrades were kept in a state of constant readiness. They practised alarms. No NCO or yeoman was allowed to go unarmed for more than half a mile from the base without specific permission. When General Sir Ian Hamilton, General Officer Commanding-in-Chief Central Force (Home Defence) inspected the regiment, he intimated that they would go abroad as soon as they had completed their musketry training.

But it was not to be. Instead, the North Devons did what they could to enjoy a glorious autumn – the harvest was good that year – before, in November, moving into the seaside resort of Clacton, a place of grand hotels and people's palaces, well suited to providing billets for troops and stables for horses. Day began at 5.45 with 'stables', a twice-daily ritual during which the horses were fed, groomed and had their feet picked out. New recruits were made well aware that equines were more valuable than humans, given that the latter could be hired for a shilling a day while the former cost forty pounds. This might be followed by three hours in the riding school. A razor-backed mount, such as Lieutenant Leonard Gamlen had been allotted, could rasp the tender skin off the sensitive parts of an anatomy unused to long periods in the saddle, giving a new meaning to the term 'raw recruit'. Gamlen was fortunate that his batman had been a dentist's assistant in private life and could apply bandages, while one of his aunts rallied round to the point of personally visiting Mr Ross, the family tailor in Exeter, who had made Gamlen's clothes since he was at school. Mr Ross prescribed pants made of chamois leather, with holes punched in them for ventilation, which became 'coveted by the whole Squadron' (fragments of which Gamlen was still using, long after the war, for polishing silver). The staff sergeant major was a 'holy terror', but once Gamlen had got the hang of both him and the riding exercises, he found it 'really rather fun'.

One of the prime functions of cavalry was scouting, and this they practised, leaving a couple of men in a field while the others hunted for them. Long hours were spent learning semaphore for rapid communication in the field. Like the rest of the British cavalry, the North Devons were also drilled in infantry techniques, digging trenches and trying out the bayonets with which they were issued in November. Shooting skills were honed on the rifle range. In France, it was found that neither the French nor German cavalry were so useful on foot as the British. Mastery of foreign tongues was another matter. 'Commenced trying to learn French talk,' noted one trooper, presumably thinking that they might be going to France. 'Find it very difficult.' Leonard Gamlen was unusual: he had lived in France.

Inevitably, although the regiment remained on the qui vive for invasion, a certain lassitude set in. The Master of the Devon and Somerset Staghounds, Major Morland Greig, had some of his pack sent up from the kennels and ran a drag from time to time; there was also the occasional day's hunting. But the fun was rather spoiled by the authorities' not unreasonable insistence that government-owned horses could not be used for the purpose. Instead, there was drill. No doubt the North Devons needed tuning up. (One North Devon yeoman, when asked who was the officer commanding his brigade, replied, 'I bain't rightly sure, sir; but I zim 'tis the old gentleman with the red band to his cap that rideth about with Squire Bampfylde,' who was in fact his aide-de-camp.) Even so, Lord Kitchener's edict that any man who showed sufficient surplus energy to kick a football about was to be fallen in and drilled again forthwith must have dismayed a man as sporty as Archie. All drill and no action beyond the occasional sighting of a Zeppelin overhead: he and others must have felt themselves going stale.

Further along the coast, exercising their horses on the sands at Thorpe-le-Soken, near Frinton-on-Sea, were the 1st West Somerset Yeomanry. They and the North Devons formed part of the 2nd South-West Mounted Brigade. One of the West Somersets was young Private H. C. Brittain, who joined in early 1915, a year and six months below the official recruitment age of nineteen. Before the war, Brittain had worked as a gardener for a 'good and kind lady', Baroness Le Clement de Taintegnies, at Minehead. (Pleased that he was doing his bit when he was sent abroad, she arranged for supplies of cigarettes and tobacco to be sent to him from the Army and Navy Stores, in Victoria Street.) When Brittain's regiment, with the North Devons, eagerly volunteered for service in the Mediterranean, his enthusiasm was tempered by surprise and dismay: their horses were to be taken from them. Dismounted, both regiments were to be refitted as infantry, the only consolation being that they would retain their cavalry pay.

★

At last the North Devons were going overseas. But where? When lightweight cotton drill uniforms were issued, the men knew one thing if no more: they were not going to the Western Front. We see Archie in a photograph taken at this time, wearing his new sola topi, a plume to one side, his three sergeant's stripes on his sleeve. His usual cap badge had been unpicked and sewn on to a new helmet. Gone is the brawny confidence of the conquering sportsman: he looks as eager as a schoolboy. Every soldier was given fourteen days' leave to say goodbye to their loved ones – although in Brittain's case he did not have the courage to break it to his mother that he was going to the front. There was a final parade, and – if the North Devons were anything like the Royal 1st Devon Yeomanry – 'a tremendous lot of kissing went on amongst the men & the girls they were leaving behind them'. As the historian of the Devon Yeomanry, writing a dozen years later, Benson Freeman would pass the following judgement on the war so far: 'It is probably not too much to say that no one in either regiment enjoyed his year in Essex.'

The North Devons, like the rest of the South-West Brigade, climbed into their railway carriages without any idea where they were going. They watched the names for enlightenment. After Colchester, they discovered that their direction was north; this, some of them realized, meant Liverpool. The men whose loved ones were at that moment hurrying to Plymouth, to see them off from their native Devon, were aghast; on the other hand, the more sensitive were pleased to be spared the pain of seeing familiar landmarks disappearing into the distance. Pint mugs of tea for the men and 'tea baskets' for officers were served at Crewe. Once at Liverpool, the regiment posted its letters – the last to avoid the eyes of the censor – and the men struggled to the docks under the weight of their kitbags.

Anyone who was inclined to regret leaving home would not have had his spirits raised by the weather. Damp was the word to describe it – mist turning to rain. It might not have seemed so depressing if the men had realized this would be the last proper rain the regiment would experience until November. Out of the drizzle loomed the immense bulk of the RMS *Olympic*, 300 yards long, her steel hull rising like a cliff above the docks. The country boys could hardly

believe the size of her. From the top of her four funnels to the water-
line, the whole of her exterior was painted in clashing colours and
streaking geometry, the proto-Jazz Age dazzle camouflage invented
by the marine artist Norman Wilkinson (later notable for his advertising posters) to confuse the enemy. A naval air was supplied by the
presence of two twelve-pound guns, mounted fore and aft, and eight
machine guns around the deck. But nothing the navy had done could
disguise the beauty of the ship, one of an entirely new breed of sleek
superliners, sister ship to the RMS *Titanic*, launched and sunk only
three years before. The identical twin sister in fact, since every detail
was to the same pattern, down to the Royal Crown Derby plates in
the first-class dining room. All of Britain had heard of *Olympic*, which
had rolled down Harland and Wolff's Belfast slipway in 1911, the year
before *Titanic*. As the first of the Olympic Class ships in the sea (the
third being RMS *Britannic*), she attracted far more attention than her
twin: it was only when disaster struck the *Titanic* that her fame was
eclipsed. For a time she was the fastest ship in the world. As the
U-boat threat increased, speed in the water was an ever more desirable quality, and so the Admiralty had ordered her out from the yard
at Belfast, where she had been sent for the duration of the hostilities.
She was now HMT (His Majesty's Troopship) *Olympic*.

Naturally, exploring this wonder of the seas was the first priority
for many men, who took a schoolboyish interest in the boiler and
engine rooms, clanking over metal floors amid the thrilling novelty
of the castings, pipes and tubes. They may have taken a particular
interest in the modifications that had been made since the *Titanic* disaster, which included the addition of watertight skins and bulkheads,
and extra lifeboats. In time, the men who sailed in HMT *Olympic*
would call her *Old Reliable*, perhaps not the most flattering of names
for such a paragon of marine engineering, but an affectionate one.
They had no reason to extol their berths. Archie's sleeping quarters
would almost certainly have become 'very stuffy and uncomfortable'
as the voyage progressed. On the lower decks, 100 men had to sleep
in a room that measured 40 feet by 20 feet, with no possibility of
opening the portholes once the voyage had started.

Accompanying the North Devons were eight other yeomanry

regiments, as well as a quantity of Canadian doctors. It made quite a crowd, 6,000 troops in total. 'I am sure a finer body of men were never gathered together anywhere,' observed the ship's Captain, Bertram Hayes. In the bustle of departure, men explored the decks and staircases, trying to memorize a route back to their rooms. Rifles were now stored in the armoury and helmets in the helmet room. No doubt Archie was among those who went back on deck for the excitement of the departure. As the ship started to move, someone played 'Home Sweet Home' on a cornet, a moment of sentimentality which only the leatheriest of old soldiers found unaffecting. An elderly sentry on the quay felt moved to take off his cap and wave it on top of his rifle, an unmilitary gesture of encouragement for which a brigadier, who happened to be on the bridge, roared at him.

Another soldier, the young sculptor Charles Sargeant Jagger, who would survive service with the Worcestershire Regiment to create the Royal Artillery Memorial on Hyde Park Corner, had left Southampton shortly before Archie on the Cunarder RMS *Franconia*. In a letter to Connie, his future wife, he described the departure as 'one of the greatest days I shall live to see . . . [When] we passed out of the Sound the air was simply rent with cheer upon cheer from the shore.'

There was a marked difference between the conditions enjoyed – or endured – by the officers and the men. The former were housed in 'great luxury', as was only to be expected on such a glamorous ship. 'Hosts of friends on board,' noted the North Devons' commanding officer, Colonel Robert Sanders, who was familiarly known, for some reason, as Peter. He was a Norfolk-born barrister who had taken a first at Oxford but masked his cleverness beneath the image of an Old Tory hunting squire. 'We had an MP's dinner and a Master of Hounds dinner on way out.' As for the latter, the North Devons were able to contribute 7 Masters and ex-Masters to the 24 who sat around the central table. When someone produced a horn, it was passed around the table and blown by each in turn. Rumour had it that the passenger list represented more wealth than had ever been on the ship before, not excluding its time as a transatlantic liner at the height of the season. Captain R. S. Hawker, a machine-gunner with the Royal 1st Devon Yeomanry, could hardly believe his luck. 'Officers were well catered for in the way of amusements,' having, 'a swimming bath with nice clean water in it & a room on the boat deck with all kinds of things for taking exercise, riding, rowing, camel riding, spine massage, biking, Ball Punching'. This last took place in a gymnasium rather empty of exercise machines by today's standards, but with walls that were wood panelled; the punch ball was suspended from a circular plate beneath the ceiling. Occupants of the old First Class section swept to dinner down an elaborately carved staircase, beneath a glass dome, the atmosphere that of a country house. The à la carte restaurant was in the Louis XVI style of the fashionable Ritz Hotel, richly panelled, carved and gilded, while the immense, white dining saloon – the largest room afloat in 1911 – evoked an earlier age, the Merrie England of Elizabeth I.

The kitchens appear to have operated to much the same standard that they would have done when *Olympic* was the pride of the White Star Line. When Captain Hawker wanted to celebrate his promotion and recent marriage, he could order a dozen bottles of champagne. 'Our food continues wonderfully good & such a remarkable variety of dishes too!' exclaimed another young officer. 'In this respect I fancy our experience must be unique.' It was certainly a contrast to circumstances on the lower decks. There, the 'voige', as one soldier spelt it, did not seem to be a pleasure cruise. The men had to queue for the canteen, there was little choice, and supplies ran short. Some country boys felt distinctly underfed. The worst of it was the close atmosphere when the portholes were closed, which became increasingly oppressive as the ship steamed through the Straits of Gibraltar and into the Mediterranean. Still, the meals of soup, meat and potatoes were not despised by all, and were probably an improvement on the fare served in some homes – it would also prove better and more reliable than soldiers would find on shore. And one had to remember, as *The Shipbuilder* observed when *Olympic* was launched: 'Third-class passengers today have greater comforts provided than had first-class passengers before the great modern developments in passenger carrying, for which the White Star Line is largely responsible.'

The buoyant-spirited ambulance man Frank Phillips enjoyed 'an experience of quite a new kind'; it was rather fun to sleep in a hammock (or 'hamlet', as one soldier persisted in calling it), and the other ranks had a swimming pool too. Each soldier was allowed a dip of ten minutes, timed by blasts on a whistle. There were a few rounds of boxing, for those who liked it – Archie, no doubt, included.

There was, however, one experience that everyone shared, once the ship reached the Bay of Biscay. It is a place notorious for its heavy seas, the Atlantic rollers having had 3,000 miles of uninterrupted ocean to gather strength. On *Olympic* mal de mer was no respecter of rank. 'All the men frightfully seasick and going into their quarters was just awful. Where they vomited there they lay like logs & one fairly waded in it!' The officers also suffered, if in more stylish surroundings. Someone threw up over Captain Hawker's boots, before he himself went aft to lean over a rail. But the next day, a cheerful machine-gunner, James Tozer from the Royal 1st Devon Yeomanry, could record the weather as 'beautiful & sea quiet'. Three days later, on 30 September, he wrote in his diary: 'Voyage up to this point *simply delightful.*'

He was not the only person on board to appreciate the journey to war as if it were a cruise. He felt the incongruity:

We are a cheerful crowd, and it is hard – nay impossible – to believe we are going to risk our lives within a very few days. I don't suppose to find a better illustration of the typical English temperament than here on the boat. Here we are in the smoking room chatting, laughing and playing bridge as tho' it were just a pleasure trip we were taking.

One episode did remind the troops of the dangers of war. On 1 October, *Olympic* stopped to rescue nearly three dozen French sailors who were adrift in an open boat off Cape Matapan, their collier having been torpedoed that morning – 'a rather rough looking lot, in all coloured jerseys', as they seemed to the insular British troops. Brass hats in the British army did not approve of the risk incurred by slowing the ship, but the French government later awarded the ship's captain the Médaille de Sauvetage en Or de 2ème Classe. Their rowing boat provided a 'little target practice' for the machine-gunners, who were disappointed to find that it did not immediately sink, despite being riddled with bullets. If Archie had been below deck, he would have heard, shortly afterwards, a 'crash, and a bang'. Everyone rushed on deck, and rumours flew. Had the ship been hit by a torpedo? There was another boom, caused by one of the ship's guns, which turned out to be responsible for the first sound too. *Olympic* swung round in her course. Money-Coutts's cup of tea slid off the table as the ship keeled over. *Olympic*'s quartermaster had seen the conning tower of a submarine. Many of the men were convinced that they had glimpsed a torpedo streaking across *Olympic*'s wake. Similarly, the gunner swore that he had hit the target. Cooler heads regarded both assertions with scepticism, although, writing about the episode after later investigation, Colonel Sanders agreed that a submarine had probably been there. From now on, the ship zigzagged, in an attempt to confuse the enemy. The captain must have regretted that the three destroyers who escorted *Olympic* – doing their best to keep up with her spanking pace – on the first part of the voyage out of Liverpool had taken themselves elsewhere. (In May 1917, *Olympic* would take revenge by ramming a U-boat whose crew had to abandon it.)

Around noon on 2 October, Olympic reached the island of Lemnos, where, according to Greek mythology, Hephaestus, the god of fire and smiths, fell to earth when banished from heaven by Zeus, leaving him forever lame. Jason and the Argonauts supposedly enjoyed the company of the island's women, all of whom had murdered their husbands. As late as 1912, Lemnos, less than a hundred miles from Istanbul, had belonged to Turkey, but that year the Greeks captured it during the First Balkan War. It was never much visited by travelling Britons, but the purse-like enclosure of Mudros Bay, enclosed by two submarine nets, provided an excellent natural harbour. As *Olympic* steamed into it under a blazing Mediterranean sun, a band on a French ship played a welcome. 'It sounded lovely across the water,' sighed Frank Phillips.

The bay presented a 'superb' spectacle, according to the war correspondent Ellis Ashmead-Bartlett. It was crowded with ships of every description, from the battleship *Queen Elizabeth* with her immense and devastating guns, to cruisers, torpedo boats, trawlers, tramp steamers and any number of smaller craft, some more elegant than others, but all full of interest to men who had been cooped up on *Olympic* for a week – particularly a rowing boat carrying three local girls. Conspicuous among the vessels was a large hospital ship, which stood out in nun-like simplicity against the warships, dressed not in 'razzle dazzle' but virginal white, marked with a large red cross on its bow and flag. To add to the colour, that whale of the skies, a dirigible, floated overhead, advertising the presence of a large Royal Naval Air Service airship station. Positive as ever, Frank Phillips found the scene to be 'just lovely', the land dotted with lines of tents for a long way down the coast. Some people saw in the landscape a resemblance to Dartmoor, although the crags were not green so much as colourless in the shimmering heat. F. D. Baker was not one of them. He was not the least bit tempted to go ashore, 'so barren, bleak and totally devoid of interest does this island base appear'. His assessment would have been reinforced by the views of those who had spent any time in the dusty tents and hutments, which were the lot of troops who did find themselves on Lemnos, en route to the front. For a week, Archie and his fellow soldiers were not allowed to leave *Olympic*; but at least the engines had stopped.

There was a surprise for the officers who had painstakingly issued their men with tropical kit before leaving: it was no longer wanted. The breezy assumption by the War Office that the Mediterranean was bound to be hot had been unfounded. While the days here could be baking, the nights, as autumn set in, were correspondingly cold. So cap badges had to be removed and sewn back on to regular hats. Still, it gave the troops something to do. Having arrived, Colonel Sanders found himself without orders. This meant that the North Devons had to wait in the bay, along with the other regiments, much to the frustration of all. There was little to occupy the men beyond drill. A lecture on precautions to be taken in the trenches advised that it was 'very unhealthy' to gaze over the top, as soldiers who had seen their comrades collapse beside them, a sniper's bullet in their head, would have confirmed. Captain Hayes ordered *Olympic*'s boats to be lowered so that the men could have some exercise rowing about the bay. Ominously, he heard General Sir Bryan Mahon, who came on to *Olympic* from the battlefield, remark that his best friend's heels stuck out of the sand within six feet of his dugout, because bodies could not be buried adequately. (As it happened, Hayes knew the best friend in question, a lieutenant in the 10th Hussars.)

Deprived even of newspapers, unreliable as the reporting was, and with only patchy wireless transmissions to connect them to the outside world, all manner of notions abounded about the progress of the war and the North Devons' future destination. Almost all of it was untrue. Five times the sun sank behind the hills on one side of the bay, seeming to cover the sky in gold leaf; five times it rose again from behind the opposite hills . . . and the North Devons were still there. But on the evening of 7 October, they were issued the iron rations on which they could draw when desperate: a pound tin of bully beef, some tooth-breaking biscuits, and a tin containing tea, sugar and Oxo cubes. They would disembark in the morning. Reveille on 8 October was at the unpopular hour of 4 a.m. A smaller troopship, the Khedivial Line steamer *Osmanieh*, drew up alongside *Olympic*, looking 'like a pygmy beside a giant'. It could now have been no secret to the troops that the North Devons were heading for the Dardanelles.

The Dardanelles strait is a long, narrow file of water, clamped between the Gallipoli peninsula and the easternmost part of Turkey. Known to classicists as the Hellespont (Sea of Helle), it runs for sixty miles. Generally the water is about three miles wide, although in some places much less. Otherwise dusty classicists, such as the eighteenth-century historian Edward Gibbon, thrilled to think of 'the adventurous Leander . . . [braving] the passage of the flood for the possession of his mistress', or Xerxes spanning the channel with 'a stupendous bridge of boats, for the purpose of transporting into Europe an hundred and seventy myriads of barbarians'. While Gibbon never actually visited the Dardanelles, Lord Byron did, famously imitating Leander's feat by swimming the Hellespont himself.

In 1914, Turkey threw in its lot with Germany and the Austro-Hungarian Empire. To the Allies, the importance of the Dardanelles was in the entrance the strait provided from the Mediterranean to the Sea of Marmara and the Turkish capital of Constantinople, now Istanbul. If Istanbul fell, it would be possible for Allied ships to slip through the Bosphorus into the Black Sea. An attack would at the very least open another front in the war, at a time when the armies in France and Belgium had become bogged down in the mud of the trenches. Had an attack been successful, it would have knocked Turkey out of the conflict, brought Romania into it (on the side of the Allies, before 1916) and opened another route into Russia. Although it is unlikely that the planners foresaw the fall of the Romanov dynasty, the ability to bring munitions and other supplies to the ports of Novorossiysk (in Russia) and Odessa (in Ukraine) to alleviate the shortages in Russia might have delayed the Russian Revolution until after the end of the war. In any case, seizing possession of the Dardanelles would have materially shortened the conflict.

Even to think of an attack took daring, because conventional wisdom had it that the Dardenelles were impregnable and could not even be forced by the might of the British navy. But the First Lord of the Admiralty, Winston Churchill, was not a conventional man. The strategic prize was too great for his boundless optimism to resist. Unable to convince the army to share his vision, he persuaded the Cabinet to allow him to launch an attack using the navy alone. In February 1915, an Anglo-French fleet began to bombard the Ottoman forts at the narrowest point of the strait; a month later, eighteen battleships attempted to force their way through. It was a disaster. Ten days earlier, an extra line of mines had been sown in the strait. The French battleship *Bouvet* hit a mine and sank. HMS *Irresistible* struck another, and so did HMS *Ocean* on its way to rescue her; it was the end of both ships. Several other vessels were severely hurt. Although they were down to their last ammunition, the defenders forced a powerful fleet to turn back.

The Allies' intention as regards the Dardanelles was now declared. They meant to control the strait, and to do so would have to silence the Turkish guns in order to sweep away the mines. The Turks hurriedly set about reorganizing their defences, and had several weeks in which to do it, before a Mediterranean Expeditionary Force could arrive from England and France. A maze of trenches was dug above the beaches. Barbed wire was strung out. The war correspondent Ellis Ashmead-Bartlett summed up the result.

The whole position was indeed one of the most formidable which an army has ever attempted to take even under normal conditions. But when it is remembered that the men had to be rowed ashore and landed from boats without a particle of cover, the feat becomes even more inexplicable.

The troops included the last of the original British Expeditionary Force, the old professional army, which had gone to France in 1914. They were, Ashmead-Bartlett believed, almost too good for the job. They succeeded in landing where others would have failed. If they had been repulsed on the first day, the whole Gallipoli campaign, with its suffering, needless heroism and waste of human life, might have been called off.

As a member of A Squadron, Archie must have watched the departure of the rest of the battalion on *Osmanieh* with regret; he was one of the detachment of five officers and forty men who stayed with Major Bayly at Mudros for a further five days. Whatever excitement the encampment on land had to offer a young man experiencing his first taste of a foreign country would soon have been exhausted.

But let us follow the rest of the battalion. Despite the early start, it took until the early afternoon for the 1st Devons to file down the companion ladders and into *Osmanieh*; the North Devons left *Olympic* around 3.30 p.m., followed by the West Somerset Yeomanry. Those who had been sick during the voyage cast a nervous eye at the choppy water – with just cause, as it would turn out. But initially the sixty miles to the Gallipoli peninsula were covered without incident. As they arrived in the gathering darkness, some British torpedo boats off Cape Helles, firing at Turkish positions in the hills, gave them their first sight of action. Cape Helles is at the southernmost extremity of the peninsula; the South-West Brigade headed towards the north of the peninsula's Aegean coastline, in a scrubby sweep called Suvla Bay.

There is a sandy beach at Suvla Bay but little else beyond sand dunes, some wisps of vegetation and, to one side, the bald expanse of a salt lake without a particle of cover. Further inland rise the Anafarta Hills. Anzac Cove lies four miles to the south: the Australian and New Zealand force, their night landing having taken place on the

wrong beach, had been bottled up there since April. In August, the
British had attacked Suvla Bay using a new kind of shallow-bottomed
craft known as the 'beetle'; for once, the initial plan had been successful, the Turks having been so distracted by subterfuge and diversions
that this section of coast was only lightly defended. Perhaps they
wondered who might want to land in such a desiccated and un-
promising location. But the poor reconnaissance that bedevilled the
Dardanelles mission meant that the strength and whereabouts of the
Turkish positions were unknown. One of the morning's objectives,
Chocolate Hill, was captured at sunset. General Stopford – a man of
sixty-one years, yet a mere novice in terms of his experience in the
field – trod cautiously, fearing stiffer opposition than existed.

The next day, Sunday, proved to be a day of rest. The men had
been overcome by the fatigue and thirst of the roasting summer heat.
The formidable Turkish commander Mustafa Kemal (later famous as
Turkey's nationalist and first President, Atatürk) knew exactly what
use to make of the invaders' slow progress: he reinforced. The slopes
of the hill, wooded and cracked by ravines, could hide thousands of
defending troops. An unforeseen horror emerged when the shells
from ships set alight the scrub on a feature called Scimitar Hill. The
war correspondent Ellis Ashmead-Bartlett saw crawling figures disappear into the black clouds of smoke.

> When the fire passed on, little mounds of scorched khaki alone
> marked the spot where another mismanaged soldier of the King had
> returned to mother earth.

The British dug in beneath high points such as Chocolate Hill, in
positions that afforded little if any shelter from shelling. 'The muddle
is beyond anything I have ever seen,' gasped one weary officer. The
assault was to prove the last big British push at Gallipoli. Although
they did not know it, the North Devons had been sent to shore up an
army whose eventual evacuation was already more or less certain.

The first idea was to land the South-West Brigade at night. Two
squadrons of West Somerset yeomanry climbed from *Osmandieh* into
the flat-bottomed lighter as it bobbed about on the waves. The wind
was getting up. The Military Liaison Officer, who should have

coordinated the operation, had been having dinner when *Osmandieh* arrived, and then decided it was too rough for him to go aboard. So without orders, Colonel Sanders had to leave the troops on the lighter as it was tossed about on the waves, straining at her warps, sometimes crashing into the side of the ship, and smothered in spray. 'The snorting and rumbling of her motor engines, running free, sounded like the morose complaining of a discontented elephant.' *Osmandieh* dragged her anchors and 'the disadvantages of an excited Greek skipper were apparent' as he screamed, stormed, quarrelled with his mate and wrung his hands. Not surprisingly, the men in the lighter were appallingly sick, and given that the gangway was too short to reach the boat, which was rising and falling by a dozen feet on each wave, they only got back on to *Osmandieh* with difficulty. Two of them fell into the sea and lost their rifles and packs in the process, although happily they were saved. That night, the troops on *Osmandieh* slept where they could in passageways, 'packed like herrings'.

Next morning, the troops could see the shore described by the poet John Masefield the following year.

> Those who wish to imagine the scene must think of twenty miles of any rough and steep sea coast known to them, picturing it as roadless, waterless, much broken with gullies, covered with scrub, sandy, loose and difficult to walk on, and without more than two miles of accessible landing through its length. Let them picture this familiar twenty miles as dominated at intervals by three hills bigger than the hills about them, the north hill a peak, the centre hill a ridge or plateau, and the south hill a lump. Then let them imagine the hills entrenched, the landing mined, the beaches tangled with barbed wire, ranged by howitzers and swept by machine guns, and themselves three thousand miles from home.

The sea was now calm (if not calm enough for some of the queasier troops). On the beach, a Red Cross team could be seen re-erecting tents that had been blown down in the storm. On the rocks were the remains of some of the lighters which had been wrecked, leaving only two for the troops. Under the cover of the battleship *Queen Elizabeth*, whose guns, each weighing 100 tons, could propel 2,000 pounds of high-explosive shell across a distance of over 16 miles (making quite a din in the process), the North Devons were lucky enough to get ashore without being shelled. This was an extraordinary piece of good fortune, given the losses that other regiments had suffered before so much as reaching the beach. The Turkish guns, they were told on arrival, usually opened up around teatime.

Frank Phillips wrote a description in a few lines in his diary of the scene he found upon landing.

> We came amidst a host of army stores of all sorts, and men working with picks, etc., and Indians who looked very queer sort of men with queer dresses driving mule carts hither and thither.

Old Indian hands were less astonished by the sight, and could communicate very well in Hindustani. Phillips's diary entry continues:

> Then as we advanced, in the open at 10 yds apart, in case of shells, we came across all sorts of dugouts, some looking very cosy indeed, and then we found ourselves in a deep valley, known as the Valley of Death, when the landing was effected here nine weeks ago. There we flopped down, jolly glad to rest after coming up the hill with full kit and also kitbags.

Although an ambulance man, he concluded with unquenchable optimism:

> We are really at war now, and so far, although it is a very rough and dirty life up here, I have quite looked on the bright side of it, and rather enjoyed the various experiences.

We shall see whether that view was modified with time.

To begin with, the North Devons, part of the 11th Division, were principally engaged in making roads and improving trenches as part of divisional reserve. But every third night a squadron manned part of the trenches. They lay on a ridge that ended with a prominence (in Turkish possession) known as the Pimple; to the south, the division linked up with the Anzac forces, in the hills above their beleaguered cove. The arriving troops cannot have been heartened by any exchange of pleasantries with the men they relieved; the latter were weary, bitter and sick. Because so many senior officers had been killed, they were also inadequately led. The men, in Colonel Sanders's words, 'seemed to have no go in them'. It is little wonder they had become disheartened.

The ground that the North Devons now occupied could hardly have been worse: overlooked by the Turks and with little natural cover. Even the digging of proper trenches was impossible, because earth only covered the rock to a depth of three feet; sandbags were needed to build parapets, but sandbags were few. Timber was even more difficult to obtain. Later, the North Devons were to find that some parts of the line consisted of what, in a term that the commanding officer would have relished, were known as 'grouse butts'. These were isolated posts made of sandbags, capable of holding five or six men each. The groups in the grouse butts had to remain all day without communicating with the rest of the regiment, contact being only possible at night. Even then, the Turks were recognized to be 'top dog' in the dangerous activity of patrolling no-man's-land after nightfall.

Archie and the rest of A Squadron arrived from Mudros on 13 October. Ominously, scores of the North Devons had already fallen sick – there would be seventy-five cases by the end of the first week. In their static positions, the Allies suffered from the ailments that had bedevilled besieging armies for centuries. In all armies, the numbers of men lost in action were traditionally much fewer than those who died through disease: in the American Civil War the ratio was 1:24. On the Western Front, the improvements in medicine and hygiene brought the ratio down to near parity; but the conditions on the Gallipoli peninsula made the job of the Royal Army Medical Corps (RAMC) next to impossible. Normal hygiene hardly existed. In the trenches, a mere teacupful of fresh water was allowed for washing every twenty-four hours. To eat, men had to crouch and slither their way through the communication trenches for a mile or more, down to the coast. Here was the only medium for washing either body or clothes: the sea. Soldiers complained that even their razor blades rusted in the seawater. There was so little water for drinking that, in the usually relentless heat, it became a precious commodity – and it was often muddy. An officer with a friend in the navy might take advantage of his cabin to bathe and shave; life on board ship was civilized in comparison to that on land, and it did not go unobserved that the commander-in-chief, the same General Sir Ian Hamilton who had once inspected the North Devons in Essex, rarely went ashore.

The Revd Arthur Rose Fuller, the North Devons' chaplain, forty-one years old, educated at Eton and Oxford, and a curate at Holy Trinity, Sloane Street, before becoming vicar of Paignton, took these privations in his stride. 'There is no dressing or undressing of course, in fact I haven't undressed for about 4 days and not likely to for some time. I am hoping some day to meet again all my kit . . .' The only piece of baggage that he kept with him was the portable altar.

Another witness is the resolutely droll F. D. Baker, whose letters home drew out what strands of wry comedy he could find among the horrors and hardships of the front.

> For this life out here one requires a permanent air-cushion fitted to one's hinder parts & amputation of both hip bones. The ground is very very hard & chairs & beds only exist in the super-dug-outs of very super-Staff Officers with lots of red about them. For my meals, my chair is a rock, & my table another rock. I sleep on aforesaid hard ground, which no amount of rugs seems able to soften or mould to the human form. At present I'm sitting in a trench on our 2nd line, having just 'lunched' off bully beef, dry bread & water tasting strongly of 'Boots' sterilizing tablets. Oh what a life!

Most of the North Devons' men were of farming stock, outdoor types who would not normally be knocked over by a spell of wet or cold; Archie, a tough young man in the peak of physical condition, should have been able to withstand the suffering better than most. But there was more to come, some of it inflicted by the Turks, some brewed by the poor sanitation amid which they lived.

Turkish snipers proved masters of disguise, plastering their faces with mud and attaching branches to their clothes, making themselves extremely difficult to spot. Otherwise, the British troops were not unduly concerned about the rifle fire they faced, which was not very accurate. There was, however, little protection against shells. The North Devons' first bad experience of it came on 17 October. The day before, an aeroplane had flown over the valley, its pilot presumably reporting on how fully it was now occupied. One of the senior officers, Major Greig, had been talking to two sergeants in the lines when the bombardment began. One of the first shells hit him on the skull before bursting, blowing his head to pieces. A palm-sized piece of his face landed beside a trooper who was three paces away. Colonel Sanders in his diary lamented the loss of 'one of the best and kindest hearted fellows that ever existed', burying him that afternoon 'on the North side of Karakol Dagh overlooking the sea, in a spot not unlike the Exmoor combes that he loved so well'. Even the innately sunny Frank Phillips judged this to be a 'very black day indeed'. He recorded in his diary how he personally attended to a man who, although horribly wounded, was still conscious and talking: 'It was an awful sight. To enumerate some of his wounds – His left hand and arm was blown to a pulp, his right leg similar, and his inside hanging out, and holes where jagged pieces of metal had been embedded.' Near him was another casualty, with equally horrific wounds, who was begging to be put out of his misery.

Death and mutilation were soon commonplace. The Turkish enemy kept largely out of sight. By 27 October, 2nd Lieutenant Jagger, having been in such buoyant spirits on board the *Franconia*, was now falling into the pit of despair:

> . . . we have got many men who fought in France and I believe they would sell their soul almost to get back to Flanders again. You biddie people at home have no idea what sort of Hell this is. It strikes me as being the home of the damned.

There were, despite the constant danger, odd moments of normality, which seemed bizarrely out of place in this small patch of land, where explosions, bodily torment and human indignity had become commonplace. A sheep would wander across no-man's-land, gladdening the hearts of West Countrymen like Archie. Some soldiers, though not all, continued to grasp at the idea that this barren land-scape looked in some way like home. The postal service was good enough to send a tortoise home to the commanding officer's daughter. But the horror was pervasive and inescapable. In this land it was impossible to bury all the dead.

The ground between the British and Turkish trenches was strewn with corpses. Burial parties were shot to pieces when they attempted to bring them back. Men became inured to the ghastliness, as they did on the Western Front – although even Frank Phillips was struck by unwonted thoughtfulness after seeing a captain, evidently killed while putting a field dressing on his wrist, with 'his left hand up in the air, now quite black looking, stone dead and unburied'. The thin soil meant that only shallow graves could be dug. 'A heap of dirt by the side of the cookhouse, with the notice "Do not disturb, covering dead men" tells its own awful tale.' Admittedly, Phillips's reflection on mutability did not prevent him opening a parcel he had just received, and tucking into the contents (biscuits and cheese, and a cake). But more than sensibility was at stake. Flies were everywhere, in everything. 'The flies are very very very very awful,' observed F. D. Baker; he could hardly see his mess tin when he opened it in the trenches. No wonder, just a week after landing, the North Devons had seventy-five men sick. 'The irregular equation', remembered by Lord Rowallan, was: '1 Gallipoli tummy = 3 Gypo tummies.' The 'prevailing complaint' was so commonplace that Baker could make light of it to his mother, describing how a sergeant, having 'gone to a certain place', was 'hit on the ear by a piece of shrapnel whilst "in situ"'. While his broad Cornish could not be repeated verbatim, the burden could be paraphrased as: 'It was a rotten shame that you couldn't live without being worried out of your life four times before breakfast and it was adding insult to injury to be fired at during such a troublesome period.' But for many, the consequences were more serious. They came down with the disease which had plagued besieg-ing armies since the Middle Ages and even earlier (a consequence of poor hygiene and unburied bodies): dysentery. Disinfectants would have helped to control it, but when the North Devons' staff captain indented for them, the reply came 'None available'.

Captain Money-Coutts got dysentery within a few days of landing, before he had even reached the trenches. He survived to leave
a polite account of the symptoms:

> . . . one evening as we sat down to supper in the dug-out I became
> conscious that food was hateful to me. A sensation of extreme fatigue
> and lassitude was followed by a painful and sleepless night. Next day
> I toiled wearily up and down hill between my dug-out and the latrine,
> at increasingly frequent intervals, and by evening it began to be appar-
> ent to me that before long I should be too ill to make the journey.
>
> The 1st Devon M.O. came and did what he could; as I was no bet-
> ter in the morning he sent me down on a stretcher to the nearest field
> ambulance.
>
> There I stayed for four or five days, tormented by my disease, very
> sick making an effort to avoid complete collapse and defilement.
>
> The F.A. was near the beach, and many Turkish shells passed over
> it. The Turks respected the Red Cross in Gallipoli, but occasionally
> a 'short' burst very close to the F.A. tents. Little its wretched inmates
> cared.

For a fortnight, Archie had been getting used to the harsh landscape and makeshift amenities of the peninsula. He and the rest of the
squadron had been labouring behind the lines, to make roads and
repair the trench system. Every so often they were sent up the communication trench to a position at the front, sipping foul-tasting
water and battling both the enemy and the flies. After only two
weeks, though, he began to feel stomach cramps, accompanied by
diarrhoea that seemed to dissolve his insides. Soldiers knew the
symptoms, but there was little they could do for the suffering. Archie
was carried to the dressing station, knocked out with an injection,
put on a motor lighter that took him to a small hospital ship, and
then transported to the big hospital ship at Mudros or the hospital at
Alexandria.

One of the small hospital ships was the *Essequibo*. Sister Mary
Fitzgibbon, who worked on her, saw many mangled bodies, brought
down the steep hills on stretchers or on the backs of mules. But her
greatest pity was reserved for the dysentery cases.

Their insides had simply turned to water, and all they had been able to do to them on shore was to tie their trousers tight round their legs with a piece of string. We had to rip their trousers off with scissors, and then we washed the boys as best we could. We couldn't do very much for them because we only had them for a few hours – just the length of time it would take to get them back to Mudros. Of course, they were all running a high temperature and they wanted to drink, drink, drink. All we could do was to strip them off, clean them up and put them to bed.

There were not many proper beds, only stretchers, which were laid out along the decks; the nurses had to step over them as they did what they could to reduce the soldiers' misery.

We had wounded as well, of course – because there were many wounded – but it's the sick I remember. I'll never forget them. Just pouring with dysentery – sick, miserable, dehydrated and in terrible pain. It was pitiful to see them, so weak, and blood and water pouring out of them. We had medicine that we gave them, but we could really do little for them.

The North Devons, who had expected to be part of a big 'push', were dismayed by the stagnation that they found on the battlefield. There was little to keep up their spirits. As in Essex, football was out of the question, but this time because there was nowhere to play it; there was not so much as a recreation room. Men got discouraged. In September, before the North Devons had arrived, Ashmead-Bartlett described a collapse in morale.

The whole Expedition is moribund. The sooner we evacuate the Peninsula the better, otherwise we shall lose the equivalent of the whole army from sickness, misery, and the enemy's bullets.

But they fought on. Their worst trial came on 27 November. In the afternoon, the heavens opened and torrential rain fell for the rest of the day. The trenches were soon swamped. Dugouts collapsed on top of their occupants. Young Private Brittain, on guard duty, found himself standing in water.

I could have cried with the pain, being gradually frozen where I stood, and felt myself sinking, my feet were useless, and my hands were as bad. I tried my hardest to pull myself together but Jack Frost had beaten me . . . They found me frozen stiff with my rifle underneath me.

Trooper J. W. Shambrook, writing on 13 December, thought his parents would be 'surprised to hear that I came here yesterday from Suvla Bay with frost-bitten feet and legs . . . Going on A1, although I expect I shall lose all my toes on my right foot.' Soldiers arrived on the hospital ship with their feet bandaged in their puttees, unable to put their boots on. Although storms are common towards winter, no account had been taken of them by the General Staff. But the misery had not long to continue. Kitchener himself arrived to approve the evacuation; it was perhaps the one action of the Gallipoli campaign that was carried out with exemplary efficiency.

Padre Fuller was as frustrated by the waste of labour and life as anyone.

> It almost made me cry to see the deserted dugouts . . . Looking over the area covered by Salt Lake and the ridges up by Chocolate Hill and the plain where our fellows are now, one thought of 100's of lives laid down, and now we are running away and leaving what they had gained – it's a big tragedy.

Colonel Sanders's judgement, recorded in his diary, was terse: 'And so ended one of the greatest failures in the history of the British Army. I heard of no one who was sorry to leave Gallipoli.'

Archie's contribution had ceased some months before. Despite being a strong and athletic man, unlike many of the poor physical specimens who were taken into – or rejected by – Kitchener's army, he died on 27 October, less than three weeks after he had landed at Suvla Bay. It was dysentery that killed him. He was buried in Alexandria.

3

The Old Army

— CHARLIE BERRY —

On 8 July 1916 a compact, brown-haired, weather-beaten man, just over five feet six inches tall, waited at the altar of St Petroc's Church. Two days later, his new bride would have the pleasure of stitching a lance corporal's stripe on to the sleeve of his tunic. But for now, 28-year-old Charlie Berry, native of Kent, was still the private that he had been for the last eleven years. For a man who had spent all his adult life soldiering, and had recently narrowly escaped death on several occasions, marriage was a quite different order of challenge. He had had no experience of domesticity since childhood.

Charlie's father had been a boilermaker, probably at the naval dockyard at Chatham. The family lived just outside it, at Brompton, whose name denoted 'the place where the broom grows'. The village had swelled in the eighteenth century and boomed in the nineteenth, astride the fortifications protecting Chatham. This was the country's leading dockyard during the Dutch Wars of the mid-seventeenth century, and had built HMS *Victory*, as well as HMS *Achilles*, the first of the ironclads to be constructed in a government facility, launched in 1863. In 1907, HMS *C17* had run down the slipway, one of the first British submarines.

As a boy, one of fourteen children, Charlie had begun by learning his father Charles's trade, as a boilermaker's assistant, but it did not suit. Nor did the navy. On the last day of August 1905, at the age of eighteen years and three months, he went to Gravesend and there, amid the old sea captains' houses, he joined the army. It offered a life of order, excitement and regular pay, after a crowded and none too prosperous childhood. He knew something of what to expect, having already joined the East Kent Regiment's territorial battalion.

Now he was posted away from his native county to the Worcestershire Regiment, based in Aldershot. His contract was for a period of nine years. It would send him not only out of Kent but out of the country.

One word was emblazoned on Charlie's new buttons and cap badge: Firm. The regimental journal *The Worcestershire Star* was unsure as to which feat of arms – at Vimiera or Corunna in the Peninsula War, or against Tipu Sultan in India – had merited the award; suffice it to say that it was one of the oldest, if not the oldest, in the British army and a source of intense pride to the regiment. Charlie was posted to the 2nd Battalion, then in Ceylon; he arrived there in the last days of 1906, along with 274 other men, 4 officers, 3 women and 8 children. The battalion had already been abroad for nine years.

It was now white ducks and sola topi for parades. A fresh-complexioned boy, Charlie must have struggled with the intense sun, the suffocating humidity that preceded the monsoon, the unrelenting deluge when the rains came, and the bitter cold at night. But he was only hospitalized, with minor ailments, on a couple of occasions. Other soldiers died of the diseases that were always the scourge of the British army in India. Some relief from the heat came when the battalion went to camp in the hills. It was here that they trained – and train they did. The 2nd Battalion thought of themselves, with reason, as model soldiers, well drilled in the musketry that had become the cornerstone of the British system. Like the rest of the British infantry, they could shoot both accurately and very fast; thirty rounds a minute was not unknown. On the ranges, a target within 1,400 yards was officially considered to be within 'effective' range, while 'distant' (so distant in fact that it required a special long-range sight) meant anything up to 2,800 yards. They were masters of the seventeen-inch blade that could be attached to the barrel of their rifles; in action, this might not produce a statistically great number of enemy deaths, but it certainly created a degree of terror in the troops facing it. Only India gave them no chance to use it. It was not considered an exciting posting.

A soldier of the 2nd Battalion has left a mournfully evocative account of his time on the subcontinent which, while dating from the mid-1930s, evokes a life that would not have been very different from that of thirty years earlier.

All told we sweated it out in India for seven years. Apart from the north-west frontier and a couple of short breaks in Hill Stations among the beautiful scenery and clear air of the Himalayan foothills, most of our lives were spent in boredom and monotony on the hot, dusty, fly-blown plains, in drab military cantonments. To combat the melancholy of this existence we used to play football or hockey six evenings out of seven, after the heat of the day. Social life was totally non-existent and every evening, except when on guard, patrol or picket, was spent in the barrack room, writing, reading, cleaning equipment or playing cards, and a few men managed to find some sort of hobby.

The Worcestershire Star confirms the picture, with its accounts of musketry competitions, inter-regimental football, hockey and cricket. The polo players looked forward to the arrival of another British regiment as 'there are certainly rather too few players at present'. It was due to arrive in about eighteen months' time.

One of few big moments came in October 1907 when the Viceroy of India, the Earl of Minto, gave new colours to the battalion, which was then in Bombay. But they did train. Following the Boer War, the Commander-in-Chief, Lord Kitchener, set about getting the army in shape. He introduced the 'Kitchener Test', which consisted of a long forced march followed by an assault. In December 1907 the 2nd Battalion performed the test in a 'very satisfactory manner', justifying the 'good opinion' which the General Officer Commanding the 6th Division had formed of them. After divisional manoeuvres at Poona the next year, the GOC was moved to describe the 2nd Battalion as 'unusually well fitted for service'. And so it was: the comments recorded in the battalion's Historical Record on physical training, musketry, signalling and appearance were never less than glowing. The endless drills, parades and manoeuvres, which honed the efficiency and discipline of the battalion, would prove their value after 1914.

Altogether the battalion had been away for a total of seventeen years before it sailed home from Karachi during the trooping season of 1912–13, those monsoon-free winter months when it was possible to reposition the British army around the globe. Aldershot may have been all but forgotten in the interim, but the battalion soon knew where they were, and who was in charge. They were under the eye of the future Commander-in-Chief, General Douglas Haig. Everybody knew there was a war coming, and Haig made sure the 2nd Worcesters, already good troops, were doubly ready for it. As it happened, Charlie's nine years in the army were due to expire in August 1914, but this had become academic; he was recalled before he had so much as left the regiment.

The 2nd Worcesters received their orders on 12 August. Early the next morning, Charlie and the rest of the battalion marched down to the government railway siding, long puttees wound around their calves and ankles, their torsos encased in the standard leather harness made from thick belts and straps. A variety of items necessary to his duty as a soldier and his survival as a man were attached to the webbing: pouches containing 150 rounds of .303 ammunition, a water bottle, an entrenching tool, a bayonet, and a pack to hold the limited comforts of a portable home (greatcoat, groundsheet, iron rations, equipment to shave his face of everything except the obligatory moustache).

In one respect, Charlie was typical of the men who comprised the British Expeditionary Force. It was a professional army. Conscription did not come to Britain until 1916, and the BEF was dwarfed by the armies of France and Germany, each of which had more than a million soldiers in the field. But the men in it were elite troops; disciplined, used to the uncertainties of service overseas, inured to harsh climates and – after training at places such as Willsworthy Camp, as well as in India – exceptionally well able to handle a Lee-Enfield rifle. Not everyone, though, had Charlie's length or continuity of service. Regiments were not kept at full strength during peacetime, so as much as half the army now going to France was made up of reservists, called back to the colours from civilian life. Other soldiers might only have served a year or two. Of all the hearts of oak going to France, Private Charles Berry, with his nine years' experience, was one of the most seasoned.

Acrid smoke and hissing steam, a shriek from the whistle, emotional displays by wives and loved ones – and the train taking the 2nd Worcesters from Aldershot to Southampton was off. It sounds as though Sergeant John McIlwain of the 5th Connaught Rangers, companions to the 2nd Worcesters in the 2nd Division, enjoyed it: 'A leisurely sail on a sunny day along the Channel near our coast, past Brighton, St Leonards, Hastings, etc.; then abruptly across to France.' An officer with the 2nd Battalion of the Oxfordshire and Buckinghamshire Light Infantry, who sailed in one of the same ships as the 2nd Worcesters, gives a more mixed review; they started about 8 p.m., after 'a very uncomfortable meal on deck'.

They woke on the morning of 14 August to find that they had not got further than Portsmouth. While the navy, operating at a remove, blocked either end of the Channel and kept German ships bottled up into their ports, the captain still had to play a cautious hand in order to avoid U-boats, as well as mines such as the one which had sunk the destroyer HMS *Amphion* on the day war was declared. It was not until early afternoon that the ship reached Boulogne. But it was a beautifully warm day and crowds of local people turned out to welcome the soldiers, as they had been doing since the first BEF troops had arrived two days previously. Small though it was, the BEF was much needed – desperately, as it turned out.

It had been arranged that two English speakers from the French army would be attached to each regiment as interpreters (not that ordinary soldiers would have had access to them). Instead, most soldiers of Charlie's rank had to rely on a repertoire of gestures to communicate by sign language, with varying degrees of success. A soldier later wrote home without irony: 'I am getting on first-rate at the lingo. "Parlez-vous" means "Good Morning!"'

The soldiers of the 2nd Division had their first taste of France's cobbled streets when they marched up to the fields above the town where Napoleon's troops had camped as they waited to invade England. Boulogne may have been crowded with British soldiers, but in other respects it was as yet wholly unaffected by the war. Officers rode in the countryside or had an 'excellent bath at the Hotel de Paris'. For a day or two, something of a holiday mood prevailed as the division accommodated itself to France. As another Oxs and Bucks officer, Harry Dillon, wrote to his Uncle Frank: 'It seemed extraordinary to be marching over the same Bridge I motored over . . . 22 months ago, returning from Monte Carlo.' Privates such as Charlie were supposedly confined to the camp but some enterprising individuals managed to evade the sentries to see what this foreign port had to offer. It did not take a great linguist to master, '*Promenade, mademoiselle?*' (To which the well-brought-up answer was, '*Après la guerre.*')

On the 15th, two luxuriant moustaches came to Napoleon's column – officially the column of the Grande Armée – each attached to a 62-year-old man. They were a study in contrasts, the upward sweep of the one giving the impression that its proud owner meant to enjoy life, the other drooping with worry. These fine and revealing facial appendages belonged to the Commanders-in-Chief, Joseph Joffre and Sir John French, who inspected the division that evening. Around midnight, Charlie marched back down to the railway station where, in official language, the 2nd Worcesters 'entrained'. Even the regimental history records that the 'crawling train journey', made in very hot weather, was not a comfortable one. Through Amiens and Arras they jolted, to Wassigny, the Picardy town south-west of Boulogne where Sir Douglas Haig, commanding the 1st Corps, had made his headquarters.

The next five days were spent marching north, with any spare time that Charlie and his comrades might have had being devoted, on the Kitchener principle, to drill – unless completely exhausted. At Pont-sur-Sambre they rested and bathed, not knowing that this was the last time they would be able to enjoy either activity for many days. The march to war was an intimation of the foot slogging that was to come: 'We marched and marched through the live long night walking 100 yards and then stopping, everybody was most fearfully tired & dozens of men fell out,' recorded Dillon. When the Connaught Rangers had their feet inspected, 'the French people marvelled at the sight'. Sitting on the ground, the men revealed 'a very ugly line of blistered and bunioned feet'.

It was particularly difficult for Charlie. His chest had never been of the strongest, and early that summer he had been hospitalized with pneumonia. With few X-rays to diagnose it properly and no antibiotics to treat it, it was a more dangerous disease in 1914 than today. After he had spent thirty days on the sick list, it was deemed to have 'cleared up', according to his medical notes, producing 'no marked effusion'; but now the chest pains behind the ribs were returning. It was an awkward time for the battalion to lose Charlie's services – more awkward than they knew – but there was nothing for it. He was sent to the 4th Field Ambulance, which would soon be the first port of call for many of his wounded comrades.

A field ambulance was a collection of horse-drawn wagons, their canvas sides marked with a red cross, tended by stretcher-bearers and orderlies under the command of a doctor from the Royal Army Medical Corps, with perhaps a padre attached. Edgar Drage, an orderly, has left an account of the one that Charlie attended a couple of weeks after he went to it. Drage crossed to France on 27 August, noting with naive enthusiasm that 'the sea was perfect and I think everyone enjoyed the voyage'. By the time he caught up with the Field Ambulance a week later, the complexion of events looked very different. It was only slightly less hazardous working as an orderly, tending to the wounded, than it was at the front.

> We had only just stopped when a battery of Field Artillary [sic] who were coming over the Bridge just by to take up a better position passed us on the road we had come down. Whether they meant them for the Artillary or for us I don't know, but shells began to burst all around us, of course we had to see about clearing, but not without loss, a driver of the army Service Corps who was driving a wagon was hurt and died afterwards, he had his leg blown off. Lieutenant Howel who stayed to attend to him had a part of his foot blown off. We went back to the Village, we had to run for it of course. The horses were fagged out and couldn't pull the wagons up the hill leading to the village, so we had to help pull the wagons up. We were nearly done

too, but news had been brought that some Engineers & Artillary were wounded, where we had just left, they had been shelled as they were crossing the Bridge, so the Major took 16 of us back and one to carry the Red Cross Flag. Lieutenant Lovell also came . . . it was terrible to see. Horses & men laid dead in heaps, just as they had been struck, there were two officers both dead and their horses too.

But that account from 14 September anticipates events. On 22 August, the stretchers were as yet fresh and unstained.

The doctor at the Field Ambulance sent Charlie to the town of Landrecies which had become the new corps headquarters. Landrecies was not destined to give him much rest. In the evening, three days after he had arrived, a picket of the Coldstream Guards challenged a convoy of wagons. The drivers replied in French, and talked their way closer – then bayoneted the picket and captured the machine gun. They were German transports, sent ahead of the main force in the belief that the town was unoccupied. The machine gun was quickly retaken, but the German army had found a very nearly open door. Word was rushed to Haig. Weak from the explosive effects of a laxative he had taken the previous day, he was for once less than calm. Roads were barricaded, secret documents destroyed. A well-placed machine gun and a howitzer held the enemy at arm's length, the one by riddling an advancing column of infantry, the other by silencing the German field guns. But it was touch and go whether Haig himself, trying to rejoin the rest of the corps in his staff car, would not be captured. Charlie had to rise from his hospital bed to join the retreat. Somehow he got on a train, and somehow reached a hospital in Nantes, far away from the fighting. He stayed there until 19 September, weak and quite possibly frustrated. He had been a soldier for eleven years without seeing action. Now that his battalion was in the thick of it, he had been let down by his health.

When Charlie rejoined his battalion, the convalescent – if such he could be called – and his comrades looked very different from each other. Charlie had been left pale and underweight by the pneumonia; but he was still as smart as though he had stepped off the parade ground. His uniform was fresh, his equipment complete and boots in good order. The men whom he found on his return bore little resemblance to their previous, parade-ground selves. There were fewer of them for one thing, after the heavy casualties that had been suffered. They were hollow-eyed from fatigue and battle strain, and while they had now been able to wash and shave, their ragged, mud-stained uniforms showed the marks of a month's almost constant fighting. They had lost caps and greatcoats. By the time 1 October came around – one of the idle days that sometimes occur in the middle of a hectic conflict – and the 2nd Division smoked their cigarettes and pipes and joked on the street corners of a village called Soupir, the battalion would not have needed to tease Charlie with tall tales of what he had missed. The truth was extraordinary enough.

The day after Charlie had left, 23 August, the British army had begun to improvise a battle – the Battle of Mons – as soon as the first units came into position next to the French line. The 2nd Worcesters had hurried up in time to form part of the reserve. They did not know what was happening at the front but soon formed an idea. Harry Dillon encountered:

> . . . an officer of some regiment who told me he had been in action all the afternoon, he thought they had lost in his regiment 500 out of 1,000 men. Soon afterwards we passed crowds of men asleep on the pavement. – I heard afterwards that they were corpses.

It was another intimation of things to come. The war had begun.

At first, the Commander-in-Chief had hardly been able to believe the reports he received. From the cockpits of their flimsy aeroplanes, the pilots of the Royal Flying Corps peered downwards, through the mist of their goggles, and saw column upon column of Germans marching to the front. The Kaiser and his staff were gambling everything on a swift, decisive right hook, which would punch its way through the west of the French line and on to Paris, confident that General Alexander von Kluck would roll over what the German warlord memorably called a 'contemptible little army' in the field. It was a description that the survivors of the BEF, the Old Contemptibles, would adopt with the characteristically dark humour and dogged pride of the British Tommy.

The 2nd Worcesters had not been called upon to fight at all on the 23rd, but their time quickly came. Not only did the British face overwhelming odds, but the French to their right had suddenly withdrawn. They had no option but to pull back. It was critical that this was done in good order, to prevent the BEF being overrun. The 2nd Worcesters were one of the units tasked with keeping the whole of the elite German First Army at bay as the rest of the BEF retired. It was, as Harry Dillon put it, 'a most anxious job'.

Early on the 24th, the 2nd Worcesters withdrew past slagheaps and through the unprepossessing coal-mining village of Frameries. It was in chaos. The civilian population, terrified by what it had heard of German atrocities, real and imagined, had poured out of their houses in a terror-stricken, orderless mob. 'Runaway horses and shrieking sobbing women broke up the ranks of the platoons, while the houses around collapsed under the German shells,' remembered Captain H. FitzM. Stacke in the regimental history. But the Worcestershire lads made their way through the 'stampede', halted, reassembled, closed up into columns of fours and stood at ease. Rolls were called. While shells burst in the houses behind them, the troops calmly sloped arms and set off down the road, 'exactly as if marching back to the barracks at Aldershot.' In the words of a fellow officer (who saw much fighting afterwards), 'I have always considered that this reassembly of the Battalion after the utter disorder in the streets of Frameries was the finest possible example of the discipline of the "Old Army".'

However, it was as well that Charlie had not stayed with the 4th Field Ambulance. Struggling to get down roads clogged with refugees, and possibly left without orders in the turmoil, it had been overrun and captured by the end of the month.

There began a long, managed, but urgent retreat that would take Charlie's comrades to the outskirts of Paris. Remembering Kitchener's insistence on the importance of travelling light, some soldiers discarded their greatcoats. They were to regret it: 'I shall never forget the penetrating quality of that rain of August 26th,' General Spears wrote in his diary. But as a staff officer, with a shelter, someone to carry his waterproof, and hot coffee and invigorating spirits to drink whenever he wanted them, his position was rather better than that of Sergeant McIlwain, huddled coatless in the darkness of a field, unable to make a sound because it seemed that the German cavalry was going past. It turned out that the foreign voices were French rather than German – a relief that was tempered by the discovery that the French had also taken all the billets. There was nothing for it but to find what shelter they could in a wood. McIlwain's own suffering did not numb him to that of others. 'Amongst the French that night I saw Algerian troops, hurried across from Africa on the outbreak of war, in their long cotton robes, then rags, soaked and clinging to their bodies. Many of these poor fellows had malaria, and many died, I daresay, soon after that night.'

The marching continued into September. Men who had reached the last extremity of their endurance would be helped on by their comrades, the officers often carrying their rifles and packs. Units became jumbled, more equipment and clothing were jettisoned: female sunhats, looted from shops, replaced caps. Sleeplessness and hunger wore out officers as well as men. It was impossible to escape the distressing sight and awful smell of dead horses. This horror particularly affected the British, whose own horses were recognized to be 'the finest in the world. As our cavalry and artillery passed through France it was a common sight to see civilians raise both hands in astonishment at the consistent high quality of the thousands of samples of our bloodstock prancing proudly along.'

But even British horses gave out under the demands made of them, whether pulling burdens uphill or enduring constant patrols by the cavalry. When they collapsed, they were shot. People barely had time to bury the human dead: horses were left where they fell.

Spirits rose on 4 September. 'At 7.30 that night,' remembered McIlwain, 'we *advanced*.' They were still marching, but this time in the other direction, north towards Belgium. 'The happiest day of my life,' wrote one colonel in his diary, his eyes turned to the east and Germany, 'we marched towards the rising sun.' Sir John French, under the strain of protecting his battered and exhausted force, had faltered; but the appearance in Paris of Lord Kitchener, Minister for

War, wearing his field marshal's uniform, stiffened his backbone. Joffre had set a trap for the Germans; their First and Second Armies were nearly separated and encircled, and they retreated to the river Aisne. The speed at which they fell back could be seen in the rifles, ammunition, rations, broken-down guns and wagons that they left behind. They shot the horses that they could not take with them. On 8 September, Sergeant McIlwain saw a dead German. 'He was lying sprawled in a wheelbarrow with his head hanging grotesquely sideways. He was packed like a sausage tightly in his grey uniform.' There would be countless more dead bodies over the ensuing four years. The Germans had been denied a quick victory; the war would continue.

At Soupir, Charlie found himself in the trenches east of a farm called La Cour de Soupir. Sergeant McIlwain's billet was in the gallery of the church, from where he could look down on privates sleeping on the pews of the nave. He would awake in the quiet of the dawn to see the altar candles being lit for mass, as the village congregation assembled. On 1 October, he watched 'the priest in his vestments attended by the serving boys in their surplices coming on to the altar. When mass begins, our good Catholics, who have been stretched on the pews all night, have simply to roll over and sit up and they are at divine service.' But on 13 October the trenches were handed over to French troops, still dressed in the baggy red trousers and long blue coats that they had worn in the Crimea. After a night march and a day spent hidden from the enemy, the battalion entrained at Fismes, east of Reims.

To old hands, the puffing, jolting, crowded troop train must have seemed infinitely preferable to marching over more cobbled roads. Not knowing their destination, they watched for clues in the landscape and stations through which they passed. Street lights and buildings looked ghostly in the small hours of the morning, but suggested the outskirts of Paris. The train headed north, reaching Amiens at dawn, and then west, along the Somme valley, to Abbeville. As dusk fell, the soldiers could distinguish the pine trees and sand dunes of Étaples, little knowing that it would in time become 'virtually a hospital city' for the British wounded as part of the casualty evacuation chain. From here, the train took a route along the coast, through Boulogne to Wimereux and then Calais, showing glimpses of the sea. At last it turned inland and the battalion, after its twenty-four hours' journey, could finally climb down, to find themselves on the platform of a Belgian railway station – Hazebrouk – in the level countryside of Flanders, where the BEF was straining to prevent the German army from reaching the Channel ports and threatening England.

After the church at Soupir, the Connaught Rangers found that they again had billets in a religious building: this time a convent school, whose nuns scattered the floors with straw on which the men slept. Some farm women had stayed on to milk their cows, only leaving when shells started to fall on their farm, so Sergeant McIlwain was able to drink from a tub of sweet milk. But such pastoral episodes were soon put aside as the brigade advanced towards the enemy. From dawn on the 21st and throughout the day, the 2nd Worcesters were fighting from the hedgerows around the village of St Julien outside Ypres, in the eastward bulge of the British line known as the Ypres Salient. Nightfall did not bring relief, only picks and shovels. They dug all night, until dawn on the 22nd brought a ferocious bombardment. As darkness fell, the German infantry 'swarmed from their trenches and charged', but they were beaten back. The bombardment continued fitfully throughout the night, concentrating into a crescendo of shellfire the next morning. This would be a difficult day for the men who spent it huddled in trenches, worn out through lack of sleep.

In the course of the following night, the brigade was relieved by French troops. But the 2nd Worcesters did not leave their trenches until dawn. It was at the spot later known as Hell Fire Corner that the 2nd Worcesters found the remainder of the brigade, looking forward to breakfast. They could eat it in view of a bosky plantation called Polygon Wood.

Polygon Wood takes its name from its outline; it was a plantation of fast-growing fir trees, which were used to make pit props for the coal mines. In the years to come it would be reduced to a broken skeleton of smashed trunks and jagged stumps, but as yet it was a thickly planted wood, around the bottom of which was a dense undergrowth of oak, beech and chestnut saplings. Before the 2nd Worcesters had cooked their breakfast, they received urgent orders to clear Polygon Wood of the enemy: force of German numbers had overwhelmed the 7th Division. Polygon Wood must have been bad enough to get through at any time, but as well as the physical obstacle, the battalion did not know who or what lay inside. They fixed bayonets to avoid shooting any of their own troops. At this point the regimental history reads like an adventure story.

> Suddenly in the dense wood the advancing platoons encountered the leading troops of the enemy. A swift and murderous fight ensued at close quarters; and the struggle grew more and more desperate as reinforcements for each side forced their way through bushes and brambles into the fight. At one point a party of the Worcestershire charged cheering. The cheer echoed through the wood and was taken up all along the line. Everywhere the men of the regiment plunged forward with the bayonet and the Germans gave way. Back through the wood they were driven, and after them in a long ragged line came the Worcestershires, shooting and stabbing, hunting out the broken enemy from behind the trees and bushes and cheering fiercely as they charged forward.

The cheering was a mistake; it alerted the German reserves to their presence and the battalion was 'met with a sharp storm of shrapnel and machine gun bullets'. It dug in. Now at last it could be relieved, and catch its breath in the reserve.

Elsewhere in the brigade, Lieutenant Baines of the Oxfordshire and Buckinghamshire Light Infantry described 30 October as 'one of the worst and most terrifying days' of his life. The noise of battle was so deafening that he could not make his voice carry more than five or six yards. As a result he did not know what the grim-faced men running back through the line were doing until afterwards. They were going to deal with some prisoners who had surrendered and been disarmed but then started fighting again; and they were not in the mood to waste bullets on them.

On Hallowe'en the dawn was clear; the weather, at least, would be calm. From his position in the reserve, Charlie could watch German shrapnel shells, known as Woolly Bears, bursting in deceptively innocent puffs of dark smoke above the treetops, each explosion unleashing a murderous scatter of metal balls. The battalion was in less than perfect condition. Indeed Charlie's own appearance had deteriorated since he rejoined after his month in hospital. Ten days' continuous fighting had left him and his comrades haggard, bearded and dirty; their uniforms, already muddy from the defending of trenches, had not been improved by the thorns and brambles of Polygon Wood. Puttees and caps had gone missing. There were also many gaps in the ranks. With only 500 men left to it, the battalion was at half strength. But they had plenty of ammunition, as well as confidence. They had proved themselves.

The 2nd Worcesters were not merely in the reserve; they *were* the reserve. There was no one else. Opposing the British, 80,000 fresh troops had just arrived to bolster the German forces, along with the Kaiser himself, so confident of breaking the British line that he wanted to witness the triumph in person. A captured communication stated that 'the Emperor himself considered the success of this attack to be one of vital importance to the successful issue of the war'. Five depleted British battalions, mustering little more than 1,000 men, held the trenches along the Menin Road against 13 German battalions, many at full strength. Pulverized by the artillery, some of the British units – such as the 2nd Royal Scots Fusiliers – were almost wiped out. A dwindling band of South Wales Borderers fought on tenaciously from trenches beside the Chateau de Gheluvelt, but Germans could be seen running into the chateau's grounds. A potentially disastrous gap had opened up. This took place at a time when even divisional headquarters was in disarray, a shell having burst in the chateau at Hooge that it was occupying, killing the 1st Division's commander, General Lomax, along with six staff officers, and concussing General Monro, commander of the 2nd Division. The commander of I Corps ordered the artillery to be withdrawn through Ypres in preparation for a general retreat. While this was being organized, Major Hankey of the 2nd Worcesters was ordered to Brigadier General C. FitzClarence's headquarters, some 300 yards from Polygon Wood. It was about 1.30 p.m. Realizing that the

moment *à l'outrance* had been reached, FitzClarence ordered Hankey
to counter-attack the chateau. This presented a procedural difficulty,
in that Hankey was not under FitzClarence's direct command, but
after a moment's consideration, Hankey accepted his authority. He
detailed a company to occupy a railway embankment to prevent the
Germans advancing up the Menin Road, and he led the 2nd Worcesters down into the little valley of the Reutelbeek on the way to the
chateau.

From the Reutelbeek, the land rises; the soldiers could not be seen
until they had crested the ridge. But what lay on the other side of the
ridge they knew not. They took their bearings from the tower of
Gheluvelt to the right, and the smoke rising from the ruins of its
houses. In every direction were signs of retreat, from the wounded
and stragglers who were making their way across the open ground
towards shelter, to the field guns that were being limbered up before
being sent back. There was not much that Hankey and his men could
do, other than to cross the open ground quickly. Underfoot the
going was rough. But with bayonets fixed and their officers at the
front, the 2nd Worcesters crossed it at a 'steady double'. As soon as
the bayonets were spotted by the enemy gunners, they were met by a
furious barrage; men fell, but the platoons continued through the
hedges and wire fences into the grounds of the chateau. Now the
ground sloped downwards, and the steady double quickened pace.
The enemy, which had been looking into the outbuildings and considering how to open fire on the flank of such troops as remained
around Gheluvelt, were taken by surprise. They were young, and
some of their officers would have been killed; they did not stay to
fight it out.

There was a Dr-Livingstone-I-presume moment when the 2nd
Worcesters found, to their surprise, that the South Wales Borderers
were still holding out. Their commander, Colonel H. E. Burleigh
Leach, happened to be an old friend of Major Hankey. 'My God,
fancy meeting you here,' said the major, on coming over. Quietly,
Colonel Burleigh Leach replied, 'Thank God you have come.' The
2nd Worcesters then charged the village itself. They found parties of
Bavarian troops enjoying what they had thought was a victory,

searching for water and looting. They were in no position to resist, and the Worcesters retook the village. When darkness fell, both they and the South Wales Borderers withdrew to a more sheltered position.

When the barely credible news that Gheluvelt had been retaken reached staff headquarters, the relief was intense. French had just lived through what he would call 'the worst half-hour of my life'. The cost fell heavily on a battalion that was already weakened; of the remaining strength of around 600, it lost 187 men of all ranks, killed or wounded. But the action saved Ypres. The opposing forces dug themselves into lines that would remain little altered until 1918.

Later in the war, Gheluvelt became the subject of a rousing military lecture, which concluded with a summary of the achievement.

> Thus, despite the presence on the battlefield of the Supreme War Lord, the great German attack failed. Gheluvelt was destined to sound the knell of the enemy's hopes of breaking through in the West. 31st October was practically the last of his great offensives against the British.

At Gheluvelt one in three of the 2nd Worcesters – members of an already depleted battalion – was killed or wounded. Casualties on the German side were also severe. The 16th Bavarian Reserve Infantry Regiment lost two-thirds of its troops in four days. But one of its lance corporals, promoted from the infantry to be a dispatch runner, had the good fortune to survive and was nominated for the Iron Cross. Lucky Linzer, his comrades called him; he is more familiar to history as Adolf Hitler. Through *Mein Kampf*, published in the mid-1920s, defeat for the Germans at Gheluvelt became part of the Nazi myth. For the Worcestershire Regiment, Gheluvelt became another battle honour, exemplifying the understated motto of the cap badge: Firm.

Like many Lydford people, Mary Hammett did not go by the name she had been christened with, preferring to be known as Polly or Pol. She lived at Lydford Station, the daughter of Theophilus Hammet, signalman for the GWR. With his Father Christmas beard, Theophilus's appearance was as imposing as his name; the beard was so long that he would have to lift it up before buttoning his railway uniform up to his chin and setting off on the short walk between 4 Great Western Railway Cottages and his signal box. As we have seen, the Methodist-inclined, railway-centred community at Lydford Station provided an alternative hub to Lydford itself, and many folk lived there, including no less a personage than Alderman Nicholls. Theophilus was one of the trustees of the Bible Christian chapel, Bible Christians being a sect founded in the North Devon parish of Shebbear in 1815, which was slowly becoming absorbed into Methodism.

Theophilus's wife, Jane, had died in 1905. Five years earlier, Polly's younger sister Alice had married at the age of fifteen. There had been another sister, Winifred, but she died as a child. The boys – Tom, Septimus, Harry, Edwin, Stanley and finally another Theophilus – were all out in the world, Edwin as a railway guard, Septimus as head boots at the Bideford Hotel in Taunton. So it was left to Polly to keep house. Life cannot have looked very rosy for her, a spinster of over forty, who may have thought her chance of marrying was past as she settled down to care for her father in his old age. But the war opened a new possibility for service. This kind-hearted, devout young country woman, her naturally maternal instincts having found no outlet in life, volunteered to become a nurse in London. The memory of those who used to live at Lydford Station does not reveal which hospital she was attached to; however, I strongly suspect that it was the Royal National Orthopaedic Hospital in Great Portland Street.

Still recovering, if not exactly recuperating, from pneumonia, Charlie had again found that the rigours of life under arms were taking their toll. He coughed his way through the famous Christmas truce of 1914. On 9 January 1915, he made another visit to the Field Ambulance, this time being diagnosed with rheumatism. Next day, he was sent to a clearing station, and from there to a hospital at Rouen; the diagnosis was now bronchitis. It was serious enough to be a Blighty case, one that put him on a ferry to England. He crossed the Channel on 15 January.

Victoria Railway Station in London is a hybrid of a terminus which, during the First World War, was still two stations – one for the Brighton line, the other for the London, Chatham and Dover line – built next door to each other in contrasting styles and materials. Its concourse was invariably crowded with servicemen in khaki greatcoats, knapsacks and rifles on their backs, being the capital's first and last point of contact for thousands of servicemen, including the returning wounded – so many that from February 1916, women from the Green Cross Corps (Women's Reserve Ambulance) were detailed to help those who were lost or needed accommodation. Church groups had set up kitchens to offer food and hot drinks (the vicar of St Peter's, Eaton Square, turned his chapel of ease in Wilton Road into a hospital, devoting the whole of his church's ample endowment to running it). By the end of 1915, the ladies of the Soldiers' and Sailors' Free Buffet were:

> . . . cutting bread, buttering it, spreading it thickly with minced ham, beef or potted meat; cutting cake into generous chunks, and filling the clean enamelled dishes, both for use at the buffet counter and on the platform . . . while a ceaseless stream of Tommies or Jacks, on travel bent, passes through, demanding refreshment.

Well-wishers pressed chocolate and cigarettes on the returning troops, their uniforms still caked with mud. Mugs of tea were handed out. The porters who collected the tickets were now women, as the men who had previously done the job had signed up.

From Victoria, Charlie took himself to the heartland of medical consultancy, Great Portland Street, where he crossed the imposing threshold of the Royal National Orthopaedic Hospital. In August 1914, the hospital offered the War Office between 100 and 130 beds for wounded soldiers, and was still doing its best to continue to provide both specialist and general care, despite the inevitable shortages of doctors, porters, engineers and other male staff. (The hospital itself was not entirely risk free; in 1915 a patient was killed in a lift. Inside gates were then fitted.) There Charlie was treated for pleurisy, staying for nine days. In the course of his stay he probably met Polly. A hardened soldier who had been away from his family home for ten years, Charlie had known little enough female kindness, and Polly belonged to a world of domesticity that was far removed from the horrors that he had recently lived through. If he fell in love with his nurse, he would not have been the first soldier to do so.

Once discharged, Charlie had another journey to make – rather longer in distance than his one to France. He was posted to the Worcesters' 5th Reserve Battalion at Plymouth. This had been the Worcesters' militia battalion until 1905, when it was renamed the Special Reserve. The battalion was accommodated in the Palmerstonian Fort Tregantle, built in the 1860s (principally a gun emplacement sunk into the crown of a hill and protected from enemy fire, as well as sunlight, by earth ramparts). Its purpose was to guard Britain's second most important naval station, and it was the mill through which raw recruits and newly appointed subalterns were passed before being judged fit for active service in the field. There was neither glory nor, probably, joy here for the officers and NCOs, most of them past their prime, who had the job of bringing this motley crew up to military standard. To the ranks of the recruits were added men like Charlie, all too experienced in the realities of war. Those who wanted a bit of peace to help their recovery from wounds would have found it quiet enough on Tregantle Beach, a great sweep of sand that is not much frequented during January, when Charlie arrived. Otherwise, it would have taken a military mind to regard Tregantle as a natural place in which to recuperate. A disgruntled squaddie from the Second World War remembered it as being:

> . . . as remote a place as one could ever wish to find, an old fort stuck up on the moors ten miles to the west of Plymouth. To get to it you had to cross by the old chain ferry at Torpoint. Even on the sunniest of days it seemed to be hidden by clouds of clinging mist.

But a train from Plymouth to Lydford Station took less than an hour.

We left Charlie at the altar at the beginning of this chapter; it was Polly whom he was waiting for, on their wedding day. But that did not take place until the summer of 1916, which must have seemed hopelessly distant to Charlie in the spring of 1915. For at the end of

April he was posted to the 4th Battalion, and they had already landed on the Gallipoli peninsula. Charlie was sent to join them in the Dardanelles.

Charlie was lucky not to have been with the 4th Battalion when it left Avonmouth on a 'lovely' March morning, everyone 'as cheerful as could be', coming instead as a draft to make up losses a month later. Sergeant G. Keen of the 4th Worcesters was one of those who took part in the landings on 25 April. Their objective was the tip of the peninsula, V Beach, on Cape Helles, which they reached in the mist of the early morning. Out to sea, battleships were pounding the hillsides with their shells, and the landing parties, with their binoculars to their eyes, could see some heartening results, as villages disappeared in flames and rubble. However, this was a misleading picture; as they were about to find out, the two old forts overlooking V Beach proved to be very solid, and even the ruins of the village provided good cover for sharpshooters. Keen, in company with his brigadier and brigade major, climbed nimbly into one of the four small boats being towed by a steam pinnace as it came alongside the minesweeper *Newmarket*. Already, SS *River Clyde*, an old collier turned transport ship, had been deliberately run ashore, so that the attackers could gain the sands without being as exposed to rifle fire as they would have been in open boats. Its steel sides provided protection to the 2,000 men inside – as long as they were within it. Troops in the open lighters that were being towed by *River Clyde* were all but annihilated by a hail of rifle and machine-gun fire before they could even disembark. But *River Clyde* had run into a reef in advance of the shore, leaving it still in deep water. Although a pontoon of sorts was formed by boats, under a terrible fusillade from the shore, the soldiers attempting to use it were either shot, or lost their footing and fell into the sea, to be dragged down by the weight of their packs. The landing was temporarily abandoned. Those who were still inside the ship waited as a 'whirlwind of rifle, machine gun, and pom pom fire' sent 'bullets rattling against her sides like huge hailstones. The troops on board were well aware that it meant almost certain destruction to leave the ship.'

River Clyde was the Worcesters' initial destination. But as they approached, the colonel of the 2nd Hampshire Regiment, whose men were still aboard the ship, shouted from the heavily fortified bridge that 'for God's sake' they were to go round to the other side. 'You see,' Sergeant Keen later wrote to his 'dearest sweetheart' Olive, 'the Turks were waiting for the boats just there and blowing them to pieces.' Going round *River Clyde* they saw the pontoon of lighters, but when, taking the lead, Brigadier General Napier sprang on to the nearest lighter he was immediately killed. When the brigade major followed him, he was killed too. With the prospect of the entire company being wiped out before they reached the beach, the major took shelter, leaving the men to lie down in the lighters and wait; Keen was forced to lie on top of another soldier who bore the weight philosophically. Men who had reached the beach could not get past the barbed wire, lying flat until someone raised a pair of wire cutters; but each time a hand went up, it was met by a volley of bullets. The regimental history, usually neutral and measured, describes the scene as an 'inferno of exploding shells'.

Having waited for what seemed to be an eternity, Keen found that night did eventually come, upon which he and his companions went to find the rest of the Worcesters. They waded ashore in water up to their necks, only to discover that they were alone. The rest of the battalion had not landed; so they made the journey back again, sleeping as best they could in wet clothes, with the roar of battle in their ears. Dearest sweetheart Olive would have found the rest of the letter painful reading.

Well during the morning the Major got us together what few were there and told us we would have to take ammunition, stretchers, and water for the wounded ashore and bring the wounded back, this made another walk through the water, I took ammunition and gave it to men in the firing line, and then helped to bring back a wounded officer of the Royal Fusiliers back to the big boat, which was a hard job because he was about 6ft 6 and a heavy fellow and made a struggle through the water again, I am sorry to say all the time we were walking through the water we were walking over dead bodies as that part of the sea was full of dead.

Keen managed to bring back the Royal Fusiliers officer, before landing again to join the rest of the battalion in the trenches that had been dug around the cliffs. They made some tea, and tried to sleep, but 'the night was so cold and we had no blankets and the turks firing all night [so that] we had little chance of sleeping'. About 1,000 men had got ashore during the night. When daylight came, they were able to advance roughly seven miles across the sloping scrub, but the Turks occupied the hilltops. As they tried to move forward on the next day, they were met by a 'murderous' fire, and Keen was wounded. He closes his letter with the observation of an atrocity by the Turks, whom he saw 'throwing oil over' wounded British soldiers, tied by hand and foot, 'and burning them'. The colonel of the Hampshires who had saved Keen's platoon by shouting from the grounded *River Clyde* had, soon afterwards, been shot in the head. By the end of 28 April, nine officers of the 4th Worcesters had been struck down, as well as 300 men. They were dug into such trenches as they could scratch from the thin soil, supplemented by sandbags, beside Gully Ravine, a deep, searingly hot fissure in the sandy ground, out of reach of any cooling breeze, which runs more or less parallel to the coast before debouching on to Gully Beach.

Word of these disasters had not reached Devonport by the time that Charlie and 158 other men of the 4th Battalion boarded the Orient Line's SS *Orsova* on 9 May, as part of what the author of the regimental history calls 'much needed reinforcement' to make up for heavy losses.

One of the thirteen officers on board was Lieutenant Colonel A. W. Brocks. In tiny, regular script, his diary records the detail of the voyage, including a stop at Malta, presumably to take on more coal, during which he won the officers' boxing competition. Brocks, Charlie and the others arrived off Cape Helles, on HMS *Hythe*, at 4 p.m. on 26 May. Like Sergeant Keen, they landed via *River Clyde*, but without the devastating firestorm that the 4th Worcesters had faced a month earlier. As Brocks notes laconically, 'Enemy's shells greeted our arrival but only made us jump somewhat.' As they filled their water bottles, they would have observed a cosmopolitan scene. Two-wheeled mule carts, used for transport, were driven by Indians squatting on their haunches on the footboard. Huge French Senegalese troops, very black with little round red caps on their heads, 'added to the brightness of the scene', as a private of the 2nd Hampshires put it. There might have passed turbaned Sikhs and those legends of military toughness, Gurkha soldiers, in the broad-brimmed headgear that was officially classified as 'Hats, Felt, Ghurkha'. But there was little time to look around. Straight away, the new arrivals had to make their way up to the reserve trenches through an artillery duel. The next day they moved up to the front trenches in Gully Ravine. 'Despite the nearness of the enemy's lines,' noted Brocks, 'one has a remarkable feeling of security in the trenches & the absolute indifference of the older soldiers to the whizz of bullets & shells is astounding.' In the mid-afternoon, the enemy became 'exceedingly lively' and the Turks charged a working party of the Essex Regiment, to the Worcesters' right, with fixed bayonets. The Worcesters were able to enfilade them and drive them back.

The morning of Thursday 3 June was spent improving the rear trenches, to make an assembly point. As Brocks notes: 'All kinds of preparations made for a big attack which we are about to make along the whole line. Great Excitement reigns.' By the end of the day, they had moved forward for the attack that would take place on the morrow. They would advance, for the third time, on the little village of Krithia, in the hope of taking the height of Achi Baba, which dominates the southern part of the peninsula. Maps were issued. At 8.30 a.m. a bombardment opened up, which stopped abruptly nearly three hours later. Brocks describes the scene.

> Immediately the artillery ceased firing at 11.20, all the Infantry in the first line trenches & we in the second, commenced to cheer, fix bayonets, pretend to go forward & anything else that would lead the enemy to think we were going to attack. This was calculated to mislead the enemy so that their supports & reserves would be hurried forward, & would receive the full benefit of the artillery fire which was to follow ... [The artillery then let rip] the most terrible bombardment it is possible to imagine, aided by the French & British Fleet, for half an hour.

The Turkish trenches were enveloped in smoke and flame, until, at the stroke of noon – with the sun glaring down from the heavens – Charlie and his comrades swarmed over the parapet. In the words of the battalion diary, 'It was just glorious and magnificent to see our gallant lads get out of the trenches "not a slacker amongst them" [sic].' They soon took the first Turkish trench. 'On we went gaining trench after trench, despite a frightful hail of shrapnel & bullets from the enemy. We gained about 10 lines of trenches, a distance of about 800 yds.'

But the effect was simply to expose the Worcesters in a forward position. Not all the Turkish machine guns had been destroyed by the bombardment and, on the left, the tall Sikhs fell in swathes; on the right, the King's Own Scottish Borderers also found it hard going. So there was nothing for it: the Worcesters had to fall back 300 yards, to a Turkish trench that, elsewhere, was still occupied by the enemy. As Brocks wryly observed, 'Needless to say it is a warm corner.' With its flank exposed, the battalion organized a new line along the slope of Gully Ravine. A body of Turks counter-attacked, but were driven back at the point of the bayonet. As a result of their action, the line now had a pronounced bulge in it, but Krithia remained distant. The losses had been nearly as bad as at the landing a month earlier: 5 officers killed, 3 missing and around 300 other ranks killed or wounded. Among the last was Charlie Berry.

Charlie had been hit in the left arm. The bullet had broken his humerus. It was a Blighty one again, and he went back the way he had come, via Malta. From there, after landing at Dover, he was dispatched to Graylingwell at Chichester, originally a mental hospital built by Sir Arthur Blomfield in the 1890s. Like other such establishments, it was supplied by its own farms, two of them, on which patients could work in exchange for tokens to buy cigarettes and sweets in the hospital shop. The grounds contained some fine specimen trees, including a cedar of Lebanon and Spanish cork oak. By the spring of 1915, however, the psychiatric patients had gone, as Graylingwell became one of the fifteen psychiatric hospitals to receive casualties of war, most of them coming straight from the Western Front. The medical superintendant, Harold Kidd, found himself made an honorary colonel for the duration.

Charlie's wound was not very serious. It gradually healed and he was able to move his elbow and shoulder. After three months, he could go. By now it was late September; on 13 October, he was posted back to Plymouth. And back to Polly.

Service life was also to take another direction. At the front, Charlie must have noticed the kudos that was attached to machine-gun crews. These elite operatives were badly needed. While the British were supreme at rapid rifle fire, the Germans began the war with more machine guns, and they were coordinated to give a withering concentration of fire. The British quickly upgraded their weapon from the Maxim to the Vickers machine gun, tended by a crew of four and capable of discharging, when properly cared for, over 600 rounds a minute. They supplemented the Vickers with the gun which Colonel Isaac Lewis of the American Coast Artillery had designed three years before the war started: a lighter weapon, it may have been less reliable but required fewer people to work it, was easier to carry, and could be manufactured more quickly. The Birmingham Small Arms Company made 200 Lewis guns each week. A circular magazine on top of the gun – which, from the radiator wrapped around the barrel, looked like a stovepipe with a stock attached – contained either forty-seven or ninety-seven bullets (depending on the type of magazine), driven round by a portion of the gas from the propellant each time a bullet was fired. By July 1916, there were sixteen Lewis guns to each battalion, meaning one to every platoon. A tactical breakthrough was made when they were used in attack, to cover the advance of the infantry.

Retraining on a machine gun might not have been easy for Charlie. 'In a matter of hours, the memory of the soft time in hospital was purged from me into a half-forgotten dream,' remembered George Coppard, a wounded machine-gunner who was brought back to the peak of efficiency at the Machine Gun Corps camp near Grantham. Drills would have familiarized him with the gun, enabling him to strip it to replace a barrel or broken parts, and then reassemble the pieces at high speed, sometimes blindfolded, because in the trenches this might have to be done at night. Charlie clearly flourished in his new role, since he earned a promotion. To the happiness of marrying his sweetheart from Lydford Station, Charlie could soon add that of becoming a lance corporal.

Cupid works quickly in wartime. The imminence of parting and threat of death are apt to bring matters to a head. Polly had probably long ceased to think of marriage, and seized her chance while she could. Perhaps Charlie, who had lived for so long abroad, and within the last year had fought in appalling conditions, suffered two serious illnesses and been wounded, felt a keen desire for domesticity. Let us hope that Charlie and Polly were happy in their union, spent at the home which came with Polly's father's job. They would have little enough time to enjoy it.

On 20 July 1916, twelve days after his marriage, Charlie Berry returned to France, this time with the 3rd Battalion of the Worcestershire Regiment. He took with him a new item of kit, in the form of the steel 'soup plate' helmet that had recently been introduced: its broad brim was meant to offer protection against the shrapnel shells or Woolly Bears that burst overhead, sending hundreds of metal balls hurtling down on to whatever might be below. His uniform had also changed: leather for belts and straps was now replaced by canvas. Leaving Polly, he would soon be part of a different sort of union – the small close-knit team responsible for operating a Lewis gun. Although more portable than the Vickers, Lewis guns still needed to be worked by more than one man, notably because thirty or so drums of ammunition had to be carried to keep them firing.

Charlie was part of the thirty-third reinforcement draft. It was badly needed. Only the day before Charlie had left, Brigade Major A. E. C. Johnston (responsible for the 7th Brigade, which Charlie would be joining) had confided to his diary: 'Hope we shall get some drafts at once to fill the place of the 74 officers and 2,000 men we have lost the last few days.' The brigade was in the centre of the Somme. He had heard that they were 'definitely not to be sent north to take over a quiet bit of the line, but, as a compliment for what we have done, are being kept in these parts, shall be filled up with reinforcements at once, and will again take part in the "great push", which,' he concluded with his positive attitude undimmed, 'is excellent news.' Excellent, one wonders, for whom.

By the time Charlie reached them, the 3rd Worcesters were at rest, north of Albert. But rest of a kind only: to Johnston's frustration, orders kept arriving for them to undertake pointless marches. A thousand soldiers were sent as working parties to help the tunnelling companies carry the sandbags of earth dug from their mines and empty them in places that the Germans would not notice. Although Charlie, with his new skill as a machine-gunner, would probably have escaped these duties, it meant that many of the men got no rest. 'In fact,' cursed Johnston, 'if they want to get good value out of us in the next fight, I can't imagine the "powers that be" doing anything more foolish.'

As luck had it, the 3rd Battalion had not taken part in the attack of 1 July, the first day of the Somme. But in the course of the month it still suffered the loss of 15 officers (6 killed, 8 wounded, 1 missing) and 366 other ranks (46 killed, 282 wounded, 38 missing). Its fighting strength had been reduced by half. Johnston would have been pleased to see Charlie, an old sweat; he was not impressed by the quality of some of the rest of the draft. Conscription had begun that spring. It was producing a different kind of soldier from the professionals of the BEF and the volunteers of Kitchener's army, and this new kind of soldier was not always warmly received; the regulars and the volunteers feared he would let them down. Johnston's fears were confirmed some days later, when he found a party of 10th Cheshire recruits wilting under their first experience of shelling, machine-gunning and 'crumping', as slang for bombardment by German heavy howitzers had it (the Last Crump would be the end of the war). 'They aren't a bad lot really,' he reflected, 'and when they have been blooded a bit, and had some discipline knocked into them, they will be all right; but it is not easy to do all this while actually in the trenches.'

Charlie was among the reinforcements who arrived with the battalion during the muggy day of 24 July. He found the wood where the 3rd Worcesters were camping to be a different France from the one he had left at the end of 1914. During the retreat from Mons and the Race to the Sea, which took the BEF to Flanders, Charlie had marched – or, when he was down with pneumonia, been carried – through a countryside that was still going about its usual business, crowded with refugees, columns of soldiers and wagon teams on occasion, but not yet scarred by war. Since that time, the front had lost its fluidity. Soldiers dug themselves into the ground for protection, much as they would have done during a medieval siege. Polygon Wood, when Charlie sheltered in it, and fought through it, had been as bosky as a copse in his native Kent. The wood outside Mailly-Maillet where the 3rd Worcesters were bivouacked was different: beech, birch and larch grew on the reverse slope of the hill, but none had a top which reached higher than the crest. Anything that rose above the hill had been blasted off. The trees on the slope facing the trenches had been, as the novelist Frederic Manning described, 'all shattered by shell-fire, only the truncated bases remaining'.

Sounds of menace greeted Charlie and the rest of the draft from the bombardments at Pozières, High Wood and Guillemont. The composer George Butterworth had been killed at Pozières twelve days before. The site that had been the village, of which nothing remained except the branchless trunks of trees that had once grown in orchards and gardens, was to fall on 26 July.

On the evening of 25 July, Major Johnston was out on his bicycle. Coming back after dark from visiting the 1st Wiltshires in their trench at Beaumont-Hamel, he found himself 'caught in a barrage of these new German gas shells'. He decided simply to push on through the miasma as quickly as possible.

> . . . the gas was pretty thick but fortunately, unless one is caught asleep at the bottom of a dug-out, these gas shells are not so very dangerous unless one gets a concentrated mouthful of it into one's lungs. The gas seems to have rather a sweet sickly taste; got through it in about 3 minutes, and bicycled back to B[riga]de HQ without further incident, and had a good sleep.

Luckily for Johnston it was only tear gas, but he felt the consequences the next day. Men who, like the Canadian dental officer Wilbert Gilroy, found that 'the smell of the [gas] helmet is something awful' soon decided that it was better to put up with it.

In March, an officer in the Cambridgeshires had written: 'I could almost cry sometimes at the universal mud and the utter impossibility of escaping from it.' But the ground conditions were quite different now. It was hot but cloudy when Charlie's battalion took over the trenches previously held by the 10th Cheshires on 29 July. Some 500 yards from the German line, these trenches had been the scene of a disastrous episode on 1 July, when the Newfoundland Regiment, from a province that had not yet joined Canada and felt itself to be intensely British, formed the third wave of an attack that had already failed; stumbling to their starting place, some of them had to come out of communication trenches that were already full of dead. Those men were machine-gunned before they had so much as arrived at their own front line, let alone the German trenches. That day, none of the brave Newfoundlanders got near the enemy. The regiment was all but wiped out as it toiled over no-man's-land. Their dead bodies, blackened and bloated, still lay unrecovered, decomposing in the hot sun and swarming with flies.

Since the failure of 1 July, the Allied line at Beaumont-Hamel had not moved. It was now regarded as a quiet sector, the sort of place where inexperienced recruits could be introduced to the peculiar rituals and casual horrors of trench warfare, to toughen them up for more arduous duties. The 3rd Worcesters set about improving the trenches that they had taken over, which included mending their own barbed wire and cutting that of the Germans. Newly arrived soldiers in the working parties were, understandably, disturbed by the 'Hun Minenwerfers and guns from the THIEPVAL direction . . . particularly as these new drafts are not very steady yet.'

Trench life had developed elements of a routine. Dawn and dusk were the most dangerous moments, since it was then that the enemy might emerge from the half-light, in the hope of catching the defenders unawares. 'Stand to' at which soldiers stood to arms, lining the trench wall and ready for anything, took place at each of these times. Men who had been asleep were roused, and sentries peered out across no-man's-land from the fire step – a raised shelf at the foot of the trench which enabled soldiers to see over the parapet. Daytime was spent with heads below the line of the sandbags that made the forward lip of the trench. Charlie was lucky that he was five feet six inches tall; if he had been a foot taller it would have been more difficult to keep hidden. Tall men tended not to last long, a fact that went apparently unnoticed by the headquarters staff which kept sending them there. (Why were they not posted to the artillery?) A variety of lairs provided shelter against shelling, from funk holes dug in the side of the trench to fully developed dugouts which might be many feet below the surface and possibly protected by a concrete slab. The geology of the Somme was kinder than that of Flanders – a solid bed of easily quarried chalk lay beneath the soil – although it provided equally promising terrain for the tunnelling companies of either side to lay mines.

In terms of developing the position, the busiest time came at night, when parties from both sides crawled out into no-man's-land, hoping that the moon would not shine. Work was done, as far as possible, in dead silence. Sometimes it was necessary to raid an enemy trench, in order to ascertain the identity of an opposing regiment; this might mean capturing one of the enemy. But if the raiding party alerted an opposing sentry to their presence, a white rocket called a Very light (named after its inventor, the American Edward Very) would be sent up to illuminate the scene; before its brief radiance had dimmed, a machine gun would have started to rattle out potential death. Men crawled and crept their way around the shattered landscape, from shell hole to shell hole, among the corpses. It could be a terrifying ordeal although Robert Graves would volunteer for it, reasoning that a wound from a stray unaimed bullet was likely to be better than one from a sniper, a machine gun or a shell. In the summer months, when the nights were short, the British had to be careful about when they set out. Occupying positions to the west of no-man's-land, they might think that the light had failed more completely than it had, and show as silhouettes against the last rays of the sun. Similarly, Germans had to take care at dawn. Mistakes on either side could be severely punished by snipers. Snipers kept soldiers in a state of constant anxiety. Comrades who allowed their heads to be glimpsed through loopholes might suddenly crumple to the floor, shot dead.

The weather was getting hotter, and although Charlie, as an old India hand, was used to the sun, even he must have felt uncomfortable in his thick serge tunic and tightly wound puttees. Water was in short supply: nothing new for him there, of course, after Gallipoli. That which did arrive was tarnished by having been carried up in petrol cans, which imparted their own unwholesome taste to the contents. On 3 August, the din of war was punctuated by a monstrous explosion in the German-held village of Courcelette on the other side of the Thiepval Ridge. A column of smoke rose 2,000 feet into the shimmering heat of the clear sky – presumably the British artillery had hit an ammunition store. Next day, Brigade Major Johnston was still worrying about the state of the recruits; he had heard that they were about to be relieved by the 6th Division, which he regarded as 'a pleasant surprise, though we are very comfortable here'. Four days out of the trenches did offer the chance to get some training done – not that he thought it would be enough.

At last the day arrived when the 3rd Worcesters could march back to Bertrancourt, five miles behind the lines; on Sunday 6 August the village was overrun by Allied soldiers. With its faded plaster and ragged thatch, it could not have looked smart, even in peacetime. Standard practice was to operate a four-stage rotation of troops, with two spells in the front trench, one in the reserve line and one at rest. Charlie and his comrades had been holding the front trench for nearly a week, longer than the three or four days that came to be regarded as the norm – the maximum period that anyone could be expected to function. In that time, considered 'quiet' by the standards of the front, they had lost 26 men (8 killed and 18 wounded).

That Sunday at Bertrancourt, Charlie's path crossed that of J. R. R. Tolkien, who attended mass at the Roman Catholic church there. Tolkien had come out in June – not hurrying to do so – as a 2nd lieutenant in the Lancashire Fusiliers. The presence of field ambulances had caused a cemetery to be created here. The weather continued to be stifling, but at least now the troops, having trained in the morning, could relax in the afternoon. Johnston spent some of his time visiting other battalions and listening to regimental music, the band of the 2nd Irish Guards and the pipes of the Scots Guards. 'It does one good to see all these Guardsmen about, fine big smart looking fellows, and there are any amount of them too.' But by 9 August he was feeling the heat. 'Another tremendously hot day,' he gasped. Expecting the division to be relieved by the Guards, he pondered the usual subject: 'I wonder if we shall be out long enough to really train these drafts.'

Whatever the state of their training, the soldiers were quite able to cheer. This they were required to do on Saturday 12 August when the King came to Sarton. As one of the two senior regiments of the brigade (the other was the 1st Wiltshires) the 3rd Worcesters lined the route. Having spoken to a few senior officers, the King drove past the troops in a staff car. With him was the Prince of Wales, who looked 'splendid, quite the typical healthy young Englishman. Everybody likes him immensely, and one hears that those who are looking after him have a time of it, as he is always going up in front if he gets half a chance.' Had the men honoured the royal party by polishing their buttons? It took the military authorities some time to appreciate that the sun glinting off a brass button could provide a target for German snipers in the trenches, and that buttons were better left tarnished. The next day would be another scorcher.

On Monday 14 August the 3rd Worcesters practised bayonet training, bombing (grenade throwing) and drill at Sarton. When they marched down the Roman road to Puchevillers, however, they found something else to practise because, as well as a casualty clearing station and a railhead, it had a dummy trench system. The General Staff had perhaps already learnt one of the lessons of 1 July: that troops, particularly from the new armies, were not sufficiently prepared for the sort of fighting they would encounter when storming enemy trenches. If experienced Tommies like Charlie thought that Puchevillers was a preparation for going over the top, they were right. On Friday 18 August, on a cooler day than those they had been used to, the 3rd Worcesters left soon after dawn for the front line: a position known as the Leipzig Redoubt.

At Pozières, there had been a stout windmill which the Germans had used as an observation post, scanning the ridge and marking their photographs with salient points such as Thiepval. This had been reduced to the stump of its foundations, but even this made a formidable machine-gun nest that would only be taken, by the Australians, at great cost. Similarly, the Leipzig Redoubt, on the spur of high ground known as the Leipzig Salient, was created around an old quarry. A century on, it may form little more than a blemish on the smooth sweep of the Picardy downs, but at the time it was a fearsome obstacle, having benefited from the improvements made to this section of the German line by Major Hans von Fabeck, the nephew of Field Marshal Paul von Hindenburg. On arrival in April 1916, von Fabeck ordered that every German dugout should be deepened to over seven yards. Dugouts were clustered into groups, connected by tunnels and with multiple entrances; the largest of these complexes at St Pierre Divion could house 1,000 men.

To visitors in a car, the rise of the salient may hardly be obvious today; but the upper slope commands a broad view of the gently swelling landscape, now only cropped fields and woods, but then crossed by the straggle of trenches, barbed wire, dugouts, bunkers and machine-gun posts that constituted the British front line. Observation was critical to this artillery war: the gunners either needed to see their target or have an observer with field glasses in a forward position, attached to them by a telephone wire, to direct their fire. High ground was therefore heavily defended, and above the Leipzig Redoubt was a second, star-shaped redoubt known as the Wunderwerk or Wonder Work, stiff with machine guns. The capture of the Leipzig Redoubt on 1 July had been one of the successes of the terrible first day of the Somme. The Highland Light Infantry had followed closely on the heels of the final 'hurricane' bombardment and rushed the fortification while the defenders were still reeling up the steps of their dugouts. (The success was followed by appalling loss of life when the HLI tried to push on, in the face of devastating machine-gun fire from the Wonder Work.) The poet John Masefield thought the quarry was 'very evil-looking', and the 3rd Worcesters may well have agreed. The Wunderwerk had still not been taken, so the British holding the Leipzig Redoubt were overlooked by that higher strongpoint. It made for an uncomfortable position.

On the day that the Worcesters arrived on the salient, a British attack was in progress to the right, at Authuille Wood. It did not stop Brigade Major Johnston from registering his disgust at the state in which the trenches had been left. It had rained in the night, so they were wet; but more than that, they had not been kept clean. Poor housekeeping probably meant that tins of unfinished bully beef had been left lying around, encouraging rats. There could also have been issues of hygiene; not all soldiers were fastidious in their habits, and poor discipline in the matter of latrines did not make the trenches any pleasanter to occupy. It also encouraged disease. But Johnston soon had other things on his mind. 'Very busy day getting ready for these two attacks we are going to make,' he records on the 20th. (An acceptable addition to this exemplary officer's burdens that day was to receive the Croix de Guerre.) But already the bombardment in advance of the morrow's assault had begun. Unfortunately it fell short and caused as much trouble to the British as to the Germans.

Today the Leipzig Redoubt is hidden by scrub. Through it, a farm track leads past enormous round straw bales, and up to a wood above which, from some angles, you can see the top of Lutyens's memorial to the missing of the Somme, the Thiepval Arch. Some of the bitterest fighting of the Somme was over the Thiepval Ridge that rose a few tantalizing feet above the Leipzig Redoubt. A step towards it was made by the attack of 21 August; this was undertaken by the 1st Wiltshire, immediately to the right of Charlie's battalion, as well as 1/4th Gloucestershire of the 48th Division. Charlie and his fellows also had a role to play: the Worcesters were tasked with laying down covering fire to keep the Germans in their trenches, as part of which the machine-gunners would have provided a barrage. While the first day of the Somme had been catastrophically overambitious in some areas, planners were now – following the doctrine promulgated by Henry Rawlinson, Lieutenant General of the Fourth Army – content to bite and hold small objectives. At six in the evening, for three minutes, the shelling by the British artillery reached a furious pitch. When it stopped – indeed shortly before – the 1st Wiltshires got out of their trenches and pushed their snipers into 'crump holes' to shoot any German sentry who ventured to look over the sandbags. Having left too soon, the men had to stand exposed until the moment that 'they hopped into the German trench'. On this occasion, the gunners 'shot magnificently, and there was not a single short round'. As a result, the

British soldiers were able to surprise the Germans, bayonet the sentries and throw incendiary fumite grenades into the dugouts. 'The fumite bombs were excellent for clearing dugouts,' noted Johnston with the casual callousness bred by the trenches, 'except that they usually set the woodwork alight and the occupants were buried and burnt to death; this was rather a pity as one wants to use these dugouts oneself after capturing the trench.' Rather a pity, too, for the defenders.

The attack was also remarkable for the use of a push pipe, as described by Johnston.

> It is a contrivance which bores a pipe at the rate of 18 yards an hour underground under the German trench, the pipe is filled with ammonal, and as the boring makes no noise the Huns have no idea of its presence. When the 1st Wilts started, this was touched off and in addition to blowing up the German block, it made a ready made communication trench in their line, up which our bombing parties rushed on to the astonished Bosche.

Although not quite everything on the list had been captured, a 'good many' trenches were taken, along with 100 prisoners who, badly fed and weary from being shelled, were not sorry to give themselves up. Incredibly, the 1st Wiltshires suffered only one death (the wounded figures are not known). A British success, however, was invariably followed by a counter-attack, on the German commander Erich von Falkenhayn's principle that every part of the German line would be defended to the last man, whatever the cost, and whatever the strategic value of the disputed ground. In the Leipzig Redoubt, the Worcesters caught their share of the heat, with 1 man dead and 8 wounded. That night, as the bombardment continued, few of the men slept.

Next day, with only part of the German trenches captured, the 1st Wiltshires were still fighting against bombing raids. To prevent a single weapon being able to shoot down the length of a trench, trenches were dug in a Greek key pattern, so that there were constant corners. Where only part of a trench had been taken, men could make their way around the bulwarks until they encountered the opposition, then throw a grenade. Johnston, however, was pleased to note the damage inflicted by the artillery, which had even penetrated some of the German dugouts. The 3rd Worcesters now moved up to relieve the 1st Wiltshires; the operation was completed by 9 a.m. but lost the Worcesters 54 men, 5 of them killed. The objective was to provide a larger force to attack the Thiepval Ridge. Johnston made frantic arrangements for dumps of bombs, ammunition and other material to be available at the front. Always on the lookout for a counterattack, the 3rd Worcesters knew that they would soon be among the troops seeking to take the Hindenburg Trench, which comprised the next German line.

The war correspondent Philip Gibbs wrote of this day:

> The doom of Thiepval is near at hand. By a series of small, sharp attacks, in short rushes, after enormous shell-fire, our troops have forged their way across a tangled web of trenches and redoubts until now they are just below the southern end of the village. They have bitten off the nose of the Leipzig Salient.

Before them stood what remained of the village of Thiepval: a hundred gaunt and splintered trees, no buildings visible at all. Throughout the morning and afternoon – as on so many previous days – the heavy artillery had, almost casually, been sending over a shell every minute or two, and soldiers would have heard the rush of air as they passed overhead. As Gibbs noted, 'before the roar of the explosion, a vast volume of smoke and earth vomit[ed] up from the place between the trees where the enemy's trenches lay'. A forward observation officer studied the accuracy of the shellfire through a telescope, and relaid his comments to a telephone operator, hunched at the bottom of the trench, whose messages crackled over fragile strands of copper wire to the gunners, several miles behind the line.

The Hindenburg Trench was 300 yards away at its furthest point, 50 at its nearest. But it ran along higher ground. Before British troops could break out of their trenches, they had to assemble, and the position where they would do so was overlooked by snipers and was also shelled. Enemy machine guns swept the ground. Troops had to wait until 4.10 in the afternoon, but then the earth seemed to convulse.

British heavy artillery, field guns and trench mortars had unleashed a storm of fire – a two-minute battering of shattering ferocity intended to drive the Germans underground. The infantry moved up behind the shelling and then, as soon as the 'curtain' lifted to fall again on deeper German positions, they bombed and bayoneted their way into the trench. 'Look! They're away,' breathed one man on the fire step. 'Oh, splendid fellows!' So far the attack had been a copy of the previous one, but this time the enemy put up a determined resistance. A German sent up a rocket, calling a hail of 'crumps' to fall on no-man's-land. A machine-gun team attempted to set up their weapon to spray the trench, only to be themselves mown down by a British Lewis gun seconds before they were to start firing. There was a fierce 'bombing' fight, which was particularly intense at the two ends of the trench section, adjoining the German parts. As soon as it was captured, the trench had to be consolidated before the expected counter-attack; that meant reversing the arrangement by raising a parapet with loopholes at what had been the back (now the front) and building fire steps to enable soldiers to look over and shoot. 'Magnificent,' said a French officer, summing up the achievement. 'By God, your men are fine.'

The last day of Charlie's life was very warm, but the overcast sky gathered into clouds and broke in heavy rain. The threatened German counter-attack was preceded by a pounding from their artillery. In the measured words of the regimental history, 'the bombardment was most trying to men exhausted by twelve hours of battle; but the troops stood it gamely, cheered on by the example of their young officers', several of whom were decorated. Watches, for those of the stoical troops who had them, ticked on to 5.30 p.m. Just as the British had done the day before, the Germans unleashed a devastating barrage before the intended attack, and the glint of bayonets could be seen above the parapet of their line. But the British were ready for them. So devastating was their artillery reply that nobody risked going into the open. It went on and on. The counter-attack never materialized. At 7.30 p.m., a daring patrol of the 3rd Worcesters crept forward, from shell hole to shell hole, to discover what was happening over the way.

They found the German trench smashed and broken, filled along its whole length with killed and wounded. But amid their stricken comrades a remnant of the enemy were still holding on, still waiting with fixed bayonets for the order to attack. They were the 5th Grenadier Regiment of the Prussian Guard.

These shattered but unbroken men belonged to the elite of the German army. They were utterly defeated. British tactics had worked.

But there had been a price to pay, and that seasoned soldier Lance Corporal Charlie Berry was one of those who paid it. Perhaps he died at his Lewis gun preparing to repulse the enemy. A survivor of Gheluvelt and Gallipoli, he had finally run out of luck; one fewer of that proud but diminishing band of Old Contemptibles was left alive. Since he had left his home village eleven years earlier, at the age of eighteen, he had known little except soldiering, with the all too short exception of a fortnight's marriage. It would have pleased him to have read the Commander-in-Chief's assessment of the day's action, as expressed in the official communiqué.

> The success of our defences is largely due to the steadiness and determined gallantry of Wiltshire and Worcestershire men, who, in spite of being subjected to a very heavy bombardment, steadily maintained their positions, and repulsed the determined assault of the enemy.

Charlie has no headstone; his body, probably hastily buried, was never recovered from ground that was constantly being reshaped by shelling. Later, Thiepval's reputation as a site of strategic importance and desperate fighting was confirmed when it was chosen as the place at which to erect the British and South African memorial to the missing. Charlie is among over 72,000 soldiers to have their name chiselled in Roman lettering on to the Portland stone facings of Lutyens's Arch of Victory. He is also remembered at Lydford, both on the war memorial and in the churchyard, where the headstone of Theophilus Hammett also bears the name of his daughter Mary Elizabeth Berry, 'widow of Charles'.

4

Canada Is at War

⸺ SAMUEL VOYZEY AND MANCEL CLARK ⸺

It is highly unlikely that Charles Berry ever met Samuel Voyzey or
Mancel Clark. Sam was born in Lydford and Mancel grew up there,
their names, like Charles's, attached to the war memorial; but life had
taken them far away from their Devon homes, and they would only
have been a memory in the brief time that Charles spent in the village. To Charles, a boilermaker's son from near Chatham, the army
had offered adventure combined, for a young man whose prospects
in England hardly looked rosy, with a form of security. Sam and
Mancel had taken a different path in the years before the First World
War, even stonier in some respects, which had led one to the Canadian city of Montreal, the other to the rural province of Manitoba.
It was in Canada that they signed up. In September 1916 they were
fighting on another side of the spur of downland of which Thiepval
is the crowning glory. The capture of the Hindenburg Trench took
the British nearer the ruined stumps of walls that made up all that
was left of the village; Sam and Mancel were some of the Canadian
troops who were trying to come at it from the back.

The Lydford around which Sam and Mancel had spent some of
their early years was poor. Throughout the centuries, the village – or
town, as it had been – relied on two mainstays for its support: mining
and farming. The tin, which had once given a proud independence to
the stannaries, had run out long ago. It had been replaced by other
minerals: lead, even silver. In 1825 it was announced that the 'rare
mineral Tungstate of Lime [scheelite], rarely if ever before met with
in England' had been found, but as yet there was little use for it,
beyond jewellery. Copper enjoyed a boom in the late nineteenth

century. When that faded, arsenic – a dreadful element to work with – was about the only thing left; and then even that became uneconomic. One of the last of the area's mines was Peter Tavy, which went into receivership, for the second time, a few months before war broke out. Wheal Friendship kept going until 1924, mining arsenic and pyrite (or fool's gold), which provided the crystal in crystal radios, but only intermittently. Originally, the people who worked the Dartmoor mines often came from elsewhere; now their descendants moved away again, if they could not find other employment. Their skills were in demand wherever minerals could be exploited.

Across Britain, farming had been in decline since the 1870s, and was doing particularly badly in the undercapitalized farms of the West Country's damp hills and windswept moors. Even so great a landowner as the Duke of Bedford threw in the towel. In May 1911 it was announced that he was selling the greater part of his estate in Devonshire. Frank Ward of Burnville House, outside Lydford, took the majority of the sales, commenting that the town of Tavistock, most of which the Duke owned, would be broken into lots: 'It appeared to be the wish of the people of Great Britain that the community should own the property instead of the individual.' The Duke had earlier told an audience at Woburn, in Bedfordshire, that he would never 'betray your trust' by allowing the House of Commons to 'acquire the despotic power over the people at which they aim' by denying the House of Lords' power to veto budgets. The Duke of Bedford's land sales were the first in what became, after the First World War, an avalanche of similar sales across the country, at the end of which it was said that a quarter of England had changed hands: a bigger transfer of ownership than the dissolution of the monasteries by Henry VIII. The prestige of owning land did not compensate for its responsibilities, at a time when agriculture was struggling.

Lydford had never been part of the Bedford estate; many of the cottages belonged to Millaton, a house in the adjacent parish of Bridestowe, which, in the mid-nineteenth century, was notable for its collection of rare birds that had been shot on Dartmoor and then stuffed. The owner, J. G. Newton, also kept a pack of hounds to hunt otters. But by the early twentieth century, the income from an agricultural estate such as Millaton was not sufficient to support the life of a country squire without selling some of the capital. That duly happened. Cottages and farms were disposed of. For the rest, there was little money left for investment. Repairs may have kept Lydford's builders employed, but only the absolutely essential were carried out. Little money circulated around the village economy, beyond that brought by the select number of visitors who chose to take a room at Lydford for their summer holidays.

Mancel Clark measured only five feet four and a half inches. This was not exceptionally short by Edwardian standards, but it does suggest that he did not enjoy an abundant or nutritious diet when growing up. Born in 1891, Mancel had, before the age of ten, suffered the death of his father, James. As a result, the money coming into the cottage at Lydford, where he and his younger sister Maud were living with their mother Emily in 1901, was scant. At some point Mancel learnt to be a tailor, untroubled, one hopes, by the loss of half a finger on his right hand. Every village had a tailor, making and repairing the heavy corduroys and tweed clothes which kept the Dartmoor weather away from male bones. He would usually sit cross-legged on his work bench, surrounded by snippets of cloth, just as Beatrix Potter describes in *The Tailor of Gloucester*. But the real-life tailors were not much richer than their fictional representation; besides, it would need to be a large village to provide work for more than one. At the age of twenty-two, Mancel decided that he had to make his way – if not his fortune – in another corner of the British Empire. Hands were stretching out across the oceans to make this possible.

There had been emigration from North Devon since the economic depression that followed the end of the Napoleonic Wars in 1815. It has been estimated that between 9,000 and 10,000 people left during the years 1830 to 1855; hardly a huge figure in national terms, but considerable for a sparsely populated area whose biggest town, Barnstaple, contained fewer than 9,000 inhabitants. Far from being dismayed, the authorities regarded emigration as a convenient solution to the problem of surplus population. The Devon diaspora was not as dramatic as that from the Highlands of Scotland, where whole communities were cleared from their huddled clachans, and their huts pulled down to prevent reoccupation; the Devon people, at least, made their decision independently. But they equally left their native land – never, except for those who prospered exceedingly, to return, or hear more news than could be supplied in the occasional letter. Many were Nonconformists, reflecting the numbers in Devon as a whole. By 1831, enough Bible Christians had reached Canada for two preachers to be sent to minister to them. As we have seen, there had been a strong Bible Christian presence at Lydford, until absorbed into the Methodist fold.

By the beginning of the twentieth century, the concept of emigration was nothing new to Devonians, many of whom would have had associations with people who had already left, particularly in Canada. Canada, a country of over 3 million square miles, occupied by fewer than 5½ million people, was actively recruiting new entrants. In 1911, one of the hundreds of booking agents who existed across the country held a well-attended meeting in the schoolroom at Lydford, addressed by Mr R. Willoughby, a farmer from Alberta. He described:

> . . . in a realistic manner the benefits and prospects of the West, pointing out that the men needed were those of the farming classes able and willing to work. For such the opportunities were boundless, and whilst men with capital were needed, yet for the man whose only capital was a healthy body and vigorous mind there were far better chances than obtained in other parts of the world generally.

The *Tavistock Gazette* was full of advertisements, placed by the Dominion government and the Canadian Pacific Railroad, for 'Ready Made Farms for British Settlers in Canada. Payments arranged on a twenty year instalment system.' On one occasion, the paper also ran letters from settlers for whom Canada had been a disappointment. But there were clearly opportunities to be had. As railways opened up the interior, mines and forestry developed, towns grew and wheat ripened on the prairies, and the Canadian economy boomed in the years between 1900 and 1913. Mancel left for a new future in the rural province of Manitoba in the summer of 1913, aboard *Royal George*, landing at Quebec on 24 June; he gave his final destination as Winnipeg.

When Mancel got there, he may have been agreeably surprised by the egalitarian character of Canadian society. However, it was not to all tastes. 'If the man who works for them eats with you and uses the same fork for his meat and pudding, why you get accustomed to it,' sniffed Agnes Nash, while visiting a daughter who had married a Canadian farmer. The Nashes' social standing in Shropshire had been considerably higher than the Clarks' in Devon. Inside the house, the decoration had yet to be completed, but Mrs Nash noted that in due course 'Alf will buy paper and the Vicar will come and paper inside the house. It is an odd country.'

Canada still brought out the pioneer spirit in its settlers. It took Agnes Lee a week of sleighing across the snow to reach the farmhouse at Hanceville, in British Colombia, which her newly married husband Norman brought her to in 1903. The building was a cabin which would later be used as a chicken coop. Her face fell.

> A house built of logs in the midst of a wilderness, with a trading post just across the road. This was my home in the New World.
>
> Having come straight from an English drawing room I was soon very homesick, especially when Norman talked pidgin-English to the Chinese cook and various dialects with the Indians. But I never let him know I was unhappy in the home he had provided for me. Riding was one of my greatest joys in this strange new world and I often rode out to the Indian cemetery nearby. There I'd sit on the rail fence and cry my heart out.

But Mancel did not come from an English drawing room, and would not have been worried by such matters as the high cost of servants – he was unlikely to have employed one. A world in which even Old Etonians had to tend vegetables, work as cowboys on ranches, or become motor mechanics, might have had an appeal for a young man who was at the bottom of the class system at home.

★

Sam Voyzey's experience was different. He was older than Mancel, having been born in 1875. There had been Voyzeys around Lydford since the eighteenth century; Sam's great-great-grandfather, William Voyzey, died at Bridestowe in 1796. A Hardyesque character with mutton-chop whiskers and bowler hat, Sam's father, also named Samuel, would only ever be seen with a pipe clamped between his teeth (it was not even removed for the photographer). His wife, Mary Anne, with hair braided across the top of her head, is shown with the expression of grim determination that you might expect of a woman who had brought up six children (Sam was the eldest boy) on a labourer's wages. The Voyzeys were farmhands and always had been, except for a spell when William worked in a quarry. But Sam had different ideas. He had no intention of staying in the Bridestowe nest longer than he could help. By the age of twenty-three, he had enlisted in the army: not the Devonshire Regiment but the 3rd Battalion of the East Surreys. He did not stay in it long. In 1898 he married Elsie Evelyn Isabella Meena Jane Bute, known as Isabella Blackmore – Isabella because she had a wide choice of names and liked that one, and Blackmore because her parents divorced when she was two years old and she took her mother's maiden name. 'Oh yes, my dear,' she told a granddaughter years later, speaking of what it had felt like to be in love. 'It's a ticklish feeling around your heart!'

Isabella's early life had been difficult. Following her parents' divorce, the household collapsed and she was taken in by Dr Barnardo's charity, which had been founded to help destitute children. In time, she was sent to the United States to work in the house of a doctor, but the family had four boys who beat her. Returning to England, she lived with her mother's father, then in his eighties. She was working as a nanny or nursemaid for a well-to-do family when she met Sam. He had come to do some work in her employer's house as a plumber. That was now his trade, and it served as a declaration of his direction of travel in life; there can have been little demand for plumbing in a village which still took its water by bucket from Squire Radford's taps. As a plumber, Sam left the hardships of the countryside behind him and set his sights on the expanding cities, where the piped water and hot baths on demand that would have seemed a glorious luxury in Lydford were taken as part of the necessities of everyday life.

Sam and Isabella lived in the respectable suburb of Streatham on its airy hill, to the south of London. They seem to have prospered, to judge from the wing collar and watch chain that Sam wore on formal occasions. They had six children there, the first of whom, William, arrived within a year of their marriage. We see Isabella in a photograph taken in front of a window that is heavily draped with lace curtains. Around her are the children: plump boys (William, Harry and Ernest) are bursting out of their suits; little Elsie Eveline in a pinafore holds a doll; the twins, Nell and Arthur, repose in a snowy expanse of white gowns on Isabella's knee. And there is a photograph of Sam in shirtsleeves that shows a shrewd-looking man, five feet six inches tall, his face deeply creased by experience, a grin twinkling in his deep-set brown eyes and stirring beneath his thick moustache. This is a man at home, untroubled by the tousled state of his grey curly hair. Kneeling beside his daughter Elsie, with baby Nell on one arm, he seems to be, by the standards of the time, an active father.

Perhaps it was for the sake of the children that Sam and Isabella decided to emigrate, Sam leaving first on the SS *Sardinian* which docked at Halifax, Nova Scotia, on 3 May 1907. From there, Sam made his way to French-speaking Quebec City. It cannot have been easy for him, but he found a job building what would prove to be an ill-fated bridge over the St Lawrence river (the southern arm later collapsed, killing seventy-five workers). He then moved to Montreal.

It was left to Isabella to pack up the household and follow Sam on the SS *Corsican* in November 1908; she sailed steerage with the children. Not only were Sam and Isabella leaving their native land behind them, but also their rural childhoods. They had made the change from country folk into townspeople. Some of Montreal may have spoken French; as it was already developed, it may not have offered the boundless opportunities of pioneer settlements, but it was the largest city in Canada. And with the increased population went opportunities for plumbing. In tune with the mood of opportunity and change, Sam revised the spelling of his surname from Voyzey to Voysey, a more modern-seeming variant perhaps.

In Montreal, two more children arrived; Mabel would be four when war broke out, Edward just two. By now, the Voyseys were living in Clark Street, in the Mile End district of Montreal. This was an area which, residentially, had been conjured into existence by the advent of the railroad, and then blessed by the electrification of the tramway service in 1893. Shortly before the Voyseys' arrival, the streets of brownstones had been organized into their own town, St Louis, with a town hall to match its ambition. If St Louis did not prove to have a sufficient independence of character to resist being absorbed back into Montreal in 1909, it had at least declared itself as a town to be reckoned with. As the eldest of their children entered his teens, Sam and Isabella could congratulate themselves on having done well in a foreign land. But the strain had told, and the 'ticklish' feeling had gone. In 1913 they separated. Sam may have felt himself to be absolved from family responsibilities and released for adventure when war in Europe was declared the next year.

Canada's emotions were not in all respects so different from those in Devon. 'When Britain is at war, Canada is at war,' the Prime Minister at the time, Sir Wilfrid Laurier, had declared in 1910. 'There is no distinction.' The then Leader of the Opposition, Sir Robert Borden, who succeeded him, took the same view. Although many immigrants must have had mixed feelings about the countries they had left, a surge of patriotic sentiment swept Canada on the declaration of war. Crowds filled the streets of Montreal, singing '*La Marseillaise*' and 'Rule Britannia'. The question, for the government, was how to harness this enthusiasm, given that Canada was an essentially non-military nation, with a standing army of exactly 3,110 men, all ranks, and 684 horses at the beginning of 1914. Fortunately, the militia had been transformed from its condition at the end of the nineteenth century, when a British commanding officer had called it 'unsatisfactory in the extreme', and it now trained 55,000 men a year. But the country was unprepared for war. There were too few guns, too little clothing, barely any vehicles. The one department in which it was moderately well equipped was the rifle, although of a type designed by Sir Charles Ross, rather than the .303 Lee-Enfield that was the imperial standard.

The crisis was met by the Minister of Militia who went into overdrive. Without waiting for cabinet approval, he immediately let contracts that would provide clothing for a force of 50,000 soldiers. The Ross Rifle Company worked at capacity. More than 850 farm wagons were purchased. Motor transport was bought from the United States. The Director of Veterinary Services collected over 8,000 horses. A total of 25,000 MacAdam shovels – a patent entrenching tool which could double as a body shield, with loops for observation and shooting through – were sourced from Philadelphia. It was a heroic effort, and enabled a battalion called Princess Patricia's Canadian Light Infantry after Her Royal Highness, the daughter of the Governor General, to leave for England on 28 August.

By the time the Patricias had reached France on 21 December, after training on Salisbury Plain, much of the equipment so energetically assembled in Canada had been jettisoned in favour of British issue. Boots were an urgent priority. The Canadian pattern proved not to be strong enough for hard marching on metalled roads, nor sturdy enough to withstand the continual soaking to which they were exposed in an English winter. The overshoes sent from the home country – 48,000 pairs of them – wore out in ten days. With every man having only one pair of boots, there was no opportunity to waterproof them with dubbin, which could only be done when they were dried out. The Canadian boots were replaced by ones made to imperial specifications. It was a wise precaution, as the dental officer Wilbert Gilroy, attached to Mancel's division, who made the mistake of wearing Canadian boots to the front line, could attest.

> Ordinary boots are no good over here. The boots I wore in England are very good boots but over here they just last three weeks. Every three weeks I have to have them half-soled. The roads are terrible on boots as you can imagine. So now I wear the issue army (British) boot. It has heavy steel plates on heels, and is steel studded on sole. Mine weigh just 64 ozs. so if you weigh your own some time, you will get an idea as to what mine are like. They are nice for walking in, when one gets used to them. Over the sharp stones, there is from 3-6 inches of muddy slush and water, so that boots are water-proof and well up over ankles.

The new footwear impressed those who were not used to it. 'Some boots,' joked a nineteen-year-old from Mancel's battalion, 'the first five years is the worst, after that they get seasoned and you can wear them for a whole day without stopping!' The MacAdam shovels, having proved wholly impractical, would be sold for scrap metal.

But by one means or another, the Canadian Expeditionary Force was equipped and under way. It would quickly grow to a force of over 260 infantry battalions, 13 mounted rifle regiments, 13 railway troop battalions and 5 pioneer battalions, supported by field and heavy artillery batteries, ambulance, medical, dental, forestry, labour, tunnelling, cyclist and service units. And despite the steep learning curve, they were regarded as some of the best troops at the front. Mancel may have been on the short side, but many of them were physically robust, brought up in farming country, not smoke-blackened industrial cities. They came with the self-reliance and positive spirit of the settler. Gilroy wrote to his mother:

> I do wish you could see our men. We have in our brigade 5000 of the finest men in the world. I mean that. There are none finer. An old English officer inspected them with Gen. Steele the other day and he said they were perfect specimens. Every time I see them on parade, I get a lump in my throat, I feel so proud of them. They really are wonderful. One battalion started out the other night at 8 o'clock on a night march. It was very dark and they marched all night and got back at 5 in the morning, and had covered 25 miles. That was just a little side issue with them, and they started in and did a day's hard work after that. So you see they are in good condition, and as willing as can be.

These were the men beside whom Mancel and, no doubt, Sam would fight.

With the exception of Princess Patricia's Canadian Light Infantry and the Royal Canadian Regiment, infantry battalions were numbered. On 23 May 1915, Lieutenant Colonel F. A. Gascoigne of the Victoria Rifles was authorized to raise the 60th Battalion at Montreal. Sam seems to have resisted the first call to arms; he was, in any case, forty-three and therefore too old to serve. But on 11 August he presented himself at the Northern Electric Barracks on Guy Street and signed up, giving his age as forty. He said goodbye to his children on the porch of their home, because he was not allowed to go inside. The eldest of them, William, was impressed by the figure his father cut: although still only seventeen, he joined the 148th Battalion the next year.

Meanwhile, Mancel Clark was already in England, training for France. On 13 May, the 27th Battalion (City of Winnipeg), which Mancel had joined in the new year, marched off to the Canadian Pacific Railroad sidings from its barracks in the Old Agricultural College at Tuxedo, and set off for Quebec, cheered by a crowd of 2,000 well-wishers. Once belts, braces, ammunition pouches, haversacks and entrenching tools had been issued, the battalion, nearly 1,100 strong, could board the RMS *Carpathia*, crossing in company with the 31st Battalion (one of whose number, 'known to be slightly demented', jumped overboard in the course of the passage). Except for a day of mal de mer, the time at sea was not wasted. Lectures on kit, sanitation, first aid, drill, military reports, physical training, field training, field defences and mounting guard were interspersed with rifle practice and a patriotic band concert. 'We have a crack band on board and every little while it bursts out with a hymn to remind us it is Sunday,' wrote Gilroy. He concluded that, 'This old boat isn't a palace but believe me it is very comfortable and the crowd is very fine.' Forage caps were replaced by steel helmets and balaclavas. Soldiers followed the course of the trip using their compasses, and were exasperated to observe that, towards the end of the voyage, the ship started to zigzag. The manoeuvre, they discovered afterwards, had been adopted to avoid a German submarine that had already sunk a large freighter, mistaking it for the troopship. Those who knew of the incident must have felt some relief when, on the morning of 28 May, the English coast came into view: the Devon shore which Mancel had left two years before. When *Carpathia* steamed into Plymouth that afternoon, the brigadier's orders 'not to cheer on Entering Port' were '*not*' obeyed. Imagine,' noted the battalion war diary, 'men keeping quiet when entering an English Port on a Troopship and are cheered by all the Boats in the Harbor. Especially Canadians!'

So while Sam was undergoing the medical for the 60th Battalion, Mancel was already on the South Coast, near Folkestone, preparing for France at Shorncliffe Camp. For three months he was drilled for eight hours a day in bayonet practice, entrenching, route marches, night marches, musketry practice, rapid fire, physical exercise and semaphore – a means of battlefield communication seemingly as old-fashioned as the carrier pigeon, which (like the latter, used in tanks) could nevertheless have its place. The drill put Private John Row through his paces.

> We are getting up at 3 now as we have to get down to the ranges in time to get our shooting over by noon so as to let another bunch shoot in the afternoon, consequently we have to get to bed early. It is about six miles to the ranges with a long climb of about a mile up hill, done with heavy marching order, to say nothing of the 7 pounds of boots. It was pretty warm coming home today, my tunic and shirt were soaked with sweat. We have to keep two suits of underwear on the go, wear one suit while the other is drying out. All the boys are in first class shape and feeling fine. I can fire my rifle with one arm now. That bayonet exercise beats the physical exercise all hollow.
>
> This is the darnedest country for hills you ever saw. Our camp is on a sort of plateau so no matter which way we come home we have a long weary climb . . . I can easily see why some people live for 60 or 70 years and never go 3 miles off their own farm. A ten mile route march is equal to about 25 at home.

The brigadier, who was a golfer, encouraged Gilroy to entertain Gladys Ravenscroft, the 'amateur golf champion of Great Britain and America', which he did willingly, observing that she was 'a fine type of an English lady. And quite refined too.' (Nothing came of it except an invitation to her wedding, due to take place in London on 12 August, to a wounded officer who was going back to the front.) Miss Ravenscroft was running a YMCA tent for the men. 'And there are many examples of such work about here,' Gilroy continued.

> The wife of one of the prominent Lieut. Cols over here is working at the Military Hospital at Shorncliffe. Maids are hard to get, so she

scrubs floors on her knees every morning, so that the nurses can attend the wounded men. And believe me the places are filled with wounded these days. They are coming over by shiploads every day.

A diversion was provided by Charlie Chaplin films at the cinema, although the 'picture houses' were not as good as in Winnipeg. Occasionally, one of the large airships that patrolled the coast would float over the camp, airmen's heads sticking out of the portholes of the cabin underneath; the Canadian band might have saluted them by playing the national anthem. (That November, another kind of dirigible passed over the camp: a German Zeppelin which dropped bombs packed with scrap iron, killing 13 men and 38 horses.) In late July the troops moved to nearby Otterpool camp, which was judged to be 'dandy'. On that day, Gilroy reported on the mood in London, which could be paraphrased as: 'Oh well, we will win and there is no hurry. We always have won and we can't lose.' Whether hurrying or not, the 27th Battalion would probably have been pleased to leave camp. Eventually came the hot, bright day in mid-September when the battalion marched to Folkestone Harbour. Their ship sailed at 11.30 a.m.; fourteen hours later it reached Boulogne. They were en route to Ypres.

Sam Voysey would soon be en route to Europe too. But first, the 60th Battalion collected itself for basic training at Valcartier, sixteen miles north-west of Quebec City. Valcartier was a town composed of tents, built on the site of small farms, originally granted to British soldiers after the capture of Quebec, beside the Jacques Cartier river. Over 30,000 men lived under canvas. There were 1,500 targets on the rifle range. 'I'm still having a glorious time here performing all sorts of "stunts" with a rifle and attacking imaginary Germans,' wrote another private in the 60th Battalion, John Sudbury, to his mother on 2 August, 'but oh! It's a grand life and the more dangerous the attack the more we enjoy it.' The 60th Battalion was part of the 9th Canadian Brigade, in the 3rd Division; it sailed from Montreal on 25 October on the SS *Scandinavian*.

After docking at Southampton, the battalion had only a short journey to Bramshott in the New Forest. Boys who had known only Canada marvelled to see the hedges and stone walls, the green grass that grew all year round, the roses still in bloom, the ivy scrambling over the old-fashioned houses, the tall trees, the ubiquitously paved roads, and the steam engines that were doing the work of horses in 'Mudsplosh' Camp, as it became known. Bramshott was one of four Canadian camps around England. It was a ramshackle affair, made of slate-lined huts, which would be rebuilt along better lines in 1916; but if the 60th Battalion's experience was anything like that of the Seaforth Highlanders of Canada, they would have enjoyed a warm reception, 'with as good a meal as ever was tasted'. It was, according to one of the Seaforths, 'a bit like home . . . its soil very sandy, and the surrounding country wild moorland and gorse. There were good bathing and fumigating arrangements.' When the Canadian Grenadier Guards arrived, they laughed at the size of the trains – 'vest-pocket editions' of those in Canada. 'We thought our training in Canada had amounted to something,' recalled a member of the Canadian Grenadier Guards. 'We found we might just as well have been playing croquet. We learned more in the first few weeks in England than we did from November to April in Canada.'

In the case of the Canadian Grenadiers, battle-hardened Canadian officers who had been wounded in the retreat from Mons or the Battle of the Marne were supplemented by a number of 'Imperials', as the Canadians called British soldiers, from the Grenadier Guards. The 46th were also exposed to an Imperial, in the shape of a cockney who trained them in bayonet fighting: 'Fink it's yer muvver-in-law,' he screamed as the recruits lunged at the sack dummies. The roads were thought to be 'good but hard for marching'. The battalion left for France, then Belgium, on 20 February 1916.

It had been a hard winter for the 27th Battalion. 'Everything is sopping wet and some of the fields look more like a slough than a field,' observed John Row on 12 December 1915. 'I have just drawn my third pair of boots since coming to France so you can imagine what it is like.' Rain was followed by a bitter freeze, perhaps appreciated, after a fresh snowfall, for the ermine mantle that it threw over the shattered landscape, but hard to endure, particularly by soldiers who may have trimmed the bottom two feet off their greatcoats to save weight when marching. John Sudbury was one of the Canadians who marvelled – and carried on with as much of a smile as he could muster.

> Again I am back in the trenches but they have put upon themselves a very changed aspect for on the night of my arrival it snowed all night so that when I emerged from the dugout to go on guard about 2am the scene was one of dazzling whiteness in spite of the moonless night. One had great difficulty when coming from the lighted dugout into the white darkness to detect the path, with the consequence that several collisions between parapets that seemed suddenly to take a pace forward or backward and myself who little realizing their pranks stepped or stopped in the wrong place at the wrong moment, lost my equilibrium and at once became engrossed in a minute study of a snow covered trench mat.
>
> Such experiences and tumbles are a matter of everyday occurrence with me, snow or rain, mud or fine, so apart from making me smile I just carried on as usual. To lose one's equilibrium of temper is a thing too absurd to be thought of let alone acted upon and if one does, well it just increases the comedy 2 fold.

It was still snowing in mid-March, when, in one of those flashes of humanity that illuminated life in the trenches, 'one of the boys' showed John Row 'a robin as it was not much bigger than a sparrow and all puffed out on account of the cold'.

Snow did not halt the shelling, the shrapnel, the terrifying night patrols or the blowing of mines. Four thicknesses of blanket were not enough to keep out the noise of the high explosives, as the dental officer Wilbert Gilroy tried to sleep behind the lines. 'Were it not for the slight danger attached I wish you could all be here, just to see the sights,' he wrote to his sister Emily.

> It is really beautiful. For miles around the sky at night is all lit up. It is just like when the heavens open up with lightning. When it is real dark one can see the shells bursting and it is just like fireworks on a large scale. Better than [the] Toronto Ex[hibition]. Then too the shells and their noises are a study. The small ones whistle, larger ones shriek, while the big ones roar like an express train. The beauty of it

is that you can hear them coming and have plenty of time to take shelter. I had to laugh at one of our boys the other day. He was riding his horse along the road when he heard one of these expresses, as they call them, coming. He jumped off his horse, and scrambled into the ditch, and pulled the horse in on top of him. Then he had the pleasure of seeing it burst away out in the field beside the road. He was so badly scared that he galloped his horse at full speed right into town. Some sport isn't it?

Gilroy records making only one visit to the front trenches, but the filth of a Belgian farmhouse could seem bad enough to a hygienically minded Canadian, his hair cropped as close as a billiard ball, who spent most of his time behind the lines.

The idea of the Belgian farmer, so far as I can make out, is to choose a big dirty foul-smelling manure pile and then to build his buildings around it. The closer to the pile he can get his back door the more up-to-date his plant is. Then his stables and outhouses all open into this square. To reach the back door you must plod thru this muck. The other three sides of the house are surrounded by the proverbial moat, filled with dirty water, covered with green scum. There is no official entrance to the front of the house, but there is a door opening into the moat, used principally to throw the refuse thru, into the moat.

At first we tried to eat in the kitchen, in fact we ate two meals there, but we could not stand it. The smell . . . was too much for us, so we went out into the yard, and ate in a shack. Then the old lady would not let us use her stove so we had to dig trenches and cook over them. I don't want to commence on the inhabitants but I will say they corresponded favorably with the surroundings. And flies, I mean FLIES! They are entitled to capital letters all the way thru, they were so much in evidence. The first day I went in to buy some bread, as we were short of the issue bread. Over on the table in the corner I saw something black, which after she had taken up in her hands, turned out to be bread, which had been literally covered with the brutes . . . We were only there three days but if we had to stay there longer, I would be in favor of letting the Germans have the blamed country.

The Canadians were, according to battalion orders, expected to leave their billets 'scrupulously clean'; they hoped to find them in that condition too. Generally, the cleanliness of the Belgians suffered criticism from the 27th and 60th Battalions – 'I have since seen Kenya Africans eating from a common dish but never so disgustingly as the peasants in Belgium,' noted Sudbury.

But even the fastidious Gilroy could sometimes be lucky. 'It is beautifully clean,' he commented of the office he secured as a surgery on the high street of a Belgian town, 'and the people are very friendly, and above all other things CLEAN.' His own billet was found in the parish priest's house. 'I gave the old Abbé a cigar today and he immediately ordered the housekeeper to bring down a pillow. Another cigar produced a white slip and I think if I had had a box of cigars with me could have had the house.' Condescending though Gilroy could be, he reveals his own lack of sophistication in the matter of the lighting arrangements; the cluster of electric light bulbs hanging from the ceiling was evidently a novelty. 'I think we would call it at home a chandelier. Turning on a button is easier than lighting a candle, only it is awkward until one gets used to it.' Next door was a convent, with a bath tub and hot water – a blessing, since Gilroy had generously given his heavy woolen underwear to an officer leaving for the trenches, forcing him to make do with his single set of light cottons. (Unfortunately the officer was compelled to throw the present away because it had lice.)

Underwear is a constant theme of letters home from all ranks. 'We have a bath and change of underwear about every two weeks and I really couldn't carry any more in my pack as it is heavy enough now,' wrote Fargey of the Cameron Highlanders of Canada, a kilted battalion (the 43rd) in the same brigade as the 60th. Another preoccupation was socks.

Gilroy's trip to the front, which took place on 8 December 1915, was obviously something worth writing about, and he describes it in detail in a letter to his mother, beginning with the arrival of a friendly quartermaster:

> . . . with enough stuff to equip an arctic expedition. He had heavy
> woollen socks, long rubber boots, up to the hips and fastened on to

my belt. One of the boots was an 8 while [the] other was a size 10. However I put on two extra socks on the ten foot and came out about even. Then he had a leather vest, fleece lined sheepskin over-vest, mitts and waterproof cape. I could not wear all the junk. I could not stand the smell of the sheepskin, so left it at home. However I managed to get into most of the stuff. Oh yes and Gov. underwear, which, by the way, I wear all the time now.

Having the rank of captain, he could start, as he put it, 'à cheval', leaving as it got dark at 4.30 in the afternoon.

It was some ride and I was glad I could ride, otherwise I should have had a very unpleasant time of it. As it was I was ditched several times, jammed between wagons, and that is where the heavy long rubber boots came in handy. We went a long way about and had the transport with us. It is certainly an experience to go along a narrow road, pitch dark, and meet all kinds of traffic. Wagons, guns, ambulances, lorries, and we passed hundreds of troops. And all in pitch dark as no lights are allowed on these roads leading to trenches. It is too dangerous as the road is often swept by German guns. At one place we helped to pull an ambulance, full of wounded men, out of the ditch. And we were held up dozens of times.

After two hours, he had covered the four miles to battalion headquarters, where he took tea with the colonel. He and his guide then set off again at about 11 p.m., this time on foot.

And believe me it is some road to the trenches. Never in all my life have I seen such mud. You can scarcely imagine it unless you have been thru it. I went up in absolute darkness, which of course, did not make it any easier. Several times I went in up over my knees, and more than once the water came in over my hip boots. When you are going down you wonder when you will stop, then you wait for breath, and begin to pull yourself together again. Then too, at this point, immediately behind the trenches the bullets are flying overhead in all directions, which does not add much to your pleasure. However one is practically safe as they are all stray bullets. Nearest they came to me was some 10 - 12 feet when one landed plump into soft earth beside me.

>After some puffing we arrived at front line trenches. They were quite a revelation to me. They should not be called trenches. Ditches, ravines or some such name would be more appropriate. Several have running water in them, and if one slips off the narrow sidewalk, good night, and it's up to the knees at least. However less said better, and I stayed there until 4 am. The dug outs are quite lively with rats and mice, and they are absolutely tame. I visited several dug outs while up there, and they are not any too choice.

That night he snatched three hours' sleep, and then made a tour of 'the battalion frontage from end to end'. The day ended with a 'terrible' meal, shared with officers in a dugout under heavy shellfire. The two different Christmas cakes that he was able to sample were only scant compensation. He got back to his billet at 7 p.m., soaked to the skin; but unlike the men he had visited, he could soon change, 'and my man had a big hot dinner ready for me. I polished off two large tenderloins in very few minutes.'

The visit was enough to persuade him that, when the time came, his brother Alf would be better off in the artillery than the infantry. As he shrewdly observed, 'This war is an artillery and aerial war. It is much more pleasant to be behind a "howitzer" than in a trench, and one can do better service behind the gun.' He himself would be hospitalized home with a bad case of measles in the spring of 1916. When he returned the next year, it was as a member of the Royal Flying Corps, with whom he flew until wounded in October 1917. (At the end of the war, he resumed his dental practice in Winnipeg.)

The 60th Battalion was still on the Ypres Salient on 12 August when, with the help of a barrage of twelve-inch artillery shells that came shatteringly to earth just behind the enemy's front lines, they beat off some 'strong' battle patrols that were attacking Hill 60. Such Germans as did reach the Canadian trenches were killed or driven out. But the battalion war diary had to admit that the Canadian casualties were 'heavy': 2 officers and 26 other ranks killed, and 2 officers and 56 other ranks wounded or missing. The corps commander congratulated the 60th on its 'steadiness and tenacity': not bad for troops such as the plumber Sam Voysey, who had been pursuing the peaceful trades of civilian life only a year before. By the end of the month, both the 60th and 27th Battalions had been withdrawn from the line, but the relief would be short-lived. They were now in training for the Somme.

On 6 September 1916, the 27th Battalion reached Albert, the little town that had become famous for the gilded Madonna on top of the basilica church. Like all high points that could have been used for observation, the church tower had been the object of German shelling, which had dislodged the Madonna, but not toppled her; instead she leant out at a right angle over the town, hovering as though in benediction, or perhaps prostrate with pity for the wreckage below. The legend grew that the war would finish when the statue fell. Mancel found himself bivouacked in the areas of desolation that were the brickfields outside the town.

> On the Brickfields the men quickly discovered that boxes of Small Arms Ammunition could be built into substantial walls: and when a tarpaulin was thrown over them an adequate hutment was the result . . . Huddled within their improvised shelters, they paid little heed to the long-range shelling which was scattered indiscriminately over the area.

During the day, they were kept busy, preparing themselves for the attack that was to come. One of the reasons for the failure of the first day of the Somme had been the inadequate training given to Kitchener's new armies: to relieve pressure on the French army, which was suffering catastrophic losses at Verdun, Haig had reluctantly agreed to launch the battle several weeks earlier than he would have wished. By contrast, the 27th Battalion, already battle hardened, had several days in which to perfect mock assaults on a practice ground in the brickfields. They moved out to take up their position on the front line at 2 p.m. on 14 September. That evening, just at the time that the 27th set off for their assembly trench, Sam and the 60th Battalion marched into the brickfields. Bashing the keys of his smudgy typewriter, the battalion adjutant later recorded: 'During night very heavy artillery fire in preparation for big attack to take place at 6.20am tomorrow morning.'

Water was important now: they had seen too much of it since they arrived from England, but the farmers – and plumbers – among the Canadian troops would have known its importance in other circumstances. One of the logistical problems for both sides on the Western Front was keeping the miles of trenches supplied with adequate amounts of food and water. The inadequacies of the food were reflected in the gratitude with which soldiers received parcels from home. Dental officer Gilroy was kept busy by the 'hard tack' which 'certainly plays havoc with teeth and gums'. Men also needed something to wash down their bully beef and tooth-breaking biscuits. In Belgium, even the abstemious Canadians had been reduced to drinking wine in preference to the water, which they found worse than unpalatable – and that was in billets. At the front, boiled water was needed to fill the dixies with that elixir of the trenches: tea. Even the machine guns would have seized up without the water that served as a coolant. We have seen the state of the water brought up to trenches held by the 3rd Worcesters: the little that there was tasted of petrol from the cans used to transport it.

The sons of the Canadian prairies who served battalions such as the 27th kept a keen eye on the landscape: soon those who survived the attack would report to their farmer families at home on the state of the harvest, which was progressing slowly with only women and old men to bring it in. The Canadians admired the French horses but deprecated the ploughs. They would certainly have understood the significance of a factory to process sugar beet – it needed water, and that was not a commodity to be found everywhere in chalk downland. There was a sugar factory, or the ruins of one, outside the village of Courcelette. Beyond its significance as a strongpoint, it had a strategic value as the centre of a network of wells and water channels going out into the surrounding fields.

Not that anything was left of the farmed landscape. As the 27th Battalion moved forward, they saw a section of the earth that seemed to have gone into spasm and spewed up its own innards. What had been features of an orderly and productive scene now existed in name only; woods, farmhouses and villages had been reduced to a universal sterility, above which floated countless observation balloons. If the

1. Lydford's church choir and bell ringers on an outing, 1908. Third from left, back row is Frank Fry, whose son, Wilfie, died in 1918. Jim Stephens, thought to have died in 1925 from eating an infected camel's liver, is fifth from the left in the third row.

2. Villagers outside the Post Office, Lydford. At the time of the First World War, the sub-postmaster was Arthur Petherick, whose nephew Richard died on the Somme.

3. (*top*) Tourists in front of the White Lady falls in Lydford Gorge. Families like the Hunters of Cheltenham stayed at Lydford for many weeks. Captain Nigel Hunter, MC, who died on the Somme, is remembered by an inscription at his favourite spot on Dartmoor.

4. (*bottom*) The Lydford village band. It was founded by the musically inclined schoolmaster William Kenner, who played the cornet.

5. Archie Huggins, in the tropical kit with which the Royal North Devon Hussars were issued before going to Gallipoli in September 1915. The uniform was found to be inappropriate: although warm by day, the peninsula was bitterly cold at night.

6. Archie Huggins's grandfather, Roger.

7. The Huggins family, stonemasons and builders, shown in front of the extension which they built to the school. Archie Huggins stands on the far left, trowel in hand.

8. (*right*) Picnic outside
Lydford in the 1920s.
Signalman Theophilus
Hammett occupies the chair,
with his daughter Polly to his
right. Polly married soldier
Charlie Berry on 8 July 1916;
he went back to the trenches
on 20 July and was killed on
24 August 1916 near Thiepval.

9. (*left*) Charles Sargeant
Jagger's bas-relief of the
Battle of Gheluvelt, 31
October 1914, when the
2nd Worcesters, of which
Berry was part, saved the
British line outside Ypres
from collapsing. Jagger was
himself a member of the
Worcestershire Regiment.
Although heroic, the
sculpture is grimly realistic
in its details.

10. Horse ambulance at Courcelette, on the Somme. Mancel Clark emigrated to Canada
before the First World War; he joined the Canadian army and died in 1916 at Courcelette, the
first battle in which tanks were used.

11. (far left) Sam Voysey in the uniform of a territorial cadet. From a family of agricultural labourers, Sam escaped Devon by joining the 3rd Battalion, East Surrey Regiment. He subsequently trained as a plumber.

12. (left) Sam Voysey emigrated to Canada in 1907, to be followed by his wife and family the next year. He is shown here with his two daughters soon after his family arrived: Elsie Eveline, born 1904, is on the left, Nell, born 1907, on his knee.

13. (left centre) The family which Sam Voysey left behind, photographed around the time of his death in 1916.

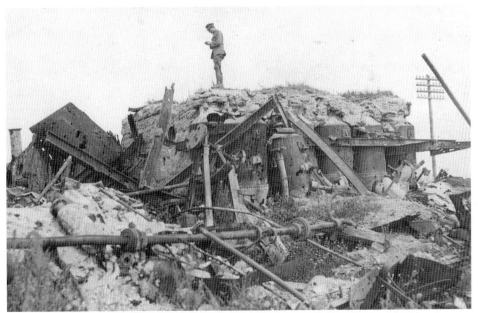

14. A soldier stands on top of the ruins of the Sugar Factory at Courcelette, 15 September 1916. The Sugar Factory was at the apex of Sugar Trench and Candy Trench, with the Fabeck Graben beyond. Sam Voysey and Mancel Clark were among the Canadians who died capturing these defences around the village of Courcelette, which opened a back way to Thiepval.

15. Lieutenant Richard Radford Turner, whose father, a vicar, married Lily Radford, daughter of Lydford's squire.

16. Captain Nigel Hunter, MC. He loved Dartmoor, which he knew from family holidays.

17. (*right*) Bridge House, Lydford, built by Daniel Radford, who had made a fortune from selling coal.

18. (*below right*) This memorial to the 177th Tunnelling Company of the Royal Engineers stands at the edge of Railway Wood, where eight Royal Engineers and four infantrymen were killed underground during the defence of Ypres between November 1915 and August 1917. Dickie Turner died leading men to the front when the Germans blew the mine that created the Hornby Crater on 3 February 1917.

19. Footballers from the Royal North Devon Hussars, 1907, perhaps showing a non-commissioned officers' team. Archie Huggins is third from the right in the back row. The RNDH was a territorial regiment, which several of Lydford's young men joined before the First World War. The government helped soldiers pay for the cost of their horses.

20. Builders collecting water from a Dartmoor stream. Dartmoor supplied many materials, including the granite slabs which masons cracked from the outcrops on the surface of the moor. It was a slow process and the resulting gateposts, lawn rollers and lintels did not fetch more than a few shillings.

21. The Pethericks outside their Lydford farmhouse in the first years of the twentieth century. The father, Herbert Petherick, was a house builder; Richard Petherick, who died on the Somme, holds the horse.

22. Petherick boys and their sheep: probably Richard and his brother Herbert.

balloons could have been joined dot to dot, the line would have roughly replicated the windings of the front trenches. 'All around were the evidences of what was involved in a great offensive – artillery parks, ammunition dumps, horse lines, watering troughs, stores of gasoline, engineering material, and everywhere, khaki-clad soldiers.' The chimney and storage towers of the sugar factory were no longer to be seen, but the stubs of the walls that were left had been fortified by the Germans, manned with numerous machine-gun teams and turned into a formidable redoubt. It was this – and what had been christened Sugar Trench and Candy Trench, to either side – that the 2nd Division had been sent to attack. Beyond it lay what was left of the village of Courcelette (the source of the thunderous boom from, probably, an exploding German munitions dump which Charles Berry had heard on 3 August on the other side of the Thiepval Ridge).

It was no easy matter for Mancel and his comrades to take up position in the assembly trench. A little way beyond the ruins of the windmill at Pozières, the trench was a German strongpoint which the Australians had succeeded in capturing on 4 August. The communication trenches were jammed with soldiers, all trying to move forward. The last of the battalion did not arrive until 4.25 a.m. Providentially, this gave the late arrivals only two hours to wait until the assault. Immediately to the right of the 27th Battalion was the 21st, where Private Lance Cattermole was in the third wave of attack (each wave was twenty yards apart). Because they were attacking from the west, the Allies had an advantage at dawn: they could see the silhouette of the German positions before the Germans could see them. It enabled Cattermole and his comrades to crawl over the top of the parapet and line up:

> . . . on a broad white tape, just discernible in the growing light, immediately in front of the trench and behind the first two waves which were already in position. It was almost Zero Hour. I looked at my wrist watch and saw we had about three minutes to go. I never heard our officers' whistles to signal the advance, and I don't suppose they heard them either because of the terrific crash that the creeping barrage opened up, exactly at 6.20am.

The air over our heads was suddenly filled with the soughing and sighing, whining and screaming of thousands of shells of all calibers, making it impossible to hear anything. We stood up and I looked around behind me; as far as the eye could see, from left to right, there was a sheet of flame from the hundreds of guns lined up, almost wheel to wheel, belching fire and smoke. It was an awe-inspiring sight.

As at Thiepval, the attackers moved up behind this cataclysmic artillery barrage, and then rushed the trench, in the face of a brief outburst of rifle and machine-gun fire. 'As soon as our men reached the trench,' records the battalion war diary, 'the Germans threw up their hands and surrendered. At least 70 dead Germans were counted in this trench.' In front of the sugar factory, Private Cattermole's experience was rather different.

Suddenly we came upon an enemy trench to our left. In keeping with our 'no prisoners' order, in view of the past German treachery, this trench was being mopped up and the occupants eliminated. The trench was already half-full of dead enemy and here and there little columns of steam rose in the cool, morning air, either from the hot blood let or from the urine I understand is released on the death of any human body. Two Canadians stood over the trench, one on the parapet and the other on the parados, and they exterminated the Germans as they came out of their dugouts.

One young German, scruffy, bareheaded, cropped hair and wearing steel-rimmed spectacles, ran, screaming with fear, dodging in and out amongst us to avoid being shot, crying out 'Nein! Nein!'. He pulled out from his breast pocket a handful of photographs and tried to show them to us (I suppose they were of his wife and children) in an effort to gain our sympathy. It was all of no avail. As the bullets smacked into him he fell to the ground motionless, the pathetic little photographs fluttering down to the earth around him.

At 6.27 a.m., the 27th Battalion reported to headquarters that its first objective had been taken. It went on to capture the Sunken Road, with little opposition; the battalion's Lewis guns were to prove their value in holding it. The four heavy Colt machine guns came up with the third wave of the attack. In the words of the battalion war diary, it was then that Sergeant F. W. Haines 'pointed out a German machine gun and crew with a number of snipers dug in in a shell hole 200 yards away. Pte Stewart opened up with a belt knocking out a number of the party.' Haines and Stewart then dashed forward and captured a new model German Maxim, recovering the bolt, which the crew had flung away, from the mud of a shell hole. The gun was then turned on the Germans' own snipers, to considerable effect.

For the 27th Battalion, it was a successful operation; but the compiler of the battalion war diary seems barely to have noticed the withering fire into which the men walked – perhaps, by this stage in the war, it was par for the course – nor, indeed, the feature for which Courcelette is generally remembered. Both are described by Private Donald Fraser, fighting with the 31st Battalion, mopping up to the immediate left of the 27th Battalion. The artillery had not driven all the German soldiers off their fire steps; Fraser was astonished by the number who were still at the parapet. He recalled:

> The air was seething with shells. Immediately above, the atmosphere was cracking with a myriad of machine-gun bullets, startling and disconcerting in the extreme. Bullets from enemy rifles were whistling and swishing around my ears in hundreds, that to this day I cannot understand how anyone could have crossed the inferno alive.

As Fraser approached the German lines, he caught sight of a new weapon of war, which offered the hope of nullifying the rifle and machine-gun fire which scythed down so many of his comrades.

> Away to my left rear, a huge gray object reared itself into view, and slowly, very slowly, it crawled along like a gigantic toad, feeling its way across the shell-stricken field.

This was a tank. At the time, the word meant only a metal container for water, or possibly a swimming pool, and was used as a code name for Winston Churchill's 'landships' to put the enemy off the scent. Many people thought it had made its debut prematurely, and ought to have been unleashed in massed ranks that would stun and demoralize the enemy. But the appearance of this singleton, the

Crème de Menthe, had a morale-rousing effect on the Canadians who saw it. Fraser continues:

> I watched it coming towards our direction. Down and up the shell holes it clambered, a weird ungainly monster, moving relentlessly forward. Suddenly men from the ground looked up, rose as if from the dead, and running from the flanks to behind it, followed in the rear as if to be in on the kill. The last I saw of it, it was wending its way to the Sugar Refinery. It crossed Fritz's trenches, a few yards from me, with hardly a jolt.

The tanks were not problem free: carbon monoxide could build up inside them, and the danger of bullet 'splash' or flying rivets when under fire was so great that the crew were issued with chain-mail helmet and goggles to protect their faces. Tanks were also unreliable. But *Crème de Menthe* showed the way of the future: it survived Courcelette to go into action again at Cambrai.

Tanks or no tanks, the toll on the 27th Battalion had inevitably been heavy. The runners taking messages to and from headquarters suffered the worst, as was usual: a casualty rate of 75 per cent. But they did their job. Altogether, the battalion lost 394 men, killed, wounded or missing. Of these, 72 were known to be dead. Among them was Mancel Clark. At Ginchy, elsewhere on the Somme, the Prime Minister's son Raymond Asquith died the same day.

If Mancel died as part of a successful set-piece attack, Sam Voysey lost his life in the murk of an unscripted operation, which took place as part of the follow-up three days later. By the morning of the 17th, the 60th Battalion found themselves occupying a trench known as Fabeck Graben, after Major Fabeck, whose vision it had been to fortify the German trench system so securely; it ran towards Courcelette from the Ferme du Mouquet, or 'Mucky Farm' as the Tommies called it, another of the stubborn obstacles on the way to Thiepval. This had not been the original objective, but their planned attack had been abandoned when another by the 42nd Battalion failed. Even getting to Fabeck Graben had caused 'severe casualties', according to the battalion war diary. Eventually they found their intended jumping-off point, which had been impossible to do before because heavy shelling had refashioned the landscape, and the two men guiding the battalion had become casualties. But now it hardly mattered, and the battalion did what it could to regroup and secure its new position. The war diary takes up the story.

> The weather was extremely bad on the night of the 17th -18th. Strong patrols were sent out and also covering party supplied for the 58th Battalion, who dug a trench . . . connecting with the Chalk Mound Trench. A bombing post was established . . . and we dug a trench, connecting it with Fabeck Graben.

Routine stuff. It was while out on patrol, crawling beneath the barbed wire of no-man's-land on a dirty night, that Sam was killed.

The Thiepval Ridge was taken by Canadian troops on 26 September. Eventually, on 11 November, they captured Regina Trench, and then Desire Trench a week later. The weather now made it impossible to fight on. The battle of the Somme was over. Or almost. On 24 November it claimed the life of Archie Huggins's young friend Dickie Petherick, a fellow member of the Royal North Devon Hussars. The North Devons had been broken up and distributed around other units – in Dickie's case, the 5th Battalion of the Dorsetshire Regiment. His family were in the same line of business as the Hugginses, being builders, responsible for renovating the Bible Christian chapel at Lydford Station in 1909. Playing billiards in the Reading Room in January 1914, he had produced the 'best performance' by beating Harry Heathman, proprietor of the Dartmoor Inn. 'Situation normal' reported the 5th Dorsetshire war diary for 24 November. A working party had gone out at night to improve the front line near the recently captured German bunker complex of St Pierre Divion. There were '22 casualties'. One of them was Dickie.

In military terms the Somme offensive fulfilled its objective, by drawing German troops away from Verdun, preventing them from being deployed against other Allies, and wearing down their numbers through sheer attrition. The failure of the German Chief-of-Staff, Erich von Falkenhayn, to repel the Allies caused his dismissal; he was replaced by men whose doctrine of total war, including unrestricted submarine attacks against merchant ships, brought the United States into the conflict on the Allies' side.

So vast, though, are the casualties that both sides inflicted in the course of the Somme that the sacrifice of individual soldiers such as Mancel, Sam and Dickie could be overlooked, anonymously merged into an unspeakable immensity of destruction and loss. But they were remembered in Lydford. They were remembered in Winnipeg and in Catherine Street, Montreal, where Sam's children read their father's name on the big sign which listed the fallen, and ran home to tell their mother.

5

The Golden Gorse Flowers Bud,
and Bloom, and Fade

⎯ RICHARD TURNER ⎯

Railway Wood, lying about two miles east of Ypres, is a pleasant place to visit on a sunny autumn afternoon. You walk up to it past a field of maize, which hides a large dairy farm – although you could guess its presence from the rich country aroma. Look back, and you can see the towers of Ypres, silhouetted against the setting sun. The Flemish old masters painted landscapes that were not dissimilar – big skies, cattle at pasture, ancient woods – in the seventeenth century. On the edge of the wood, the blackberries are sweet, but their thorns somewhat insistent if you try to penetrate the interior. If you do, though, you will find a dingle or hollow, one of many around here. Badgers have tunnelled in the banks. It is a place of darting dragon-flies and birdsong, a micro-wilderness where the rotting branches of trees that have collapsed into the bowl sink into a deep layer of spongy leaf mould; a rabbit's skull has been placed on a decaying stump. Nothing much disturbs the peace of Railway Wood, unless it is the noise of cars driving along the road that has been made from the old railway track, for which the line has now been dismantled.

In other woods, you might think the declivity was anonymous; but this hollow has a name – both a name and a history. It is Hornby Crater, created at 1.30 a.m. in the early morning of 3 February 1917; the Germans blew it in response to the efforts of the Royal Engineers, whose miners were also busily at work in this sector. Few people have heard of Railway Wood, or the triangle between the railway and the Menin Road, by the village of Hooge, but it was one of the most active sectors on the Western Front. In dispute was a stretch of ridge, slightly higher than the rest of this low-lying land-scape, in which a rise of three yards could constitute a strategic advantage. By 1917 it had become the only piece of high ground which the British still held in the bulge in the front line known as the Ypres Salient. The fight for it was continuous, but largely pursued underground. On a front of little more than half a mile, the German and British forces exploded some three dozen mines in their attempts to undermine each other, to interrupt the other's tunnelling efforts, and to seize – or keep control of – the ridge. Hornby Crater was made by one of them. On the February night when the mine was blown, the young officer in the Royal Sussex Regiment required to lead up reserves and stop the enemy occupying the ridge was Richard Turner.

He is remembered as R. R. Turner on the Lydford war memorial. The second 'R' stands for Radford which, for a boy who probably never spent very much time in the village, helps explain his presence here. St Petroc's churchyard is full of Radfords; Richard was the nephew of Squire Radford, the only son of his half-sister, Lilla or Lily.

In Lydford terms, the Radfords were new. Richard's grandfather Daniel Radford began to buy land here in 1871, fascinated, presum-ably, by the gorge. Already the gorge had acquired a degree of fame, having been described by topographers, rhapsodized by poets, painted by artists and studied by geologists. In the language of the Picturesque Movement, the extreme natural scenery would have merited the word 'sublime'. The age of Ruskin would have been equally enthralled by the rocks. Geology, which had begun to unfold a history of the early world completely different from that described in Genesis, was a subject of intense concern. ('If only the Geologists would let me alone, I could do very well, but those dreadful Ham-mers!' Ruskin lamented in 1851. 'I hear the clink of them at the end of every cadence of the Bible verses.') There is no reason to suppose that Daniel Radford was a Ruskinian. A chapel-going Congrega-tionalist who migrated to the Church of England in his prosperity, and appears to have supported every church or chapel cause that was presented to him, he hardly seems a man of doubt. But as a quick-witted businessman, he would have been alert to the intellectual currents of the time. Besides, the fast-flowing stream would have engaged him as much as the banks through which it passed: one of his relaxations from business was fishing. So frequently did he pass his time with rod and line that he was eventually buried in Lydford churchyard under a boulder that had formed his favourite seat by the river (looking, to the uninitiated, as though it had been placed to stop him getting up again). Dropping precipitously through potholes and chasms to rushing water that sometimes seems to boil as it froths over the black rock of the gorge, this section of the Lyd isn't the best place for trout, but it does have some. And a fisherman will always be drawn to a river.

Although new to Lydford, the Radfords were not new to Devon. There had been a conspicuous Radford during the Wars of the Roses. Nicholas de Radford, born around 1385, was a lawyer. At one point he was close to the Courtenay family, Earls of Devon, being a godfather to the 4th Earl's son Henry, and serving as steward of the Courtenay estates during the minority of the 5th Earl. But when de Radford was seventy, Sir Thomas Courtenay paid him a visit. While de Radford was offering food and drink, his men ransacked the house, rolling his sick wife, Thomasine, out of bed in order to use the sheets to wrap the loot. Nicholas then had his brains beaten out before being stabbed, literally as well as metaphorically, in the back. The gang returned, this time with de Radford's godson Henry, to mock the body before casting it naked into a pit. Later, they stole the money that de Radford had left in Exeter Cathedral for safekeeping. It is gratifying to learn that the 5th Earl and his family all met grisly ends – from poison, beheading (two family members) and death in battle – as a result of which this branch of the family became extinct in the male line.

This was only a moral victory as far as the Radfords were concerned. They did not recover their prominence until Daniel was born in 1828, to an improvident marine whose strong-minded wife ran a bakehouse in Plymouth. Daniel moved to London, went into coal, initially failed, but then became one of the earliest merchants to spot the potential of Welsh coal, with its high calorific properties, when it was first delivered to Paddington Station. This made his fortune.

We see Daniel at Lydford in 1885, chin, tie and coat collar obscured by a grey bib of beard, his clothes ample and baggy. He is a man at his ease in the company of children and friends, sporting floral hats or watch chains according to sex. Gazing intently into the camera, he looks shrewd, if not as stern as you might expect from his portrait in oils. He is fifty-six years old. On his leg he still bears the open abscess that developed when he was a boy: neither the wise woman's prescription that he should carry a Queen Anne shilling around his neck on the grounds that it would provide a cure for the King's Evil, nor a doctor's attempt to cauterize the wound with a hot iron, proved effective; he carried this stigmatum all his life. But as his relaxed attitude in the photograph suggests, the days of struggle to establish himself in the coal business are behind him. His second wife, Emily, is only thirty-five, although they have been married thirteen years. Lucy, the first wife, had borne Daniel a succession of children, in a succession of houses around London which necessarily got larger at each move, but also more genteel. By the mid-1860s, they were taking holidays in Devon. Lucy died a fortnight after childbirth in 1868. Daniel was left with a family of ten.

In the way of these things in the Victorian world, a selfless unmarried female relation arrived to take care of the children. But Daniel was intent on remarrying, and began to court a twenty-year-old Emily Allen. She was the daughter of Thomas Allen, the secretary of the Ruabon Coal Company and a deacon at the Congregational chapel at Hanwell: he had helped Daniel find a house at Ealing and the pair had built a cottage hospital together. Daniel's attentions to Emily did not cause universal delight. As he admitted in his autobiography, Emily was 'just half my age, a handsome and cheerful girl, and it seemed to her friends unreasonable and even wrong for her to marry a man so much older and with a large family'. Relations were broken off between Daniel and the Allens for some time. But as soon as Emily reached twenty-one, he proposed. They were married in 1872. This time, the honeymoon was at the Dartmoor Inn, on what is locally called the 'top road' at Lydford.

Daniel had begun to buy land at Lydford the previous year. It lay a little way out of the village, down the precipitous and then narrow defile down to the bridge that vertiginously spans the gorge. An architect called Mr Snell built a commodious, very solid house out of Dartmoor stone, with a bay window to enjoy the view to the west, and plenty of gables. Daniel continued to acquire farms, until in 1882 he owned 2,000 acres. It was not a particularly productive investment: farming had entered the long depression that would last, except when prices spiked during the First World War, until 1939. The farming around Dartmoor was particularly backward. Daniel did not follow the example of some of his contemporaries by sinking money into buildings, organized on factory lines, and buying expensive machinery: capital-intensive High Farming was more an article of faith than business sense, and would not have suited Devon. He did, however, have his own ideas, sending a Mr Ash up to Falkirk to buy Highland cattle – twenty-seven of them. When they reached Dartmoor, they liked it. Tourists venturing on to Dartmoor can to this day be menaced by farouche, long-horned, ginger-coated beasts: probably not the progeny of Mr Ash's herd, but following in its footsteps.

These days, newcomers to villages try to fit in and respect local sensitivities. A benevolent Victorian paternalist felt differently: Daniel had no hesitation in making his presence felt. Now part of the landed interest, he not only worshipped in Lydford's medieval church, but contributed substantially towards its enlargement. A new north aisle and vestry were built, along with a new barrel roof, at the end of the 1880s. But when he fell out with the High Church curate, Revd Chafy-Chafy, he promptly took himself off to the chapel, where he delivered the sermons himself. Whatever the village thought of the sermons, they must have been pleased with his gift of a water supply, delivered from taps set into what look like tall granite headstones bearing Daniel's name and the date 1881 (one survives outside what used to be the butcher's shop); a tap on the street was better than a bucket hauled up from a well. On Daniel's death in 1900, Revd Sabine Baring-Gould, squire-vicar of nearby Lewtrenchard, called him 'one of the noblest and kindest of men, and one of the most modest . . . one of the best men whom it has been my happiness to know'.

Daniel also shaped Lydford's modern character by opening up the gorge. Previously its woods had been impassable: anyone struggling to the edge of the ravine would have risked falling into the Lyd. He cut paths through the woods, an initiative that gave employment to the men of the village and, in the words of his obituary in the *Tavistock Gazette*, made the gorge 'what it is to-day, one of the beauty spots of England'. And the public could enjoy it free of charge.

At home, Daniel was anxious to take care of Emily. Not only had he lost Lucy, but twenty months after her death his eldest son, Frank, had died at the age of seventeen: rowing with some of his brothers, at Littlehampton on the South Coast, he had lost an oar, gone over the side to retrieve it, become detached from the boat (he could not swim) and drowned. After Tom's birth, Emily was ill for months, if not years. Tom was her third child, and her last. Perhaps with Emily's health in mind, the Radfords were spending more time in Devon; from 1881 they lived mainly at their town house in Exeter, rather than London.

A family such as the Radfords – with Lucy's children veering towards intellectual pursuits, and Emily's towards field sports – was big enough (as well as lively enough) to provide its own entertainment. Occasionally neighbours were invited to share their 'hospitable board'. That phrase was used by the Revd Sabine Baring-Gould, when dedicating the book of folk songs that he had gathered in Devon and Cornwall, *Songs of the West*, to Daniel, whose idea it had been.

Baring-Gould's Lewtrenchard, a village hidden away among dripping trees beside the Lew, lies a couple of miles west of Lydford's Norman castle. It was inevitable that Baring-Gould would become Daniel's friend. They were men of a similar stamp. Both liked procreation; both were men of strong mind; both worked hard. (Baring-Gould's labours were as much literary as pastoral: he wrote 40 novels and 60 other works on religion, travel, history and Dartmoor.) While Daniel might have been suspicious of his friend's Tractarian sympathies, he at least had the reassurance that Baring-

Gould's fifteen-volume *Lives of the Saints*, comprising 3,600 entries arranged in order of the saint's days, was put on the Index by the Roman Catholic Church. Eight years younger than Daniel, Baring-Gould inherited Lewtrenchard in 1881, on the death of his uncle. Characteristically, he designed the house that he built there himself, creating a seemingly indestructible Elizabethan-style mansion of local stone. He also rebuilt the church of St Peter and most of the village. So far, so Victorian, but Baring-Gould's interest in folk culture was ahead of his time, even if he did not hesitate to rewrite the words of any folk song that he considered indecent.

In the photograph for which he posed in 1885, Daniel looks relaxed, but not entirely at ease: there is an awkwardness to his posture, which suggests that he is about to move on. Perhaps he was temperamentally restless; perhaps – despite Baring-Gould's company – he felt country society to be too restricted. At all events he left Bridge House in 1886 and took his family to Tavistock, occupying Mount Tavy House (now Mount House School). He immediately set about restoring the property, building greenhouses and conservatories, lodges and drives. Soon he founded the Tavistock Cottage Hospital, held a bazaar to raise money for the National Schools and received a letter from the Duke of Bedford: 'You will – I trust – forgive me, if I venture – as a ratepayer of Tavistock, to express the hope that you may *not* be unwilling to allow yourself to be put in nomination for the County Council?' He was not unwilling; nor, given that the Duke owned most of Tavistock, was it a surprise when he was duly elected. As his obituary in the *Tavistock Gazette* on 5 January 1900 would conclude:

> No inhabitant of modern times has been such a public benefactor to this district. Blessed with ample means, he never turned a deaf ear to any application for assistance for any benevolent or philanthropic object, and to-day many institutions will mourn the loss of a generous-hearted supporter.

In all this whirl of good causes, Lydford was not quite forgotten. There remained the matter of the church. Its restoration had been completed but the debts incurred for doing so, despite Daniel's generosity, had not been cleared. Besides, the Bishop of Exeter had yet to consecrate it. When Lydford had a new rector, in the shape of Revd Richard Turner, a New College man of affable demeanour, it was natural that the Radfords would see something of him. Aged thirty-seven, Revd Turner was of particular interest to an unmarried Radford daughter called Lydia, known as Lilla or Lily. Her sisters had all married at the conventional time, in their twenties. Lily, however, had attended Newnham College, Cambridge (unusually, in an age when women could not become full members of the old universities), and she had brains. She chose to linger at home, to accompany her parents on holidays to North Wales and the Lake District, and to follow hounds during the season. She had written an account of a journey to visit an 'intimate friend' (daughter of an Exeter clergyman) who was living in Shanghai, under the title *Letters from the East*. But at thirty-five, she must have been losing hope that she would have a family. Having met Revd Turner in 1893, she married him the next year. Presumably they moved into the Lydford rectory, a turreted building by that great builder of parsonages George Edmund Street: it looks about as comfortable as you would expect of an echoing Victorian rectory on the edge of a moor. (It was even mocked by Baring-Gould.) A daughter, Dorothea, was probably born there. But they did not stay at Lydford for long. In 1895 they moved to the parish of Bickleigh, forty-two miles away, in the Exe Valley. In March 1896, when the trees were naked of everything except lichen and moss, but snowdrops shyly speckled the banks, a son, called Richard after his father and Radford after his mother, came into the world. Richard, or Dickie, Turner would have only twenty years to enjoy it.

Despite the bookish propensity of his parents, Dickie enjoyed much the same wind-blown Devon childhood as other boys. Ponies featured largely. But the place was not always as healthy as it might seem. In 1902 Revd Turner became vicar of Colyton, near the Devon coast. 'We are having a rather depressing time with a horrid lot of sickness in the parish,' Lily wrote in a letter of 1905, 'the death bell tolls cheerfully and I run around with bronchitis kettles and soup.'

Dickie escaped those risks when he was sent to Temple Grove School, then occupying a small country mansion at Sheen, on the outskirts of London. Established in 1810, it had claims to being the oldest preparatory school in the country. But if Temple Grove removed Dickie from some dangers, he encountered others after winning a scholarship to Westminster School in London: at one time, a rat bite gave him blood poisoning. On learning of this, his mother flew to his bedside, staying with family including her brother Herbert and sister-in-law Dora: 'Mrs Turner is still here,' the latter wrote on 7 November 1911, 'and not exactly a cheerful guest.' Dickie recovered, but lost six months' school. Then in 1912 his father died, and since they lived in a rectory – then at Barnstaple – the family home was broken up. By the standards of the time, he had been unusually close to his father. Yet his academic performance was soon back at its peak.

That summer, the Turners spent their holidays in Switzerland with Dickie's uncle Sir George Radford, MP. Dickie was present at the opening of the Britannia Hut on the Allalinhorn, given by the English members of the Swiss Alpine Club to Switzerland. The occasion is described in the pages of the family history.

> This strange ceremony, with its cosmopolitan crowd of Alpinists and guides collected round the little hut, perched on a rock among the everlasting snows, greatly impressed and delighted him; above all the magnificent singing of the various national anthems to the accompaniment of the thunder of avalanches down the mountain sides.

They often returned to Switzerland. Having damaged his knee lugeing, Dickie had to restrict his own Alpine activities to walking with others, like '*des vrais chamois*', and attending a New Year's Eve fancy-dress carnival on ice, robed as a kind of anachronistic Harry Potter, in 'a high black hat and cloak'.

Meanwhile, Dickie's studies continued. He gained the Duke of Devonshire's prize, open to all public school students for an essay on an imperial subject, Dickie's theme being aviation. Like his father, he wrote verse, often contrasting the wild countryside of his youth with the trials of city life.

... The spring is on the bracken,
And the moorhen's nest is made,
And Badgeworthy is bursting into green,
But the toilers in the city, their work will never slacken,
Though the golden gorse flowers bud, and bloom, and fade.

As his photograph suggests, he was sensitive as well as clever.

Already a member of the Officer Training Corps at Westminster School, he wanted to sign up as soon as he could. Fearful that the bad knee might get him rejected, he had it put right by Mr H. A. Barker, later described by his mother as 'the famous manipulative surgeon'. His headmaster succeeded in cooling his ardour, persuading him to postpone enlisting until he had won a scholarship to his father's old college at Oxford. So it was in January 1915 that he joined his battalion, 3rd Royal Sussex, in Dover. The shooting skills which he had no doubt honed in Devon caused him to be put in charge of the rifle range.

By 17 October 1915, the regiment was in France, having its first exposure to what Victorians had called the 'smell of the Continent', its camp being 'situated close to an amazingly dirty little French town which', as Dickie heard an American put it, 'smells "fit to beat shambles"'. Officers, equipped by their families, were better clothed than their men, to some of whom they looked, on the parade ground, like gods. They could also pack a sausage-shaped bag known as a valise with personal effects, although it was generally left in billets rather than taken to the front line. A letter survives from a lieutenant in the 2nd Devons to an artillery officer, still in England, describing the garments that worked best in the trenches. Gumboots were 'absolutely essential'; being heavy, they could be sent by post if necessary, and would arrive in less than a week. A short overcoat known as a 'British warm' was also vital. A mackintosh might be worn over it, but the length had to be judged nicely: too long and the skirts would get clogged with mud, too short and it would drip on to the knees.

Bedford cord is the only thing for breeches. Some people have coats of it as well. Have double brace-buttons sewn on. Night-glasses are useful for our work, but probably not for yours. Get a waterproof flap for the back of your cap, the men all make them. I brought one out with me. For a mounted officer it is advisable to have your service jacket fleece-lined. Have your boots plenty big – at least we need them so, – for 2 prs of socks, & the swollen feet we get.

Dickie was also distinguished from his men – and many officers – in knowing French; it enabled him to order omelettes for breakfast, if not quite to satisfy 'an honest Briton's desire for bacon and eggs'. Not that lack of the language was necessarily a deterrent to a soldier of determination; on one occasion, Dickie's servant, 'Ginger' Phillips, managed to return from a shopping trip with a sketch block, two electric batteries and a tube of rubber solution, with no more command of French beyond 'Alleman no bon.'

At the end of the month, Dickie learnt that he would be sent on a bombing course. The bombs in question were what we would now call grenades. At the beginning of the war, grenades had been aptly described as 'jam pots'; some were literally made out of old jam tins, stuffed with gun cotton, nails and a detonator. Industrially produced versions had become available by the spring of 1915, although the earliest of them were apt to fail in wet weather. During the course of the war, grenades – so valuable to trench raiding parties – were made in a variety of shapes, the Germans favouring a stick form known as the Potato Masher. The British staple was the pineapple-shaped Number Five Grenade or Mills bomb, named after its inventor, William Mills. They were issued in long wooden boxes: rows of unprimed grenades to one side, and detonators and five-second fuses (inserted before use) to the other. They could be thrown about thirty yards, and also fired from a rifle. 'When the smoke cleared, there were six Jerries on the ground,' wrote a corporal who had just killed a Maxim gun team which threatened to mow down a raiding party. 'The rest hid, they wouldn't argue with a Mills.'

Because early grenades were almost as dangerous to the man throwing them as to the enemy, the bombing officer of that time enjoyed privileges and, if only in his own mind, prestige. He was likely to be under the direct control of headquarters, being attached to a company only when it was conducting offensive operations. This gave him an envied independence. Even during a raid, the bombs were so dangerous that only he would be allowed to touch them. The bomber would go ahead of the riflemen, throwing bombs into the enemy trenches. Once a trench was taken, he would then race along its length bombing the dugouts in which, with luck, the German troops had taken shelter from the artillery bombardment and were preparing to emerge. The Mills bomb was considerably less volatile (although, as we shall see, not perfect). Even so, Dickie's mother was alarmed. 'Please do not think that I am going to blow myself up bombing,' he wrote to reassure her on 7 November. 'Although it may sound very dangerous, it is really not more so than rifle shooting, if you take proper care. Most of these high explosives you can hit with a hammer quite safely, which I should not like to do with a rifle bullet.' One of the jobs of the bombing officer was to train other soldiers in the company in the use of grenades. The bombing officer may have lost some of his elite status, but, shorn of his self-importance, he perhaps got a better reception from his unit as a result.

In fact Dickie was soon to find, if he did not know it already, that the bombing officer was likely to have a strenuous time as he made his way between the bombers whom he was supervising. On one occasion they were stationed at either end of the line which the battalion was holding. 'This meant a walk of about half a mile along the trench, and half a mile is no light thing in a trench, equal to about three miles on top.' It was, however, dry and, apart from 'a fair amount of shelling', reasonably quiet. Only one man was lost to a sniper, but Dickie himself 'potted a Hun who was working on a trench'. He was pleased enough to get back to his billet at 2 a.m. He then slept until 11 a.m. – the first 'proper sleep' that he had managed for the four days he had been in the front line.

By Easter 1916, the brigade clearly thought that bombing ought to be recentralized, because Dickie:

> . . . got a job with 'Brigade Grenade Company', a collection of confirmed anarchists, culled from each battalion of the brigade. I spend my time instructing, and paying periodical visits to the front line to see that the bombers are holding the saps, mine craters, etc., all right.

One of the most daunting tasks that faced any soldier was patrolling in no-man's-land, 'a nasty wet job crawling about on one's tummy between the lines'. On one occasion, the Germans 'threw a bomb at us, but did not hit us, and we returned safely, but I was rather frightened at the time when I thought I saw strange people crawling about. Of course, they were really only thistles.' By Christmas, the men were having to contend with another enemy: mud. 'In one part of the line,' reports Dickie, 'eight men got completely stuck. One man left his boots *and* trousers behind him, and had to walk back to the dressing station weirdly garbed in a shirt and numerous sandbags.'

Life at the front was cheered by the arrival of letters and parcels. Neither was guaranteed to reach their destination: the presence of U-boats in the Channel interrupted the service. But some comforts got through. 'The slippers and gloves arrived safely, and are adorning my fairy feet,' Dickie told his mother. 'I refer to the slippers, not the gloves.' He thought it would be 'rather a good idea' to be sent weekly parcels of tobacco, magazines, food, socks 'or anything that may be lying about, looking as if it wanted to go to France.' In later correspondence there was mention of books and mittens, cigarettes, mince pies and Turkish delight. A hoped-for supply of gramophone records never made it, but issues of the magazine *Punch* seemed more humorous than ever in those surroundings, 'a magnificent tonic'. The traffic was to some extent two-way. Although he could not fulfil an aunt's request for souvenirs, being able (he wrote) to find nothing smaller than some very heavy German shells, he did offer to send her, perhaps sardonically, 'an English bullet which was successful in its mission'. He had 'picked it up on patrol on the other side of a German's coat'. The following year, in December 1916, he would send home two Belgian shell cases, decorated by a brass worker, 'to beautify the Christmas board'.

Brigade routine, for Dickie as for other British soldiers, was to have two battalions in the front trenches, one in the reserve and one resting in billets. The cellars of ruined houses were thought to be safer than the rooms above ground; Dickie's company had been sheltering in some on the support line, he wrote on 7 December 1915. The town where he was then billeted was 'somewhat shattered, and is also extremely noisy, as lots of our batteries are posted in it. This morning

I woke up and found half the ceiling lying across the foot of my bed.'
Billets allowed men an element of respite, pursued amid the shattered
ruins of streets that were still being shelled. The previous month, at
Lillers, west of the coal mining town of Béthune, Dickie had enjoyed
'a good billet over a grocer's shop with a good lady who provides me
with coffee and an excellent bed'. It was, he felt, 'not a bad little town
with some quite decent shops, and a full-blown theatre, in which we
had a regimental concert last night.' He took part in the concert as
part of a maritime quartet, *en costume*: 'with four school-children's
sailor hats, four blue and white striped jerseys, trousers, "emergency,
blue pairs four," and a quantity of yellow tow, we sang "Four Jolly
Sailormen." It was – very literally – a howling success.'

In the new year of 1916, Dickie came home for a short leave. On his
return to the front he was made a wiring officer. Barbed wire had
been invented about 1870 to help American ranchers parcel up the
Great Plains, a land too vast for post and rail fences, stone walls and
hedges. By 1914, it had been recognized as a defensive obstacle which,
though quick to install, was very difficult for infantry to cross. Thousands of miles of it were unrolled across no-man's-land, in front of
the trenches of both sides. On the Somme, the failure of British artillery to cut the German barbed wire would be a major factor in the
colossal losses of 1 July 1916. A machine-gunner remembered looking through his field glasses to find that it was a 'black mass' – so
dense 'that daylight could barely be seen through it'. The soldiers had
a grimly humorous song, which, after reviewing the comforts and
whereabouts of the officer class, concluded:

> If you want to find the old battalion,
> I know where they are, I know where they are.
> If you want to find the old battalion,
> I know where they are.
> They're hanging on the old barbed wire.
> I've seen 'em, I've seen 'em,
> Hanging on the old barbed wire,
> I've seen 'em, I've seen 'em,
> Hanging on the old barbed wire.

Dickie's new job, which involved maintaining the British wire and reporting on that of the Germans, was therefore highly important. Wire entanglements could take various forms, from strands nailed to trees or posts, to coils of Dannert wire extended like a concertina. In a letter of 12 March 1916, Dickie describes going 'out for a walk' (a euphemism, surely, for a night patrol spent crawling through shell holes):

> . . . just to examine our own wire, which was awfully bad, and then to examine the Bosch's. Well we examined. He had, we found, an awfully cunning contrivance, quite likely to hold us up completely in case of attack. First, fifty yards from trench, 'knife rest,' *i.e.*, iron crosses joined by a long pole and covered with wire. Three rows of these and a smaller row on top. This of course quite concealed a second ordinary entanglement thirty yards behind, which in a bombardment the artillery would not destroy as they would not know of it. Rather cunning idea, eh!

Having seen five or six Germans get out of their trench to work on the parapet, he was about to fire when he spotted what might have been a loophole for a machine gun, 'so we decided to return'. Generally, German wiring, like the engineering of the German trenches, was of a superior order to the British effort, described by an officer in Flanders as 'the usual series of iron thickets' versus a 'brambly pretence'.

The next night Dickie 'felt rather cheap and seedy', but he carried on. Soon, however, he was running a temperature of 102 degrees. This got him sent to the Meerut British General Hospital at Rouen, on the journey to which he inadvertently shared a carriage with a man suffering from measles. As a result he was put into quarantine: a frustrating period, because he wanted to get back to the regiment before anyone else took his job as brigade wirer.

Almost as soon as he had returned, another piece of misfortune fell, literally, out of the sky. On 3 April he found himself as part of the reserve battalion, in the cellars of a ruined house. 'To-day was nice and fine and I slung my hammock in the back garden in the sun. But a silly ass of a battery behind sent over some shrapnel which burst too soon, and gave me a slight wound in the leg. I'm afraid it won't mean England.' The Field Ambulance was located in a hospital that otherwise belonged to a coal mine; the proximity of both the mine and a crossroads meant heavy shelling, and Dickie's servant (not Ginger Phillips) disappeared. When Dickie had moved on to Number 33 Clearing Station, his spirits perhaps lowered by his experiences, he heard what had happened and recorded it in a letter home.

> [He] had reached this hospital – nearly, he was down on the books – Admitted – dead. Admitted – dead. All the tragedy of the war seems to be in those two words. He was one of the best young fellows I have come across out here. Bright, clean, and brave, like a hundred thousand before him, and a hundred thousand to follow him – admitted dead. But it doesn't bear thinking of.

Like other young soldiers, Dickie would rather have been up and busy, so that thinking time could be reduced.

By the end of the month, Dickie was back, training soldiers to throw bombs. But on the afternoon of 27 April, a rifle grenade exploded prematurely while they were practising; it wounded sixteen men, including Dickie. Four or five pieces of the grenade hit the fleshy part of his right leg, the one that had already been caught by the shrapnel. He wrote to his mother: 'In the words of the immortal and illustrious Dan Leno, "Here we are again."' The wound, he assured her, 'doesn't hurt much. I am rather sorry I got it, as the Brigade Bombs were quite a good job.' Shortly afterwards he developed scarlet fever. There was nothing for it but enforced, tedious rest at Number 25 Stationary Hospital at Rouen, with a travelling chess set sent to him by Aunt Gracie – 'rather a clever little apparatus, but I can only do problems on it, as there is no one who plays but me'. A visit from his sister Dorothea, who was serving as a nurse at Étretat, cheered him; but otherwise, there was little amusement beyond the gramophone, magazines and a Methodist orderly 'of peculiar tastes with a high falsetto voice. He is believed to use rouge, and a box of face powder was once captured from him by a jeering crowd of patients.'

One of the nurses must have liked him. On her day off, she picked a large bowl of 'bee orchids, lizard orchids, and other curious flowers,' which she gave to him. In a letter dated 19 June, he wrote: 'They are the most wonderful things – especially when opened and looked at with a strong magnifying glass. It seems a pity such wonderfully delicate colouring should be wasted right inside the flower where it can be hardly ever seen.' But even such attentions only dented the boredom. As he wrote on 25 June: '*J'y suis, j'y reste, et je m'ennuie* . . . If only someone would blow up a mine in the garden I should feel much happier, it would be so much more home-like.' But now at least he was beginning to hobble around, wearing a red flannel dressing gown and with a blanket around his legs, so that 'I look like a cross between John Jorrocks and Abraham'. Early in July he was sent to Netley Hospital in Hampshire. There followed six weeks' leave.

It was high summer. Much of the leave was spent in the West Country, in Cornwall, Dartmoor and North Devon – perhaps with his Uncle Tom and Aunt Crystal at their home Ingo Brake. There was a fine crop of whortleberries that year. Doctors and vets were finding it difficult to get around the countryside on their petrol allowances, and the Tavistock Rural District Tribunal was kept busy hearing cases of wheelwrights, farm workers, tree fellers, horsemen and waggoners who wanted, on grounds of hardship or because their employers could not manage without them, to be made exempt from conscription. Dickie's Aunt Dora was sorry that her nephew was unable to wear the gold stripes of men who had been wounded in battle; since Dickie's injuries had been caused by his own side, he could not. This period of freedom came to an end in September, when Dickie was deemed fit to rejoin the regiment at Newhaven, to teach musketry. This included a course of revolver shooting with officers, which he described in a letter written on 11 November as 'not the least dangerous job I have had for some time'. Like other battle-hardened soldiers, he was amused by the energy of some young officers, one of whom concluded a lecture with the rhetorical question: 'After all, what are we here for?' upon which 'one of Sussex's brightest specimens rose slowly to his feet and delivered the subtle suggestion, "Cause it's raining, sir."' By December 1916, he was ready to return to France, looking, to Aunt Dora, 'awfully fit'.

★

The next months were busy. Dickie was now attached to the 12th Battalion, which was short of officers; for some time, therefore, he acted as a temporary captain. His sector was now the Ypres Salient, that awkward bulge in the line which had in part been formed by the 2nd Worcesters' heroic action at Gheluvelt. The 12th occupied a position beside the 11th Battalion, responsible for a narrow but active arc of trenches, between the Menin Road and a railway embankment. It was a freezing winter, the worst for many years. This is a watery land, and the terrible pummelling that it had taken from the heavy artillery had destroyed the field drainage systems: later in 1917, what would misleadingly become known as the Battle of Passchendaele, a village that occupies only one part of the Ypres Salient, became a byword for mud. There was, however, little mud to be seen that January. The ground was frozen solid, and so thickly covered in snow that the men of the 11th Battalion were sent some camouflage for night patrols: on opening the package, the men found a consignment of ladies' nightdresses.

The Sussex trenches – 'miserable British breastwork', according to Edmund Blunden, an officer of the 11th – occupied the crest of a low ridge, which, in this flat countryside, had the strategic value of giving an uninterrupted view of Ypres. Historians have largely passed over the operations taking place in this corner of the salient in the first weeks of 1917; nothing came of them. But the British had heard from an impeccable Belgian source that a German attack was brewing; perhaps the Germans thought one would come from the other side. The miners, men of all ages, plucked from other regiments and drafted to the Royal Engineers because of their experience in digging underground, were kept hard at work. The RE's 177th Tunnelling Company had been there since 1915.

Soon Dickie was the only officer in the company, doing the duties of all. At least the accommodation took the form of 'quite good dugouts in the garden of a château, never yet shelled, because it belongs to an Austrian Count'. That is perhaps a rather fanciful description of Potijze Château. 'It boasted a handsome cheval-glass and a harmonium, but no roof,' remembered the poet Blunden. (The observers in the upper floors of the building, gazing through a telescope across a landscape of devastation, were much to be envied: their day could not begin before first light or go on after sunset.) But there were other compensations. 'My tea is just coming in,' Dickie exclaimed on 5 January 1917. 'Toast, butter, mixed biscuits, jam (surely not, is it? yes, not plum but marmalade!). I don't do so badly here, you see.' He also had a horse, 'which is rather pleasant, when I have time to use him, but just now I have not. However, it means a little less fag when marching anyway.'

Blunden describes the trench system in *Undertones of War*.

> Its arrangement was simple – a breastwork front line, running across the Zonnebeke road to a railway bank on the south; a support line; two good (or not too bad) communications trenches – Haymarket and Piccadilly . . . If one lived much in the district, one evolved a sense when to use the Haymarket communication trench, when Piccadilly. The men, unable to keep their footing on the glazed boards, bound sandbags around their boots; but the 'practice' had to be 'discontinued forthwith.' Going forward, one finds St James's Street, the support trench, none too comfortable: it is narrow, its sandbags are worn out (and the thaw will come presently), its dugouts are only dugouts by name, for they are small hutches of galvanized iron and revetting materials, blackened with wood-smoke, and inside dusky and suffocating. Sit down, and cower, for the 'air' is best near the floor.

Even by the standards of this war, the front line was 'crude and inhuman', with a low parapet that made the soldiers stoop for its whole length. 'There were no dugouts in the front line, and even recesses for bombs and ammunition were scarce.'

In the fortnight after his arrival, Dickie had two spells in the front trenches. During the first, it snowed heavily; 'during the second [there was] the bitterest frost and keenest wind I have ever known outside Switzerland'. Heavy shelling made it 'rather a stiff time', and the two officers who were now with the company were inexperienced, being fresh from England. The rule was now four days in the trenches, four days behind the lines. The regular captain had returned by the end of the month, and in a letter of 30 January, Dickie asks wistfully about a subject dear to his heart: 'Is chocolate frightfully expensive at home now? Out here it has risen to 5d. an ounce. It used once to be my staple food out here. Now I shall have to give it up or go bankrupt.' He ends with a story of a soldier who took a tot of rum on an empty stomach and fell into a manure heap; 'his nostrils being assailed by an intolerable odour, he emitted a loud yell of "Gas".' This got him court-martialled for raising a false gas alarm, but the court had sufficient sense of humour to acquit him.

Below ground, the 177th Tunnelling Company was hard at work, pushing forward the gallery known as 16WA. It was one of more than a dozen that they had on the go. The tunnellers, disappearing through entranceways which other troops were strictly forbidden to penetrate (the makeshift doors were daubed with slogans such as 'Keep Out – That Means You') were known as stubborn men, and had to be. The tunnels linking the quarries around Arras had been dug through limestone and did not need to be shored up; this was also true of the hardened chalk around Thiepval on the Somme. But the tunnellers on the Ypres Salient were digging through clay. This required different expertise. Rather than coal miners, these conditions needed men who had dug beneath the Thames, where the contractors Price and Reeves had finished the Rotherhithe Tunnel in 1908. In Flanders, the Royal Engineers developed a technique known as clay kicking: the tunneller put his back against a wooden frame facing the surface of the clay and dug down with a short spade into the space between his knees. As the tunnel progressed, the work was performed in conditions as close to silence as possible. Clay is impervious to water, but the walls and roof had to be supported; eventually the tunnel became, except for the floor, entirely encased in wood (or sometimes metal). But gaps initially had to be left between the props to allow for the expansion of the clay, as a result of the water vapour introduced from outside. The clay swelled, extruding itself between the wooden supports, until it could be sliced off like cheese. If the walls had been close panelled straight away, even thick timbers would have been snapped by the pressure.

If the tunnellers went deep enough, they got to a level of blue clay; they were spading their way through it in February 1917. This gave them a particular problem; the earth that was taken to the surface could not simply be emptied around the tunnel entrance. It was too distinctive. But neither could the sandbags be left lying around. 'If you collected a pile of sandbags with blue clay you had to get rid of it quickly,' recalled Captain M. Greener of the 175th Tunnelling Company, 'because the Germans would shell it just to see what was in it. You had to take it out and distribute it as best you could at night, behind the trenches, well away from the line, so that the trenches didn't look any different.' The tunnellers worked in silence, but the Germans listened for them; they could hear telltale noises through their geophones – listening devices similar to a stethoscope. The tear-shaped crater formed when the German tunnellers exploded their counter-mine was of sufficiently impressive dimensions (75 feet in diameter, 25 feet deep) to be named after Major General M. L. Hornby, who commanded the 116th Infantry Brigade, 55th Division, when they took over the line. The explosion disrupted work on gallery 16WA, causing damage to 30 feet of its length. This was competitive mining: blow up the enemy's mine or risk being blown up yourself. They were at it again later in the month when, on 25 February, the Germans blew the even bigger mine that created Gordon Crater, 100 feet in diameter and 30 feet deep. This time the damage to the British system was worse: 320 feet over three levels. Two of the tunnelling company were killed and three wounded.

There was another military advantage in mining. The craters formed strongholds that could be occupied by troops, in advance of the front trench and perhaps overlooking the enemy line: it was with that purpose that they were sometimes created. So while the last particles of frozen earth thrown heavenwards by the Hornby mine were still settling, the British infantry rushed the crater. A runner scrambled his way back through the communication trench – not an easy job in the dark – with the order for Dickie to bring up some more men. Presumably the Germans knew that this was likely to happen, which is exactly why they shelled the trench. During the First World War 70 per cent of casualties were caused by artillery shells. On this occasion, the Germans did not try to occupy the crater themselves.

It was a bad night for the 12th Battalion. They lost fifteen men; one of them was Dickie.

Thereafter, the official communications followed the usual pattern. First, a 'deeply regrets to inform you' telegram from the War Office; next, because he was an officer carrying the King's Commission, a telegram from Buckingham Palace, signed by the Keeper of the Privy Purse. These were followed by letters from the commanding officer, invariably stating that the individual was killed instantly, and the battalion chaplain. Dickie's mother also received a warm letter from his servant and a request from his runner: 'Have you by any chance any sort of photograph of him? I have nothing in memory of him, and if you should have one to spare I should very much like one.' At one point Dickie thought he had been put in for the Military Cross, but he never got it.

'Time and again,' comments George Radford, Dickie's nephew, 'my parents would tell me that the brightest and best were killed in the war.' After Dickie's death, his sister Dorothea wrote to her cousin Ursula: 'I know how much you loved him. I think you know him better than any of his other cousins. Those times we have in Switzerland are among the happiest we ever have.' Years later, Ursula would remember: 'There was nobody to go out with, there was nobody to dance with, they were all dead.'

6

Death in Every Imaginable Shape

— RICHARD HOBBS AND EDWARD WHITFORD —

The woods on the hillsides at Coryton were planted soon after the Newmans came to the manor at the beginning of the nineteenth century. At the start of the next century they were ready to harvest, and Squire Newman established a sawmill. Shortly before the First World War, a fair-haired man in his early thirties, Edward Whitford, came to run it.

While Samuel Voyzey and Mancel Clark left Lydford and sought their fortunes across the Atlantic in Canada, Edward was a newcomer to the area. He had been born in Sherborne, Gloucestershire, in a village dominated by the mock-Elizabethan Sherborne House, the seat of Lord Sherborne, on a tributary of the Windrush called Sherborne Brook. Earlier, the family had been living in the respectable town of Cheltenham. When Edward was just a few months old his mother, Elizabeth, and elder siblings (a sister and three brothers) took lodgings at Northleach, six miles away. According to the 1881 census, they were living in the house of a 'Draper, Grocer and Bank Manager' called Jonathan Wane. History does not reveal what became of Edward's father, who did not feature in Edward's childhood; presumably he had not died, because Elizabeth considered herself to be a wife, not a widow. However, Mrs Whitford was fortunate to have some means of support, and by 1891 she was back in Sherborne, 'living on her own means', as she told the census enumerator, at Sherborne Gardens. Edward's eldest brother, Frank, was by this time a solicitor's clerk, and the family had an estate agent's clerk as a lodger. Perhaps the Whitfords' aspirations to enter the growing ranks of the Victorian middle class came to less than they might have hoped, since, by the age of thirty-nine, Frank had become an estate agent's clerk himself. It was then 1911 and he and his wife, Edith, and their little daughter, Kathleen, were living in the queen of suburbs, Ealing. With them was Edward, 'sawmill foreman', aged thirty-two.

Ealing had been a place of orchards and market gardens until the nineteenth century. Then came the Grand Junction Canal, followed by the Great Western Railway, and it was rebuilt as semi-detached villas, with good drains, an electric tram service, drinking fountains and a town hall that was opened by the Prince of Wales. A growing borough (as Ealing became in 1901) needed building materials. From as early as the eighteenth century, a timber yard had existed on a wharf on the river Brent. This went through various ownerships, and faced the rivalry of other concerns, until taking the name of James Montgomery and Son. Was this where Edward was sawmill foreman? If so, he would have had a motive for moving before the First World War: in 1911 James Montgomery and Son sold out to Water Softeners Ltd, making another product needed in the capital. We do know, however, that at one point Edward was working for a hardwood importer called W. W. Howard, with offices in the City as well as yards at Canning Town, Poplar and Southampton, and a veneer depot in the Euston Road. He was evidently well regarded.

From Frank's house in St Stephens Road, Edward went to another of his brothers, Frederick, 250 or so miles along the London and South Western Railway track at Lydford Station; resplendent in watch chain and uniform, he was the stationmaster. Through him, Edward was introduced to Lydford. Dartmoor must have seemed a rugged and untamed place for a bachelor to make a home in after the gentility of Ealing: the moor itself was windswept, with few trees. There had been a controversy over forestry on the moor at the beginning of 1914, with Revd Sabine Baring-Gould observing that only sycamore seemed to prosper, and that was regarded as a weed by foresters. Trees needed the shelter of the valley at Coryton in order to thrive.

Edward had interests beyond his work. Like Archie Huggins, Dickie Petherick and Jim Stephens, he was a member of the reserves. His regiment was not the Royal North Devon Hussars but the King's Royal Rifle Corps. He was thirty when he enlisted, and the place where he did so was East Ham, then in Essex, now part of the eastern aspect of London. One imagines him living there when working for W. W. Howard in Canning Town. When war came, he went, after a judicious pause, to Winchester. Here, on 11 September 1914, he volunteered for overseas service with the 13th Battalion. Fair-complexioned, taller than many of his contemporaries (he was nearly five feet ten inches tall), he started as a plain rifleman but was soon promoted: to lance corporal on 13 October 1914, to corporal on 28 January 1915, and to acting sergeant on St George's Day, 23 April 1915. He was promoted to full sergeant in July 1915. At the end of that month, the battalion crossed to Le Havre.

Edward's service papers were nearly destroyed during the Blitz. But a charred telegram survives, instructing him and three privates to report to 'C.R.E. forests at Rouen for duty'. The Chief Royal Engineer would have had need of specialists such as Edward to improve the supply of timber to the trenches. As well as being an artillery war, which devoured millions of human lives, the First World War was a war of logistics. The statistics are prodigious. Nearly 7,000 miles of railway line were built in France for military use; over 51,000 rubber stamps were issued; precisely 137,224,141 pairs of socks were given out. Stupendous quantities of armaments, uniforms, rations, horses and other stores were distributed – and consumed on an epic scale, particularly during a big push. Even the static lines were a monument to the supply of materials. One mile of trench was defended by 900 miles of barbed wire. A Canadian soldier wrote a doggerel verse to 'Our Pal – the Sand-bag', celebrating its many uses, from makeshift clothing to tablecloth.

> He makes the dugout cosy
> And soaks up all the damp
> I've even seen him used as wick
> Inside a handy lamp.
>
> We use him as a dishcloth
> To wipe our mess tins clean
> And he makes the warmest stockings
> That anyone has seen.

As blanket broom or brush
He's really very fine
Likewise as helmet trimming
To cover up the shine.

It was as well to make friends with him, because he was present in almost unimaginable numbers: 6 million for each mile of the line. That mile would, in addition, have been lined by 36,000 square feet of corrugated iron, and propped up and floored by a million cubic feet of timber. 'That timber is an essential munition of war is demonstrated forcibly by the enormous quantities of wood which were required by the Allied armies in almost every phase of military operations in France,' wrote the American Lieutenant Colonel W. B. Greeley in 1920.

> The great military bases behind the lines consumed lumber in vast amounts for camps, hospitals, shops, and warehouses. No advance could be undertaken without large supplies of railroad ties for extending railheads into conquered territory, of bridge timbers, and road plank for throwing forward quickly built roads over streams and shell-torn ground, and of lumber, logs, and pickets for constructing fortifications.

Foresters had been worried by Britain's strategic shortage of trees since John Evelyn published *Sylva* in 1664. Nelson's navy was built of oak trees, which took more than a century to reach maturity. Admiral Collingwood, who took over command of the Mediterranean fleet after Nelson's death at Trafalgar, was so concerned about shortages in supply that he filled his pockets with acorns before taking a walk in his native Northumberland, so as to scatter them in the hedgerows as he passed. Those acorns might have grown into mighty oaks by 1914 but what was needed now was large plantations of straight, fast-growing pine. Britain did not have sufficient quantities, and in due course created the Forestry Commission to cover the mountainsides of Scotland, Wales and Northern England with geometrical blocks of Sitka spruce, a native of North America. In the meantime, it had to source timber in France. There was no shortage there. As Greeley observed:

If France had set about deliberately, 60 years ago, to supply the armies of the Allied nation with timber during the Great War, she could hardly have built up her forest resources more effectively than her thrift and foresight had actually done.

But the trees still had to be felled, sawn and distributed. A sawmill foreman such as Edward was in demand.

We do not know how long he spent with the Royal Engineers. It is certain, though, that he had returned to his battalion by the time of the Somme offensive. R. D. Mountfort, a non-commissioned officer in the same brigade as Edward, summed up his experience in a letter to his mother.

> After having been up against the push since I wrote you last, & seen in 3 days more wonderful, more pitiful & more horrible sights than would suffice any ordinary mortal for lifetimes, we tried a push ourselves yesterday morning. I hadn't pushed far before a machine gun pushed a bullet through my shoulder as I pushed [paper decayed]. Am in hospital at Rouen . . .

That was written on 16 July 1916. Next day, Edward might have used the same words himself, having received what his service papers note as being a 'GSW' (gunshot wound) in the back. It sent him home to England, where he was admitted to the Duchess of Connaught Canadian Red Cross Hospital at Taplow, Buckinghamshire, on 20 July. He stayed there until September; then it would have been back to Lydford, where his mother was also staying, until he was strong enough to return to France. He did so on 24 November, the day that Dickie Petherick died at St Pierre Divion. It was back to the Somme.

The sweeping downland of Picardy was not the only sector on the British front. The gardener Richard Hobbs, married at St Petroc's, Lydford, on 10 August 1915, served amid the coal-blackened landscape of Artois – a far cry from Whitchurch, where Richard grew up with his mother and invalid sister. Today the earth still erupts into the grey pustules of slagheaps (not cleared away like those in Wales and

other British coalfields). They are a blot surviving from a past that
people prefer to forget, left as a sombre monument to the area's history of mining. The settlements were never picturesque: they were
grim of face and pinched, like a number of their inhabitants. A lad
from Devon would have found the hard-featured town of Vermelles
uninviting at the best of times. And these were not the best of times.
If there had been architecture to appreciate, little enough of it was
now left. Robert Graves had been billeted in the cellars of the town
in June 1915, claiming that it had been 'taken and re-taken eight times'
since the previous October. Even by then:

> Not a single house has remained undamaged in the town, which once
> must have had two or three thousand inhabitants. It is beautiful now
> in a fantastic way. We came up two nights ago; there was a moon
> shining behind the houses and the shells had broken up all the hard
> lines of roofs and quaintly perforated the grim walls of a brewery.
> Next morning we found the deserted gardens of the town very pleas-
> ant to walk about in; they are quite overgrown and flowers have
> seeded themselves about wildly.

There were currants, which Graves felt inhibited from eating in
the presence of a non-commissioned officer, since the latter was not
permitted to eat in front of an officer. He later played cricket using a
parrot cage (with the dead body of a starved parrot inside) as a wicket,
before using a glass case containing artificial fruit – a precious Victorian heirloom, perhaps, of a family who had fled – as a target for
revolver practice. Almost every back garden had two or three wooden
crosses marking the graves of soldiers who had died in fighting from
one house to another.

The journalist Philip Gibbs had been there soon after the Battle of
Loos, which was notable for the Germans' first use of gas, commenting that he 'never went without foreboding into that village of ruins
where the French fought like tigers from garden to garden and house
to house before the capture of the château'. A young French lieutenant is supposed to have swung a marble Venus around his head during
the melee.

Shells made smaller dust day by day of all these rubbish-heaps and bigger holes in the standing walls. The smell of poison-gas reeked from the bricks and the litter. Other smells lurked about like obscene spectres. At any moment of the day or night death might come here, and did, without warning . . .

Sadly, it came to Richard Hobbs, serving with the 2nd battalion of the Devonshire Regiment – not during the Battle of Loos, but a year later, on 7 September 1916.

The battalion had arrived from the Somme, their new life not being characterized by rest so much as by frequent mine explosions, German raiding parties, trench mortar bombardments and 'aerial torpedoes'. By September, the 2nd Devons were supposed to have achieved the psychological advantage. The battalion war diary 'speaks of the Germans as unaggressive, of their snipers as completely dominated by the battalion's, of dispersing his working parties, of effective bombardments by our artillery and trench-mortars'. The entry for 7 September reads:

> Our Artillery was fairly active during the day and enemy replied with a few Minenwerfers, doing little damage.
>
> Our Stokes and 60lbs. T[rench] M[ortars] very active, receiving practically no reply. We sent several patrols during the night with a view of capturing a 'Bosch', but none of the enemy were encountered.

They had the upper hand all right, but losses were part of the routine:

CASUALTIES: – 1 O.R. Killed. 2 O.R. Wounded.

The '1 Other Rank Killed' was Richard.

About twenty miles to the south-west of Vermelles is Rollecourt. In the beautiful days of March 1917, Edward found himself at rest in the countryside there. For nearly a month, the division drilled in the mornings, but spent the afternoons playing football. They were weeks of untypical peace: gunfire could not so much as be heard, and the conditions among the farmhouse barns in which some of the brigade were living were 'almost civilized'. Rumours were getting around, though, that something exceptional was in store. It involved a village: the battalion spent a week practising mock attacks. As a sergeant, Edward was privy to the name of the village, although it remained a secret from other ranks: Monchy-le-Preux.

You cannot miss Monchy-le-Preux if you take the Cambrai road out of Arras. It is an old Roman road, as straight as a ruler: a challenge to the engineers because the landscape through which it leads is so flat that they would have been hard put to find a natural feature to line up with. But to the left of the road from Arras, a small hill swells up, dome-shaped and wooded; among the orchards can be seen the red pantile roofs of Monchy-le-Preux, a place of farmhouses and barking guard dogs, where you are as likely to see a tractor as a car, and the orchards are full of geese. This modest eminence commands a panorama of fields in three directions, to the north, south and west; another hill rises, Infantry Hill. It is only five miles from Arras, but in 1917 that was also five miles behind the German line, which sat on the outskirts of what had been an important wool town in the Middle Ages, famous for tapestries (in Shakespeare's *Hamlet*, Polonius is killed 'behind the arras'). For normal purposes, it was impossible to visit Monchy, but Whitford and his platoon knew what it looked like. They were given street maps. They could study photographs, some taken from aeroplanes, but others showing the streets themselves, with the German soldiers who were attached to the divisional headquarters in Monchy loitering in the vicinity of the estaminets. The photographs could only have been taken by spies within the village. The spies had provided other information too. Large maps showed the position of the bigger cellars in the village, together with details of how many men each would hold and roughly the size of shell it would take for the cellar roof to cave in.

On a sunny day in early April, Edward marched his platoon to a point ten miles from Arras. Now the low rumble of the guns could be heard in the distance. A sergeant from every battalion was chosen to inspect the town of Arras, and more particularly what lay underneath it. Unlike the farmers' village of Monchy-le-Preux, making do with red brick, magnificent Arras could afford limestone. There was a ready supply of it around the town. The quarries lay below the earth, and extracting the stone had created a series of underground caves and chambers. Since the end of 1916, tunnelling companies (largely from New Zealand) had been at work creating passages to link the quarries, until they could have sheltered the whole population of the town. But most of the townsfolk had fled. The object of the tunnels was to hide 24,000 soldiers, and bring them directly on to the battlefield in an audacious surprise coup. They would surge up fresh – even if, after a long wait in the dripping caverns, chilled – immediately behind the first wave of attack, without the usual difficulties of clogged communications trenches and enemy shelling of reinforcements. It was not, however, just the tunnels which impressed Sergeant John Coast, from the 10th Battalion, The Royal Fusiliers, part of the same brigade as Edward's 13th King's Royal Rifle Corps. As one soldier observed:

> He said that Arras was simply packed with troops of all divisions and Regiments, that not a single member of all those thousands was allowed to be seen in the streets during the daytime on account of Hun aeroplanes getting an inkling of the coming attack, but directly it was dark the streets full of men getting walking exercise after being cramped up in cellars and tunnels allday [sic].

Arras, so near the German line, had been constantly shelled; the squares were now lined with what the troops called doll's houses. With the facades of the handsome stone houses gone, you could look straight into the rooms, still furnished for their pre-war life. It was now clear that the Germans were about to receive a severe dose of their own medicine. An immense arsenal had been assembled, including field guns, howitzers, tanks, armoured cars, cavalry, miles upon miles of Army Service Corps and Engineers' stores and rear ammunition dumps: 'It reeked of something big coming off.'

That year 6 April was Good Friday. During the morning, the brigade moved nearer to Arras, their ears becoming attuned to the slow crescendo of the barrage that would build towards zero hour, when every gun in the orchestra would open up simultaneously in a cacophonous fortissimo. Life in billets remained, for the time being, domestic, if in a way that seemed strange to a Tommy. As one of the brigade, young Sergeant R. S. Whiteman, remembered:

> . . . we spent the evening in a combined living-bed-dining-sitting room, round the usual type of efficient French stove that burns anything from dust to cabbage stalks. The 'Madame' was of the type termed stout; it was said that she had to deflate herself to get through the doorway! The old fashioned draped bed was occupied by an equally old fashioned white headed man who appeared to think he had the room to himself judging by his actions.

Next day, in Duisans, Edward's battalion moved into a hutment – a row of semi-cylindrical corrugated-iron huts of the kind recently invented by Major Peter Nissen, RE. Kit was thrown on to the floor because the walls had no hooks or pegs. On Easter Day, while the chaplain of the 2nd Battalion, Suffolk Regiment, held a service in Wellington Quarry below ground, Edward's platoon was struggling to make headway along roads that were crowded with men, horses, wagons, ambulances and guns. 'Our Artillery bombardment on German lines East of ARRAS was in full swing,' comments the battalion war diary jauntily. Eventually they reached an open field about a mile from the town. That afternoon, the colonel explained the method of the attack that would begin at 4.50 the next morning. It was to be carried out 'leapfrog' style: the first attacking division, on gaining its objective, would stay there; the next division would then pass through them, take its objective and stay. The third wave of the attack was to capture the third line of the German trench system, designated as the Brown Line. The 111th Division, to which Edward belonged, was to proceed to the Brown Line, reorganize itself and from there take Monchy-le-Preux.

As a sergeant, Edward had much to do. Every man had to be issued with fifty extra rounds of ammunition. Lewis guns had to be inspected to check that they were in perfect order. Iron rations had to be drawn from the quartermaster's stores: for the next couple of days, men would be living off what they carried in their haversacks, hoping that something would be found for them thereafter. As the evening drew in, the artillery made the firmament ring with what seemed, to Sergeant Whiteman of the Royal Fusiliers, who was situated half a mile from the guns, practically a phenomenon of nature: 'the whole of the eastern horizon was lit up as by summer lightning and the thunderous roar of the heavies'. Candles flickered and the sheets of the bivouac tents bulged. The gunfire got gradually worse, until at midnight, most of it suddenly stopped. Although a few guns were still firing, the comparative hush seemed deathly. This state of peace prevailed until zero hour the next morning.

It was a cold night for the men, both above ground and in the tunnels. They had rolled their overcoats into bundles and handed them to the quartermaster: it was thought that they would have been too bulky to wear during the attack. But that Easter Monday the weather changed. Edward awoke to a miserable morning, pitch black, bitter, with a sharp wind blowing. It was three o'clock and he had to wake those of his men who might still be sleeping. With chilled fingers, all now began searching for their equipment, stumbling over other men's possessions, disentangling the knots that webbing and straps formed themselves into when left for a moment on the floor. Waterproof sheets were rolled and strapped on to haversacks; water bottles were filled from a cart. The cooks of the field kitchen had a breakfast of boiled bacon ready by 3.30, but it was not easy to distribute it by the light of the candles that kept blowing out. Thank goodness for tea. It 'made everyone feel twice the man he was before'. But dawn, when it broke, was singularly cheerless. The leaden sky matched the apprehensions of the men, who knew that attacks in this war were never accomplished without casualties.

They reached their position, about 300 yards behind the first line of heavy artillery, at 4.40. Nobody spoke. Watches ticked towards zero hour. Then, 'with a roar the heavens and earth seemed to be rent asunder, every gun along that fifteen miles of front opened fire simultaneously, from Vimy to Croiselles.' The bursting of shells caused the German line to erupt in a single sheet of flame. Within seconds, the Germans put up a desperate pyrotechnic display of rockets: 'Single red rockets, rockets that burst into numbers of red balls, strings of green balls, golden rain and Very lights rose high above the inferno of flame and smoke – but to no avail, our artillery once started could not be stopped.' When marching past the huge fifteen-inch howitzers, the din alone was devastating (in later life, gunners were often hard of hearing, suffering from what they sometimes liked to call 'gunner ear'). Noise was not the only physical manifestation of the firing. As Sergeant Whiteman explains: 'In cases like this it is always advisable to keep one's mouth open otherwise the concussion on the stomach may lead to disastrous results, it also seems to lessen the effect on the ear drums which otherwise feel as if they must burst.' When it started to rain, he wondered whether that had not been caused by the colossal clangour of the guns.

Edward's platoon now halted. Some of the men tried to make a fire from twigs and branches, but these were wet. Clearly the first wave of the attack had gone well, because parties of bedraggled German prisoners started to go past them. Their terror-stricken faces revealed the practically dementing effect of the 'satanic barrage'. When the battalion fell in again, they could see the artillerymen loading their gun limbers, so as to keep within range of the retreating Germans. On the outskirts of Arras, they passed dressing stations, busy with the first of the wounded. They left Arras as quickly as they could; it was not considered, in soldier's parlance, 'healthy' to linger in such an obvious target. Their way then led into a trench cut through a cemetery, along which they proceeded in single file. Orders were passed down from man to man. Sometimes the direction of travel was reversed, sometimes they stopped. To no one's surprise 'Shell Shock' Fowler of the 10th Royal Fusiliers collapsed – he invariably did. Not understanding mental illness, his comrades thought his condition would be improved if they walked over him. Behind them, a terrible explosion rent the air as one of the ammunition dumps in Arras was hit. Eventually they reached what had, until earlier that morning, been the British front line, 'vacated that morning by 15th Div', littered with pieces of kit that had been discarded at the last minute to reduce weight. As they stood on the fire step, they could look out over the old no-man's-land, without fear of being shot in the head. The only people now to be seen in front of them were scattered bands of grey-coated prisoners being brought back under escort. As they gazed out, they saw the little village of Feuchy, occupied by the Germans, 'enveloped in a cloud of multicolored smoke & dust'.

When the battalion stumblingly crossed the next 500 yards of ground, a gentle slope which had been blasted into an obstacle course of pits and mounds, they were puzzled. Where had no-man's-land ended? The German line had been so pounded that what had once been a trench was filled in, what had once been solid ground thrown up in heaps of brown earth. Duckboards, dugouts, barbed wire, the usual detritus of discarded cans – all had been so blasted and buried that there was nothing to be seen of them. It was no longer possible to make out the line of the trench. The wounded of both sides, enmity forgotten, were now helping each other back to the dressing stations. There was another pause; cigarettes were lit. Sergeant Whiteman and the 10th Royal Fusiliers were well placed to enjoy:

> . . . the sight of a straggling column of about 40 German prisoners coming down the slope, unarmed, & escorted by a tiny Jock in kilts – still in his teens I'll swear – who could not have had more swagger had he won the War himself, as he headed the column with his rifle, bayonet fixed, slung carelessly over one shoulder.
>
> When about 100 yards from us he calmly handed his rifle over to the nearest German – a great big chap – and, still walking in front totally unarmed, slowly proceeded to fill his pipe.
>
> It is such incidents as these, coupled with the appreciation thereof, that make War at all possible, for without them one would go melancholy mad.

The Artois countryside which seems flat to the motorist is not completely so, as Edward found. Like many of the men who, over the months, had served in the British line, he and his comrades wondered what was on the other side of the rise. They found, as is so often the case, that they were confronted by another ridge. For most of the afternoon they waited in front of it. Only at four o'clock did they get the order to advance. From the crest, they looked out over open country, covered in long grass – yes, real grass that had not been ploughed by shelling, on which grew trees that would soon be coming into leaf. Monchy-le-Preux, its red roofs peeping out from amid the foliage, could be seen two miles away. 'There is something wonderfully fascinating about the first sight – from a distance at least – of a position one has to capture,' reflected Sergeant Whiteman, 'it makes one conjecture as to the future, if it does nothing else.' Strangely, despite the maps and photographs, it looked quite different from what they had expected.

The weather, which had been fine since midday, now turned bitingly cold. As the brigade formed up for its attack, a rattle of machine-gun fire showed that a trench, supposed to have been taken by the 12th Division, was not empty. There were three machine guns in total, capable of catching the approaching soldiers in a withering crossfire. In front of the trench was a deep tangle of barbed wire, five feet high and as wide as a street, which formed an impossible obstacle to overcome. Men took what shelter they could, some in the gutter of a road. With mounting consternation, they wondered why no artillery was supporting them. When the outlook seemed at its bleakest, an angel appeared – a strange, slow-moving angel, which looked more like a scrap-metal yard come to life: in other words, a tank. Edward and his men looked forward to seeing the tank plough through the barbed wire, which it would then trail behind it as though it were a washing line. It was not to be. The tank came to a standstill before it had reached the trench. But the crew were able to kill one of the machine-gun teams. Perhaps they themselves had been killed or wounded, by flying rivets or splinters of metal inside their steel crate. Or perhaps the tank had simply broken down.

Night was falling, and the order came to entrench. Edward liked the outdoor life, and may have found that digging warmed him up. But the warmth was soon lost. It was too cold for sleep. Without overcoats, the men had only their waterproof capes to wrap around them. They opened tins of bully beef and munched biscuits, but there was nothing warm to eat. No tea. No rum. 'Thus a long & tiring day was succeeded by a cold wet night with snow & frost, during the whole of which there had been no shelter for officers or men,' observes the battalion war diary. When Captain Norris walked to the top of Orange Hill to reconnoitre, he could see a hundred or so Germans digging a new line of trench in front of the village. 'We were satisfied that MONCHY would be defended.'

During the morning, the 10th Royal Fusiliers took some joy from retreating to a railway cutting while the trench was cleared; hacking some of the railway sleepers into splinters, they were able to start a fire. Someone then found a well, and they boiled some water. At last they had tea – black and sugarless, perhaps, but good. Advancing towards Monchy that afternoon, they passed through a brigade of cavalry, excited and cheerful to be in action. Monchy lay a mile and a half away. It was the last quarter of a mile that proved the most difficult. The 10th and 13th Royal Fusiliers led the attack, supported by the 13th King's Royal Rifle Corps. A light field gun was eventually put out of action by the Lewis gunners, but a sunken road sheltered a row of machine guns. The men concealed themselves in shell holes, newly created and still smelling horribly of the hot, suffocating gases of the high explosives. To attempt to move, or even raise your head, was fatal; trying to improve his position, Sergeant Coast was shot through the head. Sergeant Whiteman noticed:

> Away on our right things seemed to be much the same as with us, for looking out of our shell hole we saw a platoon of the York & Lancs regiment suddenly rise out of the ground, and, forming into fours, run towards the village; they had gone but a dozen yards or so forward when their numbers seemed to literally melt away under the machine gun fire which they had attracted; the few that were left standing saw that to advance was hopeless, so went to earth in the nearest shell holes. From start to finish this little incident occupied a matter of 3 minutes yet in that short time they must have lost 15 of their number out of a total of 23 or thereabouts.

There was nothing the attackers could do but keep down.

It was now snowing; this had the benefit, at about five o'clock, of creating a blizzard. It was impossible for anyone to see more than twenty yards. The attackers saw it as their chance; they moved forward as one man. But they were still 150 yards from the village when the snow eased. Suddenly, they were visible again. The machine guns started. Any sign of life was punished. From the not very considerable depths of his shell hole, one corporal realized that snow had collected on the back of his helmet. He turned the helmet around, raised his head slowly until his eye was level with the ground, then fired a couple of shots. The heat generated by the gun melted the snow at the front, so to avoid being seen his head had to go down again. But by now, more snow had collected at the helmet's back, and the process could be repeated. His skill at deception – and luck at survival – was not shared by everyone. Only handfuls of men were left to reassemble into battalions that night.

When order reasserted itself, the battalion war diary records that the 13th King's Royal Rifle Corps were told to dig themselves in, 'the most advanced troops being only a few yards from the enemy's trenches. One troublesome machine gun was here silenced by "B" Company with Rifle grenades.' The medical officer and stretcher-bearers struggled against snow and sleet to take away the many wounded. As the men finished entrenching around 4.30 a.m., they thought that they might at least get some rest. They had not slept for the previous two nights. But the brigade major brought the order that they were to attack again in half an hour. This time, one of the two leading battalions was Edward's. In front of them was a stretch of snow-covered ground, leading to the scattered trees that grew at the foot of the village. There were more hedges then than today, but they still offered scant protection. Exhausted, unshaven and frozen to the marrow, the battalion were being asked to make a superhuman effort. And they did. Their senses quickened by the whip of machine-gun fire and the possible imminence of death, they now ran on adrenalin. A Lewis gunner riddled a window of a house in front of the village with bullets, killing the German machine-gun crew inside the room. Two tanks then growled forward, one making for the village. As the other laboured towards the sunken road, the machine guns abruptly stopped firing. Infrantrymen ran ahead of it – and on, up into the village. The streets of Monchy were now thronged with crowds of Allied soldiers. The last of the German garrison could be seen making off to the east of the village, across the snow.

Now was the time for celebration. Did Edward join in? Probably not; it is all too likely that he was killed during one of the first attacks that morning, at a time when, according to the battalion war diary, 'the enemy's shell fire was very effective, whilst the German machine-guns & riflemen swept the level ground'. A and B Companies lost all their officers, leaving only C company and Brigade Headquarters to absorb the straggling groups of survivors. But even those who did live to swarm into Monchy's streets were not able to enjoy the moment for long. For the eighty or so men who gave chase to the fleeing Germans, a terrible penalty would be exacted as they drew near a hidden German trench on the next ridge. The tank that came in support burst into flames, hit by an artillery shell. Having taken Monchy without artillery support, the troops discovered that the British gunners had now sprung into action. Only they were working to the wrong coordinates and shelling their own side. Cowering in shell holes, they saw a contact plane fly overhead, sounding its klaxon: a technique by which the army attempted to discover the position of its own front line, so as to direct shellfire in front of it. The idea was that the ground troops would send up a rocket to identify their whereabouts. One soldier was just about to do so when he realized it was a German plane. Just as the few survivors from the pursuing force managed to duck back into the village, the Germans started to shell it.

The cavalry that had been seen earlier in the day was now in Monchy. Some of the men could take shelter in cellars; not so the horses, which streamed, riderless, out on to the plain. The cavalry had done a good job of clearing the village, but the toll was great. One of the enduring images of the day, if not the campaign, is a description made by a young infantry company commander who saw Monchy for the first time the next day.

> I stopped. The sight that greeted me was so horrible that I almost lost my head. Heaped on top of one another and blocking up the roadway for as far as one could see lay the mutilated bodies of our men and their horses. These bodies, torn and gaping, had stiffened into fantastic attitudes. All the hollows of the road were filled with blood. This

was the cavalry . . . nothing that I had seen before in the way of horrors could be even faintly compared with what I saw around me now. Death in every imaginable shape was there for the examining.

On the first day of the Battle of Arras, the British advance of three and a half miles was, by the standards of trench warfare, spectacular. Two days later, the capture of Monchy was also a remarkable feat of arms for what Field Marshal Haig called the 'utmost gallantry' of the attackers. But neither the initial effectiveness of the tactics, nor the endurance and courage of the men, could produce more than the usual stalemate. The artillery were not able to move forward quickly enough; communications were poor; there were too many lines of German trenches for the cavalry to be able to break through. When planned, Arras was intended to draw off German troops, to make it easier for the French to break through at the Chemin des Dames; but that attack was a disaster. In the end, the British had to keep going to prevent the demoralized French army from buckling. The Allies lost 150,000 men, the Germans almost as many.

After Monchy, the generals found another obstacle to take: Infantry Hill, with its commanding view of the Douai plain. The capture of Monchy was furious, but also fast; Infantry Hill was only taken after another two months of heavy fighting.

The next year, C. S. Lewis was stationed here, and in his poem 'French Nocturne (Monchy-le-Preux)' described how the 'jaws of a sacked village, stark and grim' seemed to have swallowed up the sun. The poet imagines an aeroplane flying towards a land of dreams that is the moon, then being pulled violently back to earth.

> What call have I to dream of anything?
> I am a wolf. Back to the world again,
> And speech of fellow-brutes that once were men
> Our throats can bark for slaughter: cannot sing.

Like nearly 36,000 other soldiers from the British Empire who fought at Arras, Edward Whitford's body was never found; his name is inscribed on the wall of the Faubourg d'Amiens cemetery, designed by Sir Herbert Baker.

7

Oh It's Lovely, This Bed

⟶ HARRY LAKE ⟵

Once, more tobacco was imported through the little Devon port of Bideford than anywhere else in England, except London. That, however, had been in the first half of the eighteenth century and trade had fallen off since then. 'Pleasantly the old town stands there, beneath its soft Italian sky, formed day and night by the fresh ocean breeze, which forbids alike the frosts and the fierce thunder heats of the midland,' wrote Charles Kingsley in 1855 at the opening of *Westward Ho!*, making this Devon seaport sound like Portofino.

While Tanton's, on the river, was 'well spoken of', the Old Ship Tavern was merely 'unpretending', according to Baedeker's *Guide to Great Britain* of 1901, and there was 'little to arrest the tourist'. Malefactors, however, would have found that they were arrested in another sense. In 1901, the year that Edward VII ascended the throne, the majesty of the law in Bideford was upheld by, among others, PC Frederick Lake, aged twenty-six. In that breeze-kissed settlement of 9,000 inhabitants, his lot, if not an entirely happy one, might have been much worse.

With PC Lake and his 25-year-old wife, Lucy, in the New Road Police Station was their baby daughter, Flossie. But the daughter had an elder brother, aged three: George Henry Taylor Lake, known as Harry. Born at Marystow like his mother – perhaps she had gone to her parents' home to give birth – he was not brought up by his parents at Bideford; perhaps they felt the police station was too small, or perhaps they were too busy, or the family finances were too stretched. His early years were spent with his maternal grandparents at Coryton, where his grandfather, William Lethbridge, was a quarryman in the slate mine. With only one single daughter living with them at the turn of the century, the Lethbridges were able to help out with the care of young Harry, as grandparents often did.

Coryton, further from the moor than Lydford, presented a different aspect. Much of the land was used to grow arable crops, with partridges running through the stubble. Since 1809, the manor had been owned by the Newman family, wine importers and ship owners, whose fortune was big enough to employ Anthony Salvin to build a colossal mansion on the Devon coast at Mamhead; they were more often at Mamhead than Coryton. But they came to Coryton for the shooting every winter, helping to stage the Elizabethan pageants that were held at Sydenham House in Marystow each summer. By Newman standards, the house was so small, despite being extended in 1907, that they called it Manor Cottage. A bazaar was held in the same year, in aid of the church bells, giving local men – perhaps Harry Lake was among them – the chance to demonstrate their marksmanship on a shooting range. So many bullseyes were hit that a hole was worn in the metal plate behind the target; the next direct hit shot a chicken in the head, and the one after that killed a rabbit. Few people could have forgotten the fête held on 29 July 1914: not because of the heavy rain, which caused a masque about the restoration of Charles II to be cancelled, but because of the political ferment in Europe.

> The thunder and lightning was at its very heaviest, when serious news came through about the war situation on the continent. In the minds of those present it seemed that the thunder was an omen and that there would soon be 'Fire over England'.

Coryton, though, was not only a place for the Newmans to play, but also a property to develop commercially. There had been, at different times, a limestone quarry from whose product many of the estate cottages had regrettably been built (it was a poor stone – men who knew about it could tap on walls to tell which had become rotten and hollow), and a manganese mine. In the dank, freezing tunnels, the walls running with water from overhead streams, the miners had to crawl through slime, guided only by a candle, which would quite often blow out. When the mine closed in 1889, the bodies of two miners, who had died in different accidents, were still entombed in it. By comparison, the slate quarry offered attractive, open-air employment – although an avalanche brought on by heavy rains killed two men and a boy in 1874. It was a very old quarry, having been worked as early as 1300. Although the pink slate that could be extracted from it was prone to flake – builders in Lydford would regularly be called upon to repair roofs after storms, because slates had disintegrated – it was widely used across Devon at one time. When Harry was growing up, as many as fifty men were employed at the quarry. An old white horse would plod around the whim to drag up trolleyloads of slate from the deep workings. Sometimes the men would take shelter, and the rumble of dynamite could be heard exploding in the quarry wall. Large volumes of roofing slates were cut, as well as slabs for floors that could withstand hobnailed boots (a better use, since the problem of flaking did not arise).

The stone cottages in which the people of Coryton lived are now roofless, their ruins swallowed up by a wood. But at the beginning of the twentieth century they formed 'a snug little community', according to the squire, Thomas Newman. Harry would have gone to the Coryton school, along with other children from the quarry – the Lashbrooks are remembered as having seven or eight on the school roll. They were taught by Mrs Westaway, the headmistress. Once Mrs Westaway overheard six of her charges, whose route home took them past a notably fierce sheepdog called Smissles, making a pact with the Almighty: 'Dear God, if you will stop Smissles rushing out and barking at us, we promise not to bust up any more birds' nests.' Harry would have been unusual among his classmates if he had not, however deplorable it may now sound, gone birds' nesting. No doubt he played the ancient local game, which required the participants to form a ring while reciting a verse that began:

Old Sir Symons the King, Old Sir Symons the Squire,
Old Sir Symons who chases Mrs Jenkins who sits by our home fire . . .

Once this had been sung with sufficient gusto, everybody was required to shake each part of their body in turn, an activity which

was 'very simple and very foolish, but nevertheless great fun', Winters
were made colourful by the appearance of a family of gypsies at
Hedgecross, to which they returned in their brightly painted caravans
every year, as well as the Lamerton Hunt who would draw the local
coverts, then stream along the hills and moorland beside the river Lyd.

By 1911, Harry's father was no longer the New Road bobby in
Bideford. For whatever reason he had given up the force, and he now
listed his trade as carpenter. Perhaps he had trained before becoming a
policeman. He and his family, which in 1911 added another daughter,
Nellie, had necessarily left the police house; they had transferred to
Lydford Station, living opposite the chapel in a dwelling called Wastor
Cottage. Harry, though, did not join them there. Now thirteen, he was
still living with his grandparents; he was a Coryton boy.

When the war came, Coryton would send over thirty of its men to
serve the national effort in one way or another. Squire Thomas Newman prepared a list in 1940. The net, for this purpose, was cast wide,
and caught men such as his own father, Robert Lydston Newman,
who was Deputy Governor of the Bank of England from 1914 to
1917. Wars cannot be fought without money, and Britain's state of
unpreparedness in 1914 made the raising of it particularly acute.
'Robert Lydston Newman worked at the Bank most days from 8 in
the morning to 1 o'clock at night. It was a hair-raising period and
enough to break any man's stamina and morale.' One director of a
small bank who could not take the strain went mad in his office.

> It must be remembered that Germany entered the war fully armed
> with a well-trained and well-equipped army of over one million men.
> England entered the war with a small army, practically no munitions
> and very little equipment. The burden of suddenly producing a vast
> sum of money to remedy the difficulty was thrust upon the Bank of
> England in one day. There was always the danger of inflation and the
> ruination of England and her allies. Lord Cunliffe [Governor of the
> Bank of England] and R. L. Newman were able to surmount innu-
> merable difficulties. Few people realise that England partly owed her
> victory to those two black-coated gentlemen ensconced away amongst
> a sea of papers and letters at the Bank.

Coryton saw little of Robert Newman in that period. But the pressure told. Overwork, combined with lack of exercise, caused Newman's health to break down to the point where he was compelled to resign from the deputy governorship, although he remained a director of the Bank of England (serving for a record length of forty years). Thomas Newman's list of war service also includes Ralph Alured Newman, who was too young to fight but worked on the land from 1916 to 1918, a time when the West Devon Agricultural Committee was urging landowners to increase production – for example, by planting corn and potatoes on the exposed, rain-lashed pasture of Longham Down. (It was a manifestly poor choice, and the order was revoked on appeal. The last of the corn and potatoes were eaten by rabbits.) But the remaining thirty-four names served in the armed forces. Ten of them were in the Royal Navy, including William Gale who died when his submarine *K17* sank after a collision on 31 January 1918. The rest went with the army to Belgium, France, India, Arabia, Gallipoli, Egypt, Salonica, Palestine and the West Indies. Harry is the only other Coryton man who was killed but Squire Newman's record of the wounded, made by one who knew the men personally, is a graphic account of shattered lives.

BLATCHFORD, Walter Alfred, 6th Batt. E. K. Regt., 'The Buffs'. Servant. – Served in France. Wounded three times – Loos 1915, Somme 1916, Arras 1916.

COLE, Richard John Henry, Australian 5th Light Horse. Trooper. – Served in Egypt, Gallipoli, and France. Enteric Fever in Gallipoli and shell-shock in France.

COLE, Thomas, First Batt. Devonshire Regt. Signaller. – Served in France and Belgium. Wounded twice – Vimy Ridge 1917, Aschell-la-Petit 1918.

GERRY, Harry, Royal North Devon Hussars. Trooper. – Served in France. Wounded at Ypres 1917; gassed at Ypres 1918.

GROVES, Edwin Cecil, First Royal Irish Regt. Sergeant. – Served at Salonica and in Egypt. Malarial fever.

GROVES, Lionel, R.F.A. Driver. – Served in France and Germany. Wounded once. Gassed once.

GROVES, Reginald Albert, R.E. Sapper. – Served in France and Germany. Wounded once. Gassed once. Shell-shock three times.

MOUNCE, Harry, 8th Devons. Private. – Served in France. Nine wounds. Lame for life. Slightly gassed.

SANDERS, John Mark, Royal Marine Light Infantry. HMS *Berwick*. Sergeant. – Served in West Indies, Mediterranean, and France. Two wounds. Prisoner in Germany for twenty months. Awarded Military Medal.

TURNER, Thomas James, 6th Royal Munster Fusiliers. Sergeant. – Served at Dardanelles. – Suvla Bay. Wounded in the head.

WALTERS, Alfred James, Canadian Field Artillery. Gunner. – Served in France. Wounded several times.

After 1918, the community at Coryton reabsorbed its menfolk, to find that some of them were not only damaged in their limbs and their lungs, but also in their minds.

In Thomas Newman's list, Harry is recorded as having belonged to the 2nd Battalion of the Royal Warwickshire Regiment. This was not, however, his first regiment; sometime in 1916 he had originally joined the county regiment, the Devonshire. Perhaps, having reached eighteen, he was a conscript. His career is difficult to follow because his service papers were among the records destroyed during the Blitz. We do know, however, that from the Devons he passed into the Machine Gun Corps. As we saw with Charles Berry, the machine-gun crews formed an elite and the army needed the best men. Had Harry been one of the sharpshooters at the Coryton bazaar? If so, he might well have been chosen for his skill in marksmanship.

The Machine Gun Corps was a new creation. At the beginning of the war, the British army's complement of machine guns was distributed evenly through the regimental structure. Each battalion had a section containing, initially, two machine guns, then four, the Vickers Maxim gun being quickly replaced by the lighter and mechanically improved Vickers machine gun. But attaching machine guns to battalions meant that large numbers of them could not be brought to bear on specific objectives; nor could their fire be concentrated in the manner that the Germans had shown to be so devastating. Besides, the lighter Lewis gun was a better weapon to use in attack. The army's solution was to gather the Vickers teams into a central Machine Gun Corps, whose men and weapons could then be deployed in number, according to priorities at the front. Theirs was a quietly exalted lot. 'They lived apart from the companies and except in emergency were excused fatigues,' wrote one machine-gun officer. 'In trenches they were responsible only for their immediate surroundings.' The carnage they could unleash would later be recognized in the inscription, slightly adapted from 1 Samuel 18: 7, controversially chosen for the Machine Gun Corps memorial on Hyde Park Corner: 'Saul hath slain his thousands, but David his tens of thousands.' The importance attached to the corps was such that it was 'continually recruited from picked men . . . The Corps represented, and necessarily so, the cream of the National Army.'

The men in the teams had to rely on each other. This developed a close bond. Machine-gunner George Coppard remembered there were usually six soldiers to a team:

> Number One was leader and fired the gun, while Number Two controlled the entry of the Ammo belts into the feed-block. Number Three maintained a supply of ammo to Number Two, and Numbers Four to Six were reserves and carriers, but all the members of a team were fully trained in handling the gun.

There may have been, in the eyes of ordinary soldiery, a mystique to operating a machine gun but the Vickers was, above all, an efficient and reliable weapon. A water cooling system that was condensed through a tube into a canvas bucket meant that it could be used continuously for long periods. The importance of preventing the coolant

from running dry was graphically propounded by an instructor with
the Royal Warwickshire Regiment. 'From a tap; from a tap; from a
tap,' he muttered, when one of the recruits offered that as an answer
to where the water might come from.

> He stopped to face us all, looked studiously at the floor, raised his
> head slowly to scan the whole group then met the gaze of his victim.
> 'My dear young man, by the time you have been where you are all
> going,' his voice began to get louder as he finished the sentence, 'After
> a few months, you will have forgotten entirely **what a tap looks
> like!** You will collect water from anywhere that you see it, from rain-
> filled water holes, upturned steel helmets, water bottles taken from
> enemy bodies, tea cans, water rations, your friends' water rations,
> anybody's water rations and if all this fails,' he stopped, stepped for-
> ward and leaned down towards the lad, then practically with noses
> touching he quietly said, 'YOU WILL PISS IN IT!'

In *Goodbye to All That*, Robert Graves started the canard that wast-
rel machine-gunners would fire off a belt of bullets simply to boil
water for their tea: an aspersion hotly disputed by Corporal George
Coppard, an experienced machine-gunner, who observed that nobody
would make tea with oily water, and Captain Graves probably did
not understand the principles of laying down a barrage. Crews looked
on these death-dealing weapons lovingly, and prided themselves
on the care with which they stripped, cleaned and oiled the mechan-
ism. Nor did the crews resent the extra weight it imposed on them
when marching – the tripod was the heaviest element, weighing
50 pounds.

Where did Harry go with the Machine Gun Corps? We do not
know. At some point he was probably wounded and sent home, and
then assigned to the Royal Warwickshire Regiment. The 2nd Battalion was part of the 22nd Brigade of the 7th Division. A glimpse of
the sort of life Harry might have experienced if he had joined the
Warwicks by the summer of 1917 is given in a jaunty series of letters
from Private Arthur Burke, known as Pat, in the 5th Manchester Pals
Battalion (20th Manchester Regiment). In private life Pat had been a
clerk, grammar school educated, the youngest in a family which ran

the Borough Hotel in Salford. Over Christmas 1916, he took part, during a season of 'rotten weather', in one of the truces of which the authorities disapproved. As he wrote to his eldest brother, Reg, who, having been declared unfit for service, was at home running the hotel.

> Fritz & us up here are on absolutely speaking terms – he comes over & exchanges cigs etc – it got so frequent it had to be stopped & even after our orders to quit, two of our boys got 28 days for going out & meeting him half way for a chat.

When the battalion took a German dugout in June 1917, he was impressed by the engineering of 'one of Fritz['s] most wonderful underworlds – its a marvellous piece of work, nothing in creation could touch you here & yet it was won by our division at the point of the bayonet.' Soon, though, they were at rest at a 'top hole' farm where this infectiously cheerful Tommy was able to enjoy 'beaucoup promenade' with 'two of the very best Mamselles'. In the 'glorious' summer weather, it was 'the goods helping to work in the fields with the ladies (but not plenty work)'. By September, he had landed a job in charge of the officers' mess, and as such made himself so indispensable to his captain, Frank Nicholl, that he was excused all parades 'which alone is worth quids . . . I sincerely hope I shall be able to continue to satisfy him – he is so military.' In the middle of the month, he was again in billet, this time blessed with that essential precondition for a good sleep, a bed – he had not been in one for months.

> Way up these few words & devour same. I am sat up in BED writing – no not in hospital (worse luck) – we have arrived at our final destination, & Ive clicked we are likely to be here a fortnight & its the goods.
>
> . . . I can stick this, its a nice cottage – in a lovely village – like Bakewell – a lovely river – everything top hole.
>
> Ever so many thanks for that long letter it was O.K. Tots letter with raffle tickets in arrived today shall answer same tomorrow – must make the best of this BED.
>
> Sorry I overlooked your birthday again Reg – I knew when it was

but being on the move overlooked it – very many of um my dear brother

OH ITS LOVELY THIS BED.

They were still resting on the 24th and 'having a bon time', but Pat knew, probably from his captain, that they would be leaving for Ypres, 'a hellish hot place', before long.

The news when he wrote again to Reg on 4 October was dramatic.

This is the wonderful day I told you about, & no doubt you are await-ing anxiously for news. Well, its come off – its quite early yet – the battle is raging, but we are going great guns – umpteen prisoners coming down – and still they come (thats the stuff to give um). Some have got their heads bashed in – looks as though the lads have given them socks. Its too soon to give you any definite news yet – but I hear we have taken our objective & doing <u>exceptionally well</u>. Its bad luck that we should have rain today – for goodness knows the conditions are terrible up there.

Pat was not in this 'scrap', although he had been in the front line for the previous forty-eight hours, holding a position that had been taken three days before. 'It was all important to Jerry, & during our short stay in there he made 4 furious counter attacks but he was held up.' Pat had now managed to become Company Storeman, the 'soft-est' of all jobs: when Captain Nicholl said that he could not be spared from the mess Pat told him 'that was a selfish way of looking at it' and used his natural charm, supported by the credit he had won through the performance of his duties, in talking him round. 'Its the best job in the Co[mpan]y. Only go up to the line with rations & those times are exceptional – as regards going over the bags – NEVER.' Later that evening he sent his sister, 'Dearest Tot', a 'little flower got under remarkable circumstances from Hell'.

On 16 November Captain Nicholl took up his pen to write to Mrs Burke, Pat's mother. On one of the exceptional occasions when he had been given the task of taking rations to the front, Pat was killed by a shell. He was, wrote Nicholl, buried with his comrades, but his body was not recovered after the war; his name is inscribed on the wall of remembrance at the most dramatic of war cemeteries, Tyne Cot.

The day after Pat's death, Harry Lake, if already with the Warwicks, would have experienced a change of scene. At first it seemed almost a holiday. On 17 November 1917, the 2nd Battalion were put on a train that, to their amazement, took them far away from the misery of winter in waterlogged Flanders. They found themselves chugging south; as one of the brigade remembered, 'it was really grand'.

The 7th was one of five divisions being sent to strengthen the front in North Italy, where the Italians had been slogging it out against Austria in a series of no fewer than twelve battles on the river Isonzo, north of Trieste. Ever since he became Prime Minister in December 1916, Lloyd George had been arguing for an attack against one of Germany's weaker allies. This, he thought, would be a means of breaking the stalemate that had developed in France. The military view was against it; Haig believed that the war could only be won by defeating Germany itself. But his hand was forced by events. In October 1917, some elite units from the German army were sent to support an Austrian assault at Caporetto, which set the Italians reeling. French and British troops were hurried south to save the retreat from becoming a general collapse. Soldiers such as Harry Lake would have known nothing of the political or even military purpose in their redeployment. It was enough for them that they were leaving the Ypres Salient.

> Soon we were sitting on the sides of our trucks with both the port and starboard doors wide open taking in the sun en route and in our shirt sleeves enjoying the scenery and the chit-chat with the French Mademoiselles and soon the same with the Italian Senoritas. After leaving Marseilles we puffed along the French and Italian Rivieras at a leisurely pace, now and then overtaking or then passing us some other similar long train of French or our own troops and the sun was getting hotter all the time.

At Cannes they were met by residents of the British community with cups of hot coffee and cigarettes. Even once they had reached the river Piave – the new Italian line – they were able to forage for wine in the cellars of towns that Austrian shelling had reduced to rubble. The festival atmosphere was reinforced by the 7th Division's lack of artillery, the guns either having been left for their successors or lost in mud. Private E. H. Lenfestey was one of the artillerymen; for him, the journey to Italy, with frequent stops to water the horses, took eight days. Because the sergeant major had been drunk the night before, his unit had to start the first day's march without breakfast.

Private E. Smith was in the same battalion as Harry. He also remembered the journey south as a sunny time, although the deranged punctuation of his distinctly staccato account makes one wonder if his mind did not suffer from the later conflict.

What a game that was for a time – (troops) – leaving the train – when it (slowed up) - & - (scrumping in the (Vineyards) – groves etc).

The colonel was 'wild' to see troops jumping off when the train slowed down, only to be left to catch up when it accelerated, and gave offenders fourteen days CB (confined to barracks).

We had Pith helmets & Karki shorts & tunics.
    The girls gave us (vino) & 'Tolento' [polenta?] (1st was (red wine) – 2nd, a kind of flat pudding, like, (Yorkshire pud). It was O.K. with Jam (some of us were 'Kissed in plenty?)

When the train reached its destination in North Italy, the fun continued – at least, during off-duty hours.

I found a place – where (dancing) was in (progress) – had a good night, a lady, about (60) (took me round): what a 'dancer' she, was. I danced on air, it seemed to me. ? I was (23 y old), but the lady was lighter on her feet than me although I (weighed) only (8 stone, 2lbs)?

But the time for dancing soon passed:

& it was, – (march), march, (March) – for (hours) without a halt.

At the end of the day's footslogging, the accommodation was none too luxurious.

I was one of 10 men told off to (sleep) in a (cow shed) for the night & what a stink, as the 'cows' dropped (Flop, – flop, – flop) of (dung) – so (us) (10 men) (slept in the open)?

The next morning they sluiced themselves in cold water and set off again on the march. As they reached the mountains, they were met by village people, giving grapes and oranges and swapping cigarettes, although their enthusiasm faded when they found that these were *Inglesi* rather than *Americani*.

Captain N. P. Pritchard, a doctor in the Royal Army Medical Corps, took a more cultivated interest in his surroundings. 'Sun rising over the town is a wonderful sight, the towers and domes picked out in a mauve purple light through the haze,' he wrote on seeing Pavia, falling into the aesthetic mode of a Northern European on his first experience of Italy. 'One fine red brick building is perfect and just what I expected.' The 20th Manchesters (Pat Burke's battalion) found the marching tough but 'got good billets'. By 26 November, they were 'now on Italian rations – fresh meat, coffee – & soup. No jam or butter. Bread plentiful and rice.' While Pritchard gasped at the mountain scenery – 'Beautiful hills arise' – other ranks were more conscious of their feet. Fortunately, he was able to produce four ox-drawn wagons 'to take the kits of the men I had seen who could not carry them. The march was short but the day was fine & we arrived with great swish & swank thro the town [of Barbarano].' He believed in the importance of giving the inhabitants a good show. On 28 November they arrived at Villafranca, a 'comfortable place for billeting the men', with a 'very comfortable officers' mess in a very nice lady's house. The servants get on very well with the maids who can speak French a little.' The next day he notes: 'All day practically we are treating feet.' The battalion was still marching on 11 December.

The 7th Division did not go into action immediately. Instead, they remained for six or so weeks just behind Monte Grappa, in the foothills of the Alps, while they were trained in hill fighting. The 2nd Warwicks, who had arrived at Musano on 6 December before marching the eleven miles to Riese and then the short distance to Loria a few days later, played football against the 20th Manchesters on

9 December ('2/B.War. R 1 goal. 20th Manch o,' notes the battalion war diary.) Christmas was spent 'amongst French and Italian troops', remembered Private Lenfestey, 'so we got merry with plenty of wine'. Lenfestey found himself 'a bit in the forefront, being able to speak French'. More soberly, Harry's battalion could enjoy a Boxing Day concert in the Pioneers' Shop.

Guard duties through the intense cold of the Alpine night could be hard. The days, though, were sparkling and dry, although the heat of the sun made little impression on the deep white carpet of snow. This was a mountain economy: 'As the people were poor in this district with no coal or wood, they never stopped in their kitchen of a night time. They had big cows stables and a place set apart as a room where they spent their evenings with the warmth of the stable.' They were sustained by polenta, two square inches of which might, thought Lenfestey, 'weigh a ton'.

On 6 January 1918, the 20th Manchesters played Harry Lake's battalion at rugby.

Later that month, on 18 January, they relieved the 43rd Division in the line at Volpago. For the most part, this was not the line as they had known it on the Western Front. Where they were separated by the river Piave, the two sides did not need trenches. Elsewhere, they made contact across half a mile of no-man's-land: Private Smith remembered one night attack made in single file, following a white tape, and ending, predictably, in 'a fiasco'. Another battalion in the brigade, the 1st Royal Welsh Fusiliers, made a ten-strong commando raid on the town of Asiago. Faces blackened, their equipment and bayonet scabbards tied down with string to stop them from swinging, they got 'through town as far as opp number's Infantry HQ on far side of town', according to the signaller W. R. Thomas. There they found:

> . . . little mountain pack ponies standing outside loaded with enemy's rations etc., also a mobile Search light. An affair on solid steel wheels. These our chaps brought back with them shoving the ponies with their packs intact through Asiago and trundling the Search light after them.

Private Lenfestey's time on this front came to an end after his unit had been inspected by the Commander-in-Chief, the Earl of Cavan. The parade had presumably been spotted by an Austrian aeroplane. The house in which they were billeted was shelled and reduced to rubble, except for one gable. 'We were all buried under the debris and I remember having my head just above the debris.' He managed to free himself, but found blood pouring down his sleeve from wounds to his head and arm. Having walked to the first-aid post, he was put under chloroform, operated upon and packed off to Blighty. 'It was grand to travel in a hospital train along the coast from Genoa to Marseille.'

'Weather wet . . . weather wet . . . weather very bad,' reads the battalion war diary for April. But the month did include one moment of excitement when Captain T. Lynch, with 2 lieutenants and 40 other ranks, led a raid on the Austrian trenches at Ambrosini. It began at 4.50 a.m. and lasted half an hour. 'It was very successful. One prisoner was taken and also a searchlight.' By the end of April, Captain Lynch had been awarded the MC to go with his DCM and MM. But with the exception of an Austrian offensive in June, the first nine months were 'generally uneventful'.

For the Italians, the opportunity to open a decisive battle in this area was presented by the collapse of Bulgaria in late September 1918. The order was immediately given to concentrate the Allied forces, which would consist of 52 Italian, 3 British, 2 French, 1 Czechoslovak and 1 American division. The 7th Division would be one of those deployed in the intended breakthrough, which would, it was hoped, separate the Austrians in the Trentino from those on the river Piave. This interrupted the programme of regimental sports days and football matches (the 2nd Warwicks thrashed the 2nd Honourable Artillery Company by 4 goals to 1, the 22nd Field Ambulance by 4 goals to 2, and the 54th Company of the Royal Engineers by 2 goals to nil).

Subterfuge was used to hide the Allied plans from the enemy. Troops were brought up by night marches. The word was put about that W. R. Thomas's Royal Welsh Fusiliers were leaving for France and would need nails to act as hooks on which to hang their kit in the wagons during the journey. But since there was a supposed nail short-age in the British army, it was hinted that the 'only way to obtain nails on which to hang kit was to borrow or purloin from Italian stores'. Knowledge of this was certain to find its way to the Austrians through spies. British soldiers were issued with Italian helmets and capes. Over 2,000 artillery pieces were assembled along with nearly 2.5 million shells. Hundreds of barges and thousands of anchors were requisitioned. A total of 700,000 cubic feet of timber was brought up for bridge building.

The 2nd Warwicks disappeared to Treviso for special training. Officers attended a demonstration given by the Italians on 'How to Cross a River in Small Boats'. It was then the battalion's turn to march to the river and practise.

On 20 October the Warwicks were among the 22nd Brigade, which took over a line at Salletuol on the Piave. Three days later Captain Pritchard confided to his diary: 'Stunt by 22nd Inf B. to take place tonight (the 23rd/24th). Object – capture of the Isle of PAPA-DOPOLI.' This was Grave di Papadopoli, a gravelly island three miles long and one mile wide, planted with vines, peach trees and asparagus. Its name derives from that of the Papadopoli family from Corfu, who became ennobled as Venetian counts. Since Caporetto, when the Austrians were held at the Piave, it had been a kind of no-man's-land. Herons, short-toed eagles and honey buzzards flew over it undisturbed, until the Austrians fortified it as an advance post. Captain Pritchard disposed advance dressing stations accordingly.

Not only had the division been practising on the river Po with flat-bottomed boats, but they had also recruited a number of gondoliers from the Italian army, whose skills would help with the shallow crossing. The 1st Royal Welsh Fusiliers and the 2nd Honourable Artillery Company went first. Captain Pritchard noted: 'Attack success-ful & only one or two nests of machine posts left. 400 prisoners taken. Communication w. Island however is cut off by the Italian boatmen stopping work at about [2.30 a.m.].' This optimistic assessment was only an initial impression, and conceals a struggle against both artil-lery and the elements in order to cross the water. After three or four crossings, the Austrians realized what was afoot and started firing 'big stuff' which eventually found its mark; some boats were swept away in currents that were supposedly running at sixty miles an hour. Still, it could have been worse. Next day Pritchard reported a 'very creditable' level of casualties for the attack: 30 wounded, of whom 20 were walking.

The 2nd Warwicks crossed to Papadopoli at 4 p.m. on the 24th, the 'Italian Boatmen' winning special praise for the 'excellent work' which, according to the battalion war diary, 'greatly helped in the operation being a success'. Strangely the battalion war diary records the weather as 'fine'. Other accounts indicate that it poured with rain throughout the day: 'Piave swells immediately,' observed Pritchard, '& operations in the afternoon have to be postponed.' In fact the rain became 'terrific'. The previous day, he had been made adjutant by the commanding officer, and so had to cope with a stream of battalion correspondence; but his most pressing concern was the fate of his teams on Papadopoli, with whom communication had been lost. Shortly before midnight, he was detailed to take over three days' rations to them. 'I find to my delight,' he neatly pencilled into the pocket-sized diary, 'both ADS located near the beach. They complain that stretchers sent to mainland are not sent back; has none now nor blankets.'

The brigade was heavily shelled during the night of 24–25 October, and occasionally shelled during the day. But it cleared the island, and despite the appearance of enemy aircraft dropping bombs, the bridges that had been established remained open.

The crossings continued to give trouble, as Captain Pritchard found on 28 October.

> At about midnight the slight rise of Piave due to rain night before & the march of the troops rather weakened the pontoon so that all traffic was stopped while the bridge was being mended. This took a long time & during this the Huns came over & dropped bombs. On the 3 visitation they dropped one right on a crowd of Italians in the road. Great chaos. I go up to see Cpl Webster at Casa Fontebrasso & find an awful sight of blown up men mules & dead & dying & wounded. In all 40 are killed & over 100 wounded . . . never before had I been able to see the good of discipline until now when I saw the complete lack of it.

The British succeeded in throwing three bridges across the Piave. It was a considerable achievement. The Comando Supremo had hoped to achieve a total of eleven crossing places but could only manage six, including the British three. The light level of casualties that the division suffered as the flat-bottomed boats crept through the fog could not be maintained. There was serious fighting as the army reached the north side of the Piave and fanned into the plain around Cimadolmo. But by 29 October, it was clear that the Allies were winning. On that day the 2nd Warwicks reached Vazzola on the river Monticano, as the advance guard of the brigade. On 30 October, the battalion war diary records that the 2nd Warwicks marched for '30 kilometres gaining the final objective of the attack without opposition'.

The Austrians were by now in full-scale retreat, their armies bewildered by lack of orders from the despairing command. Soon the whole front had collapsed. As the future Major General A. W. Lee (then on the 7th Division staff) wrote in a letter to his family on 1 November, when the second battalion crossed the Livenza: 'We're well over the river and the Ostrich is running like hell.' The 2nd Warwicks were among the troops who pressed on into the mountains. They found a population who had been stripped of anything of value by the Austrians, who had burnt what they could not carry. *'Niente mangiare'* – nothing to eat – cried the farmers, whom Captain Pritchard and others would soon be feeding from soup kitchens. The men washed and shaved as best they could in the hedgerows but felt badly in need of a bath.

On 31 October a convoy of vehicles with closed shutters had been escorted to the Villa Giusti near Padua; in them was an Austro-Hungarian delegation, led by General Viktor von Weber, which would negotiate an armistice. Word of the armistice reached the 2nd Warwicks on 3 November, the day it was concluded. The Italians, anxious to enter Trieste and secure prisoners and munitions from the enemy armies, were in no great hurry to come to an agreement and, when they had done so, insisted that the terms would not come into effect for a further twenty-four hours. But on the morning of the 4th, the 2nd Warwicks' commanding officer was explaining his orders to an

Austrian colonel. Large numbers of prisoners, guns, horses and mules were rounded up. At 2 p.m., the battalion war diary notes that 'official news that an Armistice had been signed & would come into operation at 3 p.m. was received. Men of the B[attalio]n very cheefull [sic] but tired.'

Poor Harry Lake was more than tired: he had been badly wounded, perhaps crossing the Piave, perhaps in the fighting afterwards. He died on 14 November.

8

The Years in Between

— THE WAR MEMORIAL —

On the Sunday before Christmas, in 1921, all Lydford assembled at the newly erected memorial. The eleven-foot granite cross was draped in a Union Jack, secured against the Devon wind with tapes. Major John Colquhoun Walford, DSO, who lived at Bridestowe, performed the unveiling ceremony. An Old Contemptible, he had been wounded in two places at Éloges on 24 August 1914, only four days after arriving in France, and again at Le Cateau two days later. There, according to the announcement of his Distinguished Service Order in the *London Gazette*, 'in spite of pain from his wounds, he showed a fine example in bringing limbers and teams up under a heavy fire'. Revd Thorpe of St Petroc's held a service, while the Methodist minister Revd W. H. Tubb read a lesson and said prayers. In what the *Tavistock Gazette* later called, oddly, 'a very explicit address', Major Walford, a professional soldier himself, 'paid tribute to the great sacrifices made by men who prior to the war were engaged in peaceful pursuits'. The church choir, in surplices and hats, and the school choir, with scrubbed knees, sang 'O God, Our Help In Ages Past' before Sergeant Major White and his son, from Tavistock, played the 'Last Post' and 'Reveille'. Wreaths of greenery and flowers – not paper poppies at this date – were laid, and the national anthem was sung; at Lydford, it often is.

Nearly a hundred years later, everyone in Britain grows up near a war memorial. Only a few handfuls of thankful villages escaped loss in what is still called the Great War, and rural Britain felt an overwhelming desire to commemorate the men who would never return; it was hoped that a permanent reminder of their suffering would help to ensure that this was indeed the war to end wars. Villages are far from unique in this respect. Institutions of every kind – regiments, schools, colleges, religious groups, town halls, trades unions, factories, the Inns of Court, the Institute of Actuaries, the United Grand Lodge of Freemasons, the Great Western Railway – wanted to record the sacrifice of those they knew. Tens of thousands of war memorials were constructed, and are now so familiar that it is easy to forget what an innovation they represented.

The aisles of English cathedrals are lined with monuments to individuals, graced with allegorical figures, martial trophies and bas-reliefs of the battle scene, funded by their families or public subscription; and a few regimental memorials were erected after the Boer War. But before 1900 the lowly trooper had never been remembered by name, and for him to be so before 1914 was an exception. But the scale of the First World War was unprecedented, involving thousands upon thousands of men who, in other circumstances, would have been factory workers and clerks, tradesmen and artisans, not professional soldiers. The long and relentless lists of the killed and missing triggered a rare response in an emotionally tongue-tied nation for whom the stiff upper lip had become something of a cult. Early in the First World War, wayside shrines began spontaneously appearing at crossroads. They were a folk expression of deep feeling that would have no parallel in Britain until the death of Diana, Princess of Wales, in 1997; they can be compared to the shrines of flowers, candles, poems and art that were raised in public spaces around Manhattan after the collapse of the Twin Towers in 2001. Soon, war memorials were on the mainstream agenda. Before the end of 1915, a Civic Arts Association had been founded to promote the best standards of appropriateness and design in the building work that would have to be done after the war, memorials being a particular consideration. 'The Association is first of all concerned to demand of our memorial art that it shall be *common* art in the sense of making a universal appeal to plain men and women, that its making shall not be confused by fine phrases and talk of styles, but the natural expression of order and beauty.' A Society for the Raising Wayside Crosses was formed so that the dead would be remembered in almost every village. As its name suggests, it seemed to the society that the natural form such memorials would take would, as at Lydford, be a wayside cross.

The form was not inevitable. The great national monument in London was the Cenotaph. In the classical world, a cenotaph, as someone had once explained to the architect Edwin Lutyens after remarking that a massive stone seat in a Surrey garden looked like the Cenotaph of Sigismunda, is 'a monument erected to a deceased person whose body is buried elsewhere'. This was supremely appropriate to the memorial in Whitehall, given the government's decision that no family would be allowed to repatriate the bodies of its sons; there would be equality in death. Not everyone who passes the Cenotaph will appreciate its geometrical refinement, every line, apparently straight, being part of the radius of a giant curve. Nor do those who lay wreaths on Remembrance Sunday, before attending divine service at St Paul's Cathedral, always reflect that the monument is studiously areligious, adorned with no overt imagery beyond stone wreaths. Lutyens was not himself a conventionally religious man, and he understood that among the hundreds of thousands of British and Empire soldiers who had died were many who were not Christians; they might, like the Indian regiments, have followed other faiths, or none. Yet this austere monument, with its obscure name, was immediately recognized by the nation as a powerful and appropriate focus for its grief.

Elsewhere, war memorials took the shape of monumental arches, cottage hospitals, bus shelters, park benches, wall tablets, parks, recreation grounds, bowling greens, scholarships for the children of the dead, relief funds. Even within the single county of Devon a degree of variety exists: inevitably, perhaps, given that as many as 2,000 memorials were erected. Chudleigh Knighton built an archway over the gate to the church. Crediton purchased a field to use as a recreation ground, which became the subject of a government inquiry; it also found the money to erect an octagonal stone, sheltered by a tall, tiled roof and spire, supported on an oak frame, strongly in the Arts and Crafts spirit of Godalming. Ringmore commissioned a beautiful stained-glass window for the church: behind a kneeling figure of St George can be seen field artillery, a Royal Flying Corps aeroplane and soldiers going over the top. (The artist, Beatrice Campbell, must have been instructed on the detail of these scenes by survivors.) Shaldon went for a clock – to the irritation of the vicar, who had hoped to reroof the church. In some parishes, feelings ran high. The advocates of ceremony and religious imagery fell out with those who thought that the memory of working people would be better honoured by a village hall.

Lydford debated this very point. Ideas were canvassed at a public meeting held in May 1919. Some favoured a cross, some – on Ringmore lines – a stained-glass window in the church, but it was decided to accept an offer from Squire Radford, who wanted to give the Reading Room to the village in order to turn it into a War Memorial Institute. Tablets would provide 'an everlasting memento of the heroes who have sacrificed their lives to help win the war'. It was also intended that the institute should serve the whole of Lydford parish, which still took in most of the Forest of Dartmoor. A committee was formed; but as happens with committees, it could not make the progress that had been hoped. By September 1920, Radford had become so exasperated by the committee's failure to call a meeting to consider the tenders of the contractors that he temporarily withdrew his offer. This had the galvanizing effect he had intended. The chairman hastily convened a public meeting, at which it was found that the cost of the alterations would be £500, but the money so far raised was only £175. The War Memorial Institute was not to be. But the advocates of a memorial that would also provide practical benefits to the village had other ideas to put forward. What about street lighting? Since Lydford has resisted more than the minimum of street lighting to this day, it is easy to imagine that the opposition in 1920 would have been intense. Or a recreation ground? The bell ringers proposed adding a bell to the church tower – forgetting, perhaps, that this was not calculated to please the Methodists. In the end, after 'a lengthy discussion', the concept of the granite cross was 'adopted by a very large majority'. They were not sufficiently cowed by Revd Thorpe to have it placed in the churchyard, preferring a position at the top of the village. The person who designed it, though, was the squire. The names on it would not be those who had died throughout the spreading

Lydford ecclesiastical area, as originally conceived, but ones known to the village – if only slightly, in some cases. It would be an essentially personal choice.

Dartmoor is a land of stone crosses, raised to guide travellers across the moor. In this spirit, the war memorial was placed at a crossroads, echoing, in monumental form, the wayside shrines that had appeared spontaneously while the war was being waged.

In Devon, as elsewhere, the end of the war on 11 November 1918 had been greeted joyously. Flags were waved, bunting hung out and church bells rung – the peal in Tavistock competing with the blare of laundry and factory sirens, railway-engine whistles and the explosion of quarry detonators. The Salvation Army band paraded the streets, and a procession of marines, Girl Guides, Boy Scouts and wounded soldiers from Tavistock Hospital, conveyed in 'an illuminated and decorated waggonette', was followed by the singing of 'Praise God, From Whom all Blessings Flow' and the national anthem. Bulldog to the last, the chairman of the Urban Council expressed himself 'glad that Tavistock had proved her worth by sending out her "boys" and women' against 'the boastful, ruthless, and treacherous Germans'.

Lydford was still celebrating on 1 August 1919 when the village band, under the baton of its bandmaster, H. Bickle, marched schoolchildren and demobbed servicemen to St Petroc's for a service, followed by sports and a public tea. A dance was held in the schoolroom, before the day ended with a bonfire and the singing of the national anthem. The village was determined both to celebrate and to remember. War associations were formed, warriors' days held, and the Vestry Committee recorded in their minutes that the only tablets that could be erected in the church were ones to ex-servicemen; even the Radford family were confined to stained glass. On a May morning in 1919, Revd Thorpe dedicated a tablet on Black Rock, beyond the Dartmoor Inn, to Captain Nigel Hunter, a young officer in the Royal Engineers from a Cheltenham family who spent long holidays on Dartmoor.

Like Dickie Turner, Hunter wrote verse: he also kept a diary for the summer of 1915, recording his visits to Devon, playing golf with his father, strolling 'by the Lyd and along Widgery Tor', finding stag moss and visiting friends at Bridge House. On 2 July he attended Holy Communion at St Petroc's. Eight days later he was at Vlamertinghe, where corpses lay about in the communications trenches and he saw his first dead German. It could hardly have made a greater contrast. Only twenty, he was an exemplary officer and the next year won the Military Cross, having shown 'the greatest determination when, with his section, assisting the infantry to construct advanced strong points under heavy shell fire. When his section sergeant was wounded he, assisted by a corporal of the infantry, carried him to safety, both he and the corporal being wounded in doing so. The success of the night's work was largely due to his fine example.' He was awarded the bar to his MC for an action that took place in July 1917: 'He displayed throughout the operation the greatest gallantry and supreme contempt for danger.' Brave though he was, he hated the war, and struggle though he did to keep the worst from his parents, something akin to despair can be sensed in a letter home, written on 16 August 1917.

> How the war drags! I wish it would get on and finish, but I suppose we shall have to wait a long time for the end of it and then . . . ? I dare say it's good for me, but sometimes it gets a bit of a strain, wanting something all the time which is impossible to get. It's not shells and bullets and things which make the chief strain of the war – as you at home must know – but the ache of heart and mind, the fighting against the inexorable constraint of this war which is always making you do what you don't want to do, and go where you don't want to & prevents you doing what you long to do above everything else to do.
>
> Best love to you all. Your loving son, Nigel

Nigel died in a village near Bapaume on Easter Monday 1918. It was the time of the Spring Offensive, the Germans' last push, and as the British retreated a German machine-gun crew managed to get into some huts about 200 yards from the railway embankment that Nigel's unit was then helping to hold. Where was the gun? Without heed of his own safety, Nigel climbed on to the embankment, located it, pointed it out to his gunners – and was then hit in the stomach. He was carried back to a sunken road crossing the railway; then, with the

Germans as close as thirty yards away, the order to retire from the embankment was received. He had to be left there. Among the letters sent to his parents was one from his batman: 'I am very sorry to lose such a good master, after being his servant for two years. I miss him very much and I could not wish for a better master than Captain Hunter was to me.'

By the time Hunter's tablet was erected, most of the survivors had come home, although some had to wait until 1920. Many had been changed by their experiences, whether physically, having been wounded or gassed, or mentally; it was hard to readjust to the tranquil routine of Devon after the satanic inhumanity of the front. They found that Devon had changed too. Land that, throughout living memory, had been pasture now grew crops. It was part of the 'plough up' policy that the government had introduced to mitigate the food crisis that developed after U-boats began sinking shipping in 1915. Since the 1870s, British agriculture had been allowed to languish, as cheaper food was imported from overseas. As we have seen, at the start of the war, the country could only feed itself from its own resources for 125 days a year; the other two-thirds of its consumption came from across the oceans. In the case of wheat and flour, as much as 80 per cent was imported. Among all the other concerns that the government had in 1914, how to feed the home population did not seem the most pressing. The famously glorious summer of that year produced an excellent harvest, and many people thought the war would be over by Christmas. But rising food prices signalled a problem. The government stepped in to buy food overseas and ship it to Britain. But with merchant ships being sunk, it became clear that this would not be enough. The Board of Agriculture instigated a production drive, with the object of putting a further 3 million acres under the plough – a return to the acreage that was cropped at the end of the High Farming boom in 1870. We have already seen that their efforts, taking too little account of local conditions, did not find favour at Coryton; and they met resistance from other quarters too. The government's own figures, from the Board of Trade's Z8 reports, indicated that as many as a third of the 816,000 men employed on the land before 1914 had joined the services. As a result, farmers were being asked to produce more, with fewer people to help – and they were reluctant to incur extra costs without a guarantee that they would be covered by higher prices.

Dartmoor had not been as badly affected by the shortage of farm labour as other places. Devon, being poor, had already tightened its belt; a county of small farms, where most of the work was done by the families who lived on them, it did not employ a large number of hands.

Agricultural employment had been declining since the mid-nineteenth century, and farm labourers in Devon were poorly paid. Horses, though, were another matter. As J. Fowler, a farmer from Salcombe, asked rhetorically in January 1916:

> . . . at the rate horses are being commandeered and men enlisted, What Will Happen? The farms will become vacant. Already through a lack of labour we are unable to produce as much as we ought . . . I have already lost 50 acres of my land because it has not been tilled and the government does little but threaten to take it from me if I don't produce more food.

Those horses which had not been taken by the military were being driven harder than country folk liked. 'The poor horses are now being overworked to an awful extent,' lamented one ploughman. 'They are laden and fatigued almost to death. This is a terrible way to farm.' Such were the shortages, which included horse harnesses and ploughmen, that the amount of land farmed in Devon actually declined in 1916. Dartmoor itself could hardly be farmed more intensively, but the rest of the county was expected to do more. Returning servicemen would have been surprised by the number of tractors now in England, some bought under a special scheme from the United States. Some of the men would have been pleased to know that there was now an Agricultural Wages Board, to set minimum terms of work. Things for the poorest on the land were looking up.

But they still had to find somewhere to live. Throughout the country, enlightened individuals looked with horror at the housing stock. The return on agriculture had been so poor that the landed estates which generally owned the cottages had spent little money on improving them for decades, and none at all during the war years. 'Village slums', thundered the Tavistock Rural District Council, should be 'got rid of and replaced by habitable and sanitary dwellings'. Even that bastion of conservatism Revd Thorpe weighed in, declaring: 'Some of the cottages now inhabited . . . are a disgrace to any civilized or Christian country.'

While squalid conditions were as much an urban as a rural problem, one anonymous Devon villager believed that 'in villages the not infrequent overcrowding is harder to bear because there are less means of forgetting the terrible monotony of life which renders the cinema in towns a refuge from the home.' Poverty was no less biting because it was suffered in pretty surroundings.

> We have a church of great beauty, filled with the charm that arises and arises only, from 'the unimaginable touch of time' . . . But we have no drainage system, and our water supply consists of one tap to a small reservoir apt to run short in dry seasons . . . We are quite helpless. But one alternative remains. We can join the move to the big town, where every good thing is done for the ratepayers at a price. Town people will take our place as 'weekenders'.

The two-way migration, of poor villagers to towns and prosperous town dwellers to weekend cottages, would continue throughout the twentieth century. Lydford possessed a water supply in the shape of Daniel Radford's taps in the street, but not the piped water, brought into the house itself, in which the urban home rejoiced.

There was a peculiarly Lydford dimension to the village's own housing question: a field purchased for building cottages was crossed by the Saxon town wall. Lady Radford, the antiquarian wife of Sir George and half-sister of Squire Tom Radford, although resident in Surbiton, was appalled, and wrote vigorously to the Rural District Council to protest at the destruction of this outstanding relic. Revd Thorpe put human need above history. 'There is a very urgent need for at least the eight cottages,' he declared, 'and equal need for small middle-class houses at £25 a year rent.' A report from the Medical

Officer into rural health and the housing question in Devon agreed with the reverend: many houses were 'unfit for human habitation'. Overcrowding was compounded by general dilapidation, ground damp, insufficient larder space and primitive lavatories. The dispute at Lydford was resolved through the purchase of other land. Lydford had been quick off the mark; other villages in Devon had to wait until the 1930s. But Lydford could not offer enough jobs to pay the rent, and two of Polly Berry's brothers, Tom and Theophilus Hammett, followed the example of Sam Voyzey and Mancel Clark by emigrating to Canada.

War affected women as well as men. Having tasted responsibility while the men were away, they were not eager to give it back. The change may not have been as apparent in remote Lydford as in Carlisle, where over 11,000 women stirred the Devil's Porridge, as the explosive cordite was known, at HM Factory, the nine-mile-long munitions works at Gretna. But girls who had tried factory work often found that they liked it, in preference to the universal alternative, for a village girl, of domestic service. To the factory worker, the freedom to live and behave as she liked (once out of the factory gates) more than made up for the monotony of the work, whereas maids felt suffocated by the hierarchy, lack of privacy and remorselessly long hours of their lot. During the war, women often performed what had formerly been male tasks – destroying one of the arguments previously used to deny them the vote (suffrage was cautiously extended to some women over thirty in 1918, then allowed to all adults over twenty-one in 1928). An advertisement showing a Fordson Paraffin Tractor in the *Tavistock Gazette* captured the spirit of the times by showing a young woman on the driving seat – an eventuality that would have been unthinkable before 1914 (even if there had been tractors in Devon).

Lydford started a Women's Institute. Admittedly the radicalism of this proposition is not immediately apparent from the programme, which combined lectures on nursing the sick and first aid with socials, teas, fêtes and practical demonstrations on darning, papier mâché, ham curing, poultry trussing and the making of raffia bags. Prizes were given for the best orange marmalade, home-made pasties and jam, and if 'Jerusalem' was not as yet in evidence, the national anthem certainly was. Under the paternalistic eye of Crystal Radford, Squire Tom's wife, it could hardly be otherwise. But the WI's aim of giving training and education to rural women, and generally enlarging their ideas, which could still be mixed with a good deal of superstition and parochiality, was more progressive in the early twentieth century than it might seem now. Devon may not have been as patriarchal as Wales, but the Lydford Reading Room was a male preserve – the implication being that women did not read, or require the other relaxations away from the home (and pub) which it provided. It had taken some time for British women to embrace the WI, which had been founded in Canada in 1897. The organization's very first branch in Britain was opened at Llanfair on Anglesey in 1915. Lydford was an early adopter.

Discontent at the world left by the war boiled over into the General Strike of May 1926. In rural Devon, unions were few and far between. The strike at the Merrivale stone quarry on Dartmoor, which took place earlier in 1926 when the stonecutters, labourers and crane drivers downed their tools in protest at non-union men being paid union rates, was an exception. But travellers from Lydford Station would have noticed that something was up. Eighty per cent of GWR workers went out for the first nine days of the General Strike. There was a riot in Plymouth when blacklegs were brought in to run the trams. As a correspondent to the *Tavistock Gazette* on 22 May of that year noted, it was something of a 'miracle' that petrol supplies were preserved, particularly given the incalculable increase in demand for 'motor spirit' for every type of vehicle. Not that there was much demand for motor spirit in the Lydford of 1926. But it was rising.

Only two cars were parked in the lane to Coryton when the war memorial was unveiled. Only two people in the area owned cars: deaf Dr Postlethwaite (pronounced Puzzlewhite), who drove a Trojan from Brentor and had lost two sons in the war, and the squire. But having been let out of the bottle, the motoring genie was soon flying around the Devon lanes in an alarming manner. During the war, the local MP Sir John Spear thought sufficient numbers of doctors and vets relied on their motor vehicles for rural transport to justify asking the government to increase their allowance of petrol. In the spring of 1925, the West of England Motor Club growled through the village, looking for the way to Brentor. Normally, this peaceful byway is remarkable only for the green vault formed by the trees growing out of the stone banks, whose branches meet overhead. But it also provides a mile-long stretch of straight road which, in April, they used for a speed trial. F. W. Dixon on his 494cc Douglas reached over a hundred miles an hour. Less than a month later, an eighteen-year-old motorcyclist was killed on the same stretch. It was the first of a chapter of incidents that provided an unwelcome new burden for the village policeman, PC Madge. John Morrish, a Plymouth fish salesman, was charged with dangerous driving after colliding with a bus driven by Sam Voyzey's brother Harry. Henry Pengelly of Lydford sued a Londoner, Henry Ayland, for £26 14s 11d for damage done to his car through negligent driving, an episode witnessed by Sidney Cross from the upstairs window of the Dartmoor Inn. Cross was on holiday there. That was another change: the arrival of more summer people.

There were fewer people of other kinds as life moved on. In 1920, William Kenner retired from the schoolhouse over which he had presided for forty-one years. That year, Captain S. H. Priston, presumably a son of 'Honest John' Priston, a corn merchant from Exeter who lived in a villa outside the village, reached Bombay to take up his appointment in the Indian Civil Veterinary Department. In 1921, Frederick Whitford, Edward's brother, left the London and South Western station at Lydford after thirteen years, having been promoted to Yeovil Junction. Revd Sabine Baring-Gould died in 1924, in his ninetieth year. But above all, there were fewer young men.

Nobody to dance with; it was a memory that many women, young in the 1920s, would preserve into old age. Squire Radford's bubbly daughters would have felt the lack as much as anyone, and indeed the family's story is an object lesson in social change.

When Daniel Radford died in 1900, the Lydford property went to Tom, the youngest of all his children. Only twenty-three, he was, perhaps, the one most attached to country life. At some point, he lost an eye in a riding accident, although that did not impair his skill at shooting. In 1901 Tom married Crystal Pike, from an old Devon family, whom we have already met as chairwoman of the WI; it is said that she was named after her father's favourite hound. Although Bridge House was let, he presumably might have repossessed it. Instead, he tried his own hand as an architect, by designing Ingo Brake himself, to produce a somewhat German-looking house, with a timber-framed upper storey over a plain base. His prowess with the gun provided the decorative theme, the walls of Ingo Brake being lined with stuffed animals and birds (their glass eyes spooked visiting children). But not even Tom seems to have considered the architecture a sufficient success to risk his hand with paying clients. Old photographs show the site of the house as being practically bald at the beginning of the twentieth century; it is now decently lost behind thickly planted trees, giving the impression that this is a secret, slightly eerie place. It was, however, far from secret in Tom's day, and he and Crystal raised a warm and boisterous family.

There were five children: Mary (or Molly), Joyce, Leonard, Betty and John. They were all some years younger than their cousin Dickie Turner (the eldest, Molly, was born in 1902). They are seen at their most vivid through the eyes of Henry Williamson, the son of a bank clerk, who had arrived by motorbike at Georgeham, on the other side of Barnstaple, to visit an aunt in 1914. It was an idyllic holiday, during which he walked twenty or twenty-five miles every day, discovering the countryside to which he later claimed he owed everything. Highly strung and romantic, he was then catapulted into a horrifically different world by war service as a machine-gunner. Literary success would come with the publication of *Tarka the Otter: His Joyful Water-Life and Death in the Country of the Two Rivers*, which sold a million copies. In 1921, however, he was still struggling to establish himself, as well as to overcome the searing experiences of the war. When he shambled up to the seventeen-year-old Gwen Dennis, fishing with the retired farmer Bill Lane off some rocks near Croyde, he and his ginger-haired companion, Frank Davis, looked like tramps — if not, as Lane wondered in his thick Devon accent, a couple of ancient Britons. It was, however, the beginning of a friendship with Gwen.

At their boarding school at Bideford, Gwen and her sister Hermione shared a bedroom with Molly and Joyce Radford (it was known, with heavy irony, as the 'quiet room' from the romps that went on there). In the summer holidays, Molly and Joyce were introduced to the Dennises' new friend. Williamson put the Norton into gear and roared off to Lydford, where he stayed at the Castle Inn. He had just 'had a really ripping time', as he told Gwen in a letter, at the house of some mutual friends. One of the penalties of knowing Williamson was his habit of carrying his manuscripts in his pocket, ready for them to be read at the least expression of interest. It was therefore characteristic that he should write:

> I feel an awful fool coming here with a rotten book that no one will read. [It was probably *The Beautiful Years*.] I puff myself like a bubble and then burst myself. I feel like tying it up with cord, ringing the bell, laying it on the mat, and running away.

From the Castle, Williamson paid a visit to Ingo Brake. If he read from his novel, the Radfords put up with it, because he returned the next May, this time staying for four days. Joyce was supposed to be infatuated with him – a dangerous condition, given Williamson's reputation for being unsafe with women.

In 1923, Williamson was at Lydford in March, and then again at Christmas and New Year. Although within the same county – and in fact crossing only a small part of it – the journey from Georgeham, where he was now living, to Ingo Brake was not to be undertaken lightly at this season. 'It really was an adventure to move across this part of the world,' Williamson would remember in *Goodbye West Country*. In winter, the motorbike, driven by a rubber belt, would sink into clay mud on the unmetalled roads, so that the belt slipped off the pulley, leaving the engine to race. It took eight hours to travel forty miles to visit his Lydford friends.

In his shattered condition, Williamson, whose relationship with his own family, particularly his father, was distant, generally struggled with the ritualized jollities of Christmas. But in the exuberance of the Radford family, his spirits seem to have held up. Verses were written, and one set can only be by Williamson.

> O vinny Squire
> O lovely lad
> O plus foured Nuncle
> I am quite mad.

'Nuncle', as a nickname for Tom, presumably derives from the term of address used by the Fool towards Lear in Shakespeare's play. 'Vinny' was a cult word with Williamson, and if the meaning is obscure at this distance of time, the sentiment is clear: Williamson was having a good time. That impression is confirmed by his entry in the visitors' book:

Stayed very happily with Nuncle and his fair family, including Kilti, Patch (of vinny paintings), 'Comrade,' and 'Feathers'. Poor zany, he leaves on a broken bicycle with a broken bag, and nearly broken-hearted. Farewell ye people of Ingo, mongst the trees, I go back with only a black bottle to cheer me (but no black eyes, thank ye). The owl flys away, dam!

This is signed with his colophon in the form of an owl. (At George-ham, he lived at Skirr Cottage, named after the sound made by the wings of owls on the roof.) There were other visits, and although Tom would be remembered, towards the end of his life, as a generally forbidding figure, Williamson got on with him famously. After a storm in June 1936, he addressed a letter to:

Nuncle Radford, Esq.,
  Ingo Brake,
   'mongst trees valled down,
  Lydford

Writing in his cod Devon:

Sorry to yurr about they treeseeses. All blawed down, be m? 'Tez a proper messup I reckon. Yes didden hear thaccy bliddy broadcast about your gorge fornit agone I reckon. Twudden no cop anyhow.

Williamson set much of his spiritual novel *The Star-born* in Lydford, painting a lightly disguised picture of the gorge and his friends at Ingo Brake. When the etcher Charles Tunnicliffe came to Lydford to research the illustrations, he was given the flat over the garage. It took him two years to return the key.

During the Second World War, Tom's knowledge of architecture was put to good use; as an expert photographer, he was commissioned to record Devon churches, in case they were damaged by enemy action. By then a heavy smoker suffering from a bad heart, he was too ill to drive, but would still set off, with other family members, in his big Flying Standard motorcar. The younger ones climbed the belfries while he set up his camera. In the mornings, a favourite granddaughter would sit on the end of his bed, with a spaniel, and watch him shave.

If, at an earlier period, Joyce Radford had hoped to become Mrs Williamson, she was to be disappointed. In 1925 he married Ida Hibbert, the daughter of an official with the Cheriton Otter Hunt. He had met her while collecting material for *Tarka*; although a champion of otters (to the extent of keeping one as a pet), he proposed at the Cheriton Otter Hunt Ball. Joyce found a husband, Gordon Kidley, three years later, and left home. Her brother Leonard emigrated to Australia, 'a splendid chance for him', as his mother wrote in the family history, but agonizing for her all the same. In 1941, at the age of thirty-nine, Molly married a carpenter-cum-farmer, Thomas May. Poor Betty had to wait until she was forty-two and dying of TB before she was allowed to marry Louis Screech, an orphan who had been brought up as a carpenter.

On Betty's death, Crystal Radford kept Lou on as her chauffeur.

In the language of the time, Molly and Betty Radford 'went native' when they married tradesmen. This can be seen, perhaps, as an indirect consequence of the war, which had scythed through the ranks of potential suitors. The shadow of the conflict was inescapable, disfiguring many of the men who returned. One of them was Jim Stephens. A hint of Jim's suffering can be found on the war memorial. As you would expect, the first eleven names appear in alphabetical order, but an eagle eye will spot that after Whitford E. J. comes Stephens J. This is a mystery which can be explained by the fact that he died in 1925. It is through his death that we discover most about his time overseas, because the retired naval surgeon William Daw wrote a letter which has been bound into the thick volume of medical records containing Jim's file. Daw lived at Watervale, a house above the Willsworthy Camp, with views across to the holy mount of Brentor, the tor on which a church is poised. Jim was the son of an agricultural labourer turned cowman and worked as a groom for Miss Daw. His home ('fairly good', according to his medical records) was Watervale Cottage. But in 1925 he was too ill to work. He had been discharged from the army on 3 June 1919 as 'sick'. Aged forty-five, this staunch member of the St Petroc's congregation, whose strong features, immaculately combed hair and starched collar are to be seen in photographs of the choir and bell ringers' outings, was admitted, on 6 May, to the Devon Mental Hospital at Exeter.

According to an obituary, Jim (like Archie Huggins and Dickie Petherick) had been a member of the Royal North Devon Hussars. The date of enlistment given on his Silver War Badge is 14 December 1914; if this is correct, he spent 1915 on territorial duties, guarding the shores of Essex. When the North Devons were broken up for rein-forcements, he joined the Welch Regiment; and in November 1917 he left that to become part of the Labour Corps. The Labour Corps was a vital but unsung division of the British army, responsible for providing the manpower for the roads, railways, camps, stores, dumps and telegraph and telephone systems on which the fighting machine depended. It was formed at the beginning of January 1917 to bring the 190,000 men who were already serving in Labour battalions and Infantry Labour companies in France and at home into one organization. The speed with which this was done flustered the bureaucrats who were trying to keep records of 'thousands of men, many of whom had already been transferred several times and whose documents had not kept pace with them'. But, as Lieutenant Colonel Wetherall noted in December 1918, 'the desire to get a "move on" outweighed other considerations'. By the end of the war, the Labour

Corps contained more than 10 per cent of the whole army. Jim's presence in it probably indicates that he had been wounded; completely fit men were sent to the front. As a countryman, a rider and a groom, it was natural that he should be detailed to work with horses, and he was sufficiently good at it to be made a lance corporal. He not only handled horses, but also mules and camels, in regions that Daw describes as 'Bulgaria, Turkey, Persia, etc.' More specifically, this was part of the Salonica Campaign.

Salonica, now called Thessaloniki and the second largest city in Greece, had, until shortly before the First World War, been part of the Ottoman Empire. At the end of 1912, it was captured by the Greek army – to the mortification of the Bulgarian army, which arrived the next day. (The Bulgarians, seeking to negotiate with the Ottoman commander Hasan Tahsin Pasha, were told ruefully: 'I have only one Thessaloniki, which I have surrendered.') A combined Franco-British force landed there in October 1915 – the month during which Archie Huggins arrived at Gallipoli – to support Serbia. Serbia's importance to the Central Powers lay in its railway; Turkey had been defeated by Russia at the Battle of Sarikamish and, without a route through Serbia, she would have been cut off from her allies. By the time the French and British troops arrived, Serbia had already been overrun by Bulgaria and Austria. But they began organizing for future operations by rebuilding the infrastructure.

The First and Second Balkan Wars had left 'villages deserted, houses battered, towns destroyed and many other signs of fighting in a region which had enjoyed the blessings of peace for quite twelve months'. The railway was single track. Only two roads ran out of Salonica, and neither of them could support heavy traffic. The 10th (Irish) Division came straight from Gallipoli, exchanging the baking sand and gulleys of the peninsula for blizzards in a mountain land without roads. That winter, 1,500 men, housed in tents and not issued capes or caps until the new year, suffered frostbite. On this stagnant front the troops remained, in the words of F. A. W. Nash, 'bedded fast in slab and thick monotony like flies in treacle' until 1918. Frontline troops might have to stay in the trenches for up to a year, engaged in fighting – but generally less intensively than in France. There were, furthermore, no reserves.

To begin with, it was difficult for soldiers who had seen action in France or Gallipoli to treat the politics of Salonica with absolute seriousness. As one of them wrote later:

> The setting of the Place de la Liberté [in Salonica], with its cafés spread along each side of the brilliantly lighted square, where the Greek officers during the first mobilisation disposed themselves in brilliant uniforms with their smartly dressed women-folk, was suggestive of the opening scene of a Balkan comic opera, and the atmosphere was intensified by the general topsi-turviness of the situation.

The atmosphere was rather like that of Casablanca in the early part of the Second World War, a supposedly neutral port packed with the soldiery of many nations, thick with intrigue and espionage. H. Collinson Owen was the only newspaper correspondent to see the fighting in Salonica through from beginning to end (largely, perhaps, because it was ignored by most of the press), and he paints a vivid picture of the scene that could be observed from the balcony of the Cercle des Étrangers, a club founded by a previous British consul general.

> Looking down . . . one realised for the first time the real meaning of such words as 'cosmopolitan', 'polyglot', and 'crowded'. There were officers and soldiers of the five Allies; Turks, Albanians, Greeks (soldiers and otherwise), sailors from half a dozen navies; Allied 'native' soldiers – Algerians, Indians, Annamites, and ugly Senegalese; Balkan peasants in their rough frieze dresses, with bright waist-bands; and the innumerable all-pervading Spanish Jews and Jewesses of Salonica. The buzz of their continuous conversation, in half the languages of Europe, rose like the noise of surf on a beach. And in the cooler hours, when the populace came forth *en masse* from their villas and apartment houses and warrens, one might have waltzed on their heads.

Upcountry, conditions were entirely different, the mountains treeless, majestic and sparsely populated. It was still a land of brigands, inhabited by people wearing the picturesque clothes that enchanted Lord Byron's contemporaries, but ready to seize members of the prosperous bourgeoisie from Salonica and hold them for ransom if they were foolhardy enough to go out unescorted or unarmed. The troops stationed there felt they had been banished to the moon.

By the time Jim came to Salonica, joining the 816th Employment Company in November 1917, the British had already had two years in which to make themselves as comfortable as they could, with sandbags and corrugated iron. He was too late for the horse shows that had taken place during the summer. On the edge of the Struma Plain, the 27th Division had put on a particularly 'magnificent' one:

> . . . 'everybody' was there – nurses from the Base hospitals, delighted with the novel experience of a trip up-country, and General Sarrail sitting next to the British Army Commander in the grandstand. Aeroplanes circled overhead to keep off inquisitive Bulgar or Boche, and the weather was wonderful. It was astonishing to think that a Division very much in the field could have organised such a show. And the horses made everybody's eyes sparkle.

The horse show staged by the 22nd Division, to which Jim's company belonged, had been 'an anxious day', because the enemy started to fire long-range shells which could easily have got into the show-ground. As it was, they instead fell on the approach road, where they killed the winning team of Heavy Artillery horses shortly after it had left – 'a sad end to a day of triumph'.

As a private in the 816th Employment Company, Jim would not have seen much of the cosmopolitan clubs of Salonica. According to the one war diary which survives for his company, he spent the spring and summer of 1918 working on the land at the Gugunci Railhead. They were growing maize, in an attempt to make the army as self-sufficient as possible, given the difficulty of bringing supplies across the seas – or indeed, across the land (transport was provided by winding caravans of mules and horses, which the locally recruited muleteers often deserted). In March, they ploughed and harrowed, in April they sowed. Borrowing a Ransome's motor tractor from divisional headquarters was an event worthy of note: most of the work would have been done with horses. The rate of progress was not very rapid, and a large element of the war diary consists of a record of the other ranks who were evacuated to hospital. As noted in the diary, it was the despair of Lieutenant P. S. J. Welsford that he could not persuade the men to take basic precautions against disease: 'Find much difficulty in making sentries wear anti-Mosquito veils as they are hot & uncomfortable,' he pencilled on 16 June. 'They always advance the excuse that they cannot see through them.' Some objected to being inoculated against cholera because the injections made them feel ill. But on 19 July the men could congratulate themselves on their labours, which are recorded as:

> Weekly total of Maize issued to units, grown on land in vicinity of company beginning Sunday 14th July 1918 ending Saturday July 19th 1918 by this unit. Tons 8 cwt 15 stone 1 lbs 10.

Apart from the snowstorms and thunderstorms, and the raging heat and disease in the summer, the company seems to have pursued a gentle, pastoral existence.

The military stalemate only ended in September 1918 with the Battle of Doiran, fought in the steep hills around Lake Doiran, north of Salonica, where the British, supported by the Greeks and a French Zouave regiment, set themselves the all but impossible task of driving the Bulgarians out of their mountain positions on the Pip Ridge, a row of little eminences known as Pip 1, 2, 3, 4 and 5. The effort could only be contemplated once the Labour Corps had prepared the road – although, in the words of the official history, it remained 'still narrow and, into the bargain, steep and winding'.

Although now forgotten, Lake Doiran was as bloody as the battles on the Western Front, requiring the Allied force to make a frontal assault on all but impregnable positions with inadequate artillery support. The first two battalions to throw themselves at the heights were annihilated. It was then the turn of the Welsh Brigade.

> No feat of arms can ever surpass the glorious bravery of those Welshmen. There was lingering gas in the Jumeaux Ravine (probably ours!) and some of the men had to fight in respirators. Imagine, if you can,

what it means to fight up a hillside under a deadly fire, wearing a hot mask over your face, dimly staring through a pair of clouded goggles, and sucking the end of a rubber nozzle in your mouth. At the same time heat is pouring down on you from a brazen sky. In this plight you are called on to endure the blast of machine-gun fire, the pointed steel or bursting shell of the enemy. Nor are you called on to endure alone ; you must vigorously fire back, and vigorously assail with your own bayonet. It is as much like hell as anything you can think of.

The British and Greek attacks were utterly repulsed, leaving over 7,000 dead. However, the Franco-Serbian army was more successful to the east, and when it seemed that the Bulgarian army would be divided, the defenders were forced to fall back from Pip Ridge. In the ensuing rout, the British were dismayed to discover the atrocities perpetrated on the Bulgarian sick and wounded as the Serbians retook their homeland. They marvelled at the neat little gardens that the Germans had laid out in the part of Serbia which they had occupied, as well as Swiss-style chalets on the sides of ravines. The Labour Corps followed the British advance, helping the Royal Engineers to repair bridges which the Bulgarians had destroyed as they fled. Some of them then moved to Constantinople; it may be that Jim Stephens's unit was sent to Mesopotamia (Iraq) or Palestine.

At some point, the men became detached from the rest of the regiment, and it was assumed Jim had been killed. In fact he had managed to survive, but only by eating a diseased camel liver: ' . . . all vomited except Stephens', noted Daw; 'the others remain well'. It may have been this, or simply his close contact with animals, that transmitted what appears to have been a zoonotic disease – one that jumps the species barrier from animals to humans – whose symptoms were similar to anthrax. Blisters appeared on his hands and spread to his whole body. The case puzzled the specialists in the London Hospital, the South Devon and East Cornwall Hospital at Plymouth, the Tavistock Infirmary, the St John's Hospital for Diseases of the Skin, London, and the Charing Cross Hospital.

Before entering the Devon Mental Hospital Jim had been in the Tavistock Infirmary, exhausted through lack of sleep, unable to stay in bed and convinced that people, sometimes the nurses, were trying to kill him. He raved nonsensically. He had gone blind. His skin had been so rotted that it practically ceased to exist, being replaced instead by a 'scaly eruption which peels off in flakes'. Daw had written to tell the doctor in charge of Jim's case what he knew of it. The letter concludes: 'His mother insists on seeing his body before burial, can this be prevented?'

Jim Stephens's name is not the last of the roll from the First World War. After his name comes that of William H. Daw, the naval surgeon who wrote to the hospital about Jim's case. The son of a draper, Daw's distinguished professional career can be traced through the pages of *The Times*. In 1892 it was announced that he had passed his medical exams. Two years later, his name appears as the winner of a prize in Practical Anatomy, for which he had a scholarship at the London Hospital. Having qualified, he served as house surgeon at the London Hospital and resident medical officer at the Royal Hospital for Diseases of the Chest. As a result of his experiences, he published a book on *The Cure of Consumptives* in 1898 directed against the feared disease of tuberculosis, which would carry off Betty Screech. 'The medical world has declared war against tuberculosis' announced the review in the *British Medical Journal*, Daw's contribution being 'a very useful and practical little handbook'. His route into the Royal Navy came via the Royal National Mission to Deep Sea Fishermen, after which he was appointed to the torpedo gunboat HMS *Antelope* in 1899. Daw seems not to have gone to South Africa during the Boer War; instead, he transferred to HMS *Rambler*, a gun vessel used for survey work. His heart must have leapt to have been appointed to HMS *Wildfire*, lately *Hiawatha*, a dashing steam yacht used as the flagship to the Commander-in-Chief, The Nore, Admiral Sir Hugo Pearson (the Nore being the sandbank that marks the junction of the Thames and the North Sea and the name of a naval command).

In 1901 Daw married Barbara Moses; it is not known whether she died or the couple parted, but in 1908 he married again, in Tavistock, his bride being Gertrude Nuttall. By the next year Daw was in the Mediterranean, because a son was born at the Royal Naval Hospital in Gilbraltar. There follow appointments to a succession of cruisers, culminating with HMS *Astraea* in 1913. He was still on *Astraea* when the First World War broke out on 4 August 1914. Four days later, the ship saw action, bombarding the port of Dar-es-Salaam, then part of German East Africa. This led the Germans to scuttle their floating dock in order to impede what they took to be an imminent invasion. Daw was promoted to Fleet Surgeon, and in 1915 witnessed the attempt to oust the Germans from their newly acquired colony of Kamerund (now Cameroon). A glimpse of life on board *Astraea*, which remained off the African coast, is given by Wilfred Owen's brother Harold, who served on her towards the end of the war. He describes being 'isolated from contact with the world' except for rare visits to upcountry planters who were 'more cut off than we were . . . We all suffered in different ways from the monotony of one another.' He became a victim of depression and headaches from the large quantities of quinine that were consumed against malaria.

From 1916 until the end of the war, Daw was at HMS *Vivid*, the naval barracks at Devonport, with the exception of three and a half months on the cruiser HMS *Shannon* as Fleet Surgeon.

Daw retired in 1920, and he died six years later, at the age of fifty-three. Among the wreaths at the funeral at St Petroc's was one to 'Darling daddy from Spendwyn, Pat, Ian, Darky and Fairy' (the last two presumably being dogs). Ian would go on to be awarded the MC fighting with the Devons in 1944, being killed shortly afterwards.

Strangely, although Daw unquestionably served in the navy for many years, there is no mention in the obituaries or elsewhere of his having been wounded, let alone having died of his wounds. Would his obituarists really have failed to remark on wartime injuries, if there had been any? The *British Medical Journal*, for example, details the war record of other doctors. It puts one to wondering what his name is doing on the war memorial, among the glorious dead. And the only conclusion can be that the war memorial meant something different in 1926 from what one might imagine now. It was a shrine of collective memory, on which offerings of different value could be laid; Mrs Daw perhaps contributed a widow's mite.

★

On 14 June 1929, a large Daimler rolled along the village street in Lydford, stopping at a vacant site near the United Methodist chapel. At the wheel was Harry Hammett, Polly Berry's brother; emerging through the door that he held open for them were the stately figures of Alderman Ford James Ware Nicholls, JP, and his lady, Elizabeth. Seventy years old, Alderman Nicholls had done well as a wine merchant, removal contractor and farmer; his bullocks used to be herded to the sidings of Lydford Station and loaded into cattle trucks, fifty beasts at a time. Without children, he now exercised his benevolence on the county, sitting on the bench, chairing meetings of the Tavistock branch of the National Farmers Union and the Devon Farmers Union, serving as a county councillor, generally encouraging high standards and indulging in some good-hearted philanthropy. It was a day of rejoicing, marked in the usual way by bunting and Union Jacks. For its war memorial, Lydford had been constrained to choose a stone cross over an institute, through lack of funds. Now the funds had been found. The foundation stone was being laid for a village hall, the cost of the building – £1,700 – would be met by Alderman Nicholls, while the village raised £250 for furnishing. The story has it that the offer of a hall had originally been made to the parish of Brentor, in which the Alderman Nicholls's home of Torside, near the railway station, was to be found; but Brentor had rebuffed him, and he had promptly offered it to Lydford instead. Lydford was properly grateful. It is the Nicholls Hall to this day.

The Nicholls Hall formed a new centre of gravity for the village, the natural place for teas, dances, amateur theatricals, lectures and classes to be held. In 1939 it was the scene of the WI's annual flower show, which was said to have 'maintained its reputation as one of the best in the neighbourhood'. If only, observed Mr A. J. Priston, opening the show in place of his mother, the leaders of the nations 'would learn to grow the biggest potatoes and onions, instead of the biggest guns, then sanity would prevail, and peace return to the world'. But, alas, it was the guns that triumphed.

9

Wings Over the River Styx

— THE HERBERT BOYS —

Picture a broad valley in Northern Greece, at whose edges mountains well up abruptly and soar to 6,000 feet – a valley, itself 3,000 feet above sea level, which could be described as being lost, so little is it visited by the outside world. It is Paramythia, towards the Albanian border, and an airstrip has been hidden here. There are wolves and bears in the mountains, wildflowers on the bed of the valley. A journalist who descended between 'two towering peaks' called it 'an unforgettable scene, so much wild beauty crammed into one valley. It reminded you of the Shangri-La of *Lost Horizon*.'

At three o'clock on the afternoon of 13 April 1941 – Easter Sunday – Flying Officer Richard Herbert, slight of build, habitually pale but popular in the officers' mess, climbed on to the wing of his two-engined Blenheim and settled into the cockpit. With him were his radio operator and air gunner, 'Jock' Young, and his observer, who was on this occasion Paddy Coote, the wing commander of Western Wing, wanting to take a personal look at the German advance. Their fleece-lined flying jackets would protect them against the worst of the cold in the unheated aeroplane but many airmen chose not to wear gloves, apart from silk liners, even though the controls soon became icy to the touch; they preferred cold hands to clumsy fingers. Herby, as Richard Herbert was known in the squadron, was twenty-one years old, and the very model of what an RAF officer was meant to be: cavalier about the appalling risks that he daily ran, impossible (as his group commander joked) to keep on the ground. He was good-looking too: his brilliantined hair was combed close to his scalp, emphasizing the long straight nose, rather hooded eyes and strong mouth. But he was not an overtly wild character. Instead, people were surprised that this shy and reserved individual was so insouciant about risk.

The Mercury engines, already warmed up by the ground crew, roar to a deafening volume as Richard opens them out. The bomber rumbles forward. But there is no runway, and there are some bumpy moments as the plane, engines now screaming at full power, accelerates across the valley floor. Within minutes, it is flying over the river Kalamos, known in classical mythology as the river Styx, across which the boatman Charon ferried the bodies of the dead. This would not have seemed unduly ominous to Richard. He had flown over it many times before, twice that morning en route to Kukës in Albania and Resen in Macedonia; both raids had lasted an hour and twenty minutes. Flying was in his blood. His father, Philip, had joined the Royal Warwickshire Regiment in 1903, being promoted into the Sherwood Foresters; but while Philip's brother George had stayed in the army, rising to become a colonel, he recognized the possibilities of aviation at an early date, joining the Royal Flying Corps in 1912. In the course of the First World War Philip was awarded orders from Russia, Greece and Egypt, and ended his air force career in 1929, as an air commodore. Having married a Devon girl, Gwendoline Hawker, who gave him three sons, he became Bailiff of Dartmoor for the Duchy of Cornwall. Like so many service families, the Herberts were used to moving; they lived at various addresses, including one at Lydford for a time, but in 1936 they were at Tor Gate, Princetown, the town in which the Lydford Parish Council had its meetings. Princetown is a gloomy settlement, created in one of the bleakest and most exposed parts of the moor, best known for its prison. But it was convenient for the Dartmoor Hunt, which the family enjoyed following. It was while exercising his horse that the air commodore was killed at the end of 1936. Two of the boys were at Wellington College, a school originally founded in the 1850s for the orphans of army officers, and one was at Cambridge. They were to sustain another blow when, only six weeks later, their mother died of pneumonia. Like her husband, she was carried to the grave in Tavistock by bearers from the Duchy of Cornwall. By request –

although not an easy one to fulfil in January – wreaths were to be made from poppies.

The social composition of Lydford, as seen through the names on the war memorial, changes with the Second World War. With the exception of Dickie Turner, the scholar from Westminster School, the men from the First World War all firmly belonged to communities within the village. They came from families of artisans, builders and labourers; they might have gone to sea, emigrated or arrived to marry a village woman, but, allowing for the divisions between Methodists and Church of England and old village and railway station, they reflected a homogeneous, not highly aspirational society, living for the most part in overcrowded, damp cottages and farmhouses, their leftovers fed to the pigs. By 1939, Lydford had moved on. There were still village families such as the Bickles, whose name appears almost ubiquitously in school logbooks and descriptions of village events. But the big houses, loosely Arts and Crafts in style, which had been built since 1900 attracted a different kind of resident: retired professionals, summer people, folk who were attracted by the landscape of Dartmoor and who kept horses. They were seen around the village, or at St Petroc's, but rarely entered the Castle Inn. They came, stayed for a few years, or months, and then went. They hardly knew the Hugginses, Hobbses, Pethericks or Frys, unless the latter were doing work on their houses, or sold them stamps in the Post Office. These families did not go to the village school. Nor did they leave school at fourteen. Over the centuries Lydford's identity had changed from an important defensive centre to being a tinners' town, and then a farming village endowed with a railway junction. It was now evolving again, a new source of prosperity having been found in the natural beauties of Dartmoor. Socially, the Herberts were typical of the new sort; they were middle class.

After Wellington, Richard trained at the Royal Air Force College at Cranwell, graduating as a pilot shortly before the outbreak of war, and joining 211 Squadron. The number 211 can be explained by the squadron's history: it was formed by the fledgling RAF out of the Royal Naval Air Service's No. 11 squadron on 1 April 1918, and as in all such cases the original number was preceded by 2. They spent the rest of the First World War raiding German targets such as the U-boat ports, not perhaps doing as much direct damage as they might have hoped but certainly making themselves an inconvenience. Even the measured words of the RAF communiqués cannot suppress the sense of Biggles-like derring-do.

9 May 1918

The weather was fine with considerable haze. 27 tons of bombs were dropped. Enemy aircraft were fairly active in the whole front . . . Lt W. Gillman and 2nd Lt R. Lardner, 211 Sqn, whilst returning from a bomb raid encountered an E[nemy] A[ircraft] Triplane. A few rounds were fired into the EA and it went down in flames over Zeebrugge mole.

19 May 1918

The weather was fine. 32 tons of bombs were dropped. Enemy aircraft activity was slight on the front . . . Lt J. S. Forgie and 2nd Lt J. S. Muir, 211 Sqn, were attacked by several EA while on a bombing raid over Blanckenburghe. The Observer fired 30 rounds into one EA, which nose-dived and caught fire on hitting the ground.

13 August 1918

Weather fine. 21½ tons of bombs were dropped by night and 20½ tons by day. Enemy aircraft active . . . A raid was carried out . . . on Varssenaere Aerodrome . . . 211 Sqn bombed the aerodrome after the low flying attack was over, and demolished the chateau.

It was already a bomber squadron, with the motto, perfumed with a sense of the Paris boulevards, *toujours à propos* – always the right thing.

Disbanded after the war, 211 Squadron was reformed at Mildenhall, Suffolk, in 1937. In 1938 they were sent to the Middle East, spending the next year at a variety of bases in Egypt and Palestine, trying to keep the sand of the Western Desert out of their engines and the sand fleas off their persons. An impression of squadron life is given in the letters, written to his parents, by J. D. W. H. Clutterbuck (Hugh) known to his comrades as Buttercluck, Clattersmack, Clutter or other variations – mostly impolite – on his surname. In August 1939 he was still training at No. 4 FTS (Flying Training School) at Abu-Sueir, Egypt, getting up at five, starting to fly half an hour later, coming back at eight to wash, shave and have breakfast, and finishing the morning with lectures.

Then we pack up for the day, having lunch about 1. Sleeping from 1.30 till about 4.

The servant (an Arab) brings me in some tea & sandwiches etc. about 4 pm. Dinner is at 8.

The servant (named Mahmoud) is very good. He is young (about 25) intelligent, honest & very efficient.

He found bicycles 'at a premium', while, by late October, the 'only effect of the War out here so far' was to inflate the price of mineral water, although it was still 'quite cheap'. By then, Clutter was based at an RAF station near Lake Habbaniya.

Two years ago this place was called Dhibban which means 'many flies', a very apt name for it, but I suppose they considered it a little too expressive & so it was renamed Habbaniya.

The flies were, as he wrote the next year:

. . . the worst thing about the desert . . . The Egyptian fly is about the most fearless & persistent insect I have ever come across & there are swarms of them although now that it is getting cooler they are slackening off a little. But if one leaves one's cup of tea for 10 minutes, it is sure to have about six flies in it.

That was in September 1940 when, as a newly minted member of 211 Squadron, Clutter was sharing a bell tent with a Canadian. Air crews relaxed by swimming in the sea and spending what leave they had in Alexandria, 'the finest town in Egypt in my opinion'. At mealtimes, the 'very good cook' put on 'quite a good effort' considering the difficulties he was working under. When Clutter joined 211 Squadron he was in his late twenties, and its oldest pilot.

Richard began the war flying missions over France. In September

1940, he flew out to join 211 Squadron via Malta, a journey that was itself intensely dramatic, leading them to encounter:

> ... all the brilliant fireworks of an electrical thunderstorm, the most dangerous phenomenon an aviator can meet ... The Blenheim whirled and bucked upwards, a wind sliced earthwards and we fell through space, some hundreds of feet, to end with a spine-snapping jerk like a puppet pulled up abruptly on its strings ... a flickering bluish flame licked around the outline of the plane: 'St Elmo's Fire' ... Herby was wrestling with the stick and throttle controls, his face a dead white ... vivid sheets of lightning illuminated the jet blackness, hissing sleet lashed protesting metal, the crack of thunder exploded above the struggling engines; then ice started to form and build on the wings.

The plane limped into Malta, its fuel all but exhausted. By the time Richard reached the Middle East, he had regained his sang froid. Flying over the pyramids he remarked over the plane's intercom, in his usual clipped tones, 'Terrible waste of stone, what?'

On landing in Egypt, Richard's impressions of his new comrades may well have been similar to those of the war reporter T. H. Wisdom, who landed on the Nile in a flying boat and met some of the squadron in the Cecil Bar at Alexandria. They were young men and happy to act even younger than their years. In his shorts and shirt, Pilot Officer L. S. Delaney, known as the Duke,

> looked like a Boy Scout ... There was Squadron-Leader 'Porpoise' Bax, the C.O., 'the Bish', 'Doc', 'Willie', 'Keeper', and many others – all with scorched skin, the burned-out eyes, and the sand in the hair that told of long days in the desert.

The exaggerated public schoolishness of the RAF concealed the fact that the service often attracted grammar school boys, more than the real thing. One apocryphal recruit is supposed to have told his mother he had become a pianist in a brothel rather than confess that he had joined the RAF. In this company, Richard, naturally reserved, would not have been typical. He was following in his father's footsteps. But he shared with the other young pilots a joyous and unashamed love of flying. He was regarded as the 'recco' or reconnaissance expert, adept, in Western Desert parlance, at 'shufti' flights.

Earlier in the year, flying hours were restricted and the squadron had more than enough time for other pursuits, such as swimming in the Mediterranean and fishing from a dhow that had been acquired for the purpose. As the Bish, the son of a general, who acquired his sobriquet from his portly girth rather than excessively correct behaviour, described in some verses he scribbled:

> I lie in the prow of a fishing dhow
> As it heaves to the swell of the sea
> I gaze at the sky where the white gulls fly
> Oh where could I rather now be?

The greatest challenge came from the Khamseen wind which blew in the spring, turning the sky to the colour of a dishcloth and the sun to a streaming ball.

> The men wore their respirators while they groped their way about the camp; the heat and the sand were appalling, the flies were an excruciating nuisance and the wind tore at the tents and ripped the pegs from the parched ground. The monotonous beat of the drumming canvas got on the men's nerves.

But in June the squadron could start a campaign, of a leisurely kind, against Italian targets along the Egyptian coast. At last the war had begun.

In 1934, Italy had created Libya by amalgamating the colonies that it had seized from Turkey in 1911. In the same year, Mussolini invaded Abyssinia; Albania was annexed in the spring of 1939. When Italy joined the Second World War in June 1940, in belated recognition of the Pact of Steel between Mussolini and Hitler, it began to advance into Egypt. There had been a rumour that 211 Squadron would be sent home, to support the war in France, but the threat to British investments in the Middle East made this impossible. Instead, the pilots spent the summer and autumn of 1940 bombing Italian ships, troop concentrations, the water tanks at Buq Buq or, on a good day, Tobruk harbour, which offered the temptingly elusive target of a floating crane.

Tobruk was the target of Richard's first 'op' on 26 October 1940. When he was briefed in the wooden shack that served as an ops room, Squadron Leader James Gordon-Finlayson addressed him, in his characteristic drawl: 'Mr Herbert, you will be going on your first trip with us, I want you to keep in close to me, you are flying number three, and drop your bombs when you see mine go.' They hit the piers and roads. When all the planes had returned, Gordon-Finlayson gave the ultimate praise; it had been 'rather a good show'.

Seen from the sky, the coastline in its beauty reminded Richard's 'observer' (navigator), James Dunnet, of 'the extended wing of a huge blue Emperor butterfly'. It was a gentlemanly affair at this stage; when the fascist air marshal and governor of Libya, Italo Balbo, was accidentally shot down by Italian gunners while attempting to land at El Adem shortly after 211 Squadron had bombed it, they returned to drop a note of condolence. Sometimes the British planes only just squeaked home because of fuel shortages or engine trouble. By November, 211 had become the RAF's most experienced bomber squadron in the Middle East.

When the Italian thrust across the desert stalled, Mussolini, anxious to prove himself as a dictator worthy of the name, invaded Greece. It was a woeful decision. When the diminutive Greek dictator Ioannis Metaxas was confronted by an ultimatum from an Italian envoy, he declared: '*Alors, c'est la guerre.*' (Then it's war.) Despite Il Duce's boasts about Italian preparedness for war, his army was hopelessly under-equipped. The Greeks were fighting for their homeland and put up a bitter resistance. Even the pilots of 211 Squadron, no strangers to hardship and danger, were almost awestruck.

> The things that the Greeks have done & are continuing to do are simply amazing. One would hardly have believed that flesh and blood could achieve such feats.
>
> To scale the mountains & to live on the tops of these mountains would be, in my opinion, no mean task in itself in the bitter cold. But to do so in the face of the enemy, pulling guns, food, ammunition & all the apparatus for war up precipitous mountain tracks & then to oust the enemy & to inflict such tremendous losses is simply incredible.

Unwilling to provoke a German reaction, the Greeks declined the offer of British troops – not that there would have been many to send. But with a hopelessly antiquated air force, they were anxious to receive support from the RAF. 211 Squadron was welcomed with almost overwhelming hospitality in the tavernas of Athens when it arrived at the end of the year. Operating from aerodromes near the capital, it bombed ports such as Valona (Vlorë) and Durazzo (Durrës), packed with ships waiting to unload their supplies; petrol depots were set on fire, munitions dumps blown up, the harbour buildings shattered, ships and barges sunk. To begin with, the headquarters of the British air forces in Greece was the Grande Bretagne Hotel. It was altogether very satisfactory. Although one of the squadron's first tasks on arriving outside Athens had been to employ carpenters to build dummy aircraft to deceive spies as to their strength, they did not miss an opportunity of baiting the German diplomats who remained in the capital until Germany declared war. The Nazi flag hanging outside the embassy was stolen, to be nailed on the wall behind the bar beside the Italian one, taken from Fort Capuzzo in the Western Desert.

Tactics changed when the Greeks called for close air support to its troops in the mountains. In January 1941, 211 arrived at Paramythia. From a scenic point of view, it was

> absolutely magnificent . . . Grand ranges of snow-capped mountains with picturesque little villages perched in seemingly ungettable (?? Spelling) places half-way up some precipice.

Dazzling though a responsive young man might have found the landscape, it made for rotten conditions in the air.

> The very fact of course that Greece is so picturesque makes it most appalling country for flying with mountains covered in cloud rising sheer up to 10,000 feet, snow-storms, rain storms & danger of the aircraft icing up & in fact when I first arrived the climatic conditions were a factor far more to be reckoned with than enemy action. But now the weather has changed & we have really hot weather & blue skies so that unless this war continues until next winter I really don't think I shall need the scarf you have so kindly knitted for me.

In terse language, the Operations Record Book details some close shaves in the missions against the Italians; an aircraft landed with undercarriage retracted (its hydraulic system having been put out of operation by enemy fire) and a smoke-filled cabin when an explosive shell set off a flare. ('Air Observer extinguished fire with his flying boot.') But frontline targets were now barely more than half an hour's flying distance away, and 'excellent' targets could be discovered. 'It was a veritable feast for the bomb aimer,' records the Squadron's Narrative Report on 15 February. 'Our bombs were not wasted.' In any case there was nothing much to worry Richard, who always came back unharmed, or his commanders. This phase of the Balkans campaign was being won.

The squadron lived in tents near the landing ground, ate bully beef off tin plates, grew beards and were as happy as they had been in the desert. Little by way of distraction was provided in the ramshackle mountain village of Paramythia, so the crews would sit on packing cases in the tent that served as their mess and dream up secret weapons; Richard favoured throwing bottles out of the planes over the Italian troops because of the blood-chilling wail that they were supposed to make as they fell to earth.

The situation changed radically in early April 1941. Towards the end of the previous year, Hitler realized that Mussolini, for all his boasting, was getting nowhere. When the Yugoslav government unexpectedly changed in a coup d'état in March 1941, Operation Marita was able to fulfil two objectives, by projecting a million soldiers through Yugoslavia and Bulgaria to invade Greece. On 10 April a German motorized column stormed through the Monastir Gap in the mountains of north-west Greece. The 80 or so operational planes, including obsolete biplanes, defending Greece were now swamped by the Luftwaffe's force of over 700. Admittedly, on the first day of the German invasion, twelve RAF Hurricanes had managed to take on twenty Messerschmitt 109s, shooting down five without loss, but nobody thought such a success rate could be maintained for ever.

The Bristol Blenheim Mk Is flown by 211 Squadron were regarded with affection. They came from the Bristol Aeroplane Company, that post-1920 avatar of the British and Colonial Aeroplane Company which Sir George White had founded in some old tram sheds outside Bristol in 1910. Before the Second World War, the Bristol Blenheim was advertised as the fastest bomber in the world, and around a hundred were given by the British government to Romania and Turkey as part of a charm offensive to persuade them to side with the Allies. (Hitler, however, had something more than charm: Romania went with the Axis, while Turkey chose to be neutral.) They included such innovations as monocoque construction (where the structural load is borne by the steel skin rather than an internal framework) and retractable landing gear, which made them, in short, 'really something to shout about'. The planes handled exceptionally well. 211 Squadron were sufficiently pleased with the aircraft's speed and agility to call themselves the Greyhounds; bars set up at their remote airfields would be known as the Greyhound Inn. But neither the Blenheims' speed nor their armaments – a single Vickers K machine gun in a turret and a machine gun on a wing – were a match for enemy fighters such as the ME109, armed with cannons firing armour-piercing shells in the wings as well as a nose-mounted machine gun.

Earlier in the day, on 13 April, the squadron had carried out two successful raids escorted by Hurricanes, but the fighters were no longer available. So almost the last of the squadron's functional Blenheims, six planes, including Richard's L4819, formed up into the usual bombing pattern – a double V of three ahead and three astern – and hoped for the best. Seven miles from Florina they came down from the clouds and attempted to bomb their target, strafing some German troops for good measure. The 4th Hussars, part of the valiant force of 5,000 British troops in Greece, cheered the spectacle. But they were not the only eyes who noticed it. Circling over the German advance were three ME109s, flown by Feldwebel Herbert Krenz, Unteroffizier Fritz Gromotka and Hauptmann Hans-Joachim Gerlach, all veterans of the Battle of Britain. The Blenheims regrouped into a defensive box formation and headed west, into the setting sun, which illuminated the Messerschmitts while dazzling their pilots. The advantage was not enough. When J. B. Dunnet, who would normally have been flying with Richard, reconstructed the encounter in 1983, the crater left by one of the planes, which crashed near the village of Karia, was still to be seen. The shell of another Blenheim, L1434, rested on a bed of reeds just over the Albanian border. When four of the British planes had been hit, the remaining two – one of them being L4819 – headed east. They were now easy prey. Richard cleared the mountains but was caught as he approached the village of Trigonon; probably out of shells, the 109s could still fire over 1,000 rounds a minute from the machine guns in the engine nacelle. The crew managed to bale out but they were too low for their parachutes to open fully. They fell to earth among forests.

None of the six planes returned to Paramythia. It was the end of 211 Squadron for the time being. Of the eighteen crew, only Flying Officer Godfrey and Flight Sergeant James survived. James was shot down again while being evacuated from Greece, while Godfrey survived the war but died in a mid-air collision shortly afterwards. Of the Germans, Gerlach was shot down the next day but survived to become a prisoner of war; Krenz died when his plane was hit by a Spitfire over the Western Desert in 1942; Gromotka defied the odds, ending the war with twenty-nine victories to his credit. Richard was his second.

Having joined 84 Squadron, Hugh Clutterbuck – Clutter – was killed in the Far East in 1942. Previously he had belonged, as a squadron leader wrote to his mother on 29 July, to 'the most famous Middle East Bomber Squadron, No. 211, and the one or two who still remain will, I know, be grieved to hear that yet another of that dwindling band has gone to join his comrades'. Richard had been in fine company.

Philip Herbert was the eldest of the brothers, born in the middle of the First World War. From Wellington, where he had been head of dormitory, he went to Trinity College, Cambridge, down the road from his father's college of Gonville and Caius. It was while he was at Cambridge that his parents died. He reacted in a way that was typical of his time and class: he hid his feelings as far as possible, believing that he should not allow his own personal grief to cast a shadow on those around him. But people who knew him felt that he 'had been faced too young with responsibility and tragedy'. A lot was repressed.

He enjoyed the country existence that he had known in Devon. Unlike Richard, he did not intend to make a career out of the RAF: at Cambridge he read Agriculture and Land Management which, given that he did not have his own landed estates to manage (unlike some of his contemporaries on the course), would have suited him for a life as a land agent. He left Caius in 1937 with a BA and a Certificate of Proficiency in Estate Management. It would have provided an eminently respectable, worthwhile if not scintillating career, ideally suited to someone whose greatest pleasures derived from the countryside. He was on the way to developing his career in the Duchy of Cornwall when war broke out. A photograph survives of him in a walled garden, perhaps belonging to a country rectory, with a dog of uncertain breed at his feet. It was his natural habitat.

Like his father, Philip rode horses: like him, too, he had a bad riding accident. It was not fatal, but broke his leg so badly that it had to be amputated. This was after he had been commissioned as a pilot in 1940. It was typical of the Herbert determination that he did not let this disability prevent him from flying. Families of this stamp did not make a fuss: they stoically made the best of what fate had dealt them. He was soon back in the air.

Although Philip followed his father in many things, he was not a natural warrior. While his two younger brothers got into the armed services as soon as they could, he, as we have seen, did not become a pilot until 1940. And even then, his chosen branch of activity was vital but not aggressive. He became a member of the RAF's No. 1 Photographic Reconnaissance Unit. It was a job for a contemplative man, who did not mind his own company during flights that were prolonged with specially fitted fuel tanks, to allow penetration in depth over enemy territory. One reconnaissance pilot likened the routine to commuting to an office. The planes did not carry arms; this put the possibility of joining in a fight beyond the temptation of the hot-headed. The importance put on reconnaissance can be seen from the fact that Spitfires, specially adapted, were used for it; painted light green and flying at altitude, they were fast and difficult to spot. But that did not mean that the work was not dangerous. When they disappeared, over enemy territory or the sea, there was no one to say what had happened.

Reconnaissance from aeroplanes had begun during the First World War. The Royal Flying Corps proved its worth even as the opening shots were being fired at the Battle of Mons: initially, Sir John French and his staff were incredulous of the reports brought back by its pilots of the astonishing German troop numbers, but he soon came to accept their veracity, and he appreciated the aviators' help in observing enveloping movements which might have trapped the British Expeditionary Force. His first dispatch of 7 September 1914 acknowledged his debt to 'the admirable work done by the Royal Flying Corps . . . They have furnished me with the most complete and accurate information, which has been of incalculable value in the conduct of operations.' To begin with, the process of taking photographs was cumbersome; it required an observer, in finger-freezing temperatures, to lean over the side of the aircraft, perhaps in a gale, and operate a camera using five-inch by four-inch glass plates, mounted in mahogany frames. But technology improved in line with the demand, and by 1918 a third of all Royal Flying Corps planes were engaged in photographic reconnaissance.

After the war, support for photographic reconnaissance, as for every other branch of the armed services, fell off. It took the persistence of an amateur, Sidney Cotton, to revive its military application in the late 1930s. Cotton was, wrote his *Times* obituarist on 21 February 1969, 'certainly one of the most remarkable men of his generation'. Born on a cattle station in Queensland in 1894, he came to England and served in the Royal Naval Air Service during the First World War. That was the beginning of 'his long, frequently hazardous, but invariably fruitful association with aeroplanes' – often combined with his other great love, photography. As diplomatic relations with Germany deteriorated, he undertook almost theatrically cloak-and-dagger flights over Germany, in a converted civilian Lockheed 12A aeroplane belonging to his Aircraft Operating Company, three Leika cameras disguised from prying eyes by being encased in the shell of an old leather suitcase. Once war had begun, he was given the rank of squadron leader (which, not being a natural conformist, he accepted reluctantly) and responsibility for two Spitfires, based, as the Aircraft Operating Company had been, at Heston aerodrome. From these beginnings, photographic reconnaissance grew to be an essential tool of the Allied war effort, collecting evidence of enemy ports, manu-facturing centres and German defences.

It was a sign of the authorities' confidence in Cotton that the Spit-fires could be spared. Before Cotton's ideas held sway, the army relied on a squadron of Blenheim IV bombers to perform long-range aerial reconnaissance. But they were slow. If they flew too high, the photo-graphic equipment iced up; if they flew lower, at a better altitude for taking a detailed photograph, they made a vulnerable target for enemy fighters. By the spring of 1940, however, a specially modified Spitfire was in production, with an extra fuel tank under one wing to increase range and two cameras under the other. Forty of these adapted planes were made.

Reconnaissance flying did not suit every airman. Whereas bomber crews talked to each other constantly over their headsets, and fighter pilots had the adrenalin rush of the chase, pilots like Philip Herbert flew long, solitary missions, without the prospect of reaction-quick-ening excitement. But although only in his mid-twenties, Philip was still older than many of the RAF's pilots, and he was temperamen-tally calmer than most. He could handle the loneliness. He came from a stoic breed.

Photo reconnaissance (PR, as it was known) could identify the position of ships – most famously, the Bismarck near Bergen – spy on troop movements and assess the effectiveness of bombing raids. Occasionally the results were spectacular; by studying a dot on a photograph of a country house near Wurzburg, it was concluded that the Germans were developing their own radar system: this inspired a daring raid by paratroopers to seize some of the equipment and destroy the rest. For the most part, though, results were achieved through patient analysis, after careful, thorough and cool-headed overflying of the target by pilots like Philip. To spare men for the front line, the WAAF might provide women to do the analysis, such as the young artist Dorothy Colles who, to her evident astonish-ment, was trained in the techniques of deciphering aerial photographs in 1941. Billeted in a 'semidetached subbubban villa' at Stanmore, in the home of a 'grandmotherly' couple who 'talk about "this dreadful war" with a kind of shocked puzzlement', she was unable to tell her parents what she was doing, but nevertheless called on them as a resource. In her letter of 16 February 1941, she sounds slightly rattled by what was expected of her.

> Please would you keep a watch on the Times and cut out & send me articles of any kind dealing with Germany or the occupied countries or industry or military matters or new weapons in any belligerent country. Or neutral journalists views. It is absolutely essential to be 'au fait' with everything. I shall order a Telegraph soon as possible. If you could let me have anything special out of the Sphere too I would be very grateful. I cannot tell you what we will do exactly, I don't know yet & when I do I'll not be allowed to; but general knowledge is so important. I think one would call it the primary qualification. The scope of one's necessary learning is amazing. I can foresee some most involved mathematical calculations ahead of me! Also naval information is of great importance. I shall have to get a book on spotting ships. There is quite a good 2/- one some publisher has brought out I believe.

Colles was later posted to the Middle East with No. 2 PRU and ended the war with the rank of flight officer.

After Heston was bombed, the No.1 PRU moved, in 1941, to RAF Benson in Oxfordshire. 'The camp itself looked very grim and bleak, as we soon found that all RAF stations do,' observed a young WAAF who arrived to operate processing equipment in the course of the year. 'Not a tree in sight.' But the dreamy Oxfordshire countryside, with its ancient villages and watercress beds, must have appealed to Philip. It is fitting that death should have come, not in the air, but as he returned home to land in these green and pleasant surroundings. His plane swerved on touching down and turned over; Philip was thrown out and broke his skull. He died two days later, on 26 January 1942. He was buried in the churchyard of Theale, his grandmother's village, in Berkshire.

The youngest of the Herbert brothers was Gerald. With his fair hair and fine features, he was photographed looking heavenward, determination on his face, RAF wings on his breast, his cap at the correct angle of jauntiness; he was remembered at Wellington as 'a dashing, skilful rugger forward, though he did not look it. It was his clear course to follow his father and brothers into the RAF.' After Wellington, he spent a year training in Canada. He received an emergency commission as a pilot officer on probation in December 1941. The emergency had been caused by the loss of so many British pilots during the Battle of Britain that summer. When 158 Bomber Squadron was formed on 14 February 1942, he went to Driffield, in the East Riding of Yorkshire, to join it.

It was a critical moment in the development of Britain's bombing capability. As yet, little more than 10 per cent of the RAF's planes were bombers. Precision bombing of individual military targets had not been particularly effective, and the morale of the bomber crews was low. There were voices within the armed forces that suggested bombers would be better employed supporting the army and navy, rather than pursuing the strategic role of destroying the infrastructure and manufacturing capability of German cities. But by the month when 158 Squadron came into being, Arthur Harris had replaced the lacklustre Sir Richard Peirse as Commander-in-Chief, Bomber Command. A gruff, difficult man, Harris had an unshakeable conviction that bombing could cripple the German war effort. In May 1942, the 158 Squadron took part in the first Thousand Bomber raid, against Cologne. Before Harris, Britain's force of bombers was so dated that, when the *Scharnhorst*, *Gneisenau* and *Prinz Eugen* broke out of Brest harbour in February 1942, they were attacked, suicidally, by Swordfish biplanes. 158 Squadron was to benefit from the improvement in equipment that Harris pushed forward. In the summer of 1942, their two-engined Wellingtons were replaced by four-engined Halifaxes.

The memory of the Handley-Page Halifax has been overshadowed by its more glamorous rival, the Lancaster; Lancasters could carry a greater bomb load, fly further and operate at higher altitudes. Even Bomber Harris was among the Halifax's critics, declaring, with characteristic lack of charm, that: 'One Lancaster is to be preferred to four Halifaxes. Halifaxes are an embarrassment . . . The Halifax suffers four times the casualties for a given bomb tonnage when compared to the Lancaster.' It was, however, the better aircraft for saturation bombing of a specific target, as opposed to scattering bombs over a wider area. There were also advantages for the crew. The fuselage was rather less cramped, which made it more comfortable to fly and easier to escape from in an emergency. As skipper, Gerald Herbert led a crew of seven – himself as pilot, with the flight engineer behind him at a lower level, checking on the fuel and tweaking performance in front of an array of dials and different-coloured knobs. The navigator sat at his desk, with the wireless operator at his instruments in the front of the plane. Bubbles in the nose and tail contained gunners, as did a turret on the aircraft's back. They could squeeze their way around the plane, stooping to avoid the unreasonable number of sharp metal corners that seemed to protrude at head height. Steel, steel, and more steel, unadorned except for a coating of black or glaucous paint, set the character of the space. Except for the leather of their seats, there were few comforts (unless a lavatory can be so described).

Gerald must have wished the Halifax had a longer range when, on 7 November 1942, he was forced to touch down at Ossington in Nottinghamshire, having run out of fuel. Eight days later, after attacking Genoa, he was again unable to reach home, the crew having to bale out over Somerset; his Halifax crashed near the coal-mining town of Radstock.

On 14 February 1943, eleven crews took off for Cologne. It was the day of 158 Squadron's first anniversary. They were now flying from Rufforth, to the west of York, where they had been based since 6 November 1942. Gerald and his crew rumbled across the airfield in an old bus, reached their Halifax DT696 and climbed in through the door on the underside of the flank.

It was shortly after six in the evening. One after another the propellers spun into action. Then the chocks beneath the wheels were removed, and the heavily laden plane lumbered down the grass runway, heaving itself into the air at 6.16 p.m. Within a few minutes it got into trouble. The port engines failed. Gerald reduced the weight of the heavily laden craft by jettisoning the bomb load near the village of Appleton Roebuck, but this was not enough to prevent it stalling. The plane crashed among the ploughed fields of this prime, flat arable country near Stillingfleet at 6.30 p.m. Halifaxes had a good record for allowing their crews to bale out or otherwise survive losses – nearly 30 per cent, compared to the Lancaster's 11 per cent. But nothing could help the crew of DT696, all seven of whom were killed. Gerald's name was carved on the same headstone as his brother's at Theale.

The War Seemed Very Far Away

⊸ RICHARD GILLETT ⊷

From the beginning of the twentieth century, Bridge House, once the home of the Radford family, owners of the gorge, restorers of the church and bringers of a water supply to the village, was let out. Having built his own house, Squire Tom Radford continued the arrangement. In 1913, the then tenant Mrs Bromwich had the misfortune to find herself in the newspapers, as a result of legal proceedings brought against her by William Usherwood, a draper. She had ordered three dresses at a cost of £23 10s, and had not paid for them. Mrs Bromwich stumped up eventually, pleading that her daughter had been unwell, but it must have set tongues wagging. Muttering resumed when Bridge House came to be occupied by Mrs Margaret Gillett. Note the use of her own Christian name, rather than that of her husband: Mrs Gillett was divorced. It was not a state that Lydford was used to.

Margaret's ten-year marriage to Aubrey Scott Gillett had begun at Cockington Parish Church, in Devon, just after war broke out in 1914. Gillett was a doctor. In 1916, he sailed back from Malta (known as the Nurse of the Mediterranean for its twenty-seven hospitals) as a 2nd lieutenant in the Royal Army Medical Corps: presumably he had been helping tend soldiers like Charlie Berry and Archie Huggins in the disaster of Gallipoli. Their only child, Richard Hamilton Gillett, had been born the previous year. His middle name paid tribute to Aubrey's friend from medical school, Douglas Hamilton. In the last days of 1908, Aubrey and Hamilton had left King's College Hospital together, catching a tube to their respective homes. When Hamilton got out at Oxford Circus, he realized he had taken Aubrey's ticket; he hared alongside the train as it pulled out of the platform, collided with the start of the tunnel, and was caught by the front carriages and dragged onwards, between the train and the tunnel wall. Finger-marks showed how he had desperately tried to get a purchase on the wall and claw himself free. His body was found twenty-five yards from the platform.

After the First World War, Aubrey practised in Torquay: perhaps it gave his wife, born in London, the affection for Devon which led her to take Bridge House. But the valetudinarians of an affluent, slow-moving seaside resort did not offer Dr Scott Gillett the professional stimulation that he craved. By 1923, his consulting rooms were in Wimpole Street, the epicentre of the medical establishment, while the family lived in the fading gentility of Westbourne Park, near Paddington Station and Hyde Park.

Richard was nine when his parents divorced in 1924. His father had set off down a new avenue in his professional as well as his domestic life, becoming a police surgeon. In 1924 he was sufficiently well respected to advise the Home Office pathologist Sir Bernard Spilsbury on the contents of the first 'murder bag', a leather case to be taken to crime scenes. Until then, no special measures were taken to preserve evidence from contamination; it was simply picked up by hand and, if small enough, stuffed into an envelope. When Spilsbury went to examine the remains of a woman, gruesomely dismembered and boiled down in a bungalow on The Crumbles at Eastbourne, he had been appalled to see officers rolling up their sleeves and throwing chunks of human flesh into buckets as though they were at a fish market. The idea of the murder bag was that it would provide Scotland Yard detectives with the basic tools of the forensics trade: fingerprint apparatus, test tubes, magnifying glasses, rubber gloves and apron, scissors, forceps, disinfectant, towel and soap, tape measure, compass for recording the position of the objects found. In the 1930s, Aubrey and his new wife, Lilian Smout from Lancashire, moved to the Caribbean, where he was appointed to be a member of the Executive Council of the Virgin Islands; he later occupied a similar position on St Lucia — all the while continuing his work as a forensic specialist on murders that were no whit less colourful for being in the West Indies.

It took Margaret rather longer to build a new life. Maintenance payments had been set at £400 a year for her, and £100 for Richard. Only after she had been divorced for nearly twenty years did Margaret remarry a schoolmaster called Guy MacKarness; it was then wartime, the spring of 1943, and the wedding took place in Bristol. Richard was not there; although he was given a month's war leave on 21 April that year, he could only spend it in India, transport being impossible to find during wartime and the distances being, in any case, too great to get home. Richard was by now a captain in the Indian Army, seconded from the Baluch Regiment to the 152nd Indian Parachute Battalion. The number is misleading; the 152nd Battalion was the first and only parachute battalion of Indian troops under the British Empire. They had to be exceptionally brave men to survive the training. Richard would have needed nerves of steel – or the appearance of them – to lead a company in such a battalion. It was regarded as a daredevil outfit. Events were to show that both he and his men would live up to their reputation.

While his father had gone to public school in Oxford (St Edward's), Richard followed his uncle Edward Scott Gillett to Lancing College on the edge of the Sussex Downs, catching health-giving breezes from the South Coast. He was appointed House Captain in 1934, the year he gained his School Certificate, and was a corporal in the Officer Training Corps. On leaving, he was accepted at Sandhurst but either decided against going or did not complete his course there. Was he ill? Did he join his father in the Caribbean? All we know is that in March 1940 he presented himself to the 153rd Officer Cadet Training Unit of the Grenadier Guards for training. After six months and twenty-two days, he left as a 2nd lieutenant, and was posted to the 7th Battalion of the 10th Baluch Regiment in India. This may not have seemed hugely exciting, as far as the immediate prospect of seeing action was concerned. The 10th Baluch Regiment had a proud reputation as the first Indian regiment to fight the Germans in the First World War, but in 1940 the subcontinent seemed safe enough; Japan had not yet entered the war and would not do so until December 1941. India was sending troops to fight in the Mediterranean and North Africa rather than keeping them at home, in readiness for

23. Unloading timber from a train in France. Huge quantities were required to line trenches and tunnels, as well as to build camps, hospitals, railways and bridges. So Edward Whitford's knowledge as the manager of a sawmill was in demand.

24. Cavalry move up to Monchy-le-Preux after the battle, past a hastily dug trench. Edward Whitford was one of the infantry killed during the frontal assault on this heavily protected village, as part of the Battle of Arras in 1917.

25. Sydney Carline's 'Among the Anti-aircraft Bursts at 20,000 Feet Above the Alps: A British Air Squadron Crossing the Anglo-Austrian Line Along the River Piave, Italy, 1918'. Harry Lake died crossing the Piave with the 2nd Warwickshires.

26. Italian soldiers enjoy an al fresco meal near the river Piave. It is difficult to imagine British Tommies being quite so domestic in their arrangements.

27. A mule is tied to a frame to be tested for glanders, the infectious equine disease, at Salonica. Jim Stephens, a groom in civilian life, ended the war in the Labour Corps, working with horses, mules and camels in Salonica, among other places in the Balkans, Turkey and the Middle East.

28. Swathed in its Union Jack, Lydford war memorial, unveiled on the Sunday before Christmas 1921. Only two cars in the village in those days.

29. (*above left*) Richard Herbert: shot down, aged 21, in 1941. (*above centre*) Philip Herbert: killed, aged 26, in 1942. (*above right*) Gerald Herbert: his plane crashed in 1943, when he was 20.

30. (*left*) Four members of 211 Squadron chat to a boy on a donkey in the wild valley of Paramythia, near the Albanian border in Northern Greece. Richard Herbert, otherwise known as Herby, is second from the right.

31. (*below*) 211 Squadron's airstrip at Paramythia. They lived close to nature.

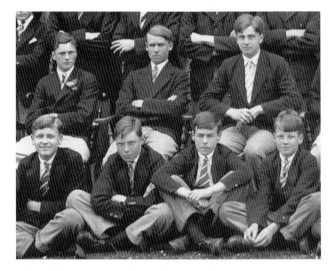

32. Richard Gillett, the son of a doctor who specialized in police forensics, at Lancing College, c.1935, second from left, front row.

33. (*above*) The early days of 152 (Indian) Parachute Battalion: something of the spirit of the Wild West.

34. (*left*) 152 (Indian) Parachute Battalion during training, c.1942. The early days of parachuting in India were extremely hazardous. Captain Richard Gillett led the first operation, against Hur tribesmen in the Sindh Desert, on 1 June 1942.

35. (*above*) Thomas Hennell's 'A Dutch Concrete Strong Point at Nijmegen, 1944'. Jack Bickle was shot in an orchard near Arnhem, after crossing the river Waal at Nijmegen.

36. (*right*) Betty Radford's mother, Crystal, strongly opposed her marriage to the carpenter Louis Screech and agreed only when Betty was dying of tuberculosis. So many of the young men whom the squire's wife might have regarded as more appropriate suitors were killed during the First World War.

37. (*left*) A cheerful Nick Taylor as a young helicopter pilot in training at Dartmouth Royal Naval College.

38. (*below*) A copy of the church kneeler at Port Stanley commemorating Nick Taylor, the first casualty of the Falklands War in 1982, whose Sea Harrier was shot down over Goose Green.

39. A padre at Nick Taylor's grave at Goose Green. Following military tradition, Nick Taylor was buried where he fell.

40. Andrew Kelly, proud member of the Parachute Regiment, who died in Iraq on 6 May 2003. It had been his life's ambition to join the Paras. He died in an accident at 3 PARA's camp near the Iranian border. This picture was taken on his own disposable camera and developed after his death.

regional campaigns. The Baluch regiment expected to see action in the Western Desert or elsewhere in the Middle East.

If Richard's experience was anything like that of John Randle, going out to the 7/10 Baluch Regiment as a young 2nd lieutenant on the *Highland Chieftain* and *Windsor Castle* via South Africa, he would have found his arrival to be 'astonishing'. After 'living like animals' on board ship, he was shown his bearer, and soon learnt the cry of *ko'i hai* – is anybody there? 'There always was someone there.'

Drinks were brought, dinner served, time languorously killed with tennis, billiards, fishing and various types of shooting: duck, peacock for Christmas dinner, even tiger. War did not prevent the Saturday night dance at the club, and Richard would still have had to equip himself with an expensive mess kit; perhaps too a light sola topi made of straw, if he wanted to avoid the weight of the pith version, externally no different from that worn by Gordon of Khartoum (unfortunately, straw topis collapsed with a crunch if sat upon by mistake). He learnt to avoid snakes, check under his pillow for spiders, put mosquito nets around his bed, place an extra fly sheet over the top of his tent to mitigate the worst of the heat, treat sunburn with lumps of cow fat, adjust himself to the peculiarities of a canvas folding bath and accept that death from 'undiagnosed fever' could visit people he knew at twenty-four hours' notice. Graves were kept permanently dug to receive those for whom India, war or no war, proved too much, coffins being weighted with stones during the monsoon season.

He learnt Urdu, though his command of the language was never more than 'elementary', according to his service papers. But he knew enough to communicate with the men, who were forbidden to speak to officers in English (on the basis that this would imply the officer had been unable to master Urdu).

By September 1941, Richard was employed in a training role. Next month, the formation of an Indian airborne brigade offered the chance of something more lively. He volunteered. It was a good move. In the 152nd Battalion of the 50th Indian Parachute Brigade – a battalion of Indian troops with British officers – he was immediately promoted to temporary captain, commanding A company. If he was in search of adrenalin, that was provided too; starting from scratch, parachuting in India was, according to one of the brigade's medical officers Frederic G. Neild (known as Eric), largely self-taught. Information on the subject was 'meagre in the extreme and on our side almost non-existent'. The immediate response to the risk assessment was to order two coffins for the mortuary. They would find that they needed many more than two.

To begin with, the only aircraft available were three twin-engined Vickers Valentia biplanes, built in 1923 and known, affectionately, as Pigs. Pilot and observer occupied an open cockpit at the front of the plane, while a 'stick' of ten jumpers waited to jump through a hole cut in the underside of the fuselage. Despite their antiquated appearance, the Valentias were not wholly to be dismissed. They were remembered as the only transports available in the early days of the Western Desert campaign; and while their cruising speed may only have been eighty-five miles an hour, this meant that they could take off and land on a very short runway, and circle over the Air Landing School outside New Delhi without having to bank at an uncomfortably steep angle. 'Jumping in the early days was quite an event.' Whenever it occurred, everyone at brigade headquarters downed tools, leapt into cars and drove out, through the squatter village, to the Dropping Zone (DZ). The DZ 'was an enormous expanse of ploughed plain, dotted with shrub bush and desiccated cattle. It was a typical part of the main plain of India, which someone once summed up as miles and miles of nothing at all with goats eating it.' Spectators would group themselves near the ambulance; the medical officer would go to the centre of the DZ and join the instructor, controlling the jumpers through a tannoy. Progress was not helped by the language difficulty: most Indian troops did not speak English, the instructors knew no Urdu. Nothing was known about the health implications of parachuting, and young medical officers were told to find out as they went along. The 'possibilities of injury were endless'.

At one point, the death rate reached one in every hundred jumps. There was a problem with correctly packing the parachutes, which could result in the dreaded Roman candle: spectators watched in horror the struggles of the trooper as he tugged on the parachute's lines in a vain effort to make it open. This had a depressing effect on the battalion's spirits, so whenever morale 'was wobbly, Brigade Headquarters did what was known as a "snobstick" when all the officers of the headquarters jumped together'. Matters improved after the commander of the Parachute Training School at Ringway, Manchester's civil airport, came out for three months. Even so, the brigade would not set out on exercises without a sufficient supply of firewood so that bodies could be burnt quickly.

The very first of the brigade's active parachute drops – indeed, the first parachute operation in the Far East – was led by Richard Gillett. It took place on 1 June 1942, over the inhospitable Sindh Desert. The object was to suppress the Hur tribesmen who, in conditions of severe drought, had begun to derail trains between Karachi and Lahore, looting and killing passengers. As yet, it was not possible to parachute by night, and the slow, daytime approach of the ancient Valentias gave the tribesmen ample opportunity to fade away into the scrubby sand dunes. Two stringent months were spent scouring the desert to no avail, other than to prove the resilience of Richard and his men. It was one of few airborne operations ever carried out by the Indian Parachute Brigade.

By now, something more significant than the suppression of banditry was in prospect. Six months earlier, Japan had attacked Pearl Harbor, declaring war on both the United States and Britain. Within weeks its armies had flooded like an irresistible tide into Burma, forcing the few British defenders to retreat across the Chindwin river and through the jungle into India. They seized Hong Kong. The fortress of Singapore fell on 15 February 1942. China, also attacked, was in disarray. The speed of the advance was mesmerizing. Even India, the greatest of British imperial possessions, would have been threatened if the sheer pace of the Japanese push into Burma had not forced it to pause to regroup. The pause lasted two years. In late 1943, General Mutaguchi Renya persuaded the Japanese High Command to press on, in the belief that a strike on India would constitute a decisive and profitable blow, at a time when the conquests of the early months of the war were increasingly threatened by the naval supremacy and industrial muscle of the United States.

The conflict had turned Delhi into an important air junction that was increasingly crowded with troops. To the relief of the authorities tasked with policing the frequent fights that took place between the 151st Battalion and the Americans, the brigade moved to Campbellpore, on a sandy plain in the north-west tip of the Punjab, beside an offshoot of the Murree Hills. There they trained for no fewer than eight airborne operations. But none of them transpired, and by the early months of 1944 the paratroopers were feeling left out of a war that had, in their sector, produced one disaster after another. On the cancellation of the last proposed operation, they were given the sop of two months' advanced jungle training in Assam, prior to being withdrawn to southern India to form part of a new division. Stores had to be reorganized to fit mules rather than aeroplanes. Officers discovered that the valises in which they carried their belongings were fitted with previously unnoticed rings by which they could be attached to saddles. Fishing rods and shotguns were packed. Men who were under par, or had their legs in plaster, looked forward to the trip as an excellent time to recuperate. They took the mess silver but not a single steel helmet or roll of barbed wire.

In due course, the cavalcade set off on a leisurely train journey that took it 1,500 miles across the northern plains. As they crossed the river Ganges, the Hindu soldiers threw coins for good luck, and children scampered along the footpath of the bridge attempting to catch them. They reached a riverhead where stores were manhandled on to flat-bottomed river boats, with no attention being paid to a dead body that lay on the sandbank, perhaps to be washed off at the next high tide. After a twelve-hour journey, the impedimenta were offloaded and reloaded again, this time on a Mississippi showboat-style paddle steamer. Then came another stretch of railway, past signal boxes manned by disgruntled Americans. Tea was made from the hot water in the engine's boiler. At Dimapur, they detrained at night, making their way as best they could, with baggage, to a transit camp where the way to the officers' mess was lined with phallic stone lingams. The last forty miles were covered by bus. The road climbed steeply through interminable hairpin bends. Packed like dates in a box, the passengers felt 'very car-sick, as there appeared to be no question of the driver slowing at corners. We gathered that it had been a case of the survival of the fittest and that the surviving drivers were pretty good.'

The destination was Kohima. Just before reaching it, the vehicles climbed the saddle of a ridge at 5,000 feet to reveal 'the most magnificent panorama eastward as range after range of green jungle-clad hills unfolded themselves before our eyes'. After a final ten-mile tramp on foot, the brigade installed itself at Chakabama, amid the Garden of Eden that was Nagaland.

> We used to watch with much amazement the local inhabitants, Nagas, who had precious little on except for many bangles, passing in single file carrying loads, their progress assisted by a series of rhythmic snorts. It was so peaceful and the war seemed very far away.

They were downcast to hear that the eccentric and unstoppable General Orde Wingate had led his Chindits – named after the mythical lions guarding Burmese temples – in a parachute landing, deep into the Burmese jungle. The Indian Parachute Brigade had been training for so long for precisely this sort of operation, and now the excitement had gone to another unit. Wingate had had to argue hard for permission to go, overcoming objections about the lack of transport planes by using gliders. But his mission soon lost its original purpose. Already, General Slim had sufficient knowledge of Japanese movements to cancel his offensive plans and put his army into a defensive posture, leaving the Chindits' deep penetration unsupported. The Indian Parachute Brigade were not to know this. However agreeable conditions may have been in Nagaland, there seemed to be very little going on.

On 14 March Richard, now Major Gillett, and the 152nd Battalion went to take up a position towards Imphal at a road junction called Sheldon's Corner which covered some tracks to the river Chindwin. The base comprised two areas of high ground: Point 7378 and a hill known as Gammon, which the 4th Maratha Light Infantry had begun work on. Richard's A Company made its home in a hideout to the rear, on the slope of Badger Hill. Their job was to stock the hideout and clear a mule track down to the road that had become overgrown. Tanks were dug and lined with tarpaulins to catch water; it was intended to bring the whole of the Sheldon's Corner position up to scratch by the end of the month. Over the next two days the battalion, according to the war diary report, 'worked all out on the defences' – and just as well. Early on the morning of the 19th, a patrol from Sheldon's Corner had an unpleasant surprise. It spotted a party of around 200 Japanese approaching Point 7378. This was obviously the advance guard of a much larger force. Nobody, however, realized how much larger. A battalion would have been bad enough, but it was later realized that there were two whole divisions. The question was: Where had they come from?

> If 'I[ntelligence]' was correct they should be some hundred miles on the other side of the Chindwin. The situation was roughly comparable to a Londoner being told that the Germans had appeared in Tonbridge, and not by parachute either. We were flabbergasted.

It was the first intimation that the Japanese had crossed the Chindwin. They had done so in force, advancing through what the British had assumed to be impenetrable jungle.

So far General Mutaguchi's plan had worked brilliantly. While the Nagas stayed loyal to the British, another local tribe with whom they had differences, the Kuki, had been bribed to go over to the Japanese. The Kuki betrayed all the knowledge they had about a series of military posts known as V-Force, established to keep a watch on the jungle; V-Force was quickly overrun, its listeners unable to pass back any warning. A feint in Arakan, 250 miles to the south, had precisely the effect intended, deceiving the British into believing that this represented the main Japanese thrust. Instead, the plan was to appear without warning and roll into the Imphal Plain, a verdant tapestry of paddy fields, plantain trees and lakes that represented the only expanse of flat land – measuring 40 miles by 20 – in that mountainous region. Having gathered his forces at Imphal, Mutaguchi intended to march on Delhi.

The 170 men of C Company, holding Point 7378, were quickly surrounded. Unfortunately, the two positions were too far apart to support each other. The soldiers on Gammon could only watch the attack unfold, unable to influence events. Richard led A Company along by a path that had previously been scouted, intending to draw some of the Japanese sting by launching a flank attack, but it was difficult to find the way through the jungle at night. He arrived at the end of the battle; the sheer numbers of the enemy, attacking in close formation and at enormous cost to themselves, had proved overwhelming. C Company's resistance had been so ferocious that the Japanese thought they were facing five times their number, and suffered 450 casualties. The denouement, however, is described in a Japanese regimental memoir.

> By mid morning the enemy's fire slackened considerably. Suddenly from the top of the hill, a small group of about 20 men charged down towards us, firing and shouting in a counter attack. However, between us was a wide ravine which they had been unable to see, and of those who were still alive some fell into it in their rush onwards while the rest had no choice but to surrender. A few escaped. At the very top of the position an officer appeared in sight, put a pistol to his head and shot himself in full view of everyone below. Our men fell silent, deeply impressed by such a brave act.

About 11 a.m., a wireless message was received from the only British officer left alive, followed by silence. The rest of the battalion fell back.

At Chakabama, the brigade had settled down as usual on the night of the 15th, expecting to be given instructions for the next phase of jungle exercises at dawn. Instead, officers were woken at midnight, and told to meet the commanding officer in the bamboo 'basha' which served as a mess. By the dim light of a Petromax lantern, they were told that Japanese forces had been spotted 175 miles south of Imphal. They had to pack up the camp – not an easy thing to do in darkness – and move off in six hours. But no orders to leave came that day. The staff of the 14th Army and 4 Corps had been taken as much by surprise as anyone else, and the precipitous roads and narrow

jungle tracks were already congested with troops being rushed into
position. Three days were passed in suspense. On the 18th, the brigade marched to Kohima. Those who then drove down to Imphal
found it was hastily being readied for war. A couple of officers studying their maps were interrupted by a bellow of laughter from the
robust second in command, Colonel B. E. Abbott – aka Abbo – with
the comment: 'It's a damned good thing you two bachelors have
brought your shotguns and fishing-rods, otherwise you will have
bugger all to do in your spare time: just look!' On the mountain road
beneath them a convoy of nuns, nurses and other women was being
evacuated. With the 152nd Battalion at Sheldon's Corner, the remaining two battalions of the 50th Indian Parachute Brigade were ordered
to consolidate at Sangshak. They drove into the jungle, marching the
last four miles, which took them 2,000 feet up. They got there just as
the attack on Sheldon's Corner was developing.

Sangshak occupies a pear-shaped plateau, on the western slope of
a mountain of 5,500 feet. Brigadier Maxwell Hope-Thompson, preferring to be known as Tim, to which the prefix of Tiger was
inevitably added, chose his ground: an area about 800 yards long and
400 yards wide, above the Naga village (whose inhabitants wisely
made themselves scarce). At the western end of the 'defensive box'
stood a small Baptist church; a narrow, slippery road ran along the
flank of the mountain to Sheldon's Corner. All around was a dense
growth of rhododendrons, amid which the enemy could be completely concealed. Scattered units of gunners and Field Ambulance
had somehow been brought in from the jungle, although the only
transport available consisted of two jeeps. That night, with imper-
turbable sang froid, officers in silk pyjamas and dressing gowns – packed
for what they had expected to be something of a jolly – made their
last inspections, before what they knew would be an attack the next
day. The brigadier himself slept in the open air, beneath a tarpaulin
in case it rained. But urgent preparations were made at first light to
prepare what defences they could. Tripwires connected to booby
traps were erected, killing zones agreed, gun sightings taken, ammunition and other stores hauled up from the river bed where they had
previously been left, and the dumps fired.

To speed our actions, we watched the Japanese appearing from over the hill down the road from Ukhrul. It was unbelievable – we might have been watching a stage play from the dress circle. They were about two or three miles away. We were curious to know what was going to happen, as we had 15th Battery of the 9th Mountain Regiment IA, commanded by Major J. P. Lock, a typical mountain gunner if ever there was one. He was a large burly fellow, with the appearance of a rugger player, wearing the most ridiculous little fore and aft forage cap and puffing contentedly at a pipe. He was in no hurry and waited until the whole length of the road was full of Japs before he let them have it. We saw the little white puffs bursting all along that road. Lock beamed – his only regret was that the guns had no shrapnel and were only firing H[igh]E[xplosive]. He said that it was the best day's shoot of his life. It was to be almost his last, as he was killed a few days later.

The stand made by C Company at Point 7378 had bought time. Richard and the rest of the 152nd Battalion arrived roughly when the Japanese did. They were assigned the western perimeter, around the church, to defend. It was already getting dark so nothing could be done until the next morning. 'As soon as it was really dark,' the battalion commander, Lieutenant Colonel Paul 'Hoppy' Hopkinson, observed in his war diary report, 'the Japanese started to attack and kept these attacks up continuously throughout the night regardless of casualties. They made no attempt at surprise, using lights to aid direction and shouting to each other.' He presumed that this astonishing tactic was designed to discover the line of the perimeter. For a while, the battle scene was lit up by the flames of the Naga village, put to the torch. When morning came, the enemy faded into the jungle, leaving Hopkinson to inspect the state of the defences. It was far from perfect. There was no barbed wire, few picks or shovels, and it had been impossible to dig some trenches deeper than three feet because of the impenetrable volcanic rock that lay underneath; there was now no time to blast them deeper with explosives. It was difficult even to find enough soil to fill sandbags. Richard's end of the site was particularly exposed. While the men worked to improve the position, they became targets for snipers, hidden in the heavy canopy of the trees. Fortunately it rained that day, allowing the brigade to collect water in its mess tins – otherwise, they would have gone without.

Water was one of the supplies that Hopkinson hoped would be dropped by air. When air drops did come, the consequences were similar to those that tormented the 1st Airborne Division at Arnhem: most of them fell into the hands of the enemy, who were just as pleased to receive them as the defenders would have been. All the planes but one avoided anti-aircraft fire by flying too high for accuracy; the exception was one whose crew had trained with the brigade and was determined that the soldiers would receive at least their load. It was quite literally a lifeline.

The mules were also becoming a worry. It was no longer possible to feed or water them; but without them, the mortars and guns would be stuck at Sangshak in the event of a withdrawal. It was difficult enough to bury the human dead: those who had already been buried were being disinterred by the Japanese shelling, and outside the perimeter lay many Japanese corpses. It was a horrific scene. The last thing that the brigade needed was a pile of dead mules, shot to prevent them falling into the hands of the enemy. The mules were eventually driven into the jungle.

Rumours of a relief column coming from Imphal proved erroneous; indeed it would not have been possible for one to make its way along the mountain roads in time, even if an available force had existed. Hope-Thompson and Hopkinson concluded that the brigade would have to fight it out for as long as possible, delaying the Japanese advance and buying the rest of the army much-needed time to prepare for the defence of Imphal. By the 23rd, the outlook was grim. 'In 152 Bn we were stretched to the limit to man our sector of the perimeter.' Offensive operations had to be confined to attack patrols that disrupted Japanese operations, but there was little enough reserve from which they could be found. 'The area of high ground by the church was subjected to almost continuous attack and I think the fiercest fighting of the battle took place here.' Several times Japanese soldiers fought their way over the perimeter wall and up to the church – once they even got inside – but on each occasion they were forced back in hand-to-hand combat.

By good fortune, a Japanese officer killed within the perimeter at an early stage of the battle had a map in his haversack. This revealed the route that two Japanese divisions would take in their attacks on Kohima and Imphal. Sangshak was being assaulted by the whole of one of these divisions and part of the other. Copies were made of the map and two men disappeared into the jungle to take them to corps headquarters.

Sangshak continued to hold up the enemy, but the position was deteriorating.

> The 25th was very similar to the previous days with enemy attacks growing heavier and their artillery fire more intense and the general situation for the defenders more and more critical. Owing to the failure of air supply, stocks of all essentials were now very low. In the Field Ambulance plasters for the wounded were being made out of blood plasma instead of water. This latter was virtually exhausted and what little was available had to be kept for the wounded to drink . . .
>
> At 4.00 hrs on the 26th the Japanese made a further large scale attack against the church position preceded by very heavy artillery, mortar and smallarms fire. They broke into the position but were driven out several times during the next few hours but still they came on and fighting took place inside the church itself. Eventually they gained this dominating point after the garrison had all been killed or wounded and we were unable to retake it. They had the great advantage of overwhelming numbers and were able to use fresh troops for each attack.

Hope-Thompson threw in his last reserves, led by Lieutenant Robin de la Haye, a dapper young man who would have been completing his Oxford degree if it had not been for the war; Robin was killed in the fight. The defenders set fire to the church with a phosphorus cartridge from a signal pistol. By now, all the company commanders of the 152nd Battalion had been killed or badly wounded. Richard Gillett was among the former.

That evening, the remains of the garrison – exhausted through exertion and lack of sleep, and often wounded – realized that the end could not be far off. The officers divided two canisters of rations, the size of kettledrums, among those who were still alive, and smoked a last cigarette before stand-to.

> We were not entirely clear as to how we had been pitchforked into this situation, but we felt that we had done our best and were glad to think that there was still a nucleus of paratroops in India around which a new parachute formation might be built. It was a lovely evening and we discussed the merits of the many club swimming-pools that we knew in India.

At that point a runner came, requiring the officers' presence at a conference with Hopkinson. The term 'runner' was, in these circumstances, something of a *façon de parler*; movement around the defensive box could only be made by crawling along shallow trenches. The officers snaked forward on their bellies to the meeting. They were told that an order had been received over the wireless set (which, since the generator had been destroyed early in the battle, was powered, bizarrely, by someone cycling on a converted bicycle). They were to break off the action. The corps commander's message ended ominously: 'Good luck, our thoughts are with you!' The field telephone rang and it was the irrepressible Abbott to say, 'See you in Imphal with a bottle of beer!' The soldiers smiled wanly – 'both contingencies seemed highly remote'. But at nine that night the last of the mortar ammunition was fired off, and those who could still walk slipped silently out of their shelters. Since the Japanese controlled all the tracks, they pushed into the rhododendrons and descended the mountain.

It was not easy to get back to Imphal, but some made it. Among them was Hopkinson. He had been wounded and his leg was in plaster; as he made his way painfully along the jungle tracks, he leant heavily on Abbott. Major Harry Butchard of the 153rd (Gurkha) Battalion met them.

> That evening we came upon two figures struggling uphill. One was Colonel Abbott, the Brigade's Deputy Commander, a large, heavily

built man with florid features who, the day before, had said to me while the battle was raging 'Harry, I am determined that I am going to die of a surfeit of port in my old age.' Here he was, half-carrying Hopkinson, who was hopping up the hill with his arms around Abbott's neck. We added them to our strength and settled down for the night in a wood.

By the time they reached it, Imphal would not have been the best place for a beer. It was the scene of another battle. But Sangshak, by inflicting horrific casualties on the Japanese, had broken the force of the attack, and the enemy was driven back. The 'staunchness' of the Parachute Brigade 'gave the garrison of Imphal the vital time required to adjust their defences', declared General Slim in a special order of the day. This included deployment of the 5th Division, airlifted from Arakan – the first time that a whole division had been so moved, an operation that lasted from 19 to 24 March. For the first time, a Japanese attack had been defeated, their armies hurled back; India had been saved.

The Scene Is Now Too Poignant

— JACK BICKLE —

After the D-Day landings, the padre to the 4th Battalion The Somerset Light Infantry used to break up old wooden ration boxes to make crosses, which he then painted white. It could be disconcerting to the more imaginative soldiers to see the number of them, piled in his vehicle, before a battle: they hinted all too plainly at the scale of the casualties that were expected, however much the clergyman might pray for the men to come through the fighting without harm. This observation was made by A. G. Herbert, a signaller with the battalion as it fought its way through Normandy and Northern France, then into Belgium and Holland, in 1944. With him was young Jack Bickle from Lydford, barely eighteen.

To most people who knew Lydford before the Second World War, the village could hardly have seemed complete without a quorum of Bickles. They were a spreading family, whose frequent appearances at the font of St Petroc's were a matter of routine in the nineteenth century. A dozen Bickles were christened in the 1880s. While the rate of reproduction dropped off somewhat after 1900, it had been enough to create a considerable clan. They sang in the church choir and rang the bells; one Bickle played the cornet, while another followed schoolmaster Kenner as bandmaster of the village band. Whenever a tea committee was being organized, or an evening of theatrical sketches put on; if billiards were being played, or songs being sung at a social; whatever the village event, the name of Bickle would be on the bill. Young Bickles crowded the pages of the school logbook – not always to their credit. In the school's early days, Mr Kenner fretted over the Bickles of Watergate, who would disappear for months at a time – 'inveterate truants' was how he described them, sitting down to report, as requested, to the Okehampton Poor Law Union. In 1906 Tommy Bickle, who had been punished for throwing stones, drowned in the Lyd, aged seven. Scholastically, the family's reputation was redeemed in 1935 when Sylvia Bickle came top out of thirty-five competitors in a scholarship examination. Sylvia was Jack's sister.

The Bickle men generally worked as blacksmiths, went for soldiers, drove lorries; but Jack and Sylvia's father, Albert, was a carpenter, working with another local family, the Mays. Jack had been christened Leslie Arthur John. Fair-haired, slight of build, he is remembered for his bravado. When local boys dammed a stream at Black Rock to form a pool, Jack was not able to swim in it, but he could dive, crossing from side to side underwater. He might also have run along the parapet of the tall viaduct near where his family lived at Mill Cottage. He was popular with everyone. A month before Britain declared war on Germany in 1939, his 27-year-old brother Ron, a lorry driver who delivered coal to the village, was killed on his motorcycle as he left a dance at Bere Alston. 'I can't get round,' Ron moaned as he lay dying. 'I can't get through.' The carpenter Frederick May was his pillion. Jack was as yet too young for dances. At the start of the war, he was only thirteen.

By 1944, however, 'little Jack', as he was apt to be known, had been called up. He was eighteen: old enough to take part in the invasion of mainland Europe that would lead to the fall of Berlin. He was not the first Lydford man to do so. The war memorial also remembers Peter Bowles. Peter's background could hardly have been more different from Jack's, so far as the association with the village was concerned. His father, Gerald, had been born at Brentor around 1890, the son of a barrister, MP and JP. With his wife, Janet, he had gone to live in Burma as an employee of the Burma Rice Company. After the Second World War had begun, Gerald and Janet sensibly relocated to India. Sometime before Gerald's death in 1951, they came back to England, living in a bungalow on the moor behind the Dartmoor Inn, providing – as village memory has it – a sit-down tea promptly at four o'clock for anyone who happened to be working for them: a legacy of India, perhaps.

Peter himself was born in Rangoon. His schooldays were spent in the UK but nowhere near Lydford. He went to Uppingham School, in Rutland – boarding, of course – and became a member of the Officers' Training Corps. He was still described as a student, nearly nineteen, when he enlisted at Gloucester on 16 September 1940. Although not obviously Scottish, this fresh-complexioned, hazel-eyed youth found himself posted to the 14th Battalion of the Argyll and Sutherland Highlanders, from which he transferred into the Black Watch. It was as a lance corporal in the 7th Battalion of the Black Watch that he went overseas in June 1942. At the end of October, he caught a shrapnel wound in the neck at the Second Battle of El Alamein; the next year he was shot in the leg at Wadi Akarit, in Tunisia. For three months, this put him out of service. But on Christmas Eve 1943, he joined the 14th Battalion Sherwood Foresters with an emergency commission as 2nd lieutenant. Three months later, on 20 March 1944, he was killed aged twenty-two, fighting with his battalion, after landing at Anzio, thirty miles south of Rome.

His image of the country he had died for would probably have been rather different from Jack's. Peter was a son of the British Empire. The fact that he had never lived in the village caused some debate about the appropriateness of including his name on the memorial. Jack's world was, by contrast, a slow-changing one – not so different from that described by Thomas Hardy. This may have been at the back of somebody's mind when the 43rd Division, to which Jack's battalion belonged, was named the 'Wessex'.

After training, Jack joined the 4th Battalion Somerset Light Infantry at Le Mesnil-Milon, to the north-west of Paris, in early September. The battalion had been fighting hard since its arrival at Arromanches on 23 June. Arromanches was one of the beaches stormed on D-Day on 6 June; the only obstacle that opposed the battalion's landing now was the weather, which had kept them at sea for five days. The scene that greeted the West Countrymen behind the sand dunes was deceptively bucolic. Corn ripened in the fields and peasants brought in the last of the hay, apparently oblivious to the military vehicles that were choking the lanes. The Cycle Company set off with its machines, only to find that they could not contend with the sticky mud; abandoned, the bicycles were never seen again. But the shellfire started west of Caen. One of the first casualties was Regimental Sergeant Major Holt (no doubt a terror to new recruits, such as Jack, on the parade ground).

After that, the battalion was kept busy, in weather so stifling that men worked with damp cloths over their mouths to keep out the dust. Under intense bombardment by artillery and Nebelwerfer rockets – known as Moaning Minnies for their banshee sound – it succeeded in crossing the steep-sided Odon Gorge, which was quickly given the nickname of Death Valley, 'not without reason'. A set-piece battle had occurred on 10 July. Soldiers were nudged awake at 4 a.m. Grenades and bandoliers of ammunition were issued, as well as the surprise of two slices of white bread. Now the mist of the early morning seemed to herald another hot day. The time had come to push on from the bridgehead that had been established on the east side of the Odon Gorge. The object to be attacked was a pimple called Hill 112 which, although only a slight rise, was regarded by one German general as the key to Normandy. It was defended by the 10th SS Panzer (Frundsberg) Division. A pale sun was shining by the time the 4th Somersets had taken up their position. Quietly, a word of command was given, and the battalion moved into the corn that stood waist high in the fields. The peaceful scene suddenly erupted into a deafening inferno of noise and flame. 'It was just beginning to get light, and the whole scene was illuminated by burning carriers and tanks,' remembered a sergeant from the mortar platoon, which alone fired 5,000 rounds. 'Practically every weapon was in action – rifles, grenades, phosphorous, L[ight] M[achine] G[uns] and Tanks,' as well as flamethrowers. Enemy snipers were hidden in the corn. When the infantry had got as far as it could, it dug trenches, struggling to break up the hard ground.

Dead bodies were now on every hand. Large bluebottles swarmed over them, clustering around the mouths of the living as well as the flesh of the dead; 'you were bound to swallow some' recalled A. G. Herbert, who did what he could with some bacon and chemically treated water. The British tanks that repulsed the counter-attack tore up the cables the signaller had laid, forcing him into the open.

He hopped from trench to trench, one of which, he soon discovered, had recently been used as a latrine. The second after Herbert had ducked into one trench, the head of a man who had been sitting on its lip as he recited his rosary was blown off. 'I had the feeling I had looked into hell, and my life could never be the same again.'

The mobile bath unit was very welcome at Fontaine-Étoupefour ten days later. 'It was pure joy to stand under hot water and let it ease some of the sore spots where my equipment had rubbed my flesh raw.' Clean underwear was issued; uniforms were dusted with DDT to kill bugs. The commanding officer succeeded in bagging a number of guinea fowl, while the second in command developed a successful method of extracting honey from broken-down hives, by means of a face veil and No. 14 Smoke Generator. Provision had been made for entertainment with films and ENSA shows; but the respite was short-lived. The battalion was soon on the move again, keeping a keen watch for snipers hiding in trees and mines underfoot. Outside Briquessard, as shells whistled overhead, they were surprised to encounter a Church Army mobile canteen. It seemed like a vision.

> The driver had been a First World War infantryman, and had driven up as near to the front as possible, 'To give the fighting men a treat' as he put it. One senior Officer asked him what he thought he was doing there, and told him to get out of the area before he had him arrested. While the Officer was trying to contact someone to eject the Good Samaritan, the man calmly started to hand out cups of tea and goods. We had no money, of course – What good is money to an infantry-man in the line. The amazing man said he would take I.O.U.s.

Tea was particularly welcome; fighting during the summertime was thirsty work.

It was to get worse. The battalion now advanced on Mount Pin-con, the highest point in Normandy, a powerful feature in the landscape whose lower slopes were cultivated with small fields and hedges and whose higher parts were scrub and woods. 'We rode on the tanks, hanging on for dear life, choked with dust and burned by the hot metal plates.' The dust was 'as thick as a London fog'. They attacked in shirtsleeves. Herbert had a bit of luck: while splicing some telephone wires together he found that one of them was still live, and the voices that he could hear on it were German. It had been left in the trench when the Germans drew back. He found an intelligence officer to listen in. It was then, while a tank ground its way noisily uphill to support the infantry, that he witnessed a remarkable procession.

> Coming down the hill towards me were two women, barefoot and dressed only in nightclothes, their hair streaming in the wind as they ran. As they drew near I could see the leading woman was carrying a large picture of Christ in a frame still complete with glass. They were both hysterical, and clutched at my uniform, begging to know where to go out of the fighting. Although I spoke no French I was able to point out the way down, and said, 'La Roguerie'! At that moment the tank had made its way up the hill and was in the act of forcing a passage up the narrow track, when it ran over a donkey which had followed the women down. The noise of the tank and the sight of the squashed donkey caused the women's hysteria to rise to a new crescendo.

As the last rays of the setting sun washed the crest of Mont Pincon with gold and red, three British tanks could be seen silhouetted on the skyline. Although the objective had not yet been captured, it soon would be.

By early September, the battalion which had landed on 23 June 1944 had changed almost beyond recognition. Gaps made by the loss of well-known characters and friends had been filled in by drafts from outside. Jack was one of those who replenished the ranks. He arrived during a fortnight's lull, while vehicles were being repaired and deficiencies in equipment made good. It was a time of kit checks and inspections, with more of the kind of training that he had been put through in barracks. The valley echoed to the sound of mortars, small-arms fire and anti-tank weapons, making it 'more noisy than the average battlefield'. In defiance of the Luftwaffe, which had been subdued by the RAF, they held open-air cinema shows after dark. There were even day trips to Paris and to the Château de La Roche-Guyon which Rommel had recently used as his headquarters. Relations with the village of Le Mesnil-Milon, which had been heavily shelled in order to destroy some German artillery, gradually thawed.

Jack's platoon commander, Sydney Jary, was only a couple of years older than him. He was, however, confident and relaxed – or seemed to be. He was certainly an individualist, as could be seen from his unmilitary dress. It had always struck Jary as odd that the British wore their most comfortable clothes for sporting pursuits and their most constricting ones for going to work. He went to his work, as a twenty-year-old lieutenant, in sand-coloured corduroy slacks and a pullover, with the pips betokening his rank stitched on to the shoulder. This approximated to the sort of clothes that were later widely adopted by the army, but then seemed highly unorthodox. In the same vein, he refused to carry the rifle or Bren gun that officers were supposed to keep by them, in order that the enemy would not single them out. Jary did not want his troops to be confused during battle as to the identity of their commander; besides, he was too short-sighted to make much use of a gun. He also found steel helmets uncomfortable, and so wore a beret. He passionately defended the platoon. As Corporal Douglas Proctor remembered, 'he wouldn't tolerate any criticism of his 18 Platoon and argued forcibly against any orders that were not to his liking'.

Jary was the third commander of the platoon since its arrival in France. When he took over, a red-faced major told him that the life expectancy of a subaltern from the time he joined his unit in the field was precisely three weeks.

It was an exciting time for Jack to have arrived. After the Allies' capture of Antwerp the previous day, 5 September became Dolle Dinsdag (Mad Tuesday), when the Germans panicked, some fleeing on stolen bicycles, others pushing handcarts of loot. Nine days later Jack and his new comrades joined the pursuit across Northern France and Belgium, and into Holland. The battalion covered over 250 miles in little more than 24 hours – an impressive rate of travel if you were squashed into a Bren gun carrier, in full kit, next to a hot and noisy engine. But swaying and rattling, they clattered through places made famous by the previous war – Albert, Cambrai, Mons – towards destinations that would always be associated with the Second World War, notably Arnhem. Their way was marked by burning buildings, wrecked tanks, blackened guns and at one point a miniature submarine and trailer, both burnt out, their intended purpose a mystery. At Linkhout, in Belgium, the battalion commander gave a briefing. It revealed the audacity of the operation that lay before them, code-named Market Garden. 'Market' referred to the airborne troops who would seize the bridges over the Dutch rivers and canals, 'Garden' to the Second Army which would secure them. From Eindhoven they would move on to Nijmegen, Arnhem, Zutphen, Deventer, North Holland and finally Germany. The object was to bring the war to a close by the end of the year.

The 4th Somersets stayed at Linkhout for three days, long enough for one of the battalion to become engaged to a local girl, who was observed shyly saying a discreet goodbye to her Romeo. There was, at this point, a giddiness to the whistle-stop liberation. Small boys and girls swarmed on to the vehicles, clinging to their backs as they moved off. The troops found the Belgians to be joyful, unlike the less demonstrative country people of Normandy, who had appeared indifferent as to which occupying force they were under. At one town, across the street from a convent, Jary identified 'what I took to be one of their pupils' dormitories: a very long room divided into small cubicles, each with a bed.' Having settled one section and the platoon headquarters into the accommodation, he crossed the road to report, when his sergeant advised against this choice of billet. It was a brothel. 'We returned immediately to find our soldiers sitting on the ends of the beds being eyed by a group of ladies in dressing gowns.'

The Dutch border was crossed on 21 September; before dawn the next day Jack and the battalion had reached Grave. At midday they were in Nijmegen, captured after heavy losses by American paratroopers. The town had suffered little outward damage, but the streets were strewn with broken glass and curls of fallen telegraph wire. A day was spent in a prosperous street, eating from mess tins and washing in bowls of warm clean water sent out by the householders. Long-range German shelling shattered the calm, and men leapt from the blankets they had been lying on to take cover, as windows from the upper storeys crashed on to the street. In the evening, they marched over the imposing Nijmegen suspension bridge, past the sprawled bodies of German soldiers who had died defending it.

The mood now changed from jubilation to anxiety. It was grim weather for flying; the RAF was having difficulty in locating and dropping supplies to the 1st Airborne Division at Arnhem. They remembered the supply vehicles that they had passed on the road, 'halted, waiting, worried, behind schedule'. They could hear the German guns shelling Arnhem in the distance.

The platoon probed a landscape of orchards and dykes, willow trees and wrecked buildings.

> The once neat gardens and cottages in the Company area were pock-marked by craters and covered with rubble, slates and dust. Cottages collapsed into piles of rubble and the paths and lanes became strewn with wreckage. Smiling faces vanished and the grey look returned once more.

On the face of it, this countryside appeared quiet, but the barns and ditches concealed large numbers of well-prepared Germans. Evening meals were consumed ravenously, amid the clink of mess tins and the hiss of the sergeant demanding absolute quiet. But the patrols who came for their breakfast in the morning had no need to be silenced. 'Wrapped in their greatcoats with their equipment hanging loosely over their shoulders, they would hold out their mess tins beseechingly for food, never uttering a sound.' Days of sunshine were spent in a state of perpetual angst.

The frustration is typified by a night when the battalion was led down to the river Waal to guard against enemy frogmen attacking the bridges. They found their way by the glow of 'Monty's moonlight', formed by shining searchlights on to the low cloud. Signaller A. G. Herbert describes the scene.

> Frogmen would have seen SLI stumbling along, hanging on to each other, in single file like a herd of trained elephants. Every now and

then someone would fall into a hidden dip in the bank, sending two or three of their companions tumbling in a cursing chaotic heap. Officers called for silence, only to be met with a muffled cry of 'Bollocks' from somewhere in the darkness.

The army was, however, right to worry about German frogmen. Some of the latter did succeed in blowing up the railway bridge at Nijmegen, although not the majestic road bridge.

The weather turned colder. Supplies were running short. Behind them, the road was cut, so troops had to be sent back to keep it open. It was clear they would not be able to relieve the airborne division at Arnhem. The western part of Holland remained in German hands. 'The great gamble to end the war in 1944 had failed.'

Jack was not the only Lydford lad fighting in Holland. The 4th Battalion Somerset Light Infantry was part of the 43rd or Wessex Division, made up of brigades from the West of England. Bill Cooke, who had been working as a builder with the Hugginses before war broke out, also belonged to it, serving with the Royal Army Service Corps; his role was to drive ammunition lorries from the dumps to the front line. He landed on D-Day and, in his ninety-fifth year, still remembers the rough sea, the scramble down nets into landing craft, the jump into waters that were already red with the blood of the men who had not made it to the beach. 'Don't take any clothes off,' he was ordered, 'we might get pushed back into the sea.' By the time the division had fought its way up to Arnhem, he was exhausted. It snowed heavily that winter of 1944/5 – the Hunger Winter for those in the west of Holland whose lack of food, compounded by German punishments, brought them close to starvation. One day, Bill lay down in thick snow and simply went to sleep. Near Nijmegen, he found a mansion that was being used as No. 3 Casualty Clearing Station. Perhaps this was the same clearing station that Lieutenant General Sir Brian Horrocks had visited, while it was being shelled by the Germans. His instinct was to take cover as a shell approached, but the Queen Alexandra's sister at his side merely continued her work. When the shell landed nearby, she simply remarked, 'What a bore – we shall have to get all that repaired.'

Bill had time to walk in the grounds. There, his attention was attracted by some newly dug graves, marked by white crosses, and out of curiosity he wandered towards them. Idly reading the names, he was startled to see that of L. A. J. Bickle. Jack had been a few years younger than Bill, although he had known him in the village. It was his first intimation that Jack had crossed to France. Jack had been killed on 9 October.

Many years after the war, Jack's platoon commander, Captain Sydney Jary, who was only twenty in 1944, wrote an account of his experiences called *18 Platoon*. It was so highly regarded that the military college at Sandhurst bought 500 copies, so that every trainee officer could be given one. Jack's winning personality had made an impression on his young commanding officer, and he gives a vivid description of how Jack was shot by a sniper.

> One morning, there was a 'Crack!' and a short interval of silence. Soon the shout 'Stretcher Bearers!' echoed through the orchard. I ran towards the commotion and saw Bickle writhing in agony on the ground. At first he looked unhurt but, as I tore open his tunic, I saw a clear wound through his abdomen, coming out by his spine. He soon became numb and was no longer in pain but was very frightened and shivered. We dragged him back behind the house and applied field dressings to his stomach and his back in case the wound started to bleed. His young life slowly ebbing from his body, our stretcher bearers, quietly and reverently, carried him away. The scene is now too poignant to remember without shedding a tear.

At Lydford, more tears were shed for Jack's sister, Sylvia, the clever girl who came top of the scholarship entrants from Lydford School. She did not take her education very far: by sixteen she was serving at Perratons, the bakery, confectionery and coffee shop in Duke Street, Tavistock. At the age of sixteen, she volunteered for the Auxiliary Territorial Services, a body of women established a year before war was declared. After 1939, the ATS supplied labour for what had previously been male jobs, the men who used to do them having been called up. Service began with a few weeks' training, during which recruits (later conscripts) learnt to march, did physical training, and learnt to salute – while riding a bicycle, if necessary. They received a uniform, described by another ATS volunteer who was, like Sylvia, sixteen on joining: 'khaki bloomers (passion killers we called them), awful pink bras that flattened everything you had, pink corsets (with whalebones), khaki lisle stockings and, of course a skirt, jacket, cap and hideous pyjamas'.

The ATS filled many roles. They cooked for troops, drove jeeps, buses, lorries and ambulances, and they maintained guns. They became radar operators, aircraft spotters and plotting officers, recording the movements of enemy and friendly aircraft. They scanned the night skies with searchlights, and they patrolled the streets of garrison towns as members of the military police. They became cipher operators, radio technicians, clerks. Beginning with a spell at camp, they were sent all over the country and sometimes abroad. For Sylvia it would have provided a chance to see something of life beyond Lydford, with more freedom than would have been possible while living under the maternal eye at Mill Cottage.

After a short written exam, Sylvia became a switchboard operator. But while in the services she caught tuberculosis. The first antibiotic against this disease was discovered in 1944 and, in the course of the next half-century, tuberculosis would be defeated in Britain. But these developments came too late for Sylvia. In 1947 Private Bickle died, aged nineteen, at Shaftesbury Military Hospital. Her funeral was held at St Petroc's, Lydford. Revd George Thorpe, now an old man, officiated – he had known Sylvia all her life – while Wilfie Fry's brother, Norman, played the organ. Fellow ATS girls were among the bearers. Her name joined that of her brother on the war memorial.

12

A Surprise Attack in Three Weeks' Time

⁓ NICK TAYLOR ⁓

On 13 November 1923, Stanley Huggins sent seasonal greetings to the *Tavistock Gazette*. He was living, aptly, at Port Stanley, in the Falkland Islands, but still had the local newspaper sent out from Devon, a reminder of his early years at Lydford. Although located 250 miles off the eastern coastline of South America, the wind-lashed, treeless islands had something in common with home. 'Out here is just the same as if one was planted in the middle of Dartmoor,' wrote Huggins. 'Tors of granite with peat bog around, very wild and desolate, no trees, and a very little gorse.' Sandy white beaches fringed the craggy shore although the weather was rarely sufficiently tempting for them to be used for sunbathing. Little could be grown except grass for sheep – and they considerably outnumbered the human population. Mutton, not surprisingly, was the chief food; the islanders could console themselves for what was otherwise a somewhat joyless existence by paying only 3d a pound for the best cuts, a price which was 'far different from England'.

By the late 1970s, when Harry and Peggy Taylor came to live at Lydford, in Greenacre, one of the big houses on the way to the Dartmoor Inn, it is safe to say that the Falkland Islands had been largely forgotten. Most people only knew them, if at all, as a geographical curiosity, one of those atolls of empire which had been marooned as the tide of British influence retreated after the Second World War. Even the British government seemed to be tired of them and had, in a desultory fashion, been holding talks with Argentina over their future. It made sense to find some new arrangement. Argentina was considerably nearer to them than Britain, which lay on the other side of the world, and the economic value of a sheep station in the South Atlantic was far less than the cost of supporting it. The Argentines, unlike the lackadaisical British, passionately wanted the archipelago. The vexation of Britain's ownership of the islands swelled in the public imagination until it took on the proportions of a massive affront to national virility. Popular emotion could be whipped into a frenzy by calling for the return of Las Malvinas (the Spanish name for the Falklands).

The problem for the British government was the inconvenient preference of the islanders themselves. There may only have been 3,000 of them but, descended from people like Stanley Huggins, they declined to throw in their lot with a volatile South American state, prone to rule by military juntas and dictators. Instead, they resolutely chose to remain British. Occasionally, the issue would wring a few short paragraphs out of bored diplomatic and overseas correspondents as Argentina pressed its case through the UN. 'The interests of the inhabitants of these territories are paramount,' Lord Caradon, British representative at the UN, thundered in 1964; but hardly anyone reading the British press would have been aware of the fact, since the meeting was scarcely reported. If the Taylors' four children grew up in ignorance of the Falklands, they were typical of the Sergeant Pepper generation for whom the distant possessions of Empire seemed as ridiculous as their governors' plumed hats.

The Taylors were newcomers to Lydford but not to Devon. Nick, like all but the youngest of the children, had been born at Lynton, on the North Devon coast, where Harry and Peggy ran a hotel. Harry Taylor had been in the army. The austerity years that followed the Second World War were a difficult period for British seaside resorts. Family tradition remembers an occasion on which Mr Taylor wheeled Nick down to the bank for a confrontation with the manager; it was so upsetting that he rushed home, stopping at the pub on the way, and left Nick there. In 1953 the Taylors sold the hotel: Nick was now four and his parents wanted to find a good day school. The family kept an association with the area, coming down every summer to spend a couple of weeks camping on farmland at Brendon, outside Lynton, owned by friends.

From Lynton, the Taylors moved to Hampstead. Its reputation for arty intellectualism suited Harry's new role as an artist's agent. This was not a quick route to riches, but Nick could still be sent to a well-known prep school, The Hall. He was an energetic, bright, naughty child who was 'unable', according to his sister Susan, 'to sit still for two minutes'. He was always in trouble at The Hall; entrepreneurial activities such as filling bottles with water and selling them to class-mates were firmly discouraged. Nick, though, was never one to be put down easily. Susan remembers: 'He couldn't bear to be told what to do. He survived by the seat of his pants.' Yet he was not one of those boys to whom native rebelliousness is an obstacle to the achieve-ment of goals. Although far from beefy, he played in the first fifteen for rugby. Academic success came easily. Others might struggle with their exams, but not Nick. Without really seeming to try, he won a scholarship to The Haberdashers' Aske's Boys' School at Elstree in 1962. The scholarship was helpful. A stalwart member of the Church of England, Harry Taylor now worked as Director of Christian Stewardship for the Diocese of London.

Needing a bigger house, at a price they could afford, the family moved to Totteridge and Whetstone, on the northern fringes of London; from the age of sixteen, Nick made the journey to school, threading through the outer suburbs of the capital, by motorbike. By now he was in the Air Cadets. He had learnt to fly before he passed his driving test for a car. Flight Sergeant Taylor, as he was known in the school's Combined Cadet Force, was one of four Air Cadets in the country chosen to make an exchange visit to Germany. In class, needless to say, he invariably came top. But school work had to be fitted around a wide range of sporting activities, including squash, canoeing and, when he could manage it, skiing. 'All the things that make the adrenalin rush.'

University did not beckon when Nick left Haberdashers'. He had his heart set on flying and went straight to the Royal Air Force Col-lege at Cranwell. His career there was chequered; although more than competent as a student, he was always 'on jankers' for one mis-demeanour or another, such as putting an ad in the local paper to announce that the college was for sale, providing a Ministry of

Defence number for interested parties to phone. The authorities grew increasingly exasperated. When, arriving late back from a sailing trip, he missed his turn as duty officer and was not present to haul down the flag, patience snapped and he was expelled. His father was furious.

After a couple of months in menial jobs, Nick applied to the Royal Navy. It is not only the RAF which flies planes in the British armed services; both the army and the navy need pilots, the navy for the Fleet Air Arm. Harry Taylor was dubious that the navy would take him. Predictably, the interview at the Britannia Royal Naval College, Dartmouth, concentrated less on Nick's flying ability, which had already been proved at Cranwell, than on what he had learnt from his sudden departure. 'To suffer fools gladly,' was his response. He was accepted. As a matter of honour, he gained a place in the rugby team, knowing that it would play Cranwell. When the match came off, he suffered a blow to his jaw, but carried on playing; only afterwards, when he was taken to hospital, was it discovered that he had broken it in three places. His family believe that it had the beneficial effect of preventing him from answering back, as a result of which he completed the course – although at the passing out ball, his mouth was wired and he could only sip drinks through a straw. He passed out top of his class and left the college as a sub lieutenant (the Fleet Air Arm equivalent of the RAF's pilot officer).

Initially, there was no vacancy for a fixed-wing pilot, so he flew helicopters from the air-sea rescue base at Culdrose, on the Lizard Peninsula in Cornwall. For a time he was seconded to the army in Northern Ireland; another secondment was to the Canadian Air Force, where he had an enjoyable time flying amphibious de Havilland Beavers in the Rockies. At home in the UK, flying Hunters, he was as irrepressible as ever, rattling chimneypots at Lydford (where his parents were now living) by swooping low over their house whenever he had the chance, or skimming the hedges below big pylons by flying under the power lines. He became a champion glider pilot, first for the navy and later buying a glider for himself. He also acquired a famous racing boat called *Thunder*, which had been designed by Uffa Fox before the Second World War. Having dated a string of beautiful girlfriends, he fell in love with Clare Downham, a Wren from North Wales who worked for the command of the Sea King training squadron based at Yeovilton. ('A very clever girl,' says Nick's sister. 'Couldn't cook.') They got married in Colwyn Bay, walking out of the church beneath an arch of naval swords. Perhaps it took a girl in the services to understand him. Daredevilry was simply part of his nature, not a matter of showing off; to navy colleagues, he was 'one of the most easy-going and pleasant blokes' that you could meet. 'It was great to be in his company.' But always he would be 'pushing himself, wanting to do something different'. He was ideally suited to becoming the pilot of a Sea Harrier, one of the most remarkable planes ever built.

After the Second World War, many aeronautical engineers dreamt of producing a plane that could rise vertically from the ground, and a number of them succeeded in producing one: a prototype frame nicknamed the Flying Bedstead, more formally known as the Rolls-Royce Thrust Measuring Rig, wobbled into the air above Hucknall aerodrome in 1953. But getting airborne was not enough by itself. A successful aircraft would also need to manoeuvre and carry a heavy weight of armament or bombs. Only the Harrier succeeded in mastering these challenges. The first generation of what became popularly known as the Jump Jet was developed by Hawker Siddeley in the 1960s. A Vertical/Short Take-Off and Landing – or V/STOL – aircraft was particularly attractive to the British military, then locked in the permafrost of the Cold War with Russia; if, as expected, Russia took out the airfields in Germany at the beginning of an invasion, the Harrier fleet would be able to operate from any open space or short stretch of motorway to bomb the oncoming troops. Not requiring a runway also made it difficult for an enemy to spot.

The world gasped when the plane was first shown, rising perpendicularly into the air like a helicopter. In engineering speak, this was achieved by means of 'vectored thrust', produced by rotating the nozzles of its turbofans. In practice, it was better for the plane to have a short run-up before taking off, rather than making its ascent from a standing start, because the plane could then carry more weight. Even so, the aircraft could be adapted for use from ships. The Sea Harrier, made by British Aerospace and introduced in 1978, was the result. It was, in all probability, the last British aircraft to have been made from an entirely indigenous design (although in fairness one has to admit that the idea of vectored thrust had been proposed by a Frenchman, Michel Wibault). Romantics warmed to the thought that it was produced from the old Sopwith Aviation Company's works at Kingston-upon-Thames, putting it in direct line of succession from such famous planes as the Sopwith Camel of the First World War and the Hurricane of the Second World War.

Since the Second World War, conventional aircraft carriers could only meet the demands of conventional military aircraft by getting bigger and bigger. They soon reached such a size that only the super-powers – the United States and Russia – could afford to build them. The Sea Harrier answered the prayers of the economically minded British by providing a plane that did not need a huge expanse of deck to land on – only, on a heaving sea, an exceptional degree of skill on the part of its pilots. It could drop down on to helicopter carriers, assault ships – any vessel, in fact, which could provide a landing plat-form. When the *Audacious*-class HMS *Ark Royal* was decommissioned in 1978, Britain was left with only two aircraft carriers, HMS *Hermes* and HMS *Invincible*, which, loaded with Sea Harriers, would hardly have been worthy of the term beside the leviathans of the American fleet. In order to allow the planes to have a rolling take-off, the ends of the decks were built up to form ramps – 'ski jumps', as they became known – not perhaps to their aesthetic advantage but allowing the planes to carry more fuel, missiles, bombs and other equipment.

The Sea Harrier could not fly at supersonic speeds, but its unique design gave it other advantages over faster aircraft. By moving the nozzles, it could be made to decelerate very quickly. It was a light plane, without a very long range, but it was fast to accelerate; it was also the 'best fighter in the world' for handling at low speed. Its small size made it difficult to spot on radar, while its smoke-free Pegasus engines left no trail to help an enemy spot it with the naked eye. These qualities had been proved in exercises with the RAF and United States Air Force. On Shrove Tuesday 1982 it seemed unimagin-able that the Sea Harrier would be tested in combat against some of the most sophisticated aircraft in the world, belonging to a previously friendly power. By Easter, that scenario became highly plausible. On May Day, it was made real.

At the age of thirty-two, Lieutenant Nick Taylor had only recently converted from flying helicopters to fast jets, but he had made a sufficient mark to be selected as a potential test pilot, with a place booked at the Empire Test Pilot's School at Boscombe Down for the autumn of 1982. However, before that came, he was swept up in the thrilling, preposterous, tragic splendour of Britain's post-colonial hurrah: war in the South Atlantic. To the Sea Harrier fleet, it was the ultimate challenge.

The Falklands War took Britain by surprise. The warning signs were read only in hindsight. To the British press, the landing of a group of scrap-metal merchants on the island of South Georgia, 800 miles south of the Falklands, at the end of 1981 – so close to the South Pole that it provided the explorer Ernest Shackleton's burial place, when he died on his final expedition in 1922 – had a comic-opera quality. The Foreign Office was too preoccupied with other matters – the Common Market, a predicted Israeli invasion of Lebanon – to give it a great deal of thought. They lodged a diplomatic protest on 9 January 1982; but this carried so little weight with the Argentine junta that the latter began planning a full-blown invasion of the Falklands within days. The old colonial power was deemed to have lost interest. To save money, it was withdrawing the ice patrol ship HMS *Endurance* which represented the British government's last presence in Antarctica. The example of Goa, a Portuguese pimple which the newly independent government of India resented on its eastern flank and had occupied, without repercussions, in 1961, offered a tempting precedent. The unpopular Argentine generals could buy favour at home by seizing a scattering of islands that, in national myth, were nothing less than iconic.

The generals were careful to order that the invasion should be bloodless, as far as the British marines and Falkland Islanders were concerned (if not their own troops). But they failed to realize the extent to which, in post-imperial Britain, consciousness of past glories still engendered a keen sense of amour propre. The memory of humiliation at Suez was still sharp. While the Falkland Islanders were few in number, they had made their democratic wishes clearly known. And as luck – good or ill – would have it, Britain still just possessed a sufficient number of ships to project its power halfway around the globe if it needed to. In Argentina, the military planners calculated that the best time to seize the Falklands would be after July, shortly before the onset of the ferocious South Atlantic winter would have made a counter-move all but impossible. But the recycling activities in South Georgia, perhaps sponsored by the hawkish Argentine navy, upset their calculations. Although *Endurance* was about to be decommissioned, it was still in the Falklands and the British government dispatched it. As a result, the generals felt they would either have to make a decisive display of force or face a humiliating climb-down. Britain's lack of urgency in other respects convinced them that it would accept a fait accompli. So the invasion of the Falklands was brought precipitately forward to 2 April. Despite a spirited resistance by the small numbers of British marines, the execution was flawless.

The Argentine generals were not the only ones to be astonished when a Task Force was assembled and put to sea three days later. So was the rest of the world. So was the British public. As the broadcaster and journalist Malcolm Muggeridge reminded readers of the *Times* correspondence pages, the words spoken by the Captain in Shakespeare's *Hamlet* seemed to sum it up:

> We go to gain a little patch of ground
> That hath in it no profit but the name.

The mobilization happened with breathtaking speed. In an age before mobile phones, some key personnel had to be stopped by police patrol cars on motorways. Nigel 'Sharkey' Ward, who would command 801 Squadron, shipped on *Invincible*, was staying with his parents-in-law. An anxious mother-in-law woke him when the call came through at 4 a.m. It was the captain of Yeovilton, who announced that Sharkey was to mobilize his squadron for sea immediately. Ward had already sniffed enough of the brewing international tensions to have ordered supplies of war paint, required to turn the undersides of his aircraft from white (easily seen during air shows) to a more military charcoal grey. However, the new AIM 9L Sidewinder missiles, hurried over from the United States, still needed to be tested. Live bombs had to be loaded. The paint, which finally appeared but in the wrong place, had to be directed to the correct location. (The squadrons would only assume their war colours after the Task Force had left; even the squadron emblems on the fin were painted out.) Planes had to be flown on to their ships at Portsmouth – not an easy task if your arrival, like David Morgan's, coincided with the passing of a large crane for loading supplies. Another obstacle was the scaffolding that surrounded *Hermes*' 'island', the sixty-foot control tower covered in radio masts and radar dishes. (The trick was to align your plane with the ship and then use the Sea Harrier's manoeuvrability to wiggle sideways.) Nick joined on 2 April. There had been no time to see his parents or siblings to say goodbye. Clare stayed at Yeovilton, volunteering for the job of breaking the news of men lost in action to their families.

Every Sea Harrier that could be prepared was loaded. Given the scale of the mission, the fleet of just twenty planes was brave but distinctly small. Twelve of these belonged to 800 Squadron, with three borrowed from 899 Squadron, the last of the dozen not being landed on *Hermes* until it was on the open sea. They included aircraft that had previously been used for training. Rather than Blue Fox or Blue Vixen radar, the noses had been filled with lumps of concrete of equivalent weight – Blue Circle radar, as somebody quipped. These had to be quickly replaced with the real thing. Nick became part of 800 Squadron on *Hermes*. The plane allocated to him was XZ450, the first Sea Harrier to fly in 1978. It had remained at the manufacturer British Aerospace's Dunsfold site ever since this debut flight, most recently being fitted, over the course of thirteen months, with the Sea Eagle sea-skimming anti-ship missile. But in the whirlwind preparation for the Task Force, there had not been time to equip what had been a test plane with some of the technology shared by the rest of 800 Squadron.

Nick arrived to find *Hermes* being prepared. People thronged the dockside; piles of equipment and provisions stood in hangars, and gangs of men were carting it on board. Grenades, missiles, flares, toilet paper, high-tech equipment, potatoes and Argentine corned beef were dumped where room could be found. Ian Martin, one of 800 Squadron's air crew, was one of those doing the legwork. 'Hello, did you see me on the telly today?' he asked his 'darling Val' on 4 April.

> I don't know if I was on, but while I was on the jetty today loading stores a load of cameramen turned up from the T.V. and the papers. They happened to arrive as a lorry load of beer was being moved on to the ship so no doubt the whole world believes we're going to throw beer cans at the invaders.
>
> Loading gear is all we've done since we arrived . . .

It was critical to keep up the momentum; Prime Minister Margaret Thatcher wanted the Task Force to sail before Britain got cold feet. A quarter of a million people spontaneously assembled to see it sail off. The fleet amounted to not the thirty ships that had been promised – many of the rest being on joint exercises with the Americans in the Mediterranean – but three: HMS *Sheffield*, one of the latest type-42 destroyers, followed by *Invincible* and then *Hermes*. A salute was exchanged with Nelson's ship, HMS *Victory*, still a commissioned warship. The crowds on the sea wall watched the ships leave in Procedure Alpha. All those not involved in actually sailing the vessels were lined up on deck, stock still – a thousand men in the case of the carriers. 'Amazing, astounding and extraordinary' is how Rupert Nichol, an instructor officer on board HMS *Hermes*, remembers it. In an untypical display of sentiment, Captain Linley Middleton had arranged for the weapons engineer to rig up speakers to play 'Don't Cry For Me Argentina' and Rod Stewart's 'Sailing' as they left; the system, however, only emitted a nasty squawk and was switched off. No matter; it was hardly necessary to heighten the emotion of the occasion.

Few people, at this stage of events, expected the Task Force to see action. Everyone, except the unusually prescient or gloomy, regarded it as an extension of the diplomatic effort, which would probably be

effective in persuading the Argentines to withdraw. This would be
followed by a deal brokered by the UN. The very idea of the armada
was magnificent but rash; powerful though it was, it did not possess
an overwhelming advantage over the Argentine forces – and it was
the latter who had punched while their opponent's guard was down.
On the cover of the 9 April issue of *Private Eye*, the captain of *Hermes*
is pictured with Defence Secretary John Nott. 'What are our orders,
sir?' asks Middleton. To which the reply comes: 'We launch a surprise attack in three weeks' time.'

It was natural that *Hermes*, the biggest of the ships in the Task
Force, should become the flagship when Admiral Sandy Woodward
joined from the Mediterranean. But *Hermes* did not inspire unalloyed
confidence in those who beheld the rust streaking down her sides.
She was an old ship, commissioned in 1962, and had been due for a
month's refit when the conflict broke out – hence the scaffolding
around the island. If the Task Force had sailed a year later, she would
have been unavailable; it was planned to decommission her at the end
of 1982. (Later in the decade she was duly sold to India, becoming
INS *Viraat*.) There was a little more space and comfort than on the
smaller *Invincible*, but not much. Despite her size, *Hermes* was
crowded. Men had to sleep where they could: some of the officers
settled in the wardroom; the press were rescued from their quarters
in the NAAFI mess and transferred to the midshipman's 'grot' (as
midshipmen's accommodation is invariably known), while the midshipmen decamped to the admiral's day cabin. Camp beds were, to
the approval of traditionalists, converted into hammocks – a memory of Nelson's day – which were slung in passages. Fortunately
Hermes was of a vintage still to have the necessary hooks, although
hammocks had been abolished in 1971. The discomfort qualified Ian
Martin and his colleagues for 'Hard Lying' allowance – a princely 55p
a day, to which could be added separation pay at £1.60 a day. There
was 'a very strong rumour that we'll be getting Local Overseas
Allowance at £4 a day. All that plus a pay rise still to be announced,
shall we get a white or blue Rolls Royce?'

A late thought had been to provision *Hermes* with cluster bombs,
known to the pilots as 'custard bombs'. This was an unpleasant

weapon whose casings split upon leaving the aircraft to scatter 147 bomblets over a wide area. They were delivered when *Hermes* was actually at sea.

In the Bay of Biscay, heavy seas produced the same sort of reaction they had done on HMT *Olympic* when she sailed to the Dardanelles during the First World War: the non-sailors were temporarily incapacitated by seasickness. Otherwise the long journey south was an opportunity to make plans. Sea Kings ferried some of 801 Squadron on *Invincible* over to *Hermes*, where they met in Captain Middleton's day cabin which was already, like the rest of the ship, cleared for action with the pictures taken off the bulkheads and movable furniture roped down. They were all too aware that the Sea Harrier would be tested to the limit and asked to perform tasks for which it had not been designed. Above all, the Sea Harrier had been procured as a fighter whose main purpose, according to the defence priorities of the time, was expected to be the interception of long-range bombers and the protection of ships at sea. It formed part of the Cold War arsenal deployed against the Warsaw Pact; nobody imagined that Britain would strike Russia first. But in the Falklands, the time for defence had passed; Britain had to attack. In the Task Force, 801 Squadron pursued the combat air patrol (CAP) function at which the Sea Harrier excelled. The fact that Captain Middleton's early career had been spent flying Buccaneer bombers tilted the interest on *Hermes* towards bombing, the first targets being the airfields at Port Stanley and Goose Green. For the Sea Harrier, this was an unfamiliar role.

The technical crews quickly adapted the planes of 800 Squadron to carry bombs. Meanwhile, the pilots debated how they could be delivered. As Sir John Curtiss, Air Commander at Northwood, admitted later, a 'long slim runway is not easy to attack'. A raid by night was proposed but eventually rejected. The use of cluster bombs was canvassed and agreed upon: some would explode beneath aircraft while the others caused general mayhem. The 10 per cent that did not explode would serve as anti-personnel devices.

A trial for the new heat-seeking Sidewinder missiles, which the Sea Harriers, when armed for combat, carried under each wing, was conducted by firing one against a magnesium flare; as the flare floated slowly down beneath its parachute, the Sidewinder accelerated to three times the speed of sound, found its target and, with a spectacular explosion, the flare disappeared. This was a better performance than that of the Sea Cats, which were intended to protect the fleet; after two failures, in front of a large and expectant audience who had come on deck to watch the show, tests were abandoned as bad for morale. Pairs of planes tried their weapons systems on each other. They practised bombing raids and ship strike sorties. None of the pilots had seen action before; some had not even finished their training. Not surprisingly, there was, as Sharkey Ward put it, 'quite a little apprehension', mixed with excitement. Tests and practice continued until a final dawn push on Friday 16 April when, with Ascension Island almost in sight, the squadron conducted a weapon-proving trial involving 10 out of 12 aircraft dropping 1,000-pound bombs and firing rockets and a Sidewinder.

Drills were rehearsed. 'Assume State One, Condition Zulu.' This command, broadcast over the tannoy, brought the whole ship to action stations. Hundreds of men burst pell-mell into passageways, life jackets and gas masks in hand, as they hurried in different directions to man all the defensive positions, operations room and damage-control headquarters. As they did so, they pulled on their white anti-flash hoods and gloves, designed to protect soft tissue against fireballs and worn since the days of the Battle of Jutland in the First World War. Steelwork clanged as watertight hatches and doors were slammed shut. The first time the procedure was practised it took half an hour; by the time *Hermes* had reached the battle zone, this was reduced to seven minutes.

Ascension Island, a volcanic outcrop in the middle of the South Atlantic, is part of a British Overseas Territory, where Wideawake Airfield had been rapidly regarrisoned by the RAF. The two-day stop that *Hermes* made here allowed time to repack her stores, while the marines practised attacks on the black sand of the beaches, in equatorial temperatures – conditions that were about as unlike those of the Falklands as it is possible to imagine. The engineers were glad of these no-flying days to repair the planes. The visit came to an abrupt end, though, on the morning of 18 April when action stations were called unexpectedly at a quarter to ten; the ship sailed immediately. A periscope had been sighted by a rating on RFA *Olmeda*; on investigation, the submarine turned out to be Russian. But a better omen, in the eyes of superstitious sailors, was provided by a pair of albatrosses that followed the ship. They were later joined by snow petrels, a bird that lives only in Antarctica. The suggestion that they should be shot since they posed a danger to the Sea Harriers' jet engines was successfully resisted by the more bird-loving officers.

Altogether *Hermes* took over three and a half weeks to steam to the Exclusion Zone. Films relieved some of the tedium: *The French Lieutenant's Woman* and even *10*, featuring the statuesque actress Bo Derek, took second place to *Scott of the Antarctic*, which offered a foretaste of the region to which they were heading. After leaving Ascension Island, *Hermes* adopted a routine of dawn and dusk action stations; the ship was now within range of enemy bombers. On 21 April, aircraft were quickly fitted with Sidewinders and sent to intercept a contact that had been made at 160 miles. It was a Boeing 707 in Argentine military colours, and even the squadron record book reflects the excitement: 'The first contact with the enemy!' Over the next five days, the 707 paid regular visits, pairs of Sea Harriers scrambling to meet it. On 26 April, the command decided that enough was enough: the rules of engagement were changed to allow the Sea Harriers to harass the plane, fire across its nose if necessary, and even shoot it down if it came within forty miles of the Task Force. But the 707 knew that it had outstayed its welcome; it spontaneously stopped coming.

On 28 April, the practice drop of a cluster bomb was performed by Nick, and produced a 'very impressive' outcome, the 'resultant area of beaten water' being a 'sobering sight'. A bomblet that detonated prematurely 'sent a white-hot slug of copper whistling past his tail'.

The squadron formed a tight group. They all knew each other, even the RAF boys who joined after hostilities had started, as reinforcements. All the Sea Harrier pilots went through RAF Wittering. Captain Middleton, a South African by birth, had spent his early career as a pilot (in contrast to Admiral Sandy Woodward, who was a submariner). Not an outgoing man, he left it to his commander to update the ship's company over the tannoy or CCTV system. RAF pilots felt less than welcome on board *Hermes* – some naval figures wanted to show that the Senior Service, which had been in line for the worst of the defence cuts, both had a role to play and could stand on its own feet.

With his submarine background, Woodward was well aware of the long-range threat represented by Argentina's two submarines, and *Hermes* went on to a war footing as soon as she left Ascension. Nobody was allowed to sleep on decks below sea level in case the ship was torpedoed during the night. Proximity to the Flag – as the admiral's staff was collectively known – was a dubious privilege for 800 Squadron, exposing it to greater control and supervision than its sister on *Invincible*, under the boisterously independent Sharkey Ward. On the other hand, 801 Squadron thought the pilots on *Hermes* were favourably treated as regards the allocation of tasks.

Poring over the essential *Jane's All the World's Aircraft* – British intelligence, as shared with the people who needed it most, was not brilliant – Nick and his colleagues knew that the Argentine forces were well equipped. The latter had recently taken delivery of five Super Étendard aircraft and five Exocet missiles from France (although the time their pilots had been able to spend flying the Super Étendards was limited). These formed part of an air force that numbered 240 planes. There were reasons for British confidence: many of the planes were stationed along the Chilean border, others were outdated, their pilots were not well versed in the most recent tactics and, with little ability to refuel in flight, any planes reaching the Falklands would be operating at the limit of their range. At the end of March, four Super Étendards had visited Yeovilton, and in the inevitable mock battle that ensued 'the Squadron was able to claim victory', according to the squadron record book. However, there were also good reasons for apprehension: the twenty Sea Harriers looked like David to Argentina's Goliath, some of whose aircraft were – unlike the Sea Harrier – supersonic.

Hermes and *Invincible*, supported by their destroyers and frigates – the core of a Task Force that would soon, with transport ships, number 127 vessels – reached the edge of the Exclusion Zone on 30 April. Two aircraft were now kept permanently in the air on combat air patrol. Two other pairs were kept on alert, on the flight deck and in the crew room. Throughout the cold South Atlantic nights, pilots waited, strapped into their jets. It was a tense and gruelling procedure, which no individual pilot was expected to endure for more than an hour and a half at a stretch; after that time he would have been too numb to fly. Cartoons in the 800 Squadron's unofficial record book reveal what the pilots felt about this cold and lonely vigil – even if, as the commander of 801 Squadron complained, it was the *Invincible* pilots who bore the brunt.

At 04.38 hours local time the next morning, the conflict opened with a coup de théâtre: the sinister shape of a black, bat-like Avro Vulcan bombed Port Stanley airfield, which possessed the only concrete runway on the islands, in an operation melodramatically code-named Black Buck. The Vulcan was an elderly plane, brought into service in 1960 to serve as Britain's airborne nuclear deterrent, ready to drop a retaliatory nuclear bomb on Russia, from a high level, when needed. It seemed almost incredible that it could attack Port Stanley, not least because the flight from the nearest British air base at Ascension Island would require no fewer than seventeen refuelling operations (not only to refuel the Vulcan, but to fill up the tankers that were doing the refuelling) on an 8,000-mile round trip. The British taxpayer faced a bill for a barely imaginable quantity of fuel. So little had the RAF been expecting to use its Vulcan force in this way that vital refuelling probes had to be borrowed from the RAF Museum in Hendon and the Imperial War Museum at Duxford (to be returned after the war). Flying over water, without land features to take radar bearings from, the crews had to navigate by sextant ('great big things like donkey dicks', as one plotter inelegantly put it). In a sense, the apparent implausibility was part of the point, sending, as Sir John Curtiss recalled later, 'a message to friend Galtieri in Buenos Aires that we had a capability of attacking at very long range'. The bombing's more immediate objective was to prevent the Argentines extending the airfield and flying Super Étendards from it. Operating from the mainland, Argentine jets carried just enough fuel to reach the Task Force (400 miles away) and return, allowing barely five minutes to operate in the skies overhead. This logistical challenge would evaporate if they could be based at Port Stanley.

The Vulcan crew had their own difficulties to overcome. One was that, as a nuclear bomber, the plane had not been designed to drop conventional weapons: nuclear bombs do not need to be delivered with great precision, whereas iron bombs do. Makeshift lines were drawn on the windscreen to provide the pilot with a visual range. In the end, the plane that completed the mission was the reserve: the pilot who had been expecting to go through with it had slid open the cockpit window while still on Ascension Island for a little fresh air and then been unable to close it properly, meaning that his Vulcan could not leave. Twenty-one 1,000-pound bombs were released in an arc over the Port Stanley airfield, one of them ripping a scar in the runway that was 250 yards long. Coming at the start of the campaign, it gave the spirits of the Harrier pilots a fillip; but the success was not repeated in the four subsequent Vulcan raids. Within twenty-four hours the crater had been repaired by the Argentines, but not sufficiently to take fast jet aircraft. The attack achieved its objective. The generals were frightened into thinking that a long-range attack could be made on the Argentine mainland, provoking a revolution. It kept most of the Mirage IIIs (which would have been troublesome to the Sea Harriers if, as expected, they had stood guard over Argentine attacks) on the mainland to defend the home turf. From then on, the use of Port Stanley was more or less limited to Hercules transports, resupplying the garrison at night. The Vulcan pilot, Martin Withers, felt that it 'wasn't cricket' to bomb an airfield that was so little expecting to be attacked that its lights were on. However, he soon broadcast the codeword 'Superfuse', to indicate a successful mission, and returned to Ascension Island nearly sixteen hours after setting off.

A couple of hours after the Vulcan had struck, Nick and the eleven other Sea Harrier pilots climbed into their working rig. First came the woolly undergarment known as a bunny suit, then sweaters were piled on. Military planes have little heating – too much weight to carry, too much to go wrong if the plane is hit – and so warm clothing is needed, particularly in the harsh climate of the South Atlantic. A G-suit consisting of inflated pouches was strapped to abdomen and legs, the object being to squeeze those parts of the body affected so that blood did not pool under the effect of gravity in legs and midriff. Shoulder holsters had been quickly run up out of thick canvas to hold a Browning automatic pistol and ammunition. Then, with difficulty, the men struggled into their green canvas 'goon suits', with a waterproof zip from groin to shoulder and rubber seals around the wrists and neck. Over this went a life jacket. Helmet, oxygen mask and gloves completed the outfit. It did not make movement easy. Despite extrovert personalities that could verge on the bumptious, the pilots shuffled rather than swaggered.

The Sea Harrier pilot David Morgan has described the flight deck of *Hermes* in his book *Hostile Skies*.

> Imagine an area of steel the size of two football pitches, surrounded by a drop of sixty feet into the sea. Place on the right-hand edge a steel tower another sixty feet high, covered in masts and radars. Add piles of bombs, missiles, rockets and torpedoes, half a dozen Sea Harriers, their engines producing an ear-splitting whine even at idle, and a couple of helicopters with rotor blades slicing the air six feet above your head. Sprinkle this scene liberally with men cocooned against the noise and weather in various coloured jerseys denoting their functions moving purposefully around their charges. Add, finally, several hundred ringbolts and lashing chains to trip the unwary and a thirty-knot wind to unbalance you.

It was a dangerous place for the uninitiated. Nick and the rest of the squadron went there at about ten o'clock, walked slowly around their planes, checking, and climbed in.

The cockpit of a Sea Harrier may be small but everything is within easy reach. Tightly strapped in, a pilot could find it 'actually quite comfortable'. Set into the riveted grey steel of the shell, the paint chipped by long use, were a closely packed array of rather basic-looking dials, knobs, switches and display screens, as well as the central control column with its buttons. The whole display produced a barrage of complicated information that had to be processed at great speed, simultaneously. But this was the pilots' natural element. Once shut into the aircraft and airborne, they could not see very much of the plane itself; as Peter Squire, commander of the RAF's 1 Squadron which joined as reinforcements, commented, 'You feel very free.'

The flight-deck loudspeakers boomed with the command: 'Start the Sea Harriers.' It was 06.40. Eight minutes later, the light beneath the jutting 'Flyco' (Flight Control) window turned green and the officer waved a green flag to the floor. The first pilot opened the throttle to maximum, and a few seconds later the Sea Harrier shot up the ski-ramp, leaving the planes behind it buffeted by the wake. Within ten minutes, all twelve planes were in the sky. Nine of them grouped into a defensive formation and headed for Port Stanley. Shortly before they made landfall, a jittery pilot nearly mistook the remaining three aircraft, which took a different course, for the enemy. Those three were heading on a separate mission to Darwin. They were after the Pucará aircraft parked on the small airstrip outside the Falklands' tiny second settlement, at Goose Green. (After the war, it was discovered that the Argentines had established a napalm manufactory there, with napalm gel, mixing machines and napalm-filled bombs.) It was, in terms of the weather, a typical Falklands day: heavy rain was falling from cloud at 1,200 feet. The three planes flew in at fifty feet, jinking to confuse the enemy, and rose slightly to drop their bombs. There seemed to be a dozen Pucarás parked around the airstrip, although some of them could have been dummies. Two or three of the Pucarás may have been destroyed; some fires were started, but without causing a secondary explosion. The bad weather prevented accurate assessment. 'Goose Green not known,' was how Admiral Sandy Woodward summed up the state of intelligence in his report the next day. The 800 Squadron record book for May 1982 is more confident: 'The Darwin aircraft cratered the field and destroyed or damaged 5 aircraft with 3 x 1000lb bombs and 6 cluster bomb units. All aircraft returned safely although FLT LT MORGAN'S aircraft sustained a 20mm shell hit in the fin, and some smaller holes in the tailplane.'

The twelve planes returned to *Hermes*. 'I counted them all out,' the BBC's Brian Hanrahan would tell the world, in the most famous phrase of the war, 'and I counted them all back.' The raid had lasted about forty minutes. The results may not have been spectacular but were considered a good start. Real reason for celebration came by the end of the day.

As soon as 800 Squadron was back on *Hermes*, the planes were switched from their bombing role back into fighters – an operation that the air crews had honed to fifteen minutes. They then took their turn as the pair kept permanently on CAP, or waiting in their cockpits on alert. Little could be done during the morning. The Argentine planes that approached the Task Force, threatening to give battle, broke away and ran for home at the last moment. But in the dying hours of the afternoon, the direction officer on HMS *Glamorgan* picked up two Mirages at twenty-five miles' distance. They appeared on the radar screens of the two CAP planes from *Invincible* at seventeen miles. One was hit by a Sidewinder and dissolved into a ball of flame and wreckage. The second took evasive action by diving spirally into cloud, but another Sidewinder had locked on to him; it exploded near the plane, badly damaging it, so that it limped towards Port Stanley. Before landing, the unfortunate pilot jettisoned his spare weapons: the garrison, thinking they were under attack, shot it down. A few minutes later, Bertie Penfold from 800 Squadron 'splashed' a Mirage V at a range of about three miles, one of a pair which had just fired Matra 530 missiles at him and Lieutenant Hale. Then, as the dusk thickened, a bearing was taken on what appeared to be incoming jets; the CAP went to investigate and found three Canberra bombers closing at 200 feet above the sea. They were attacked from behind. One was seen to explode, another disappeared into the clouds, pursued by a Sidewinder, fate unknown. That evening, the Sea Harrier squadrons could congratulate themselves on four definite and two possible kills. They were naturally elated, although not mindlessly so; Penfold was deeply distressed that the pilot he shot down had not ejected, and he did not fly again during the conflict. The day's action, though, had an incalculable effect as far as the saving of British lives was concerned. The Sea Harriers had proved their ability to dominate the skies. Argentine pilots did not risk engaging them again. Their respect can be gathered from the nickname that they gave to the Sea Harrier: *la muerta negra* (the black death). In the whole of the war, no Sea Harrier was lost to an enemy plane. The significance of the achievement can be judged by comparing the reality to the informal prediction made by the Flag Officer Naval Command who remarked before the campaign opened that he did not expect more than a quarter of the Sea Harrier pilots to return.

After the elation, the squadrons resumed the excitement of their patrols, interspersed by the tedium of their alerts. The next dramatic action happened not above the sea but below it, when the nuclear submarine HMS *Conqueror* torpedoed the Argentine cruiser *General Belgrano*, with the loss of 368 lives. The legitimacy of the attack – the ship was steaming away from the Exclusion Zone at the time – started a long-running controversy, not least in the British Parliament. However, the Argentine aircraft carrier *Veinticinco de Mayo* had been manoeuvring with its battlegroup, presumably in preparation for an attack on the Task Force, the evening before; but there was too little wind to allow it to launch its planes.

Conditions on board *Hermes* were very different from what they had been when the Task Force left Portsmouth. For some of the voyage south, officers continued to dine in what Brian Hanrahan described as 'traditional normal splendour. They wore cummerbunds and evening dress, sat at tables laid with a silver service, and ate by the light of candelabra.' Such formalities were abandoned as *Hermes* approached the Falklands. Tables were overturned and tied down, 'the chairs locked on top like barricades in a Belfast street'. The men now wore overalls, to which were attached gas mask, lifejacket and survival suit – 'an all-embracing garment made of dayglo orange rubber. It looks like a pair of baggy pyjamas, but wearing it in the chilly waters of the South Atlantic increases survival time from minutes to hours.' But to Rupert Nichol, instructor officer on *Hermes*, it seemed that certain decencies were maintained. The men liked to change regularly, if only into a different set of overalls. They always ate well. Since some of the other ships in the fleet had sailed straight from the Mediterranean, *Hermes* gave them some of her stores, including the prepared meals that could be served and eaten within twenty-five minutes. This left her with only fresh food, which – whatever the danger in wartime from ovens and friers – had to be properly cooked. The provisions had been loaded in expectation of a friendly visit to the United States, with appropriate entertainment, and included a substantial quantity of smoked salmon and even some caviar. Somebody had to eat it. Broccoli featured prominently on the list of fresh vegetables, being suitable to freeze (the captain's last meal included, by way of a farewell to the over-abundant brassica, broccoli ice cream). Claret was limited to a bottle a week but there was an apparently limitless supply of hock, of a brand called Black Tower; there was also plenty of beer.

But the opportunity to eat had to be snatched from a schedule that kept pilots, when not in the air, in an almost permanent state of readiness. Days, as Sharkey Ward recalled:

> . . . were becoming distinctly blurred. Alert, airborne, alert, airborne, night alert, airborne; although being on alert on deck was more often than not followed by a return to the crewroom. In between came the Command Briefings, squadron updates, a bite to eat, an occasional beer, and intermittent sleep.
>
> By the evening of the 2nd I was pooped.

Another bombing raid was made on 4 May. The second Black Buck bombed Port Stanley airfield in a repeat of the previous Vulcan operation; this was again followed by an attack from Sea Harriers. *Hermes* and the escorting ships, including HMS *Sheffield*, moved closer to the islands, to put Port Stanley and Goose Green within range of heavily loaded planes. Low cloud and fog kept them there, until the raid could be launched. As far as Goose Green was concerned, the confidence of the planners was boosted by a reconnaissance flight the day before, which mistakenly reported that Goose Green had no anti-aircraft defences. But the attack was a rerun of 1 May, ignoring one of the fundamental rules of war – to be unpredictable. This time the defenders were ready. Thirty seconds from the target, Gordie Batt, the pilot in front of Nick, heard the whine in his headset which told him that the radar of a pair of Oerlikon 35mm anti-aircraft cannons had locked on to his plane. He released a scatter of metal chaff to deceive it, and swung the plane violently left. This broke the lock; he continued the attack. But Nick's plane, retained by the manufacturer as a test aircraft, was not fitted with a radar warning receiver. He would not have known that the enemy radar had got a lock – probably transferred from Batt's plane as he flew through its chaff. As soon as they were back on *Hermes*, the other pilots watched, frame by frame, the film taken through the gunsight of the third aircraft as Nick's plane was hit by an explosive round behind the cockpit. The fuselage shattered. An instant later, the Sea Harrier burst into a fireball. Nick did not have time to eject; he may have been killed instantly. He was still strapped into his seat when the Argentines recovered his body; they buried him with full military honours.

His was the first British death in the war. By the time it was reported in Britain, it had been overshadowed by the loss of HMS *Sheffield*, hit by an Exocet launched from a Super Étendard, later that day (moving the carrier group nearer the islands had brought the ships within range). But Nick's death was of some importance to the development of the war. When the Argentines studied his plane, they saw that it had been fitted with Sea Eagle, a more advanced weapon than Exocet. This may have contributed to the decision to keep the Argentine navy in port for the remainder of the conflict.

In Yeovilton, Clare was the one who took the call reporting her own husband's death. She never wholly recovered from it. Eventually she rebuilt her life and found a new partner, and together they had four beautiful children. But as she lay dying of cancer, she refused to be scared by death, saying, 'I know I am going to see Nick.' Harry Taylor was almost as badly affected – although, as a military man, he insisted that Nick's body should be buried where he fell. 'His grave is tended to this day by the grateful residents of Goose Green, who regard him as very much one of their own,' reports 800 Squadron's David Morgan. 'He will never be lonely.'

13

Every Man an Emperor

— ANDREW KELLY —

There was nothing comfortable about the desert camp. Soldiers came from Kuwait International Airport by a turboprop C-130 Hercules, of a vintage when military aviation was even more basic than Ryanair. As the arriving soldiers filed out of the gaping fuselage, the heat rising from the desert airfield hit them like a wall. The temperature was about double that which they had left in the UK. Rather than an English spring, chill and damp but full of promise, they were treated to the searing, sandy aridity of the desert, where the dust stings your eyes, parches your mouth and gets into your food.

This being the army, the first thing that confronted new arrivals was a queue, and as they stood in it, their eyes had to adjust to a glare which had burnt everything to a universal shade of pale dust. The British forces adapted their colour scheme to match. Even the white Jeep Cherokee that the BBC film crew hired for the duration of the war had been repainted in the regulation sand colour. That, too, was the colour of most of the uniforms – though not all. Some units were low on desert issue so a number of soldiers, unless they were able to source their own, were compelled to wear the standard camouflage, its green and brown pattern designed for concealment among the hedgerows of western Europe rather than the empty deserts of Iraq. Sunglasses were no longer merely fashion items. Bottles of water had never seemed more valuable. In a stifling tent, the men were briefed on driving, local customs and law, health and hygiene, and the security situation. Duckboards kept men's feet out of the sand and lined the tents that they slept in. There were no beds; they rolled their bedding out on to the boards and lay on that. Fierce dust storms sometimes blew away the tents altogether, so that their occupants had to spend the night in the cookhouse. No, not the least bit comfortable. But for Private Andrew Kelly, this was the only place he wanted to be.

Andrew was eighteen. For the last three or four years, he had been consumed by a single ambition: to join the Parachute Regiment. His father Rob had spent twenty-four years in the Royal Navy, during which he sailed with the Falklands Task Force. Although Andrew was born in Plymouth, his schooling took place within the great granite cliff of Victorian Gothic that is Kelly College (architect Charles Hansom, whose brother Joseph designed the eponymous cab), a private school on the edge of Tavistock. Rob and his wife, Helen, had built up a successful chain of fish and chip shops, but finances tightened after they divorced. So at the age of fourteen Andrew switched schools, exchanging the privilege and the lawns of Kelly College for the less exalted surroundings of its state rival, Tavistock College – one of the largest secondary schools in Devon. He was not concerned about it; by then he knew that he wanted to join the Paras. But since his private school background was not likely to recommend him to his new peers, he let it be known, quite incorrectly, that he had been expelled. This changed perceptions entirely. It gave him street cred. He was also on the way to reaching six foot two.

Wherever he was, Andrew had no difficulty in making friends. Sport formed an instant bond. He was an exceptionally good footballer, playing for a team at Bere Alston; he loved in-line skating, practising jumps and moves at Mary Tavy before graduating to the big skate parks at Plymouth and Truro. He also had the knack of avoiding scraps with his peers by making a joke or finding the soft answer that turneth away wrath. Some of his closest friends were made at 'Tavi' College, one of them being Joe Smith; to Joe he seemed to be 'always laughing and joking and always looking for the funny side of things'. But adults saw that he was not entirely the typical adolescent, being exceptionally polite – always carrying his mother's shopping bags (without being asked), never letting her open the car door herself, writing her a card to thank her for Christmas. He was tidy too. Everything in his room was neatly organized. He took care over his appearance and had something of a reputation among his group for the quality of his designer-label shirts. While some boys are embarrassed by displays of affection, he was not afraid to end every mobile call to his mother with the words, 'I love you, Mum.' When teased by his friends, he replied, 'But I do.'

Until the age of fourteen, Andrew had not been sure of what he would do for a living; he had begun to investigate the Fire Brigade. Then he found a mission in life. It happened when he went to an army fair at Torpoint, in Cornwall. Among the people he met was a soldier from the Parachute Regiment. The man's physical presence and natural authority commanded respect. It was an inspirational meeting. From then on, the word 'Airborne' was never far from his lips.

Andrew was conscious of the regiment's history. Founded in 1940 at the specific request of Winston Churchill for 'a corps of at least five thousand parachute troops, suitably organised and equipped', it had played a dramatic role during the D-Day landings. Jack Bickle died at Nijmegen, trying to reach men of the Parachute Regiment who, with Polish airborne troops, had been dropped at Arnhem; their doomed struggle was told in heroic terms in the 1977 film *A Bridge Too Far*. Andrew visited the Normandy beaches and other sites. He delighted in talking to veterans, admiring the pride that they continued to take in the high polish of their shoes. For Andrew, joining the army would not have been enough: it was the Paras or nothing.

After leaving Tavi College at sixteen, Andrew spent a year at the Army Foundation College at Harrogate. There he joined Waterloo Company, one of the five training companies. His platoon – 1 Platoon – was named after the Duke of Wellington's cavalry commander, Lord Uxbridge. Other recruits had posters of footballers, female pop stars and provocatively posed young women around their beds; Andrew's space was a microcosm of what meant most to him – photographs of his immediate family, his two dogs, his grandparents, his nephews, and girlfriends from Tavi College at the leavers' prom wearing long dresses. He was now Junior Soldier Kelly. Letters to his mother would be signed 'Love, J. S. Kelly. P. S. Airborne'.

From Harrogate, Andrew went to the School of Infantry at

Catterick for the Combat Infantry Course. While there he had
to attempt the arduous Pre-Parachute Selection Test, known to all as
'P Company'. The test itself began on Wednesday morning with a
10-mile march, to be completed in 1 hour 50 minutes, while carrying
a Bergen, or backpack, weighing 35 pounds, plus weapon. That afternoon came the 'trainasium', a course that involves running across
treetop scaffolds, swinging on ropes and leaping into nets, in order to
assess a candidate's ability to overcome fear above ground level.
Thursday opened with a team event: 8 soldiers carried a 60-kilogram
log over a distance of nearly 2 miles. There was another march in the
afternoon: shorter than the one on Wednesday morning – only 2
miles – but with a helmet and combat jacket added to the Bergen and
weapon, and to be completed in 18 minutes or less. On Friday came
the 'steeplechase', a cross-country run followed by an assault course,
followed by 'milling' (60 seconds of 'controlled physical aggression'
against an opponent). On Monday, Andrew faced the endurance
march, crossing 20 miles of 'severe terrain' in under 4 hours 30 minutes. Having survived thus far, he had one test yet to accomplish: the
stretcher race, in which a team of 16 soldiers simulate the withdrawal
of a wounded comrade from the battlefield by carrying a stretcher
made of welded steel sheet, to simulate the weight of a man, over a
5-mile course, against the clock. They wear webbing and carry a
weapon. Test week is so mentally and physically demanding that
there is no shame in failure. Andrew passed. His mother was not surprised: 'He had the right mental attitude. Failure would not have
been an option for him.' Andrew left Catterick wearing the coveted
maroon beret.

Next stop was RAF Brize Norton for the Basic Parachute Course.
Most of the men on the course were destined for the Parachute Regiment. It involved nine jumps. The experience had not changed very
much since Martin Lindsay, the future commander of 151 Battalion,
made his first jump, as an early volunteer, in 1941.

Everybody was so very witty.
    'Don't do like the man who made a hole in the Brighton Road. He
pulled his tie instead of his rip cord.'
    '. . . it's guaranteed to open. If it doesn't, they give you a new one.'

. . . We climbed into the aircraft and sat on the floor of the fuselage. The engines roared and we took off . . . I noticed how moist the palms of my hands were. I wished I didn't always feel slightly sick in an aircraft.

The next morning Lindsay was woken by Private Wells, who was a fellow of Balliol College in private life.

[A] nice morning,' his voice droned on, 'and what will you be wearing today, Sir? Shall I put out your new tartan trews or your canvas overalls? If you are contemplating another descent today, Sir, I should recommend the overalls. I have cleaned off all the – ah – the – ah – *excretum vacci.*'

The difference was, Andrew had no Private Wells.

But you cannot become a member of the Parachute Regiment without parachuting, and Andrew just wanted his parachute wings. To his consternation, bad weather threatened to postpone the last jump, but it cleared sufficiently to go ahead on Valentine's Day 2003. There was no time to be lost. Britain was almost at war.

Andrew could hardly wait to turn eighteen, the age at which it is possible for a soldier to go on active service. By the time he arrived at Hyderabad Barracks in Colchester, most of the 3rd Battalion, to which Andrew now belonged, had already left for Kuwait. He made a nuisance of himself, knocking on doors, begging anyone who would listen, so as to be allowed to join them. Although a novice, he was sufficiently savvy to know that it was worth buying some of your own equipment – or those elements of it that a soldier most depends upon, such as boots. He soon had the reputation of being better turned out than some seasoned regulars, with better kit. At last his birthday arrived on 9 March. Five days later, he was on his way. He already knew Brize Norton from jump school. Wearing his maroon beret and combat fatigues, and carrying his body armour and rifle, he presented himself there on 14 March. The RAF Tristar took off, heading east.

In 1991, the First Gulf War had been fought by a broad coalition, forged by President George H. Bush, to expel Saddam Hussein's forces from Kuwait. This it achieved, but as the remnant of the dictator's broken army limped back to Baghdad on a highway littered with the charred shells of tanks and lorries, Saddam still clung to power. When the Twin Towers of the World Trade Center in New York were destroyed on 9/11, President George W. Bush launched a 'war on terror', directed not only against the perpetrators, Al Qaeda, but also the unstable and vengeful Saddam, who was thought to have been in possession of a variety of deadly weapons that he could, at any time, launch against the West. (It was later found that these weapons of mass destruction did not exist; Saddam had preferred to be attacked, defeated and deposed than to reveal Iraq's vulnerability to his many foes by admitting that his bluff had been called.) Tony Blair put Britain shoulder to shoulder with the United States, in a coalition that otherwise contained only Australia and Poland. It was not a popular course at home. Not wishing to risk a defeat in parliament, Blair barely consulted MPs, who spent more time debating fox hunting than the coming war. Even the Cabinet was sidelined, decisions being made by a small coterie of senior ministers and advisers.

Proportionately, the contribution made by Britain to a much smaller army was greater than that in 1991. Its troops comprised about a third of the total force. While they were not equipped with all the sophisticated hardware of the Americans, they had other skills. Decades of conflict in Northern Ireland had honed their ability to patrol urban streets, spotting the danger points represented by a suspect car, a lone male, the alleyway in which an enemy might be concealed. They were as skilled in old-fashioned marksmanship as Charlie Berry's contemporaries in the British Expeditionary Force. The toughness of forces such as the Parachute Regiment was legendary. As the pilots of 211 Squadron, bombing Italian positions around the Western Desert in 1940, would have confirmed, Britain had longstanding interests and experience in the Middle East. British troops were tasked with taking Basra, Iraq's second city, many of whose Shia population detested the Sunni regime, while the Americans used their ability to travel quickly over long distances and to resupply in the dash for Baghdad.

Before leaving the UK at the beginning of the year, 3 PARA's second in command, Major Mark Christie, expressed dauntless optimism. 'Whatever happens,' he told the *Daily Telegraph*, 'we will win.' In truth, there was never any real doubt as to the military outcome, given the demoralized condition of Saddam's poorly equipped forces, which had not been rebuilt after the catastrophe of 1991. This was not the Falklands. What the future might bring for individual soldiers, facing all the uncertainties of war, was another matter. They were, however, glad to be active. This was the job they had been trained to do. Their most recent deployment had been to provide emergency cover as firemen during a Fire Brigade strike. Manning the Green Goddesses — as the army's fleet of Bedford RLHZ self-propelled pumps, built in the 1950s, are colloquially known – was not their cup of tea. 'It was interesting for a day or two,' observed Major Christie. 'But Paras are not very good at sitting around.' Lieutenant Colonel John Lorimer, the commanding officer, summed up the mood of the battalion: 'Morale is high. Some of the men are as young as eighteen, but they know their job. They know what they came into the army to do.'

When Andrew joined his battalion, he was the youngest soldier in A Company, but made an immediate impression through his enthusiasm and personality. 'He showed a great deal of professional pride, and seemed a very happy soldier,' remembers Brigadier Giles Hill, who was then the company commander. 'He was very well organized. He loved being there, he loved being busy, he loved soldiering.' Andrew quickly settled into the group and made friends. 'The company felt very paternal towards him.'

On 18 March, 3 PARA moved up to the tents of Camp Longdon near the Iraqi border. In Ministry of Defence speak, the 16th Air Assault Brigade, of which 3 PARA was part, could 'deploy, and fight across enormous depth to secure a point of entry to a theatre of operations', acting as 'an enabler for the follow-on deployment of heavier formations'. Rifles and machine guns were cleaned and checked, live ammunition issued. Convoys of tanks and armoured personnel carriers crawled across the sands to the main Basra Highway. Helicopters flew in low. Simon Marsh, a 25-year-old Irish guardsman from Liverpool, wanted the action to start.

It will be a relief and a release. We know we are close and it is just a
matter of when we go. There are nerves, not fear, but obviously questions
of will we let anyone down, will we do it when it comes to the crunch.
I am sure we will, it is what we have trained for, but we never thought it
would happen.

Having spent the day on firing ranges in the desert, acclimatizing
as best they could to the ferocious temperatures, they watched news
reports on the satellite TV in the cookhouse – and knew that conflict
was becoming steadily more certain. Those with access to Land
Rover Wolfs, their roll bars festooned, in the manner of fishing boats,
with camouflage netting, would drive off to the American base to
equip themselves with items that would be useful in the forthcoming
campaign, such as GPS devices. Lavatory roll was at a premium.

The Paras had assumed that their entry into Iraq would be made
by helicopter; some of 1 PARA had even been practising jumps. In
the event they piled into four-ton trucks, rolling across the fea-
tureless landscape, cut about with canals, on roads built up on to
earth embankments or berms. Mouths were wrapped in scarves to
keep out the dust; sunglasses protected eyes from sand particles as
well as the glare. Their first objective was to secure the Rumaylah
oilfields that straddle the border. A Company advanced to the crossing point of a canal; the bridge there had been destroyed. Whatever
deficiencies were being felt as regards kit in other sections of the
army, A Company felt it had everything it needed. It was travelling
light. 'Our shovels were sharp enough, our water bottles had tops
that screwed on, we had the latest respirators and new machine guns.
We didn't have anything that we couldn't carry,' observes Brigadier
Hill. In a way that would have been familiar to Charles Berry and his
contemporaries, the company dug trenches, and waited; from time
to time, they were shelled or sniped at. Having secured the south side
of the canal, they crossed to the north.

Oil rigs could be seen in the distance, some of them sending huge
pillars of thick black smoke into the pale sky. The way was littered
with abandoned vehicles, some of them armoured. Eight Iraqi sol-

diers surrendered to the BBC crew. But there was also some well-aimed shelling, directed by apparently anonymous individuals on pick-up trucks or motorbikes, who were really spotters for the Iraqi artillery. A week was spent clearing up this sporadic opposition. Meanwhile, British Challenger tanks opened the way to Basra and British forces were entering the scatter of half-finished concrete buildings and baked earth that constituted the suburbs. 3 PARA was tasked with taking the warren of backstreets and alleyways that made up the old city.

On 7 April, the battalion assembled soon after dawn at the College of Literature. The day before, it had been seized in an operation that caused the death of three British soldiers from other units, and over a hundred of the Ba'ath party diehards known as Fedayeen. Gunshots indicated that the complex was still not completely clear, but the threat was soon dealt with. However, the men waited in their body armour until, at midday, the temperature reached forty-five degrees in the shade. Sweltering, the men then walked into the old city. They had been warned to use the patrolling techniques which they had learnt from Belfast. They split into two groups, taking separate parallel roads. A boy ran forward carrying a wad of banknotes, flinging them on to the ground and grinding his foot on the face of Saddam. It turned out to be an accurate reflection of local feeling. Soldiers crouched down, aiming their rifles at possible hiding places for Fedayeen. But the Fedayeen were not there. Instead came children, crowds of them, anxious to try out their few English phrases, asking, 'Hi, what's your name?' and, 'How are you?' High fives were exchanged. 'It's mad out there,' laughed Private Jamie Keeling, aged twenty-one, from Derbyshire. 'It's out of this world. I didn't expect this.' The soldiers were surrounded by 'smiling and happy' children.

Next to the Nadran river, an aircraft gun was protected by sandbags, but the position had long been abandoned. Occasionally there would be a burst of gunfire, but not enough to disrupt the life of the city – or to prevent looters from piling barrows with furniture or air-conditioning units. One group of men had managed to hotwire a red fire engine. Others were seen towing away a full-sized boat behind a truck. A blaze of sparks was raised by the chains attached to a generator block. Looting was felt to be unavoidable at that stage of the campaign and was the reason for the delayed start; it was deemed better to let the looters get on with it than to attempt to stop them (with possible loss of civilian life) before securing the city.

It turned out well for 3 PARA. Hand-to-hand fighting through Basra's backstreets, as fighters dodged among the civilian population, did not materialize. Afterwards, in the inevitable inter-army rivalry on such occasions, some voices claimed that they were given too much credit for the operation. The *Daily Record*, keen to play up the Scottish angle, quoted a senior officer of the Scots Dragoon Guards as saying:

> After several days of us fighting our way into Basra, it was then deemed insensitive to take tanks and warriors into the narrow centre streets, which were a lot more suited to the light infantry. As 3 PARA were sitting in reserve, it was a good chance for them to stretch their legs and prove what we already knew.

Let the cavalry say what it liked. To most soldiers, all that mattered was that Basra had been taken, and it was 3 PARA who had been brave enough to do it. Their mission accomplished, they withdrew the next day, leaving it to the infantry to keep the peace.

3 PARA moved north of the city, basing themselves at an airfield on the highway to Al Amarah, previously known as Objective Condor, but popularly rechristened Montgomery Lines after the four barracks that comprise the old regimental depot at Aldershot. Their job was to keep the supply routes open, collect weapons from towns and villages, and do what they could to establish civil infrastructure in a region whose senior figures, such as the chief of police, had often gone into hiding as representatives of the hated Ba'athist regime. A local schoolmaster or engineer might be encouraged to form a small committee to keep a town going. Meanwhile, local scores were being settled and armed groups were infiltrating from Iran. It was a period of chaos. As Brigadier Matthew Lowe, who commanded 3 PARA from March 2003, remembers:

The pattern of life reflected the security vacuum in the early summer months. Locals were initially glad to be able to go out and buy food. Children could be found playing in deserted ammunition depots. Women were out in the fields tending crops. Telephone lines would be dug up for their scrap value. There was a degree of tribal feuding, and one or two of the villages resumed intra-community firefights at night-time.

In this border area, A Company, of which Andrew was now part, was 'particularly good' at unpicking village politics and were 'the first to identify that groups of people were coming across from Iran'. To begin with it was not clear whether they represented refugees who had left in the 1990s and were now finding their way back home, or something more sinister. 'There were a couple of occasions when we detained people with advanced radios and large amounts of cash late at night. In hindsight these people may have been the precursor to the subsequent Iranian-sponsored insurgency.'

The soldiers of 3 PARA, patrolling in the heat, dreamt of food. As yet, no kitchens had been established, and for three months they had nothing to eat except rations: stews and pasta dishes designed for a very different climate from the scorching desert. Food parcels were as welcome here as they had been in the First World War trenches. Many men lost weight. There was no mention of this, though, in Andrew's letters home, which spoke only of being kept busy 'running around'. Occasionally he was able to phone. 'Don't worry about me, Mum,' he told Helen on his last call. 'Paras always go to heaven.'

They were living in a derelict building that had been abandoned by the Iraqi military. After coming back from a patrol, soldiers would clean their guns – half the company at a time so that the other half was always ready in case of attack. The men sat on the edge of the camp cots, chatting as they worked, perhaps about the parcels that had started to arrive from home, containing new socks and wine gums. On 6 May, Brigadier Hill was taking a shower from a solar-heated bag of water when he heard a loud bang from inside the building. In the echoey, concrete structure it sounded as though a grenade had gone off. He ran over to find Andrew being treated by the medic who had been only a few yards away. Tragically, a bullet had still been in the chamber of Andrew's SA80 rifle while he was cleaning it; somehow the safety catch had been left off and the trigger accidentally pulled.

It was the company's first loss, and that it should have visited such a popular, model young soldier devastated the company. Afterwards, the officer who sorted through Andrew's possessions found a couple of cans of Budweiser. They should not have been there, given the no-alcohol rule but 'somehow that summed up Andrew and the paratrooper he was – always pushing the boundaries and living life with a glint in his eye'. Brigadier Hill told Andrew's friends to crack them open and toast their dead comrade. He saw them later, around the back of the building, drinking the beer in the broiling heat and remembering their close friend 'in a way soldiers do'. It made an enduring image.

Andrew was the thirty-fourth member of the British forces to die in Iraq, and the youngest. When his body was flown home to Brize Norton, to be met by a ceremonial guard and the Duke of Gloucester, it was widely reported. Robert Kelly opened a campaign against the war, declaring that he would write to the Prime Minister to ask: '[W]ould he have put the British army into war if his son was the youngest soldier, just about to turn eighteen? What I want to say to him is that he shouldn't get away with it and I hope he doesn't.' His bitterness intensified during the summer, when the letter went unanswered for six weeks.

Outside the church at Maker, in South-East Cornwall, Andrew's best friend from Tavi College, Joe Smith, struck a different note. The military funeral would, he thought, have been 'exactly what [Andrew] wanted. He's probably looking down and thinking "How good is this".' Andrew was fully committed to the course he had chosen. 'He really felt he achieved something by going into the Paras and by going to Iraq. He felt he was doing something with his life.'

One of the possessions that Andrew kept with him at all times was a copy of the text by Field Marshal Montgomery describing the 'manner of men' who wear the maroon beret.

They are firstly all volunteers and are toughened by physical training. As a result they have infectious optimism and that offensive eagerness which comes from well-being. They have 'jumped' from the air and by doing so have conquered fear.

Their duty lies in the van of the battle. They are proud of this honour. They have the highest standards in all things whether it be skill in battle or smartness in the execution of all peacetime duties. They are in fact men apart – every man an emperor.

Of all the factors, which make for success in battle, the spirit of the warrior is the most decisive. That spirit will be found in full measure in the men who wear the maroon beret.

The cadences may be old-fashioned, but they had lost none of their potency for Andrew. They embodied an exceptionally high ideal; everyone who knew Andrew felt that he had lived up to it.

As his company commander says, 'When people take five minutes to stand before the Lydford war memorial, they see in his name youth, passion, commitment – everything that this nation should be proud of.'

Andrew, Helen and her husband Nick, together with her younger son Ross, had only lived in Lydford for a year or so before Andrew's death. It was a quieter village than the one Frank Fry had known. The farm animals had gone. The barns that used to be scattered along the village street were being converted into desirable homes or holiday lets. The school still made a respectable volume of noise at break time, but at hours other than drop-off or collection time the village was quiet; so few vehicles went past the Castle Inn that Morris dancers sometimes performed in the street, without fear of causing a traffic jam. Flocks of sheep were no longer driven through the village. Farming had become mechanized, with transport provided by lorries. Not that the times were, for those villagers who were dependent on agriculture, so much easier than they had been at the turn of the century; farming was going through another of its periodic depressions. On top of this had come foot-and-mouth disease. Memories of the 2001 pandemic, when thousands of sheep and cattle in

Devon, many of them healthy, were slaughtered and burnt, were still raw. Almost the only animals to be seen now were the dogs being walked on their way to the moor.

Lydford had not, over the past century, grown into being a picture-perfect village; thatched roofs were becoming a rarity even in Frank's day, and he was the son of a thatcher. There was evidence of new houses, not built in the traditional manner – bungalows made of concrete blocks, with nothing local about them. Planners from the Dartmoor National Park Authority now believe that these dwellings ought to be frozen in time, like the rest of the village. During the Second World War, the sidings beside Lydford Station had seen an extraordinary expansion at the hands of the American army; Theophilus Hammett would have been astonished to find that the track which he once controlled from his signal box had grown into the biggest junction west of Clapham Junction. This out-of-the-way spot was used to marshal tanks before D-Day. But the GWR branch from Plymouth had closed on New Year's Eve 1962, the LSWR line from Waterloo in 1968. The station buildings were knocked down, the track was taken up, and there was little to show that the railway had ever been there. Cars were now practically universal; it was difficult to live in the countryside without one.

Lydford's hair had turned silver, as more people lived to retirement age. Village England had become more safety-conscious; it was better housed and more comfortable, if generally less hardy and robust. It was also healthier. People were taller; their smiles did not reveal the missing front teeth that Dorothy L. Sayers observed as being 'frequently the case with country women' in the 1930s. Their homes had indoor plumbing. They were vastly more prosperous than the First World War generation. But whatever the changes that had taken place in the village and elsewhere in the country, they were no less patriotic.

Lydford remains a place of flags, where the national anthem is still sung at the end of an evening in the Nicholls Hall. Although Andrew had not been in the village long, it was natural that his name should be added to the war memorial, a tribute to a young man who was what every mother might hope her son to be. On the plinth, his story is now merged with that of the twenty-one men and one woman who preceded him, in such a variety of circumstances. They died so that the Lydfords of England would continue in their tranquil round, dictated by the slow eternal pace of the seasons rather than the urgency of military conflict.

The war memorial is only a harsh granite cross, but in some lights it seems to glow.

Roll-call of Names on the Lydford War Memorial

(Names are listed in the order in which they appear on the memorial.)

TO THE HONOURED MEMORY OF THOSE FROM THE PARISH WHO GAVE THEIR LIVES FOR KING, COUNTRY AND FREEDOM
1914–1918

C. H. BERRY — 9431 Lance Corporal Charles Henry Berry of the 3rd Battalion, the Worcestershire Regiment. Died 24 August 1916 aged thirty, in the Hindenburg Trench, near Leipzig Salient, Thiepval.

M. CLARK — 622906 Private Mancel Clark of the 27th Battalion, Canadian Infantry (Manitoba Regiment). Died 15 September 1916 aged twenty-four, at Courcelette, on the Somme.

F. W. FRY — 48228 Private Frank Wilfred Fry of the 11th Battalion, the Duke of Cornwall's Light Infantry. Died 24 March 1918 aged eighteen, at Larkhill, Wiltshire.

R. N. HOBBS — 21649 Private Richard Henry Hobbs of the 2nd Battalion, the Devonshire Regiment. Died 7 September 1916 aged twenty-seven, at Vermelles, north of Arras.

A. R. HUGGINS — 167 Sergeant Archibald Roger Huggins of the 1st Battalion, the Royal North Devon Hussars. Died 27 October 1915 aged twenty-nine, at Gallipoli.

G. H. T. LAKE — 43789 Private George Henry Taylor Lake of the 2nd Battalion, the Warwickshire Regiment. Died 14 November 1918 aged twenty-one, crossing the river Piave.

G. METTERS   Petty Officer Stoker George Metters, RN. Died
                          18 March 1916 aged forty-six. Buried at Lydford.

R. J. PETHERICK   19309 Private Richard John Petherick of the
                          5th Battalion, the Dorsetshire Regiment. Died
                          24 November 1916 aged twenty-one, at St Pierre
                          Divion, on the Somme.

R. R. TURNER   2nd Lieutenant Richard Radford Turner of the 3rd Bat-
                          talion, the Royal Sussex Regiment. Died 3 February
                          1917 aged twenty, at Railway Wood outside Ypres.

S. VOYZEY   45821 Private Samuel Voyzey of the 60th
(or VOYSEY)   Battalion, the Canadian Infantry. Died 18 September
                          1916 aged forty-four, near Le Mouquet Farm, Thiepval.

E. J. WHITFORD   R/4500 Sergeant Edward John Whitford of the 13th
                          Battalion, the King's Royal Rifle Corps. Died 11 April
                          1917 aged thirty-eight, at Monchy-le-Preux near Arras.

J. STEPHENS   388432 Lance Corporal James Stephens of the 816th
                          Employment Company. Died 11 May 1925 aged
                          forty-five, in the Devon Mental Hospital at Exeter.

W. H. DAW   Surgeon Commander William Henry Daw, RN. Died
                          14 November 1926 aged fifty-three, at Lydford.

SECOND WORLD WAR
1939–1945

L. A. J. BICKLE   14678965 Private Leslie Arthur John Bickle of the
                          4th Battalion, the Somerset Light Infantry. Died
                          9 October 1944 aged eighteen, at Elst near Nijmegen.

R. H. GILLETT   EC/1166 Major Richard Hamilton Gillett of the 10th
                          Baluch Regiment attached to the Indian Parachute
                          Regiment. Died 26 March 1944 aged twenty-four,
                          at Sangshak near Imphal, on the frontier between
                          India and Burma.

P. W. HERBERT | 82676 Flying Officer Philip William Herbert of the RAF VR, the Photographic Reconnaissance Unit. Died 26 January 1942 aged twenty-six, at RAF Benson, Oxfordshire.

S. E. M. BICKLE | W/340412 Private Sylvia Evalina Mary Bickle of the ATS. Died 11 September 1947 aged nineteen, at Shaftesbury Military Hospital, Dorset.

R. V. HERBERT | 33425 Flying Officer Richard Vivian Herbert of the RAF, 211 Squadron. Died 13 April 1941 aged twenty-one, near Lake Prespa, on the border between Albania and Greece.

G. B. HERBERT | 116456 Flying Officer Gerald Bevill Herbert of the RAF VR, 158 Squadron. Died 14 February 1943 aged twenty, at Stillingfleet, Yorkshire.

A. E. STANBURY | Sailor Alfred Stanbury of the Merchant Navy, SS *Ahamo*. Died 8 April 1941 aged seventeen, in the Atlantic.

P. C. BOWLES | 307391 2nd Lieutenant Peter Clarence Bowles of the 14th Battalion, Sherwood Foresters. Died 20 March 1944 aged twenty-two, at Anzio in Italy.

THE FALKLANDS WAR 1982

N. TAYLOR | Lieutenant Nicholas Taylor, 800 Squadron, HMS *Hermes*. Died 4 May 1982 aged thirty-two, at Goose Green in the Falkland Islands.

THE IRAQ WAR 2003

A. J. KELLY | Private Andrew Kelly of the 3rd Battalion, the Parachute Regiment. Died 6 May 2003 aged eighteen, near Basra in Iraq.

Acknowledgements

This book has taken me not only to Devon but to libraries, archives and sometimes the battlefields on which the soldiers on the war memorial fought; it has also introduced me to many people who have generously shared their knowledge of the individuals and the times in which they lived. I am deeply grateful to Graham Huggins, Fred Hammett, Richard Petherick, Susan Williamson and Helen Yallop for sharing details of family members that have enabled me to picture the fallen as they lived. George Radford's excellent manuscript history of the Radford family was of inestimable value in reconstructing the life of Richard Turner. My own researches stand on the shoulders of those of Howard Barkell, whose detective work has been invaluable in establishing the identities of some of the names, and Barbara Weeks, author of *The Book of Lydford*, both of them tireless local historians. At an early point in my work I was inspired to meet Ken and Pam Linge, who have compiled a database of over 7,000 of the names of the missing listed on the Thiepval Arch, three of which also appear on the Lydford war memorial; they have given unfailing assistance and pointed me down several avenues of research.

Lydford is a welcoming village and I have enjoyed so many conversations about its past that it is difficult to thank everyone who has helped me, but I must particularly mention Stanley Yeo, Graham May and Pam Morris, as well as the Dartmoor historian Dr Tom Greeves and Squire Peter Newman of Coryton.

In Canada, Marilyn Griesemer shared photographs as well as family memories of her grandfather, Samuel Voysey. I am grateful to Peter Barton, Jeremy Banning, Iain McHenry, François Bergez, Ian Carter, James Dunnet, Rupert Nichol, Craig Allen, Brigadier Matthew Lowe and Brigadier Giles Hill for their help with military, naval and RAF history. Jasper Hardman trawled the catalogues of the Imperial War Museum, the National Army Museum and the National Archives for references that I could follow up. I must also thank the librarians of those institutions. My colleagues at

Country Life, in particular the Editor, Mark Hedges, have been indulgent of the Lydford references that have come up in conversation and sometimes found their way into print.

The idea of making a book out of a village war memorial was suggested by Tim Binding of Peters Fraser & Dunlop; I owe him and my agent at PFD, Annabel Merullo, an inestimable debt. Happily, Eleo Gordon thought that the book could be published, and her faith has sustained the project. And my wife and sons have sustained me: their support has, as ever, been the rock upon which the edifice has been built.

Notes

Epigraph

page vii **What a shame . . . mostly boys.** From the private papers of E. Smith. Memoir describing the events of 1916–17 (exact dates unknown). Held in the collection of the Imperial War Museum, London. 13041 04/19/1.

1: On With the Show – Wilfie Fry

page 1 **Kenner always won praise . . . singing of hymns.'** Comment from the 1907 inspection, noted in the school logbook, p. 283. West Devon Record Office, Plymouth, 2053-1.

page 1 **Classes, according to the logbook . . . and so on.** Logbook, 26 July 1902, pp. 233–4.

page 1 **'Thos Bickle . . . river Lyd.** Report dated 16 February 1906. *Tavistock Gazette*.

page 2 **Their dwelling . . . coronation in 1911.** 30 June 1911. *Tavistock Gazette*.

page 2 **One of Wilfie's first ventures . . . still there.** There has been much worry about the 'k'. In Wilfie's day, Revd Thorpe would have spelt his church St Petrock's; now the saint has reverted to his older form of St Petroc.

page 3 **Once on top of the battlements . . . his father's hand.** Reminiscence of ex-infantryman Fred Hammett.

page 3 **In 1900, Sabine Baring-Gould had described . . . 'an Irish village'** . . . For a fuller description of Lydford, see *A Book of Dartmoor*, chapter 9, at http://en.wikisource.org/wiki/A_Book_of_Dartmoor/Chapter_9.

page 4 **There were around 60,000 . . . used on farms.** Helen Harris. 1998. *Devon's Century of Change*. Newton Abbot: Peninsula Press, p. 53.

page 6 . . . **a source of great amusement . . . amid much cheering.** 7 August 1914. *Tavistock Gazette.*

page 7 **Occasionally, one of the bank holiday crowd fell in . . . met her death.** See the contemporary newspaper account found in a scrapbook and posted online at http://www.lydfordparishcouncil.co.uk/ lydfordhistory.htm#accident.

page 8 **Mr Bickle Senior had caused 'great amusement' . . . at the Dartmoor Inn.** 3 May 1901. *Tavistock Gazette.*

page 10 **But by 1660 . . . a mean and miserable village'.** Dean Milles, writing in 1660, quoted in the Dartmoor National Park Authority's 2011 publication *Lydford, Conservation Area Character Appraisal.*

page 10 **The position had not improved . . . these are modern Lydford.'** Richard Nicholls Worth. 1895. *A History of Devonshire.* London: E. Stock, p. 173.

page 11 **It should not be brushed off . . . 'God has spread His table.'** Baring-Gould, *A Book of Dartmoor.*

page 11 **He got into trouble . . . suitable living.** Recorded in the Lydford Vestry Minute Book of 1914.

page 13 **It cannot have been easy . . . 'unable to work'.** See the 1911 census.

page 13 **Mary had been born at Lydford . . . was two.** See the 1891 census.

page 13 **Perhaps Plymouth offered . . . the vegetables.** Richard Hobbs's address at the time of his death in 1916 was 2 Dixon Villas, Yealmpton, a few miles from Plymouth.

2: *The Dashing Hussar – Archie Huggins*

page 16 **Archie was the sterling right back . . . and foe'.** Taken from a cutting of a newspaper obituary in the keeping of Graham Huggins.

page 16 **There is still a tribal memory . . . a brick wall'.** An expression used by Bill Cooke, although he was born after Archie's death.

page 17 **Under the inspiration of Lord John Rolle . . . and Bideford.** Joe Roe. 1992. 'Devon Soldiers'. Typescript held in the collection of the North Devon Athenaeum, Barnstaple.

page 17 **The yeomanry regiments were hastily re-formed . . . the veldt'.** Benson Freeman. 1927. *The Yeomanry of Devon 1794–1927*. London: St Catherine Press, p. 122.

page 17 **From now on, the yeomanry . . . around their yards).** As described by Leonard Gamlen in a manuscript held in the collection of the Barnstaple Museum. Later descriptions by Lieutenant Gamlen in this chapter are taken from the same manuscript.

page 20 **The sort of work . . . Forda Mill.** Terms and conditions had not improved greatly when Archie's great-nephew Graham joined his father after the Second World War. He recalls: 'Out of the £2 0s 1d I received, I had to give mother a pound, half a crown went into the Post Office, and out of the rest I had to buy my tools and clothing. I remember buying a pair of wellington boots from a van from Launceston for twenty-one shillings, and paying for them at a shilling a month.'

page 21 **Men were desperate to join . . . vacancies were few.** Hugh Burdett Money-Coutts, Lord Latymer. 1931. *Chances and Changes*. London: William Blackwood & Sons Ltd, p. 190.

page 22 **'It was a very harassing . . . squadron leaders.'** Ibid, p. 192.

page 22 **But alas, as he remembered . . . surprises from our own side were possible.** Ibid, p. 197.

page 23 **When General Sir Ian Hamilton . . . completed their musketry training.** Ibid, p. 175.

page 24 **Mastery of foreign tongues . . . very difficult.'** Noted in the war diaries of Horace Percival Crocker. Typescript held in the collection of the Barnstaple Museum. This is also the source for details and anecdotes of training at Clacton.

page 24 **Before the war, Brittain had worked . . . at Minehead.** Private papers of Private H. C. Brittain. Imperial War Museum, London. 3755 85/43/1.

page 25 **There was a final parade . . . leaving behind them'.** Papers of Captain R. S. Hawker. National Army Museum. 1988-09-86.

page 25 **'It is probably not too much to say . . . his year in Essex.'** Freeman, *The Yeomanry of Devon*, p. 177.

page 26 **Archie's sleeping quarters . . . as the voyage progressed.** Colonel R. A. Sanders' diary at the Dardanelles, 25 September to 30 December 1915. National Army Museum. 2006-04-22.

page 26 **On the lower decks . . . once the voyage had started.** See the war diaries of Horace Percival Crocker.

page 27 **'I am sure a finer . . . gathered together anywhere.'** Sir Bertram Hayes. 1925. *Hull Down*. London: Cassell, p. 179.

page 27 **As the ship started to move . . . found unaffecting.** Private papers of Private H. C. Brittain.

page 27 **An elderly sentry . . . roared at him.** In the army slang of the time he 'got awfully staffed' (see the papers of Captain R. S. Hawker).

page 27 **In a letter to Connie . . . from the shore.'** Ann Compton. 2004. *The Sculpture of Charles Sargeant Jagger*. Much Hadham: Lund Humphries Publishers Ltd, p. 20.

page 27 **The former were housed . . . on way out.'** Diary of Colonel R. A. Sanders.

page 27 **Rumour had it . . . height of the season.** Hayes, *Hull Down*, p. 179.

page 27 **'Officers were well catered for . . . Ball Punching'.** Papers of Captain R. S. Hawker.

page 28 **Occupants of the old First Class . . . country house.** See 'The History of the RMS *Olympic*' at http://www.atlanticliners.com/olympic_home.htm.

page 28 **'Our food continues . . . must be unique.'** Private papers of F. D. Baker. Imperial War Museum, London. 15400 06/120/1.

page 28 **There, the 'voige' . . . did not seem to be a pleasure cruise.** Ibid.

page 28 **Some country boys . . . underfed.** See the war diaries of Horace Percival Crocker.

page 28 **'Third-class passengers . . . White Star Line is largely responsible.'** Mark Chirnside. 2004. *The Olympic-Class Ships*. Stroud: Tempus Publishing, p. 57.

page 28 **The buoyant-spirited ambulance man . . . a swimming pool too.** Private papers of Frank T. Phillips (photocopied typed transcription of diary). 22 September 1915. Imperial War Museum, London. 4904 96/17/1.

page 29 **'All the men frightfully seasick . . . waded in it!'** Private papers of F. D. Baker.

page 29 **But the next day a cheerful machine-gunner . . . sea quiet'.**

Private papers of J. R. Tozer (photocopy of handwritten diary). 27 September 1915. Imperial War Museum, London. 1287 87/13/1.

page 29 **We are a cheerful crowd . . . pleasure trip we were taking.** Ibid.

page 29 **On 1 October . . . to the insular British troops.** 1 October 1915. Private papers of Frank T. Phillips.

page 29 **Their rowing boat . . . riddled with bullets.** Money-Coutts, *Chances and Changes*, p. 217.

page 29 **If Archie had been below deck . . . a bang'.** Ibid.

page 30 **In May 1917 . . . crew had to abandon it.** Ibid.

page 30 **Around noon on 2 October . . . forever lame.** For Lemnos, see Nigel McGilchrist. 2010. *Lemnos with Aghios Efstratios & Samothrace.* Number 12 in *McGilchrist's Greek Islands.* Ascot: Genius Loci Publications.

page 30 **The bay presented . . . Ellis Ashmead-Bartlett.** E. Ashmead-Bartlett. 1928. *The Uncensored Dardanelles.* London: Hutchinson & Co. Ltd, p. 38.

page 31 **His assessment . . . en route to the front.** Alan Moorehead. 2007. *Gallipoli.* London: Aurum Press, p. 280.

page 31 **A lecture on precautions . . . would have confirmed.** See the diary of J. R. Tozer.

page 31 **Ominously, he heard General Sir Bryan Mahon . . . could not be buried adequately.** See Hayes, *Hull Down*, p. 184.

page 32 **A smaller troopship . . . beside a giant'.** See the private papers of F. D. Baker. *Osmanieh* would be sunk by a mine as she took troops and medical staff to Alexandria in 1917, with the loss of nearly 200 seamen, soldiers and nurses.

page 32 **Otherwise dusty classicists . . . myriads of barbarians'.** Edward Gibbon. *The History of the Decline and Fall of the Roman Empire.* Originally published in six volumes between 1776 and 1789 by Strahan & Cadell, London.

page 34 **The whole position was indeed . . . even more inexplicable.** Ashmead-Bartlett, *The Uncensored Dardanelles*, p. 69.

page 34 **Despite the early start . . . the West Somerset Yeomanry.** See the diary of Colonel R. A. Sanders.

page 35 **When the fire passed on . . . mother earth.** Ashmead-Bartlett, *The Uncensored Dardanelles*, p. 189.

page 35 'The muddle is beyond . . . one weary officer. Ibid.

page 36 'The snorting and rumbling . . . discontented elephant.'
Money-Coutts, *Chances and Changes*, p. 225.

page 36 *Osmandieh* dragged her anchors . . . wrung his hands. Freeman,
The Yeomanry of Devon, p. 189.

page 36 Two of them fell into the sea . . . happily they were saved.
See the diary of J. R. Tozer.

page 36 That night . . . 'packed like herrings'. Ibid.

page 36 Those who wish to imagine the scene . . . three thousand miles
from home. John Masefield. 1916. 'Gallipoli'. Reproduced by Philip W.
Errington. 2007. *John Masefield's Great War: Collected Works*. Barnsley:
Pen & Sword Military, p. 51.

page 37 Under the cover of the battleship . . . without being shelled.
The guns of *Queen Elizabeth* were the same as those now outside the
Imperial War Museum, London.

page 37 Old Indian hands . . . in Hindustani. See the private papers of
F. D. Baker.

page 38 Ominously . . . by the end of the first week. See the diary of
Colonel R. A. Sanders.

page 38 In all armies . . . the ratio was 1:24. Richard Holmes. 2005
(new edition). *Tommy*. London: Harper Perennial, p. 483.

page 39 The Revd Arthur Rose Fuller . . . the portable altar. This
journal was sold at auction; its present whereabouts are unknown. The
quote comes from the sale catalogue at http://www.dnw.co.uk/medals/
auctionarchive/searchcataloguearchive/itemdetail.lasso?itemid=16326.

page 40 A palm-sized piece of his face . . . three paces away. See the
war diaries of Horace Percival Crocker.

page 40 By 27 October . . . home of the damned. Compton, *The Sculpture
of Charles Sargeant Jagger*, p. 20.

page 41 'The irregular equation . . . 3 Gypo tummies.' Thomas Corbett,
2nd Baron Rowallan. 1976. *Rowallan: The Autobiography of Lord Rowallan*.
Edinburgh: Paul Harris Publishing, p. 39.

page 42 He survived to leave a polite account . . . its wretched inmates
cared. Money-Coutts, *Chances and Changes*, p. 241.

page 43 Their insides had simply turned to water . . . do little for
them. See the account in Chapter 9 of Lyn Macdonald. 1993 (first

published 1980). *The Roses of No Man's Land*. London: Penguin Books. Vera Brittain also went to Mudros as a nurse (on *Britannic*) but not until after the Dardanelles evacuation. See her memoir *Testament of Youth*, originally published in 1933 and currently reissued by Penguin Books.

page 43 **The whole Expedition . . . the enemy's bullets.** Ashmead-Bartlett, *The Uncensored Dardanelles*, p. 245.

page 44 **Trooper J. W. Shambrook . . . on my right foot.'** From a letter in the collection of the Barnstaple Museum.

page 44 **It almost made me cry . . . it's a big tragedy.** Six of Arthur Rose Fuller's medals were sold at auction by Dix Noonan Webb in London on 25 February 1999. His journals are quoted in the catalogue at http://www.dnw.co.uk/medals/auctionarchive/searchcataloguearchive/item-detail.lasso?itemid=16326.

3: The Old Army – Charlie Berry

page 46 **The regimental journal . . . pride to the regiment.** See Volume 1, October 1907.

page 46 **On the ranges . . . 2,800 yards.** Richard Holmes. 2005 (new edition). *Tommy*. London: Harper Perennial, p. 379.

page 47 **All told we sweated . . . some sort of hobby.** Unnamed soldier, from papers in the Worcestershire Regimental Museum.

page 47 **The polo players looked forward to . . . few players at present'.** *Worcestershire Star*. Volume 1, October 1907, p. 15.

page 47 **One of few big moments . . . then in Bombay.** In 1909 the battalion moved from Ahmednagar to Jhansi.

page 49 **'A leisurely sail . . . across to France.'** Private papers of John McIlwain (typed record made in 1936–7 from a contemporary diary). Imperial War Museum, London. 96/29/1.

page 49 **An officer with the 2nd Battalion . . . uncomfortable meal on deck'.** Private Papers of Lieutenant Colonel A. V. Spencer, DSO. Imperial War Museum, London. 87/26/1.

page 49 **A soldier later wrote home . . . "Good morning!"'** Revd Edward Archibald Forbes. 1918. *Vermelles: Notes on the Western Front by a Chaplain*. Edinburgh: Scottish Chronicle Press, p. 16.

page 50 **Officers rode in the countryside . . . Hotel de Paris'.** Private
papers of F. F. S. Smithwick. Imperial War Museum, London. 01/59/1.

page 50 **'It seemed extraordinary . . . Monte Carlo.'** Private papers of
H. M. Dillon. Entry dated 24 August 1914. Imperial War Museum,
London. 4430 82/25/1.

page 50 **Through Amiens and Arras . . . had made his headquarters.**
Carlos Baker. 1969. *Ernest Hemingway: A Life Story.* New York: Charles
Scribner's Sons, pp. 420–21. See also Everard Wyrall. 1916 (Volume 1).
The History of the Second Division, 1914–18. London: Thomas Nelson
and Sons.

page 50 **When the Connaught Rangers had their feet inspected . . .
bunioned feet'.** Private papers of John McIlwain, journal entry dated
22 August 1914.

page 51 **His chest had never been . . . with pneumonia.** When he had
joined the army in 1905, it measured 34 inches, increasing to 37 inches
when he took a deep breath; but unlike other recruits, his physical fit-
ness did not seem to improve with the better diet and exercise of service
life. After six months, his chest measurement was 34½ inches; but the
expansion was only 1½ inches.

page 51 **After he had spent thirty days on the sick list . . . pains behind
the ribs were returning.** His army service record is held by the
National Archives (available to view online at http://www.ancestry.
co.uk).

page 51 **Drage crossed to France on 27 August . . . dead and their
horses too.** Private papers of Edgar John Drage. Imperial War Museum,
London. 11/4/1.

page 52 **He stayed there until 19 September . . . possibly frustrated.**
Details on Charlie Berry's casualty form.

page 54 **'Runaway horses . . . the discipline of the "Old Army".'** Captain H. FitzM. Stacke. 1928. *The Worcestershire Regiment in the Great War.*
Kidderminster: G. T. Cheshire & Sons Ltd, p. 5.

page 54 **They were to regret it . . . General Spears wrote in his diary.**
Quoted in the private papers of John McIlwain, recording the events of
26 August 1914.

page 55 **This horror particularly affected . . . prancing proudly along.'**
Private papers of John McIlwain, 23 October 1914.

page 55 **'The happiest day . . . towards the rising sun.'** John Terraine. 2002. *Mons: The Retreat to Victory*. Ware: Wordsworth Editions, p. 202.

page 56 **As dusk fell . . . casualty evacuation chain.** Alan Shelley. 2008. *I Never Met Ernest Hemingway*. Bloomington, Indiana: iUniverse, p. 62.

page 58 **Suddenly in the dense wood . . . as they charged forward.** Stacke, *The Worcestershire Regiment*, p. 31.

page 58 **Elsewhere in the brigade . . . not in the mood to waste bullets on them.** C. S. Baines. Typed account of the First Battle of Ypres, written some years afterwards. Imperial War Museum, London. 10/87/9, p. 146.

page 59 **A captured communication stated . . . successful issue of the war'.** Typed transcription (8 pages) of a lecture on the First Battle of Ypres given on the third anniversary of the battle. No author. It was published as 'How the Worcesters Saved the Day, Gheluvelt, 31 October 1914'. Imperial War Museum, London. 8988 Misc 23 (403).

page 60 **'My God, fancy meeting you . . . Thank God you have come.'** Anthony Farrar-Hockley. 1967. *The Death of an Army*. London: Barker, p. 159.

page 61 **When darkness fell . . . a more sheltered postion.** After the war, Gheluvelt was commemorated by the sculptor Charles Sargeant Jagger, who had himself served in the Worcestershire Regiment, although not the 2nd Battalion; the bas-relief is monumental, even heroic in conception and somewhat stylized, but the brutality of hand-to-hand fighting, as one of the principal figures plunges his bayonet into a German and another uses a broken rifle as a club, seems raw.

page 61 **French had just lived through . . . worst half-hour of my life'.** Quoted in the account of the Battle of Gheluvelt on the Worcestershire Regiment website at http://www.worcestershireregiment.com/wr. php?main=inc/h_gheluvelt.

page 61 **Thus, despite the presence on the battlefield . . . against the British.** See typed transcription of lecture 'How the Worcesters Saved the Day'.

page 61 **Through *Mein Kampf* . . . part of the Nazi myth.** John Williams. 2005. *Corporal Hitler and the Great War 1914–1918: The List Regiment*. Abingdon: Frank Cass.

page 62 **Theophilus was one of the trustees . . . absorbed into**

Methodism. See the list of trustees in the Devon Record Office, Exeter. 22760/91.

page 63 **Its concourse was invariably crowded . . . needed accommodation.** This is the very scene that Richard Jack (1866–1952), Canada's first official war artist, was to depict the next year in his epic canvas *Return to the Front: Victoria Railway Station* (oil on canvas, 1916), now hanging in the York Art Gallery.

page 63 **By the end of 1915, the ladies of the Soldiers' . . . demanding refreshment.** Described in *The Graphic*, 11 December 1915.

page 63 **The hospital itself . . . gates were then fitted.** J. A. Cholmeley. 1985. *History of the Royal National Orthopaedic Hospital*. London: Chapman and Hall, p. 99.

page 64 **A disgruntled squaddie . . . clouds of clinging mist.** Victor Gregg with Rick Stroud. 2011. *Rifleman: A Front-Line Life*. London: Bloomsbury Publishing, p. 182.

page 64 **For at the end of April . . . landed on the Gallipoli peninsula.** One of the 4th Battalion officers was Charles Sargeant Jagger.

page 65 **. . . when it left Avonmouth . . . 'as cheerful as could be' . . .** From letters written by Sergeant G. Keen. Imperial War Museum, London. 9576 Misc 37 (682).

page 65 **Those who were still inside . . . leave the ship.'** C. E. Crutchley (ed). 1973. *Machine-Gunner, 1914–18*. London: Purnell Book Services, p. 11.

page 67 **Word of these disasters . . . to make up for heavy losses.** Stacke, *The Worcestershire Regiment*, p. 86.

page 67 **In tiny, regular script, his diary records . . . the officers' boxing competition.** Private papers of Lieutenant Colonel A. W. Brocks, covering his service at Gallipoli May 1915 to January 1916. Imperial War Museum, London. 12122.

page 67 **Brocks, Charlie and the others arrived . . . on 26 May.** HMS *Hythe* sank in October as the result of a collision off the Gallipoli peninsula, with the loss of 150 lives.

page 68 **Huge French Senegalese troops . . . the 2nd Hampshires put it.** Private papers of A. W. Bird. Imperial War Museum, London. 15793 07/12/1.

page 69 **In the words of the battalion diary . . . about 800 yds.'** All battalion diaries are held by the National Archives at Kew, in the series beginning WO 95.

page 69 **By the spring of 1915 . . . for the duration.** For a description of Graylingwell as a centre for the treatment of acute battle neuroses during the Second World War, see W. Sargant. 1967. *The Unquiet Mind: The Autobiography of a Physician in Psychological Medicine.* London: Heinemann.

page 70 **'In a matter of hours . . . camp near Grantham.** George Coppard. 1968. *With a Machine Gun to Cambrai.* London: HMSO, p. 103.

page 71 **Although more portable . . . to keep them firing.** See General Staff. 1916. *Notes on the Tactical Employment of Machine Guns and Lewis Guns.* London: HMSO.

page 71 **Only the day before Charlie had left . . . is excellent news.'** Quoted by David Whithorn. 2003. *Bringing Uncle Albert Home.* Stroud: Alan Sutton Publishing, p. 51.

page 72 **'In fact,' cursed Johnston . . . anything more foolish.'** Ibid, pp. 51–2.

page 73 **The trees on the slope . . . truncated bases remaining'.** Frederic Manning. 1976 (first published 1929). *The Middle Parts of Fortune.* London: St Martin's Press, p. 159.

page 73 **. . . the gas was pretty thick . . . had a good sleep.** Whithorn, *Bringing Uncle Albert Home,* pp. 55–6.

page 73 **Men who, like the Canadian dental officer . . . put up with it.** See the letters of Wilbert Gilroy. 22 December 1915. See http://www.canadianletters.ca.

page 73 **In March . . . impossibility of escaping from it.'** John Garth. 2003. *Tolkien and the Great War: The Threshold of Middle-Earth.* London: HarperCollins, p. 188.

page 74 **Newly arrived soldiers . . . are not very steady yet.'** Whithorn, *Bringing Uncle Albert Home,* p. 61.

page 76 **Next day, Brigade Major Johnston was still worrying . . . it would be enough.** Ibid, p. 64.

page 76 **Tolkien had come out in June . . . Lancashire Fusiliers.** See John Garth's *Tolkien and the Great War.*

page 76 **'It does one good . . . any amount of them too.'** Whithorn, *Bringing Uncle Albert Home,* p. 67.

page 77 **'Another tremendously hot day . . . train these drafts.'** Ibid,
p. 68.

page 77 **With him was the Prince of Wales . . . if he gets half a chance.'**
Ibid, p. 70.

page 78 **The poet John Masefield . . . evil-looking'.** John Masefield.
1917. 'The Old Front Line'. Reproduced by Philip W. Errington. 2007.
John Masefield's Great War: Collected Works. Barnsley: Pen & Sword
Military, p. 185.

page 79 **'Very busy day . . . he records on the 20th.** Johnston quoted in
Whithorn, *Bringing Uncle Albert Home*, p. 78.

page 79 **At six in the evening, for three minutes . . . were not sorry
to give themselves up.** This account of the engagement, including
Johnston's descriptions, is based on Whithorn's *Bringing Uncle Albert
Home*, pp. 81–2.

page 81 **The doom of Thiepval . . . the nose of the Leipzig Salient.**
Philip Gibbs. 1917. *The Battles of the Somme*. London: Heinemann, p. 202.

page 82 **The infantry moved up behind the shelling . . . into the trench.**
See Stacke, *The Worcestershire Regiment*.

page 82 **'Look! . . . splendid fellows!'** Gibbs, *The Battles of the Somme*,
p. 205.

page 82 **'Magnificent . . . your men are fine.'** Ibid, p. 207.

page 83 **They found the German trench smashed . . . the Prussian
Guard.** Stacke, *The Worcestershire Regiment*, p. 188.

4: Canada Is at War – Samuel Voyzey and Mancel Clark

page 84 **In 1825 it was announced . . . little use for it, beyond jewellery.** A. K. Hamilton Jenkins. 2005. *The Mines of Devon*. Trowbridge:
Landmark Publishing Ltd, p. 89.

page 85 **'It appeared to be the wish . . . instead of the individual.'** 30
June 1911. *Tavistock Gazette*.

page 85 **The Duke had earlier told an audience . . . power to veto
budgets.** 21 July 1901. *Tavistock Gazette*.

page 86 **It has been estimated that . . . fewer than 9,000 inhabitants.**
See (1) 'North Devon Exodus' by Arthur Dark at http://genuki.cs.ncl.

ac.uk/DEV/DevonMisc/NDevonExodus.html. (2) Figures from Basil Greenhill and Ann Giffard. 1967. *Westcountrymen in Prince Edward's Isle*. Newton Abbot: David & Charles.

page 87 **By 1831 . . . minister to them.** See Dr David Shorney. 2001. 'James Thorne and the Bible Christians'. *Devon Family Historian*. November, p. 12.

page 87 **. . . in a realistic manner . . . other parts of the world generally.** 3 February 1911. *Tavistock Gazette*.

page 87 **'Ready Made Farms . . . instalment system.'** 2 January 1914. *Tavistock Gazette*.

page 87 **On one occasion . . . Canada had been a disappointment.** In January 1914 the *Gazette* published a letter in response, under the headline 'Hear the Other Side!', saying that it was not as bad as painted 'by fellows who have gone to Canada expecting to make their fortunes in a few months'.

page 87 **As railways opened up the interior . . . between 1900 and 1913.** Robert Bothwell, Ian Drummond and John English. 1987. *Canada 1900–1945*. Toronto: University of Toronto Press, p. 55.

page 88 **'If the man who works for them . . . Canadian farmer.** Barbara J. Messamore (ed). 2004. *Canadian Migration Patterns*. Ottawa: University of Ottawa Press, p. 163.

page 88 **A house built of logs . . . cry my heart out.** Quoted by Eileen Laurie in the foreword to G. R. Elliott (ed). 1960. *Klondike Cattle Drive: The Journal of Norman Lee*. Vancouver: Mitchell Press, p. xii.

page 89 **In 1898 he married . . . her mother's maiden name.** I am grateful to Marilyn Griesemer, Sam and Isabella's granddaughter, for sharing family information.

page 90 **In tune with the mood . . . modern-seeming variant perhaps.** It is spelt Voyzey on the war memorial.

page 91 **In Montreal, two more children . . . the Mile End district of Montreal.** Before the outbreak of war, in the 1911 Census of Canada, their address had been given as Jacques-Cartier, Quebec, 769 Champ Green.

page 91 **The question, for the government . . . now trained 55,000 men a year.** G. W. L. Nicholson. 1962. *Official History of the Canadian Army in the First World War: Canadian Expeditionary Force 1914–1919*. Ottawa: Queen's Printer, p. 7.

page 92 **Ordinary boots . . . well up over ankles.** Letter written by Wilbert H. Gilroy. 13 February 1916. See http://www.canadianletters.ca.

page 93 **'Some boots . . . a whole day without stopping!'** Letter written by John Row Jr to his mother, dated 15 June 1915. See http://www. canadianletters.ca.

page 93 **I do wish you could see our men . . . as willing as can be.** Letter dated 9 June 1915.

page 94 **. . . (one of whose number . . . jumped overboard in the course of the passage).** According to an entry in the battalion war diary, dated 23 May 1915. The war diaries of both the 27th and 60th Battalions have been made available online by Library and Archives Canada at http://www.collectionscanada.gc.ca.

page 94 **'We have a crack band . . . the crowd is very fine.'** Letter dated 16 May 1915.

page 95 **We are getting up at 3 now . . . equal to about 25 at home.** Letter dated 29 June 1915.

page 95 **The brigadier, who was a golfer . . . coming over by shiploads every day.** Letter dated 9 June 1915.

page 96 **(That November, another kind of dirigible . . . and 38 horses.)** 'Canadian Troops Cool Under Zeppelin Fire; Thirteen Men and 38 Horses Killed in a Kent Camp:- Bombs Loaded With Scrap Iron.' 7 November 1915. *New York Times*.

page 96 **In late July . . . judged to be 'dandy'.** Letter from John Row Jr to his mother, dated 20 July 1915.

page 96 **'I'm still having a glorious time . . . the more we enjoy it.'** See the Canadian Letters and Images Project at http://www.canadianletters.ca.

page 97 **It was a ramshackle affair . . . 'vest-pocket editions' of those in Canada.** L. C. Giles. 1986. *Liphook, Bramshott and the Canadians*. Published by the Bramshott and Liphook Preservation Society, p. 6.

page 97 **'We thought our training in Canada had amounted to something . . . good but hard for marching'.** Ibid, p. 7.

page 98 **Again I am back in the trenches . . . increases the comedy 2 fold.** Letter dated 18 January 1916.

page 98 **It was still snowing in mid-March . . . on account of the cold'.** Letter to his grandfather, dated 7 March 1916.

page 98 **'Were it not for the slight danger . . . Some sport isn't it?** Letter dated 1 October 1915.

page 99 **The idea of the Belgian farmer . . . letting the Germans have the blamed country.** Letter dated 27 September 1915.

page 100 **'I have seen Kenya Africans . . . as the peasants in Belgium,' noted Sudbury.** Undated memoir of Private John P. Sudbury at http://www.canadianletters.ca.

page 100 **'It is beautifully clean . . . until one gets used to it.'** Letter to his father dated 29 September 1915.

page 100 **'We have a bath . . . it is heavy enough now,' wrote Fargey . . .** Letter from James Fargey to his mother dated 8 April 1916 at http://www.canadianletters.ca.

page 103 **On the Brickfields . . . indiscriminately over the area.** Colonel W. W. Murray. 1947. *The History of the 2nd Canadian Battalion (Eastern Ontario Regiment) Canadian Expeditionary Force in the Great War*. Ottawa: Mortimer Ltd, pp. 113–14. Quoted in Paul Reed. 1998. *Courcelette*. Barnsley: Leo Cooper, p. 20.

page 104 **Dental officer Gilroy was kept busy by the 'hard tack . . . havoc with teeth and gums'.** Letter to his mother dated 17 October 1915.

page 105 **'All around were the evidences . . . and everywhere, khaki-clad soldiers.'** See (1) Murray, *The History of the 2nd Canadian Battalion*, p. 113. (2) Reed, *Courcelette*, p. 22.

page 105 **It enabled Cattermole . . . an awe-inspiring sight.** Reed, *Courcelette*, pp. 37–8.

page 106 **Suddenly we came upon an enemy trench . . . fluttering down to the earth around him.** Ibid, p. 39.

page 107 **The air was seething with shells . . . with hardly a jolt.** Donald Fraser and Reginald H. Roy. 1985. *The Journal of Private Fraser*. Victoria, BC: Sono Nis Press, pp. 205–8.

page 108 **Among them . . . Mancel Clark.** There is a battalion history by Bruce Tascona. 1995. *From the Forks to Flanders Field: The Story of the 27th City of Winnipeg Battalion 1914–1919*. Winnipeg: Bruce Tascona. This is in the Imperial War Museum, London. 95/1079.

page 109 **Playing billiards . . . proprietor of the Dartmoor Inn.** 23 January 1914. *Tavistock Gazette*. See also G. R. Hartwell, G. R. Pack and

M. A. Edwards. 2006 (reprinted). *The Story of the 5th Battalion the Dorset-shire Regiment in North-West Europe 23rd June 1944 to 5th May 1945.* Dorchester: The Keep Military Museum.

page 110 **They were remembered in Winnipeg . . . their mother.** Isabella's granddaughter Marilyn Griesemer recalls what happened to Sam's widow: 'After Samuel died, my grandmother received a pension from the army of $15.00 a month. That wasn't very much even in those days. She moved to Cartierville, which was outside the city and very rural at the time. She rented a little house and raised her family there. The property backed up to a river and was quite nice. She still lived there when I was a child and we went to visit often. She had a garden and grew vegetables to feed her children. She also had chickens and a pig. As the children aged they helped out financially. I went back about five years ago and where she lived is now a large park but some of the trees are still standing.'

5: *The Golden Gorse Flowers Bud, and Bloom, and Fade – Richard Turner*

page 112 **St Petroc's churchyard is full of Radfords . . . Lilla or Lily.** I am indebted to George Radford whose excellent typescript *Family History*, a copy of which is in the Bodleian Library, Oxford, forms the basis of this chapter. Unless otherwise indicated, letters quoted in this chapter are in the private possession of the Radford family. Dates have been given for the letters, where they are known.

page 112 **'If only the Geologists . . . every cadence of the Bible verses.'** Tim Hilton. 2002. *John Ruskin.* New Haven: Yale University Press, p. 167.

page 115 **On Daniel's death in 1900 . . . my happiness to know'.** Sabine Baring-Gould. 1900. *A Book of Dartmoor.* London: Methuen, p. 132.

page 117 **He also rebuilt the church . . . most of the village.** 'He sends his potatoes and his flowers to horticultural exhibitions,' commented Baring-Gould's friend, Abbé François Duine, unaware, perhaps, that this was not exceptional behaviour for a country gentleman. *Souvenirs et*

Observations de l'Abbé François Duine, edited by Bernard Heudré, was published in 2009 by Presses Universitaires de Rennes. See section on Baring-Gould, pp. 113–19.

page 120 **A letter survives from a lieutenant in the 2nd Devons . . . the swollen feet we get.** Letter written by Lieutenant G. C. Vaughan, 22 January 1915. National Army Museum. 1993-04-7.

page 121 **Not that lack of the language . . . 'Alleman no bon'.** Letter dated 7 November 1915.

page 121 **'When the smoke cleared . . . argue with a Mills.'** Martin Pegler. 1996. *The British Tommy 1914–18*. Botley: Osprey Publishing, p. 17.

page 122 **The bombing officer may have lost . . . from his unit as a result.** For bombing (in a Canadian battalion) see Mark Zuehlke. 2008. *Brave Battalion*. Mississauga: John Wiley & Sons Canada.

page 122 **On one occasion they were stationed . . . the four days he had been in the front line.** Letter dated 24 November 1915.

page 122 **By Easter 1916 . . . mine craters, etc., all right.** Letter dated Easter Day 1916.

page 122 **One of the most daunting tasks . . . really only thistles.** Letter dated 24 November 1915.

page 123 **'In one part of the line . . . garbed in a shirt and numerous sandbags.'** Letter dated 17 December 1915.

page 123 **'The slippers and gloves arrived . . . as if it wanted to go to France.'** Letter dated 30 October 1915.

page 123 **In later correspondence there was mention . . . 'a magnificent tonic'.** Letter dated 30 January 1917. Additional details in this paragraph are taken from Lydia Radford. 1917. *Richard Radford Turner*. London: Chiswick Press (printed for private circulation), p. 38.

page 124 **The previous month, at Lillers . . . a howling success.'** Letter dated 7 November 1915.

page 124 **A machine-gunner remembered . . . daylight could barely be seen through it'.** George Coppard. 1968. *With a Machine Gun to Cambrai*. London: HMSO, p. 83.

page 124 **The soldiers had a grimly humorous song . . . Hanging on the old barbed wire.** See the private papers of Arthur P. Burke, at the

Imperial War Museum, London. 1665 Con Shelf. He describes 'Xmas 1916 . . . I forgot to mention that this time in it was rotten weather, raining & thawing, what a job it was getting out there with barbed wire over our shoulder. You can't imagine the experience, falling & slipping every few yards – it was pitch dark & over we would go in the shell holes full of water. Johnnie knew of course we were out wiring, he sent Very light, after Very light, to make sure what we were doing, but he was content when he knew, he himself had umpteen out on the same job.'

page 125 **Generally, German wiring . . . versus a 'brambly pretence'.** Edmund Blunden. 2010 (first published 1928). *Undertones of War*. London: Penguin Books, p. 122.

page 128 **The Sussex trenches . . . uninterrupted view of Ypres.** Ibid, p. 124.

page 128 **At least the accommodation took the form of . . . an Austrian Count'.** Letter dated 5 January 1917. See Lydia Radford, *Richard Radford Turner*, p. 37.

page 128 **It boasted a handsome cheval-glass . . . or go on after sunset.)** Blunden, *Undertones of War*, pp. 120–21.

page 129 **Its arrangement was simple . . . for the 'air' is best near the floor.** Ibid, p. 121.

page 129 **Even by the standards of this war . . . bombs and ammunition were scarce.'** Ibid, p. 122.

page 130 **Below ground, the 177th . . . gallery known as 16WA.** For a fuller account, see the 1952 publication *History of the Corps of Royal Engineers*. Volume 5. Chatham: The Institution of Royal Engineers.

page 130 **If the tunnellers went deep enough . . . in February 1917.** The tunnelling company report actually describes the earth of 16WA as 'btd. blue clay'. (It is not clear what 'btd.' is short for.)

page 131 **'If you collected a pile of sandbags . . . trenches didn't look any different.'** Lyn Macdonald. 1978. *They Called It Passchendaele*. London: Michael Joseph, p. 19.

page 131 **The tear-shaped crater formed . . . when they took over the line.** Shown on the 177th Tunnelling Company's large maps kept at the Royal Engineers Museum at Chatham.

6: Death in Every Imaginable Shape – Richard Hobbs and Edward Whitford

page 133 **Shortly before the First World War . . . came to run it.** This is a piece of speculation. There was a sawmill at Coryton, and surely Edward would have needed a closer connection than the presence of his brother at Lydford Station to justify his inclusion on the war memorial.

page 134 **We do know, however . . . evidently well regarded.** Edward Whitford's military papers are in the Public Records Office. Among them is a letter dated 14 September 1916 from W. W. Howard Bros. asking for Edward's address from the King's Royal Rifle Corps.

page 134 **There had been a controversy . . . regarded as a weed by foresters.** 2 January 1914. *Tavistock Gazette.*

page 135 **But a charred telegram survives . . . at Rouen for duty'.** The service papers are in the National Archives, Kew. They have been digitized and can be seen online. The date stamp appears to read 24 May 1916, although it is something of a guess as to the month.

page 135 **A Canadian soldier wrote a doggerel verse . . . makeshift clothing to tablecloth.** Letter to his mother dated 7 May 1916 from Private John P. Sudbury, in the collection of the Canadian Letters and Images Project at http://www.canadianletters.ca.

page 136 **'That timber is an essential munition . . . and pickets for constructing fortifications.** W. B. Greeley. 1920. 'Timber in Modern Warfare'. In Theodore S. Woolsey, Jr. *Studies in French Forestry.* New York: Wiley, p. 336.

page 137 **If France had set about . . . her thrift and foresight had actually done.** Ibid, p. 337.

page 137 **After having been up against the push . . . Am in hospital at Rouen . . .** Letter dated 16 July 1916, from the private papers of R. D. Mountfort. Imperial War Museum, London. 10404 Con Shelf.

page 138 **Robert Graves had been billeted . . . flowers have seeded themselves about wildly.** Robert Graves. 2010 (first published 1929). *Goodbye to All That.* London: Penguin Books, p. 99.

page 138 **The journalist Philip Gibbs . . . death might come here, and**

did, without warning . . . Philip Gibbs. 1917. *The Battles of the Somme.*
London: Heinemann, p. 9.

page 139 **The war diary 'speaks of the Germans . . . artillery and trench-
mortars'.** C. T. Atkinson. 2001 (first published in 1926). *The Devonshire
Regiment 1914–18.* Uckfield: Naval & Military Press Ltd, p. 187.

page 139 **Our artillery was fairly active . . . 2 O.R. Wounded.** War diary
of the 2nd Battalion of the Devonshire Regiment. National Archives.
WO95/1712.

page 139 **They were weeks of untypical peace . . . 'almost civilized'.**
Private papers of R. S. Whiteman, 10th Battalion, the Royal Fusiliers.
Imperial War Museum, London. 3476 85/1/1. Typescript memoir
(81 pages) written in 1923. This is the main source for this chapter. See
also Major General Sir Stuart Hare. 1932. *The Annals of the King's Royal
Rifle Corps: Volume V – The Great War.* London: John Murray.

page 141 **He said that Arras . . . something big coming off.'** See the
private papers of R. S. Whiteman.

page 143 **It 'made everyone . . . twice the man he was before'.** Ibid.

page 144 **Eventually they reached what had . . . to reduce weight.** War
diary of the 13th King's Royal Rifle Corps. National Archives.
WO95/2533.

page 149 **I stopped. The sight that greeted me . . . was there for the
examining.** Quoted in Colin Fox. 2000. *Battleground of Europe, Monchy-
le-Preux.* Barnsley: Pen & Sword Military, p. 41.

page 150 **Two days later, the capture of Monchy . . . 'utmost gallantry'
of the attackers.** John Herbert Boraston (ed). 1979 (first published
1920). *Sir Douglas Haig's dispatches December 1915 to April 1919.* London:
J. M. Dent, p. 92.

page 150 **The next year, C. S. Lewis . . . cannot sing.** C. S. Lewis. 1919.
'French Nocturne (Monchy-le-Preux)'. *Spirits in Bondage.* London:
Heinemann.

7: Oh It's Lovely, This Bed – Harry Lake

page 151 **Once, more tobacco was imported . . . except London.** John
Watkins. 1792. *An Essay Towards a History of Bideford.* Exeter: E. Grigg, p. 66.

page 151 **While Tanton's, on the river . . . there was 'little to arrest the tourist'.** See Baedeker's 1901 guide, p. 166.

page 151 **His early years were spent . . . a quarryman in the slate mine.** Harry's father, Frederick, was born at Coryton.

page 152 **So many bullseyes were hit . . . killed a rabbit.** Thomas Newman. 1940. *The History of Coryton*. London: Cassell, pp. 165–6.

page 152 **The thunder and lightning . . . there would soon be 'Fire over England'.** Ibid, p. 182.

page 153 **But at the beginning of the twentieth century . . . according to the squire, Thomas Newman.** Ibid, p. 126.

page 153 **Once this had been sung . . . but nevertheless great fun'.** Ibid, p. 139.

page 154 **He and his family . . . another daughter, Nellie . . .** Flossie is called Hessie in the census of that year, and her place of birth is given as Coryton, not Appledore; but the age is the same (11 years old in 1911).

page 154 **. . . they had transferred . . . a dwelling called Wastor Cottage.** Given in the 1911 census as Bridestowe.

page 154 **Squire Thomas Newman prepared a list in 1940.** Newman, *The History of Coryton*, pp. 185–7.

page 154 **Robert Lydston Newman worked at the bank . . . stamina and morale.** Ibid, p. 187.

page 154 **It must be remembered that Germany . . . at the Bank.** Ibid, p. 188.

page 155 **Harry is the only other Coryton man who was killed . . . shattered lives.** Ibid, pp. 185–7.

page 157 **'They lived apart from the companies . . . their immediate surroundings.'** Richard Holmes. 2005 (new edition). *Tommy*. London: Harper Perennial, p. 390.

page 157 **'Saul hath slain . . . David his tens of thousands.'** The King James Bible has 'and' rather than 'but'.

page 157 **The importance attached to the corps . . . the cream of the National Army.'** C. E. Crutchley (ed). 1973. *Machine-Gunner, 1914–18*. Northampton: published on behalf of the Machine Gun Corps Old Comrades' Association, introduction, p. 1.

page 157 **Number One was leader . . . fully trained in handling the**

gun. George Coppard. 1968. *With a Machine Gun to Cambrai*. London: HMSO, pp. 37–8.

page 157 **There may have been . . . a mystique to operating a machine gun . . .** By the Battle of the Somme, the teams using Vickers machine guns were organized into the Machine Gun Corps; it is likely, therefore, that Harry Lake would have been trained to use a Lewis gun.

page 158 **He stopped to face us all . . . YOU WILL PISS IN IT!** Sergeant A. E. Henry Morgan. 2002. *Our Harry's War: 1553 Sgt G. H. Morgan Royal Warwickshire Regiment 1914–18*. Hartley Wintney: Rydan Publishing, p. 24.

page 158 **In *Goodbye to All That* . . . principles of laying down a barrage.** See Coppard, *With a Machine Gun to Cambrai*.

page 158 **Where did Harry go . . . then assigned to the Royal Warwickshire Regiment.** When Harry Lake was killed he was a private (43789) in the 2nd Battalion Royal Warwickshire of the 22nd Brigade, 7th Division, but his medal card indicates that he was formerly in the Machine Gun Corps (149019) and the Devonshire Regiment (66819). His service papers no longer exist.

page 158 **A glimpse of the sort of life . . . is given in a jaunty series of letters . . .** See the private papers of Arthur P. Burke, at the Imperial War Museum, London. 1665 Con Shelf.

page 159 **Fritz & us up here . . . meeting him half way for a chat.** Letter dated 29 December 1916.

page 159 **When the battalion took a German dugout . . . at the point of a bayonet.'** Letter dated 26 June 1917.

page 159 **Soon, though, they were at rest . . . he is so military.'** Letter dated 5 September 1917.

page 159 **Way up these few words . . . ITS LOVELY THIS BED.** Letter dated 16 September 1917 ('Tot' was Pat's sister Josephine).

page 161 **They found themselves chugging south . . . really grand'.** Private papers of W. R. Thomas (photocopied manuscript memoir). Imperial War Museum, London. Documents 7110.

page 161 **French and British troops were hurried south . . . becoming a general collapse.** See George H. Cassar. 1998. *The Forgotten Front: The British Campaign in Italy 1917–1918*. London: Hambledon Press.

page 161 **Soon we were sitting . . . the sun was getting hotter all the time.** See the private papers of W. R. Thomas.

page 162 **Private E. H. Lenfestey was one of the artillerymen . . . without breakfast.** Private papers of E. H. Lenfestey. Imperial War Museum, London. 7863 98/17/1.

page 162 **Private E. Smith was in the same battalion . . . *Inglesi* rather than Americani.** These distinctive eye-witness accounts are taken from the private papers of Private E. Smith. His manuscript memoir was written many years after the events described. Imperial War Museum, London. 13041 04/19/1.

page 163 **Captain N. P. Pritchard, a doctor . . . still marching on 11 December.** Descriptions of the journey south are taken from the diaries of Captain N. P. Pritchard. Imperial War Museum, London. 11814 03/17/1.

page 165 **But the month did include . . . a raid on the Austrian trenches at Ambrosini.** The Ambrosini raid is also mentioned in Charles Lethbridge Kingsford. 1921. *The Story of the Royal Warwickshire Regiment.* New York: Country Life, G. Newnes, p. 192.

page 166 **The 2nd Warwicks . . . Treviso for special training.** Kingsford, *The Story of the Royal Warwickshire Regiment*, p. 193.

page 166 **Not only had the division been practising . . . help with the shallow crossing.** Private papers of W. R. Thomas.

page 166 **After three or four crossings . . . sixty miles an hour.** Ibid.

page 168 **'We're well over the river . . . running like hell.'** Private papers of A. W. Lee. Imperial War Museum, London. 6762 78/13/1.

8: The Years in Between – the War Memorial

page 170 **There, according to the announcement of his Distinguished Service Order . . . under a heavy fire'.** Announcement dated 11 November 1914. Walford was also a watercolourist who painted scenes from the war.

page 170 **In what the *Tavistock Gazette* later called . . . engaged in peaceful pursuits'.** 23 December 1921. *Tavistock Gazette.*

page 171 **Early in the First World War . . . appearing at crossroads.**

Jay Winter. 1995. *Sites of Memory, Sites of Mourning. The Great War in European Cultural History*. Cambridge: Cambridge University Press, p. 80.

page 171 **'The Association is first of all concerned . . . order and beauty.'** Lawrence Weaver, architectural editor, writing in *Country Life*.

page 172 **In the classical world, a cenotaph . . . person whose body is buried elsewhere'**. Christopher Hussey. 1953. *The Life of Sir Edwin Lutyens*. London: Antique Collectors' Club, p. 391. The garden was Gertrude Jekyll's at Munstead.

page 173 **In some parishes . . . ran high.** See Todd Gray. 2010. *Lest Devon Forgets*. Exeter: The Mint Press.

page 173 **Tablets would provide . . . to help win the war'.** 19 May 1919. *Tavistock Gazette*.

page 173 **In the end, after 'a lengthy discussion . . . a very large majority'.** 8 October 1920. *Tavistock Gazette*.

page 173 **They were not sufficiently cowed . . . at the top of the village.** The work was carried out by Messrs Easterbrook, Stephens and Rook, ex-servicemen who had combined in the granite-working industry at Princetown. J. Cowling of Brentor undertook the erection of the cross.

page 174 **The Salvation Army band paraded the streets . . . treacherous Germans'.** 15 November 1918. *Tavistock Gazette*.

page 174 **Captain Nigel Hunter, a young officer in the Royal Engineers . . . long holidays on Dartmoor.** Seventeen weeks, according to an appreciation left in the guest book of Armstor House by 'Mrs Hunter & her family of eight', this Mrs Hunter probably being Hunter's grandmother. I am grateful to Barbara Weeks for this information. The quotations from diaries and letters are all taken from http://www.lydford.co.uk/hunter-ndr/hunter-texts.htm.

page 177 **As J. Fowler, a farmer from Salcombe, asked . . . a terrible way to farm'.** *Salcombe Gazette* quoted in Bonnie White. 2010. 'Feeding the war effort: Agricultural experiences in First World War Devon, 1914–17'. *Agricultural History Review*. Volume 58, Number 1, pp. 95–112.

page 178 **'Village slums,' thundered the Tavistock Rural District Council . . . Christian country.'** Article in the western *Daily Mercury* quoted in the *Tavistock Gazette* on 17 April 1919.

page 178 **While squalid conditions . . . take our place as 'weekenders'.** 'Life In A Village (By A Villager)'. 17 June 1927. *Tavistock Gazette.*

page 178 **Revd Thorpe put human need above history . . . 'unfit for human habitation'.** 8 June 1923. *Tavistock Gazette.*

page 179 **An advertisement showing a Fordson . . . (even if there had been tractors in Devon).** 25 July 1919. *Tavistock Gazette.*

page 180 **During the war . . . increase their allowance of petrol.** 28 July 1916. *Tavistock Gazette.*

page 181 **That year, Captain S. H. Priston . . . Indian Civil Veterinary Department.** 10 December 1920. *Tavistock Gazette.*

page 182 **Literary success would come . . . a million copies.** Henry Williamson. 1927. *Tarka the Otter: His Joyful Water-Life and Death in the Country of the Two Rivers.* London: Putnam.

page 183 **He had just 'had a really ripping time' . . . at the house of some mutual friends.** Tony Evans. 2000. 'The Radfords of Ingo Brake, Lydford'. *Henry Williamson Society Journal.* Number 36, September, p. 7.

page 183 **I feel an awful fool coming here . . . and running away.** Ibid.

page 183 **'It really was an adventure . . . Williamson would remember . . .** Henry Williamson. 1937. *Goodbye West Country.* London: Putnam, p. 152.

page 184 **After a storm in June 1936 . . . no cop anyhow.** This letter is quoted by Tony Evans in 'The Radfords of Ingo Brake, Lydford'.

page 185 **On Betty's death . . . kept Lou on as her chauffeur.** At least, that was how it was seen by the village. A different interpretation is that Crystal became blind in her old age and Lou looked after her like a son.

page 186 **Jim was the son of an agricultural labourer . . . a groom for Miss Daw.** He is recorded as being a groom on the 1911 census.

page 186 **His home . . . according to his medical records . . .** Exeter Record Office 3769A/H22/3.

page 186 **He had been discharged from the army . . . as 'sick'.** He was accordingly given his Silver War Badge. National Archives. WO329/3205, p. 4905.

page 186 **According to an obituary . . . Royal North Devon Hussars.** 11 May 1925. *Tavistock Gazette.* However, his name is not listed in the Devon Yeomanry book; nor is there any reference on his medal card in the National Archives.

page 186 **The date of enlistment . . . guarding the shores of Essex.** Jim
Stephens's war medals indicate that he did not enter any theatre of war
until after 1 January 1916.

page 186 **When the North Devons were broken up . . . part of the
Labour Corps.** Sadly, most of the Labour Corps' records were among
those destroyed during the Second World War.

page 186 **The speed with which this was done . . . outweighed other
considerations'.** John Starling and Ivor Lee. 2009. *No Labour, No Battle.*
Stroud: The History Press, p. 48.

page 187 **As a countryman, a rider . . . made a lance corporal.** This is
the rank given on his Silver War Badge.

page 187 **'I have only one Thessaloniki . . . surrendered.'** Richard
C. Hall. 2002. *The Balkan Wars, 1912–1913: Prelude to the First World War.*
London: Routledge, p. 62.

page 187 **The First and Second Balkan Wars . . . peace for quite twelve
months'.** Malcolm Burr, an Assistant Military Landing Officer, quoted
in Starling and Lee, *No Labour, No Battle*, p. 166.

page 187 **On this stagnant front . . . like flies in treacle' until 1918.** From
Issue 46 of *I Was There*, published 1938/9, quoted on http://www.1914-
1918.net/salonika.htm. F. A. W. Nash served with the RAMC and the
King's Shropshire Light Infantry, becoming a schoolteacher and writer
of fairy stories after the Armistice.

page 188 **There were . . . no reserves.** H. Collinson Owen. 1919. *Salonica
and After, the Sideshow that Ended the War.* London: Hodder & Stoughton,
pp. 68–9.

page 188 **The setting of the Place de la Liberté . . . topsi-turviness of
the situation.** Ibid, p. 12.

page 188 **Looking down . . . one might have waltzed on their heads.**
Ibid, p. 21.

page 189 **On the edge of the Struma Plain . . . 'sad end to a day of
triumph'.** Ibid, p. 126.

page 189 **According to the one war diary which survives . . . at the
Gugunci Railhead.** 816th Employment Company war diary. National
Archives. WO 95/4849.

page 189 **Borrowing a Ransome's motor tractor . . . most of the work
would have been done with horses.** Could Jim have worked with

camels in Salonica? Historically, camels were used there. See Sir Henry Holland. 1815. *Travels in the Ionian Isles, Albania, Thessaly, Macedonia, etc. (during the years 1812 and 1813, volume 1)*. London: Longman, Hurst, Rees, Orme and Brown, p. 326: 'Camels are sometimes, but more rarely, employed for the inland carriage of goods to a certain distance from Salonica. Their load is double that of the horse, but the progress they make in a country like European Turkey is slow, and subject to numerous obstacles. We fortunately happened to see in the suburbs of Salonica a train of thirty or forty camels, just arrived from a journey; an interesting spectacle, as well in the magnificent size and attitudes of the animal, as in the connection it has with the tales and scenery of the East.'

page 190 **Apart from the snowstorms . . . pursued a gentle, pastoral existence.** The troops did what they could to provide their own entertainment. The 22nd Division was noted for its variety troupe called The Macedons. In 1918, the division also produced *The Chocolate Soldier*, a lively musical show.

page 190 **The effort could only be contemplated . . . steep and winding'.** Starling and Lee, *No Labour, No Battle*, p. 169.

page 190 **No feat of arms can ever surpass . . . anything you can think of.** 'I Saw the Futile Massacre at Doiran'. An account by 'An unprofessional soldier' on the staff of the 28th Division. From issue 46 of *I Was There*, published 1938/9, quoted on http://www.1914-1918.net/salonika.htm.

page 192 **The letter concludes . . . can this be prevented?'** Silver War Badge records. National Archives. WO 329/3205.

page 192 **After his name comes that of William H. Daw . . . Jim's case.** The *Tavistock Gazette*'s obituary on 19 November 1926 says the H stands for Henry. But in the catalogue of the British Library, he is listed as William Herbert.

page 192 **'The medical world has declared war . . . practical little handbook'.** Review published in the *BMJ*, 1 October 1898, p. 990.

page 193 **He describes being 'isolated from contact . . . quantities of quinine that were consumed against malaria.** William Harold Owen. 1965. *Journey from Obscurity, Wilfred Owen 1893–1918, Memoirs of the Owen Family. Volume 3: War*. Oxford: Oxford University Press, p. 202.

page 194 **In 1939 it was the scene of the WI's annual flower show . . . and peace return to the world'.** 18 August 1939. *Tavistock Gazette.*

9: *Wings Over the River Styx – The Herbert Boys*

page 195 **It is Paramythia . . . an airstrip has been hidden here.** There is a description in Charles Lamb. 2001 (first published 1977). *War in a Stringbag.* London: Cassell, p. 162. See also the discussion forum 'Valley of Paramythia' – Secret RAF airfield during the Greek campaign at http://ww2chat.com/war-air/1437-valley-paramythia-secret-raf-airfield-during-greek-campaign.html.

page 195 **A journalist who descended . . . the Shangri-La of *Lost Horizon.*'** T. H. Wisdom. 2004 (first published 1942). *Wings Over Olympus.* Bristol: Cerberus Publishing Ltd, p. 124.

page 195 **At three o'clock on the afternoon of 13 April . . . settled into the cockpit.** The description of Richard is from James Dunnet. *Blenheim Over the Balkans.* 2001. Edinburgh: Pentland Press. I am grateful to Ian Carter of the Blenheim Society for giving me a copy of this book and also reading the first section of this chapter.

page 195 **Herby, as Richard Herbert was known . . . to keep on the ground.** See the *Wellington Roll of Honour 1939–45* (1949. Newport: R. H. Johns Ltd).

page 196 **The Mercury engines, already warmed up . . . ferried the bodies of the dead.** J. B. Dunnet. 1983. 'The Lost Squadron'. *Flypast.* Number 28, pp. 18–21.

page 198 **Even the measured words of the RAF communiqués . . . demolished the chateau.** See '211 Squadron in World War I' at http://users.cyberone.com.au/clardo/world_war_i.html.

page 199 **Then we pack up for the day . . . honest & very efficient.** Private papers of Flight Lieutenant J. D. W. H. Clutterbuck. Imperial War Museum, London. Documents 2282. Letter dated 18 August 1939.

page 199 **Two years ago this place . . . was renamed Habbaniya.** Ibid, 24 October 1939.

page 199 **The flies were . . . considering the difficulties he was working under.** Ibid, 12 September 1940.

page 199 **In September 1940, he flew out to join 211 Squadron . . . build on the wings.** Dunnet, *Blenheim Over the Balkans*, p. 19.

page 200 **Flying over the pyramids he remarked . . . 'Terrible waste of stone, what?'** Ibid, p. 26.

page 200 **'looked like a Boy Scout . . . long days in the desert.** Wisdom, *Wings Over Olympus*, p. 18. ('Porpoise' Bax was so called because he had a porpoise painted on the side of his plane, with part of Lewis Carroll's 'The Walrus and the Carpenter'.)

page 200 **One apocryphal recruit . . . joined the RAF.** Max Hastings. 1999 (first published 1979). *Bomber Command.* London: Pan Books, p. 21.

page 201 **He was regarded as the 'recco' . . . at 'shufti' flights.** Wisdom, *Wings Over Olympus*, p. 182.

page 201 **I lie in the prow of a fishing dhow . . . Oh where could I rather now be?** Peter A. Wright. 2011. *The Elephant on My Wing.* Bognor Regis: Woodfield Publishing, p. 13.

page 201 **The men wore their respirators . . . got on the men's nerves.** Wisdom, *Wings Over Olympus*, p. 28.

page 202 **'Mr Herbert, you will be going on your first trip . . . when you see mine go.'** Dunnet, *Blenheim Over the Balkans*, p. 30.

page 202 **When all the planes had returned . . . 'rather a good show'.** Ibid, p. 31.

page 202 **Seen from the sky . . . a huge blue Emperor butterfly'.** Ibid, p. 28.

page 202 **The things that the Greeks have done . . . is simply incredible.** Private papers of J. D. W. H. Clutterbuck. Letter dated 9 March 1941.

page 203 **The Nazi flag . . . taken from Fort Capuzzo in the Western Desert.** Wright, *The Elephant on My Wing*, p. 52.

page 203 **From a scenic point of view it was . . . the scarf you have so kindly knitted for me.** Clutterbuck, letter dated 9 March 1941.

page 204 **('Air Observer extinguished fire with his flying boot.')** 211 Squadron's Operations Record Books have been transcribed on http://www.211squadron.org. This entry is from 22 January 1941.

page 204 **'It was a veritable feast . . . bombs were not wasted.'** I am grateful to Ian Carter for showing me his copy of the Narrative Report and for reading this chapter. The original of the report is in the National Archives.

page 204 **Little by way of distraction . . . as they fell to earth.** Wisdom, *Wings Over Olympus*, p. 126.

page 204 **Admittedly, on the first day of the German invasion . . . maintained for ever.** E. D. Smith. 1988. *Victory of a Sort: The British in Greece, 1941–46.* London: Robert Hale Publishers, p. 54.

page 205 **They included such innovations as . . . 'really something to shout about'.** Wright, *The Elephant on My Wing*, p. xiii.

page 205 **When J. B. Dunnet, who would normally have been flying . . . still to be seen.** Dunnet, 'The Lost Squadron'.

page 206 **The shell of another Blenheim . . . just over the Albanian border.** In 1993, the remains of L1434 were raised and are now in the Military Air Museum at Tatoi, outside Athens.

page 206 **It was the end of 211 . . . for the time being.** Official records peter out in the summer. The squadron was re-formed in India in 1943.

page 206 **Richard was his second.** See 'Aces of the Luftwaffe' at http://www.luftwaffe.cz/gromotka.html.

page 206 **Previously he had belonged, as a squadron leader wrote . . . gone to join his comrades'.** From the indecipherable signature it appears to be Tomas Alrisdom.

page 206 **But people who knew him . . . responsibility and tragedy'.** See the *Wellington Roll of Honour 1939–45*.

page 208 **His first dispatch . . . of incalculable value in the conduct of operations.'** Sir Walter Raleigh and Henry Jones. 1922. *The War in the Air.* Volume 1. Oxford: Clarendon Press, p. 329. For a history of air reconnaissance, see John W. R. Taylor and David Mondey. 1972. *Spies in the Sky.* London: Ian Allen.

page 209 **Billeted in a . . . some publisher has brought out I believe.** Private papers of D. M. T. Colles. Imperial War Museum, London. Documents 8516.

page 210 **'The camp itself looked very grim . . . Not a tree in sight.'** Private diary of Mrs B. Dallas. Entry for 20 October 1941. Imperial War Museum, London. Documents 16313.

page 210 **He was buried in the churchyard of Theale . . . in Berkshire.** I presume it was his grandmother's village. There is a family headstone: Florence / widow of / William Dickes Herbert / died May 8th 1944 /

aged 89 years / My peace I give unto you / Also / Emily F L Herbert, / daughter of the above / died May 2nd 1952 / aged 73 years.

page 211 **When 158 Bomber Squadron was formed . . . to join it.** See Geoff Simmons and Barry Abraham. 2001. *Strong Foundations: Driffield's Aerodrome from 1917 to 2000.* Beverley: Hutton Press Ltd.

page 211 **'One Lancaster is to be preferred . . . when compared to the Lancaster.'** Quoted in Jon Lake. 2002. *The Great Book of Bombers.* London: Salamander Books Ltd, p. 192.

page 213 **Halifaxes had a good record . . . compared to the Lancaster's 11 per cent.** Lake, *The Great Book of Bombers*, p. 192.

10: *The War Seemed Very Far Away – Richard Gillett*

page 214 **Margaret's ten-year marriage . . . just after war broke out in 1914.** The marriage took place on 2 September 1914, according to divorce papers in the National Archives. J 77/2106.

page 215 **After the First World War . . . practised in Torquay:** See the UK Medical Registers for 1918 and 1919 (General Medical Council).

page 217 **If Richard's experience was anything like . . . always someone there.'** John Pomeroy Randle. Audio tape of British officer who served with 7/10th Baluch Regiment in India and Burma, 1941–6. Imperial War Museum, London. Catalogue number 28825, reel 1.

page 217 **Drinks were brought . . . during the monsoon season.** Many of the details in this paragraph come from the private papers of E. G. Leigh Brown. Imperial War Museum, London. 6243 67/377/1. For life in the regiment generally, see W. S. Thatcher. 1980. *The Tenth Baluch Regiment in the Second World War.* Abbotabad: The Baluch Regimental Centre.

page 217 **But he knew enough to communicate . . . unable to master Urdu).** Randle, audio tape, reel 2.

page 218 **Information on the subject was 'meagre . . . almost non-existent'.** Eric Neild. 1970 (reprinted by Battery Press, Nashville, in 1990). *With Pegasus in India: The Story of 153 Gurkha Parachute Battalion.* Singapore: Jay Birch & Co (Pte) Ltd, p. 5.

page 218 'Jumping in the early days . . . with goats eating it.' Neild, *With Pegasus in India*, p. 8.

page 218 The 'possibilities . . . were endless'. Major General Afsir Karim. 1993. *The Story of the Indian Airborne Troops*. New Delhi: Lancer International, p. 6.

page 219 This had a depressing effect . . . all the officers of the headquarters jumped together'. Neild, *With Pegasus in India*, p. 35.

page 221 Packed like dates in a box . . . the surviving drivers were pretty good.' Neild, *With Pegasus in India*, p. 56.

page 221 Just before reaching it . . . hills unfolded themselves before our eyes'. Ibid, pp. 56–7.

page 221 We used to watch with much amazement . . . war seemed very far away. Ibid, p. 57.

page 222 Over the next two days . . . 'worked all out on the defences' . . . See the document 'Events leading up to the Battles at Sheldon's Corner and Sangshak March 1944' (p. 4) at http://www.paradata.org.uk/media /3778?mediaSection=Documents.

page 222 If 'I[ntelligence]' was correct . . . flabbergasted. Neild, *With Pegasus in India*, p. 59.

page 223 By mid morning the enemy's fire . . . such a brave act. Quoted in Karim, *The Story of the Indian Airborne Troops*, pp. 25–6.

page 224 A couple of officers studying their maps . . . just look!' Ibid, p. 59.

page 225 To speed our actions . . . as he was killed a few days later. Neild, *With Pegasus in India*, p. 59.

page 225 'As soon as it was really dark . . . shouting to each other.' See 'Battle at Sangshak, 1944' War Diary Report (p. 2) at http://www.paradata.org.uk/media/3778?mediaSection=Documents.

page 226 'In 152 Bn we were stretched . . . the fiercest fighting of the battle took place here.' Ibid, p. 5.

page 227 The 25th was very similar . . . fresh troops for each attack. Ibid, p. 6.

page 228 We were not entirely clear . . . swimming-pools that we knew in India. Neild, *With Pegasus in India*, p. 1.

page 228 The corps commander's message ended ominously . . . 'both contingencies seemed highly remote'. Ibid.

page 228 **That evening we came upon two figures . . . settled down for the night in a wood.** Karim, *The Story of the Indian Airborne Troops*, p. 37.

page 229 **The 'staunchness' . . . declared General Slim in a special order of the day.** Quoted by Max Arthur in the obituary of Major Tom Monaghan. 16 February 1999. *Independent*.

page 229 **For the first time, a Japanese attack . . . India had been saved.** For a detailed account of the fighting at Sangshak see Harry Seaman. 1989. *The Battle at Sangshak*. Barnsley: Leo Cooper.

11: *The Scene Is Now Too Poignant – Jack Bickle*

page 231 **Scholastically, the family's reputation . . . scholarship examination.** 20 March 1936. *Tavistock Gazette*.

page 231 **When local boys dammed a stream . . . underwater.** In 'An Old Man's Ramblings', a memoir at http://www.lydford.co.uk/michell.htm, Antony Michell attributes this story to 'Jimmy' Bickle: I have not been able to contact Mr Michell to establish whether he means Jackie Bickle or Jimmy Stanbury, the boy who went down with the *Ahamo*.

page 231 **'I can't get round . . . I can't get through.'** 4 August 1939. *Tavistock Gazette*.

page 233 **Under intense bombardment . . . 'not without reason'.** Anon. 1946. *History of the 4th Battalion The Somerset Light Infantry in the Campaign in North-West Europe, June 1944–May 1945*. Taunton: E. Goodman, Phoenix Press, p. 17.

page 233 **The object to be attacked . . . the key to Normandy.** Ibid, p. 25.

page 233 **It was defended by the . . . (Frundsberg) Division.** Named after the early sixteenth-century soldier Georg von Frundsberg.

page 233 **'It was just beginning to get light . . . as well as flamethrowers.** *History of the 4th Battalion*, p. 21.

page 233 **Large bluebottles swarmed over them . . . never be the same again.'** A. G. Herbert. 'A Rank Outsider'. Undated typescript memoir. Imperial War Museum, London. Documents 7625.

page 234 **'It was pure joy . . . equipment had rubbed my flesh raw.'** Ibid.

page 234 **The driver had been . . . said he would take I.O.U.s.** Ibid.

page 234 **'We rode on the tanks . . . burned by the hot metal plates.'** Ibid.

page 234 **The dust . . . thick as a London fog'.** *History of the 4th Battalion,* p. 32.

page 235 **The valley echoed to the sound . . . the average battlefield'.** Ibid, p. 49.

page 236 **As Corporal Douglas Proctor remembered . . . not to his liking'.** Sydney Jary. 1987. *18 Platoon.* Winchester: Light Infantry, p. xvii.

page 237 **At one town, across the street from a convent . . . ladies in dressing gowns.'** Ibid, p. 38.

page 238 **They remembered the supply vehicles . . . behind schedule'.** *History of the 4th Battalion,* p. 53.

page 238 **The once neat gardens . . . the grey look returned once more.** Jary, *18 Platoon,* p. 49.

page 238 **'Wrapped in their greatcoats . . . never uttering a sound.'** Ibid, p. 54.

page 239 **Frogmen would have seen . . . from somewhere in the darkness.** Herbert, 'A Rank Outsider', p. 57.

page 239 **'The great gamble . . . had failed.'** *History of the 4th Battalion,* p. 55.

page 239 **Near Nijmegen, he found . . . No. 3 Casualty Clearing Station.** Amy 'Pam' Dunnett gives a description of No. 3 Casualty Clearing Station. Imperial War Museum, London. Interview catalogue 18784, reel 3.

page 239 **When the shell landed nearby . . . get all that repaired.'** Sir Brian Horrocks quotes this experience in the introduction to Juliet Piggott. 1975. *Queen Alexandra's Royal Army Nursing Corps (Famous Regiments).* Barnsley: Leo Cooper.

page 240 **One morning, there was a 'Crack!' . . . without shedding a tear.** Jary, *18 Platoon,* p. 55.

page 241 **They received a uniform . . . and hideous pyjamas'.** See Barbara Cawthorne's description at http://www.atsremembered.org. uk/cawthornesheetpdf.pdf.

page 241 **In 1947 Private Bickle died . . . at Shaftesbury Military Hospital.** Sylvia's death was reported in the *Tavistock Gazette* on 19 September 1947.

12: *A Surprise Attack in Three Weeks' Time – Nick Taylor*

page 243 **'The interests of the inhabitants . . . thundered in 1964 . . .** Max Hastings and Simon Jenkins. 2010 (first published 1983). *The Battle for the Falklands*. London: Pan Macmillan, p. 18.

page 244 **'All the things . . . adrenalin rush.'** Interview with Nick's sister Susan Williamson.

page 246 **'It was great . . . in his company.'** Glyn Phillips. See his testimonial at http://homepage.ntlworld.com/glyn.phillips42/heron.htm.

page 246 **But always he would be . . . wanting to do something different'.** Susan Williamson interview.

page 247 **Romantics warmed to the thought . . . the Hurricane of the Second World War.** Roger Chesneau. 2006. *Aeroguide 32: BAe Sea Harrier FRS Mk1/FA Mk 2*. Ringshall: Ad Hoc Publications. See also Roy Braybrook. 1984. *British Aerospace Harrier and Sea Harrier*. Oxford: Osprey Publishing, p. 36: 'In the minds of those who worked there, the distinction between Hawker Aircraft and Sopwith Aviation was purely a matter of financial flute-music: the product line could be traced straight back to the first fighting scout ever conceived, and beyond.'

page 247 **. . . it was also 'the best fighter in the world' . . . at low speed.** Sharkey Ward. 2000 (first published 1992). *Sea Harrier Over the Falklands*. London: Cassell, p. 58.

page 249 **As the broadcaster and journalist Malcolm Muggeridge . . . but the name.** 4 June 1982. *Times*.

page 250 **Another obstacle was the scaffolding . . . and radar dishes.** David H. S. Morgan. 2006. *Hostile Skies*. London: Weidenfeld & Nicolson.

page 250 **But in the whirlwind preparation . . . shared by the rest of 800 Squadron.** See 'Harrier Testing' by Andy Lawson at http://www. harrier.org.uk/history/Harrier_Testing.htm.

page 251 **'Hello, did you see me . . . since we arrived.** Ian Martin's letters are in the Fleet Air Arm Museum, Yeovilton.

page 251 **'Amazing, astounding . . . remembers it.** Rupert Nichol interview (audio tape). Imperial War Museum, London. Interview catalogue 23450, reel 4.

page 253 **In the Bay of Biscay . . . incapacitated by seasickness.** This is according to Morgan, *Hostile Skies*, p. 38. On *Invincible*, Sharkey Ward seems not to have noticed.

page 253 **As Sir John Curtiss . . . not easy to attack'.** Sir John Curtiss interview (audio tape). Imperial War Museum, London. Interview catalogue 17771, reel 4.

page 254 **Not surprisingly, there was, as Sharkey Ward put it . . .** Nigel David 'Sharkey' Ward interview (audio tape). Imperial War Museum, London. Interview catalogue 1280, reel 1.

page 255 **But a better omen . . . a pair of albatrosses that followed the ship.** Although on 18 May an albatross was blamed for bringing down a Sea King helicopter with the loss of eighteen members of the SAS and four other men. However, the Sea King was also heavily overloaded.

page 255 **It was a Boeing 707 . . . first contact with the enemy!'** 800 Squadron's record book is in the Fleet Air Arm Museum, Yeovilton.

page 255 **On 28 April, the practice drop . . . whistling past his tail'.** Morgan, *Hostile Skies*, p. 66.

page 255 **They all knew each other . . . as reinforcements.** Peter Squire, commander of 1 Squadron RAF, interview (audio tape). Imperial War Museum, London. Interview catalogue 28353.

page 257 **Flying over water . . . as one plotter inelegantly put it).** Rowland White. 2006. *Vulcan 607*. London: Bantam Press, p. 189.

page 257 **In a sense, the apparent implausibility . . . at very long range'.** Curtiss interview, reel 5.

page 258 **Twenty-one 1,000-pound bombs . . . 250 yards long.** Sir Lawrence Freedman. 2005. *The Official History of the Falklands Campaign: Volume II, War and Diplomacy*. Abingdon: Routledge, Taylor & Francis Group, p. 280.

page 258 **The Vulcan pilot . . . its lights were on.** Ben Fenton. 'Bombing Argentines "just wasn't cricket"'. 30 April 2007. *Telegraph*.

page 259 **Imagine an area of steel . . . thirty-knot wind to unbalance you.** Morgan, *Hostile Skies*, p. 35.

page 259 **Tightly strapped in . . . 'actually quite comfortable'.** Peter Squire interview.

page 260 **'Goose Green no known,' . . . report the next day.** Freedman, *The Official History of the Falklands Campaign*, p. 280.

page 262 **The significance of the achievement . . . Sea Harrier pilots to return.** Ward, *Sea Harrier*, pp. 160–61.

page 262 **For some of the voyage south . . . increases survival time from minutes to hours.'** Brian Hanrahan and Robert Fox. 1982. *I Counted Them All Out and I Counted Them All Back*. London: BBC Books, pp. 30–31.

page 263 **Days, as Sharkey Ward recalled . . . I was pooped.** Ward, *Sea Harrier*, p. 211.

page 264 **'His grave is tended . . . never be lonely.'** Morgan, *Hostile Skies*, p. 99.

13: Every Man an Emperor – Andrew Kelly

page 266 **Some of his closest friends . . . funny side of things'.** 'Proud Para, 18, laid to rest.' 23 May 2003. *Yorkshire Post*.

page 267 **Founded in 1940 . . . dramatic role during the D-Day landings.** Minute from Prime Minister to Chiefs of Staff, 22 June 1940.

page 268 **Everybody was so very witty . . . *excretum vacci*'.** Martin Lindsay. 'First Drop'. 21 February 1941. *The Spectator*. Volume 166, p. 199.

page 271 **'Whatever happens . . . we will win.'** Neil Tweedie. 'Whatever happens out there, we will win'. 24 January 2003. *Telegraph*.

page 271 **'It was interesting for a day or two . . . what they came into the army to do.'** Ibid.

page 271 **When Andrew joined his battalion . . . enthusiasm and personality.** I am grateful to Brigadier G. P. Hill, Commander, 16 Air Assault Brigade for fleshing out details of Andrew's military service throughout this chapter (in an interview conducted 2 May 2012).

page 271 **In Ministry of Defence speak . . . heavier formations'.** 'War on terror: Paras ready to play major strategic role'. 10 March 2003. *Birmingham Post.*

page 272 **It will be a relief . . . never thought it would happen.** David Williams. 'We've waited long enough, now we just want to get on and do the job'. 19 March 2003. *Daily Mail.*

page 273 **Instead came children . . . 'smiling and happy' children.** Martin Bentham. 'Handshakes and high fives as the Paras are swept along by the joy of liberation'. 8 April 2003. *Telegraph.*

page 273 **One group of men . . . hotwire a red fire engine.** Pooled dispatch from Nick Craven of the *Daily Mail.* 7 April 2003. Press Association. Home News.

page 274 **After several days of us fighting . . . what we already knew.** Simon Houston. 'War in the Gulf: Who won the war; Scots baffled by Basra claims of the Red Berets'. 10 April 2003. *Daily Record.*

page 275 **The pattern of life reflected . . . firefights at night-time.** Email from Brigadier Matthew Lowe to the author. 18 March 2012.

page 275 **In this border area . . . subsequent Iranian-sponsored insurgency.'** Ibid.

page 276 **Robert Kelly opened a campaign . . . and I hope he doesn't.'** Louise Barnett. 'War was fiasco, says dead soldier's father'. 8 July 2003. *PA News.*

page 276 **The military funeral . . . "How good is this".'** 'Proud Para, 18, laid to rest'.

page 276 **'He really felt he achieved something . . . with his life.'** Richard Savill. 'Mourners remember youngest Gulf victim'. 24 May 2003. *Telegraph.*

page 278 **People were taller . . . in the 1930s.** Dorothy L. Sayers. 2003 (first published 1934). *The Nine Taylors.* London: New English Library, p. 115.

Index